From Kristallnacht to Watergate

From Kristallnacht to Watergate

Memoirs of a Newspaperman

HARRY ROSENFELD

excelsior editions

State University of New York Press
Albany, New York

Published by State University of New York Press, Albany

Excelsior Editions is an imprint of State University of New York Press

For information, contact State University of New York Press, Albany, NY
www.sunypress.edu

Production by Eileen Nizer
Marketing by Kate McDonnell

Library of Congress Cataloging-in-Publication Data

Rosenfeld, Harry, 1929–
    From Kristallnacht to Watergate : memoirs of a newspaperman / Harry Rosenfeld.
        pages cm
    Summary: "An insider's account of how the Washington Post broke the Watergate story, depicting the tensions, challenges, and personal conflicts that were overcome as it laid bare the criminal wrongdoings of the Nixon administration"— Provided by publisher.
    Includes bibliographical references and index.
    ISBN 978-1-4384-4917-3 (hardcover : alk. paper)
    1. Rosenfeld, Harry, 1929– 2. Journalists—United States—Biography.
3. Editors—United States—Biography.   4. Watergate Affair, 1972–1974—Press coverage.   5. Washington post, times herald—History.   I. Title.

    PN4874.R5955A3 2013
    070.4'1092—dc23
    [B]   2013002444

10 9 8 7 6 5 4 3 2 1

For Annie

Contents

photo gallery follows page 102

Acknowledgments

Bernard F. Conners, a friend who over more than twenty years first suggested, then encouraged and finally hounded me to sit down and write this book. George R. Hearst III, *Times Union* Publisher, urged me on when Mark Felt came out as Deep Throat. Others at the *TU* who helped throughout the three years of research and writing, were Michael Spain, Associate Editor, who made available information from the newspaper's older files and provided other valuable assistance; Mark Losee, who rescued me from repeated computer crises, and Susan Wright, executive assistant to the publisher, who produced essential manuscript printouts. Sarah Hinman Ryan contributed valuable research. Jennifer Patterson performed minor miracles transcribing the sometimes hard to hear Nixon-Ziegler tape. For access to the tape, thanks go to Cary McStay, Tapes Supervisory Archivist at the National Archives in College Park, Maryland, and her colleague Ryan Pettigrew at the Nixon Library in Yorba Linda, California. Don Graham graciously opened *The Washington Post*'s library and the patient Madonna A. Lebling helped me access the paper's electronic storehouse. Peter Osnos, was the first in publishing to read an early draft, and offered useful advice on how to proceed. Rabbi Scott Shpeen, of Congregation Beth Emeth, Albany, N.Y., counseled on Jewish customs.

My heartfelt appreciation goes to Paul Grondahl, respected reporter, author, and first-rate editor of the manuscript. I could not have done without him.

Thanks to my sister Rachel Damski, the fount of much of early Rosenfeld family history; to my wife Annie and my daughters and their husbands—Susan and Dr. Stuart Wachter, Amy and Dan

Kaufman, Stefanie Rosenfeld and Paul Aiken—for their encouragement and their frank comments on the work in progress. Paul Aiken was the source of practical guidance and bolstered me when doubts weighed me down. Dan Kaufman handled the necessary legal work, his adroit skills making it easier for everyone, including my supportive publisher, James Peltz, and his colleagues Eileen Nizer and Kate McDonnell.

Prologue

Nothing in my family's history ordained the work I undertook during fifty years as an American newspaperman. My forebears in Poland were tailors and furriers, ironmongers, businessmen, and innkeepers. The most notable, according to family lore, was Yankel, who is said to have lived to the age of 114 and who worked on a greatcoat for Napoleon while the Emperor passed through during his Russian campaign. Not a scrivener among them. My father was a furrier. Born and raised in Poland, he lived in Germany for more than two decades before our family was issued long-sought official papers that opened America's doors for us less than four months before Hitler launched World War II.

On the other hand, my childhood in Nazi Germany had everything to do with my life's work.

I was not conscious of the connection as I became attracted to journalism. It was something I wanted to do, citing the ambition in my high school year book. Journalism struck me as an interesting career and a calling to a worthy public service. Of course, I was aware at a young age of my personal debt to America for providing the chance to do both. I did not pause to put my life and career into perspective until I prepared to retire in 1997. In my talk at the retirement dinner party, I first acknowledged what I owed the renowned editors—John Denson, Jim Bellows, Ben Bradlee—I had worked for as well as to the accomplished colleagues I'd worked with. Summing up, I expressed gratitude to America for giving refuge to my family. The essence of my life's work was the indelible imprint on my character of the oppressively cruel Nazi regime. America offered my family shelter and opportunity, and I had in my mind to do what I could to help assure that what happened in Hitler's Germany would not happen here. Looking back, I discerned a theme underpinning much of my journalistic labors: holding to account the accountable, the more powerful the better.

While fascism in the United States was held at bay in the 1930s, it was not because this country lacked admirers of Hitler, including luminaries such as Henry Ford. Sinclair Lewis depicted the worst-case scenario in *It Can't Happen Here,* a book I read with close attention as a youngster. Only recently removed from the real thing, Lewis's satire unsettled me. So did another book that I got around to reading when I was old enough to comprehend it. It was *Mein Kampf.*

If Europe had been spared the Nazi affliction and I had lived according to the conventions of that time and place, almost surely I would have gone into my father's trade. Attending university and its concomitant benefits would have been an extraordinary reach.

It would be many years before I fully comprehended how thin the margin of survival had been. The Holocaust shadowed all my days, more strongly with the passing years. Instead of bitterness waning, wrath intensified. I recognized myself in an iconic photograph of an unnamed young Jewish boy in Poland, dressed in a coat and cap strikingly similar to the kind I wore as a child, holding his hands up in surrender to the Wehrmacht. It could not be by the grace of God that I survived and he did not. Nothing I had done merited divine intervention, as nothing he had done earned him his pain and destruction. When my youngest grandson was named in our synagogue wrapped in my father's prayer shawl, an occasion of boundless joy, I stumbled in my prayer of thanksgiving. Even at this happy moment, in the depth of my soul I feared the world remained poised to exact its price because he was born a Jew.

These sentiments stirred in me afresh in August 2005, when I received a phone call from a stranger. On a lovely warm and sunny day I was alone at home one morning catching up on reading while my wife and our daughter and her three children were out running errands.

The phone rang. The caller identified himself as Roger Lowen. He was calling from Virginia and apologized for the oddity of what he was about to ask. For a moment I wondered what scam might be afoot. But his voice was calm and assuring as he asked whether I remembered his cousin, Gustav Loewenstein, as a boyhood playmate in Berlin in the late 1930s. I said I could not.

The caller said he possessed a letter from his cousin dated April 1939. In this letter, Gustav Loewenstein wrote: *"Liebe Tante Lehah, lieber Onkel Arthur, am Sonnabend fuhr mein Freund Harry Rosenfeld nach New York mit seinen Eltern. Ich habe gar keine Freunde mehr zum Spielen . . ."* ("Dear Aunt Lehah, dear Uncle Arthur, on Saturday my friend Harry Rosenfeld left for New York with his parents. I have no more friends to play with . . .").

My family did leave Germany that April, but I still could not place Gustav in my memory. Because of the unlikelihood of two nine-year-old Harry Rosenfelds having left Berlin at that time, I asked Mr. Lowen to tell me more about his cousin.

He said that Gustav and his father were living in Berlin and that Gustav's parents had been divorced. Now my memory snapped into place. I said I did have a friend in Berlin who boarded with his father in the home of a Jewish family. I remembered my friend in certain aspects but could not recall his name. I had a mental image of him as an apple-cheeked boy. Suddenly, Mr. Lowen, interjected, "That is your friend Gustav."

Mr. Lowen told me that Gustav and his father, Ludwig, continued to live in Berlin after we left. The Lowen family and other relatives in America tried desperately to save the Loewensteins and Gustav's two aunts by providing affidavits and sending money that would allow them to emigrate. But it was too late.

The Lowen family eventually learned that father and son were forced into hard labor in Berlin in 1941. The last time the Lowens heard from them, in a censored letter, Ludwig wrote that he was happy that he had been able to procure a warm winter coat for Gustav. Gustav's story does not end in Berlin. Father and son were subsequently deported to a work camp in Estonia where both died, likely in 1943. The aunts were deported to a death camp in Poland.

This was an all-too-familiar story. Only the details differed for what befell those who had not been able to elude the efficient German killing machine. They knew only periods of deprivation and dehumanization, of struggle and unimaginable terror, of suffering that ultimately ended in death.

A powerful emotion seized me as I listened to Mr. Lowen's account of Gustav's fate. Despite efforts to suppress my feelings, I began to weep. When I collected myself, I told Mr. Lowen what I remembered sixty-six years later about my lost friend. I remembered not merely what he looked like. I remembered that he drank milk straight from the bottle.

Based on my upbringing in Berlin, that was a strange custom. I had my milk with a touch of coffee, never straight. We called it *Kaffe Verkehrt* (Upside Down Coffee). I thought that Gustav had acquired the habit in America, where I believed he and his father had traveled before returning to Germany. Mr. Lowen said that was not so, although there was an American connection. Gustav's grandmother was born in Savannah, Georgia, and she married Gustav's grandfather on a trip to Germany in about 1890. They raised two sons, one of whom, Mr. Lowen's father, settled in America in 1906. The other was Ludwig, and the family had two daughters who perished in Poland.

I also remembered a grim experience Gustav and I shared. One day as we played at his apartment we were told to quiet down by the family where the Loewensteins boarded. The head of the household was returning from imprisonment in a concentration camp. I can still see that man clearly in my mind all these years later. Looking down a long, dark hallway, Gustav and I watched in silence as he was half-carried through the front door by male relatives, his body bent, his face almost white. A short while later, we were told, he died. The Nazis at that time were releasing some Jews, either to die or to emigrate.

That was all I could remember. Gustav and I probably met each other at the Jewish Community School, which Jewish children attended after they were expelled from the public schools in 1937. In the letter Gustav wrote to his American family, he went on to note that he had just been promoted to the fifth form at school.

I asked Mr. Lowen how he found me. He was retired from the U.S. diplomatic service and said he had meant to search for me for years but never got around to it until his daughter returned from a trip to Israel. There, she had gone to Yad Vashem, the Holocaust memorial, and consulted its computer records about her family. On her return, she helped her father to locate me.

Mr. Lowen said he would send me a photograph and other documents along with a letter fleshing out our conversation.

When the phone call ended, I was overcome with grief. I cried aloud in my anguish. In my lifetime I have mourned the loss of parents, in-laws, a young nephew, aunts, uncles, and cousins. I have lost close friends both young and old. I wept for them all—but not in the way I keened for Gustav.

Was it because of the utter sadness of the news?

Was it because it so starkly reminded me of what only by the sheerest luck I had evaded?

Was it guilt because when Gustav was conscripted into hard labor, I was studying in an American elementary school? While he was being tormented, I was being helped by caring teachers. As he succumbed, I was growing in body and health.

Did I grieve so fiercely because the image of Ludwig, a devoted father, in the end not being able to protect the life of his only child, pierced me as a father and grandfather?

Was it because I felt ashamed that I had forgotten the name of my boyhood friend? I had never forgotten him. Although nameless, he was included in a family history I was writing for my children and grandchildren. He has been a memorable part of my life. But asked out of the blue, I could not bring his name to mind.

It is surely not my singular experience that in the later decades of life memory diminishes as remembered sorrows deepen. After that remarkable phone call I vowed that as long as memory endured, the name I could not remember I would never again forget. Gustav Loewenstein, *mein Freund, mein ewiger Freund.*

I placed the photo of Gustav that Mr. Lowen sent me next to mine of the same vintage in the family album we brought with us from Germany. I wrote about him for my newspaper so that others might know his tragic story. Gustav's name comes to mind on different occasions, but I remember him without fail at the Yizkor (Memorial) service on the Day of Atonement along with my parents. As in time my children invoke memory of me on that holy day, I bid them to include Gustav, the son of Ludwig, in their prayers.

We who escaped the Holocaust bear witness to those lost lives. We commemorate slain relatives and friends to save them from namelessness. Bearing witness is an ancient Jewish trait, at least since the Israelites stood at Mount Sinai.

Unfortunately, I know few facts about my own family's history. In my youth, I was typically absorbed with the present. In adulthood, I was preoccupied with providing for my wife and children and attending to my newspaper career. I had little interest in exploring my family's past while my parents were alive and they made no effort to speak much about the European past to me either. And so in taking on the task of reconstructing my family's history, I consulted the scant archival material that I inherited. I relied as much as memory allowed on what my mother told me as a child about her early life. My sister, who is eight years older than I, was a good source because she remembered far more than I possibly could.

1

From Warsaw to Berlin

My mother Esther and father Sam were both born in Warsaw, Poland, in 1893, into divergent social and economic circumstances. My father was raised in the ghetto in a two-room apartment shared at different times by nine or ten people, with his parents' small section screened off. My father never spoke ill of his own father, but then he never spoke to me about him and only rarely on other matters. The facts as I've been able to unearth them indicate that my grandfather shirked work and used a respiratory impairment caused by smoking to spend the workday in shul, a synagogue. His grown sons helped to pay the family's bills and his wife occasionally bought and sold food items. From time to time, my grandfather was hired for temporary jobs as an ironmonger and junkyard overseer through the beneficence of my mother's brother, who owned the yard.

My mother was the daughter of an enterprising businessman, Hersz Szerman, who lived in an upscale part of town in an apartment with its own balcony, a sign of status. My father dropped out of school to go to work around age nine. My mother attended Gymnasium, where she received an education exceeding that of an American high school. My paternal grandmother wore a *sheitel*, the wig that Orthodox women donned for modesty's sake. My maternal grandmother was an elegant lady who wore no *sheitel* but bore seven children. Neither my sister Rachel nor I were ever told how our parents, who came from such different worlds, managed to meet and marry. They did share that their relationship began when they were quite young.

In a household where money was scarce, Szlama (or Solomon as my father was known in his youth) toiled as a tailor's apprentice until he was fourteen. He lived with the tailor's family and slept next to the stove under a table in the workroom. Following the apprenticeship, Solomon began to learn the furrier's trade at the business owned by his older brother Felix. At the age of seventeen, Solomon became a journeyman furrier, and he practiced this craft all his working days. Before he married he tried to smuggle himself into Germany, by placing himself in a barrel and rolling down a hill over the border from Poland. He was stopped by Polish border guards. Soon afterward he made it into Germany the legal way. For many Polish Jews, Germany was seen as the land of opportunity, a forward-looking nation compared to their backward homeland with its entrenched, religiously reinforced anti-Semitism that offered my father only a bleak future.

My parents married in Warsaw on March 24, 1918. My father was twenty-five, my mother twenty-four. During the German occupation of Warsaw in World War I, Solomon was recruited in August 1917 by one of Berlin's large fashion houses as a furrier. He returned briefly to Warsaw for his wedding. My mother was not allowed to join him in Berlin for nearly two years. She finally received the necessary papers from the German government in 1920. They lived in Germany until we emigrated in 1939.

My father's superior work at the fashion house paid off. Four years after arriving in Berlin he was able to open his own business, a grand salon. That same year, 1921, my sister Rosa Rachel, was born. I knew her first as Roeschen, then Resi, later in America as Ray. When already a grandmother, she discarded Ray in order to go by Rachel, her given middle name. By whatever name, she has been a caring and loving sister all her life, a resolute and spirited woman much in the image of our mother.

Even though business was good in Berlin, Daddy proposed moving our family to America as early as the 1920s. He wanted to join his sister and brothers who were already living in New York. But my mother talked him out of it, stressing how beautiful life in Berlin was, with its culture and entertainments that both enjoyed. Talk of leaving receded, and not long before Hitler came to power, my parents purchased a plot of land about an hour outside of Berlin where they planned to build a summer house.

I remember that my Uncle Felix visited frequently from Poland in those years. He was a wealthy man, who owned real estate in Poland and in Berlin in addition to his prosperous fur business.

He enjoyed staying at his younger brother's home in Berlin and was especially envious of my father's wardrobe, because he was an elegant dresser even as a young man living in that tiny ghetto apartment.

I was born on August 12, 1929, delivered by a doctor and a midwife in my parents' apartment. That was common practice at that time, with friends gathered for the birth. When my father went to the registry office to record my birth and name, it was supposed to be Hirsch (for my mother's deceased father) and Moritz (for my father's brother Moishe who died in combat while serving in the Tsar's army in World War I). What officially appears on the document was slightly different: it came out as Hirsch (Harry) Moritz. The explanation was that the registry clerk suggested that Hirsch would burden me in life. So Daddy compromised, but I was never called anything but Harry.

The fur business, like most other businesses during the late 1920s and early '30s, was impacted by the worldwide Depression. My father was in debt and his creditors wanted him to declare bankruptcy. He refused, and tirelessly worked to meet his financial obligations, though his suppliers did not treat him kindly. Even during these hard times my family retained two members of their house staff, a maid and a governess for me. They stayed with us because they had no other job or any other place to live. They were not paid a salary because we had no money, but they lived in the apartment and ate with our family—out of the same pot, as the saying goes.

My family's fur business emerged out of hard times, until the Nazi boycott of Jewish businesses in 1934 impacted it once more. To save on overhead, my parents that year downsized, moving the business to Ansbacherstrasse 56. My family lived behind the salon and workshop. The location was off the Wittenbergplatz, the site of the world-famous Kaufhaus des Westens (KaDeWe), and the elegant Tauentzienstrasse and Kurfuerstendamm—an upscale part of town. The store faced the Ansbacherstrasse, while the rest of the apartment windows looked into the courtyard. At the rear of the apartment there was an entrance that connected to the courtyard.

Except for one or two fragments of memory from my earliest days, what I remember most clearly about my childhood relates to Ansbacherstrasse, where we resided until we left Germany. My sister Resi, who helped raise me, recalled that I showed an early talent for making up stories. She said I regularly told tales that, temporarily at least, convinced my parents of their authenticity. One of these had me saying that a man had come into our apartment when my parents were out. Upset by my story, my parents searched the rooms before I finally confessed that I had made it up.

My mother kept me in long hair long after the common age for shearing boys had passed. Before I was sent off to school, my hair was finally cut. My parents had a record collection, but the classics were not what attracted me. The song I cherished was in Yiddish and called *Ich Vill nit gehn in Cheder* (I don't want to go school). It was sung by a young boy, whose voice broke into sobs as he sang. The song captured my attitude toward school, which I viewed not so much as an opportunity to learn as something that had to be put up with.

Along with other keepsakes, some of my school records, kept in a binder, accompanied us to America. The first page is from the 8b class, in the summer of 1936, in the No.164 State School. It was issued on October 6, 1936, when I was seven. It notes that my behavior was "very good," my attentiveness was "good," and my diligence was rated "good" too. I received a "satisfactory" in German speech and in writing, Nature Studies, penmanship, drawing, music, and Physical Training. My highest mark was in arithmetic, a "good."

I made it as far as 7b class in the public school with slightly improving marks, scoring more "goods" but never attaining a "very good." My last report card from the Volksschule is dated March 20, 1937, when Jews were excluded. I don't recall being particularly ragged by my schoolmates in public school because I was Jewish. The main difference from them, as far as I was aware, was that I was excused and left school during religious instruction. I don't remember if there were other Jewish kids in my class or that school, although there might have been some.

With the expulsion of Jews from public schools, my sister's education at the Auguste Viktoria Lyceum came to an end. I was moved to a school set up by the Jewish Community in the Fasanenstrasse Temple. In this new setting, my grades, which had been on a gradual upswing, began to decline. My final report card is dated March 27, 1939. My teacher, who up until that final report had signed herself only as K. Hirsch, now wrote Kaette Sara Hirsch. This usage followed a government decree that all Jewish women had to add Sara to their name and all Jewish men Israel. This was ordered so that non-Jews who might come into contact with Jews through means of a document would not be confused about who they were. My final report card in Berlin, a very poor one, was not returned to the school signed by my father, because we were ready to depart for America.

In Berlin, our religious observances were minimal. On High Holidays we attended a synagogue on the Kleiststrasse. We worshipped alongside other East European Jews in an unadorned hall with temporary chairs, rented for the occasion. The German Jews worshipped in the main sanctuary, with their rabbi and cantor attired all in white. Their prayer shawls were neatly folded and draped around their necks, and their heads covered not by a hat or ordinary yarmulke, but by a white high hat, almost resembling a bishop's mitre. The East European Jews wore their everyday hats or standard yarmulkes and many wrapped themselves in their tallesim, prayer shawls, as if they were sheets. These different forms of observances of Judaism were striking even to a young boy like me.

About the time that I started attending the Jewish Community school I began to go to Friday night temple services, almost always by myself, as odd as that may seem for that time and place. Although I probably was in synagogue more often than anyone else in my family, one situation arose that led my parents to think I was in danger of not adhering to Jewish traditions. It was Christmastime, and I must have asked my parents about what Saint Nicholas would bring me. In Germany, it was customary for children to shine their shoes in anticipation that Saint Nicholas would stuff them with goodies based on the quality of the polishing job. Whatever my provocation, I was swiftly dragooned into attending a Chanukah party at the home of family friends. We children received small presents, purportedly in a context to provide a Jewish alternative to the Christian holiday.

Yet the person who handed out the gifts asked questions about each kid's behavior before forking over a present, aping the Christian custom supposedly being displaced. The gift giver went further, showing up with a fake white beard and a red stocking cap, with a white puffy ball at its point, just like Saint Nicholas.

There were not many Jews living in our immediate neighborhood. The only other Jew on our block that I knew was a physician. Doctors displayed their medical specialty on a rectangular plaque affixed to the apartment building facade at street level. The background was white, with the doctor's name, specialty, telephone number, and office hours printed in black. Eventually, the German government decreed that Jewish practitioners replace the white plaques with signs with a light blue background, still with black lettering and including a blue Star of David within a yellow circle. The purpose was to warn Aryans from seeking treatment from Jews.

Another memory from childhood was collecting money from Jews for the Jewish National Fund. According to the amounts I managed to solicit, a number of stamps were pasted on a page. When the page was filled, the rows of stamps revealed a Palestinian scene. The doctor was a generous contributor and rapidly filled up a page or more in my book with his donations.

My childhood was spent entirely within an encompassing anti-Semitism that was a natural part of my world. Its absence would have seemed strange. Even as a child, I was buffeted by the overpowering racial stereotyping of Jews as disloyal, unscrupulous, obese, thick-lipped, and greedy. Although I could with a child's insight see the lies of these racist caricatures, they overwhelmed me and inculcated a sense of inferiority in me. This feeling never wholly disappeared, as in later life I disdained going into business because the Nazis proclaimed that vocation the sole talent of the Jews.

I had direct experience of that stereotyping when I was quite young. I was playing doctor with several young boys and two young girls of like ages from our apartment house. When we were discovered, there was a brouhaha. Not long afterward, as I played with one of the kids in his apartment, the mother pointedly spoke of that incident as *Juedische schweinerei*—Jewish filth. I fully understood that she was heaping all the blame for the doctor affair on my shoulders, and I was too intimidated to protest.

The closest friend I had who was not Jewish was a boy named Haenschen, who lived across the street. I recall him as a Catholic. Among the youngsters on my block with whom I played, the typical childhood games sometimes gave way to anti-Jewish outbursts, with incidents of bullying, pushing, and shoving along with lots of name calling, all of which I channeled into the background accommodating to the world I lived in. In between these anti-Semitic incidents our group of friends occasionally went off to a movie together. During the 1936 Olympics, we collected the signatures of foreign visitors, who were rather easy to spot. We also copied license plate numbers of automobiles with great enthusiasm. I can't remember the point of it, but we amassed long columns of plate numbers in notebooks. How I adjusted to the prevailing winds is illustrated by the fact that one time I joined my buddies to collect money for the Hitler Jugend.

One day I walked with friends to a wide boulevard where it had been announced Adolf Hitler was going to pass. As the crowd along the route was thick, I climbed a tree, and caught a glimpse of Hitler speeding by in his open touring car.

At one point, the Nazi Party opened a playroom for kids in an empty store on our block. A lot of young boys gathered there, and I joined without a second thought that somehow I might not belong. Shortly after I arrived, however, the pretty young woman who was in charge politely told me I had to leave. I did not make anything out of this because I was used to being dismissed from my public school room when the class received religious instruction. A few days later I returned to the neighborhood playroom and was immediately confronted again by the young woman, who firmly explained that I was not welcome there at any time. The acts that separated a Jewish child from his German playmates, although unpleasant at the time, didn't seem very important—except that cumulatively they demonstrated even to a child the increasing isolation being imposed on Jews.

Because of my age and presumed naïveté, my parents spoke discreetly in front of me about current events. When I burst into one of my parents' conversations, my mother immediately said what a fine man Hitler was, careful to repeat it several times. I quickly realized she wanted to make sure that if I recounted anything to my playmates it would be an appreciation of Der Fuehrer. Even at my young age, I detected the disingenuous nature of the Hitler compliments and noted the thin smile as she spoke of Herr Hitler. I understood why she was keeping up this pretense and knew not to say anything about my parents' true views about Hitler to my playmates.

On weekends, my family occasionally went to a kind of Jewish country club on one of Berlin's many lakes. One afternoon my family sat at a table with friends and I went to play at the dock where sailboats were moored. I wasn't watching myself as I tried to snag a rolling soda bottle, became careless, and fell off the dock. The water was over my head and I did not know how to swim. I thrashed about in a panic, bobbing up and then going under several times. I felt I was about to drown when someone pulled me out and set me down on the dock.

The man who dove in to save me injured himself, and my grateful parents paid his medical bills. I met him again when he visited our fur store. I remember solemnly shaking his hand and expressing my thanks. For a couple of weeks afterward, my mother disappeared in the middle of the day. She was very secretive and did not tell anyone where she was going. Each time, she carried a wrapped tube-like parcel. My sister later speculated our mother went to church on those occasions to light tapers in gratitude for my survival, there being no available Jewish ceremonial equivalent.

During my childhood in Berlin my parents welcomed many strangers into our home, and the visitors slept on a spare couch. They would spend a night or maybe two with us before moving on in search of safety abroad. My family traveled as well, not only to visit friends and relatives in England, France, and Poland. They had an additional reason for these trips. Mother and sometimes Resi would wear a fur coat and pack a few more in their luggage. When they arrived abroad, the coats would be sold and the earnings deposited by our English relatives in a British bank. Those deposits were substantially increased through an arrangement with diplomats connected to the American and French embassies in Berlin. Through an intermediary, cash was transported by a courier traveling on official business to London where it was handed over to our relatives minus the middleman's reasonable fee. My parents never knew who these couriers were, only that they were punctilious carrying out what they promised.

Occasionally, my mother took me with her to Warsaw, London, or Paris. On the trip to France in 1936, we changed trains when we reached the border. One strange but lasting memory of that trip is that the French train reeked of urine; Hitler's trains smelled better. When we were crossing the Channel heading to England, we were on the ship's deck when there was a sudden commotion. Mother asked a deckhand what was going on. He replied, "Madam, civil war has just broken out in Spain."

Before the Nazis took power, and even after they began targeting Jews, my parents went out on the town. My sister recalled that they kept up an active social life, apparently unbowed by the New Order. They loved opera, for one thing, and their photo album showed them in earlier times attending elegant costume parties. One Christmas Eve I remember watching Daddy getting dressed in white tie and tails, and off they went. Resi was out. So I decided to wander across the street to my friend's apartment where people dressed in party attire were gathering. Observing from the sidelines, sadness overcame me because as hospitable as my friend's family was, I felt out of place at their celebration. Disconsolate, I returned across the street to our apartment and the company of our maid.

Bit by bit, the life of Jews in Germany became constricted. After Jews were prohibited from attending public theater, we dressed up to attend special theatrical events where all the performers and the audience were Jews. I remember a uniformed SS officer rambled through the crowd before one entertainment began, his very presence a menace. He may have been Adolf Eichmann himself, who shipped countless Jews to their deaths. Books and other accounts recounted that he did that sort of thing in his effort to become the Reich's top expert on Jewry. Then, again, it may have been someone else.

Over time, the anti-Semitic incidents became more frightening. I had a teenaged acquaintance, a friend of a friend, who lived around the corner. He had a collection of nude photos, which he liked to show off. To me, much younger, the photos were more of a curiosity than an attraction.

One day, while two of us were visiting him, the teenager's mother hurriedly packed a small suitcase and made her son and husband flee their apartment immediately. They must have had a warning that the Gestapo were coming for them. As they rushed out, the mother paused to give me and my friend a half a Mark each, and asked us to pray for them. I never found out what happened to them. It is unlikely that they ever returned to their Berlin apartment.

My childhood memories come back to me in fragments that I've tried to piece together. I remember accompanying Resi and some of her Gentile girlfriends on a walk in the countryside. We passed through an area where there were military barracks, crowded with young men hanging out of the windows on a warm day. It may have been a Hitler Youth encampment, or soldiers' barracks, or more likely a youth labor facility. The teenagers and young men hooted and hollered at the young girls. I was frightened by their rowdy behavior. I pleaded with my sister to get out of there, but the girls seemed not to be bothered by the boisterous attention.

In hindsight, these incidents might appear mundane, but they stuck in my memory as reminders of our life in Germany. They are snapshots of the reality that pervaded my Berlin boyhood, and they only hint at the oppressiveness, because I was a child and sheltered by my family from the worst humiliations. The terrifying reality of life in Hitler's Germany impacted our family with an insistent knocking on the door at the rear of our apartment about five or six in the morning on October 28, 1938. The loud knocks roused the household, which besides our family included a maid, who as a Gentile working for Jews had to be forty-five or older, past childbearing age.

Two police officers, dressed in civilian clothes, were at the apartment door. They told my father that they were taking him to the police station nearby. They were courteous and said that they were only doing their job. They would not explain why Daddy was being taken into custody. I watched my father dress and heard him discuss with my mother in a low voice what his arrest could possibly be about. He speculated that it might be a complaint by a dissatisfied customer or a disgruntled former employee. After Daddy was taken away, Resi and I, silent and frightened throughout the ordeal, loudly wept in each other's arms. The Nazis had afflicted us personally as never before. Mother told Resi, then seventeen years old, to follow Daddy to the police station to try to learn why he had been arrested. It was not unusual for Resi to be called upon to undertake responsibilities far beyond her years, including smuggling a document for a family friend when she returned from a visit to Warsaw. Had she been detected, my sister could have been sent to prison or even executed.

When Resi reached the police station, she briefly glimpsed Daddy among a crowd of men. She was not allowed to speak with him in the confused situation. A police officer refused to tell her about what was unfolding. Instead, the officer advised Resi to go home and pack a small suitcase with a change of clothes for our father and bring it back to the station. As the suitcase was being packed, mother at the last minute put in a large loaf of bread. Resi returned to the police station just in time to see Daddy on the back of an open truck, along with a lot of other men, none of whom she recognized. As they were driven off, Resi ran along the side of the truck and managed to hand him the suitcase.

For the next three days we did not know what had happened to father; we had no idea if he was hurt or even alive. On the fourth day, he telephoned. He told us he was staying in the home of mother's eldest sister in Warsaw and that he was all right. He had been placed aboard a train along with other Polish Jews living in Germany who were being expelled to their motherland. The Poles, after some delay at the border, permitted the train he was on to enter the country, as they did for two other trainloads of expelled Polish Jews. Once those trains had crossed the border, the Poles hardened in their initial hesitancy and decided they did not want any more Jews, mirroring the actions of the Germans. Trapped at the border in no-man's land, with little food or shelter, in time most of the Jews perished from gunfire and other punishments inflicted by both German and Polish soldiers. Daddy had been very lucky to survive.

Later on, my father shared some details of his train ordeal. Two anecdotes stand out in my mind. Crammed into a railcar and unable to find a comfortable spot, Father opened the suitcase Resi had handed him hoping to find his slippers to change into. He saw no slippers, but he did come upon the loaf of bread. With it, he managed to sustain himself and other men during those three arduous days. Father also told us that as an SS man hovered over the prone Jews on the floor of the train, he looked up and it struck him that on the belt buckle of the Nazi guard the words *Gott Mitt Uns* (God is with Us) was embossed.

2

Kristallnacht

While Father was in Poland living with relatives, from the end of October to the end of the following March, Mother cared for Resi and me and ran the business. She refused to give in to the dire events that were confronting us. Less than two weeks after Daddy's arrest, there was another unexpected knock on our rear door. This time it came during daytime, and the person who was at our door was well known to our family.

For years, my parents had been friendly with a couple, she a German Christian, he a Polish Jew. As a prisoner of war of the Germans in World War I, he was assigned to work on the farm owned by the woman's family. They fell in love and married after the war, remaining in Germany. In time, they became friends with my parents in Berlin. Before the events of 1938 the family emigrated to Brazil.

The woman's brother, who was our visitor, was married to a woman who worked in the office of Joseph Goebbels, the propaganda minister and an instigator of Kristallnacht. Upon earlier occasions, the brother had been helpful to my parents as a result of his wife's position. He had never come to our apartment, but instead called from a public telephone booth. He tore our nameplate off the door and urged us to immediately leave our home and take refuge in the Polish Embassy. Mother guardedly alerted friends by phone and then we rushed to the Polish Embassy.

When my mother, sister, and I arrived at the embassy we found it was filling quickly with Polish Jews, mostly women and children seeking sanctuary. I spotted some friends in the crowd. It was a raw, cold November day and we tried to get inside one of the buildings to get warm. A guard stopped us and said that Mother and I could enter, but my sister, because she was older, could not because space was limited. Mother and I went in, staying a short time before mother decided she did not want to leave Resi outside by herself.

Once outside, I ran around and played games with friends I met there. Every so often I saw open trucks passing in the street beyond a high iron fence that surrounded the embassy. The trucks were filled with singing Brownshirts. We remained in the compound for many hours until word came from the Polish authorities that it would be safe to return to our homes. My mother, sister, and I walked home in the dark, along with some others who took refuge in the embassy, and got a sense of what had taken place while we had diplomatic protection. We passed vandalized stores. The sidewalks in front of the stores were littered with the broken plate glass that was to give the night its chillingly memorable name: Kristallnacht. No one bothered us.

Mother showed remarkable strength in those fateful days and nights and in the weeks ahead. She was a short woman, standing just shy of five feet. But her height was no measure of her stature, her resolve, and her calm. As we walked home, she said, "I hope everything is smashed into little pieces. I hope nothing is left." This was a pointed remark and it puzzled me because my parents took pride in their Art Deco furniture, handcrafted out of ebony and mahogany. They were expensive pieces and outfitted the apartment in grand style. They also owned Persian carpets, many valuable pieces of Dresden porcelain, and a large collection of fine crystal.

In that moment of trouble, mother was able to look beyond her attachment to her possessions, and let them go as if they never had meant anything to her, underlining her fortitude.

When we arrived home, we found the fur store and our apartment undamaged. It appeared that our shop was one of the few Jewish-owned businesses that did not suffer some damage. There are no certain explanations for our property escaping harm, but there are several possibilities. First, the Nazi gangs who committed the destruction generally came from other parts of the city, so they might not have known that our store, whose front was shuttered from top to bottom, was a Jewish establishment. Jewish businesses were commanded to have the owner's name painted in large white letters on their front window.

Also, we may have been spared because the man who came to warn us tore the nameplate off the apartment door. The door itself was steel-sheeted on the inside, with many bolts, intended to forestall burglars. My sister much later surmised that our neighbors liked our family and did not turn us in to the Nazi raiders, as other Jewish stores in the neighborhood were smashed up.

Our Polish nationality might have been another reason that we were spared. It later became known that the German leadership had instructed their minions to leave non-German Jews alone. While that order was not always obeyed (the first Jew to die on Kristallnacht was Polish), it more or less was followed.

After Kristallnacht, our store's shutters were not raised again.

The next morning, I nagged Mother to let me go outside with a friend who was about my age (since 2005, after my encounter with Gustav's history, I have come to believe that it probably was Gustav). I can't explain why she gave me permission to walk the streets in the aftermath of Kristallnacht. At the time it seemed natural to me; looking backward now, it is difficult to understand. My friend and I walked past stores with shattered windows. One was a large department store along the upscale Tauentzienstrasse. As we passed, the shards were being swept up. We headed for our school in the Fasanenstrasse Temple. We saw the synagogue burning, smoke enfolding its massive Moorish dome. German firemen and their apparatuses were standing by, at the ready, not to put out the fire but to make sure that the flames would not spread to nearby Aryan properties. We joined the crowd of people gathered to watch in silence the desecration of a central symbol of the Jewish community. Goebbels's diary later revealed that he had personally ordered the attack on it. It was the foremost liberal temple in Berlin. At its construction more than two decades earlier, it was regarded as a symbol of the confidence Jews had of their place in Germany.

As harsh as Kristallnacht was for us, it was far from the worst thing that befell Jews in Germany. Jews were killed throughout the country during those days and nights. Tens of thousands were sent to concentration camps. A collective fine of a billion Reichsmarks was levied by the German government on the Jewish community. The massive penalty was represented as an indemnity for the assassination of Ernst vom Rath, second secretary in the German legation in Paris. The assassin was Herschel Grynspan, the son of a Polish Jewish couple who, like my parents, lived for many years in Germany and who were deported to Poland and wound up in the no-man's land with other Polish Jews expelled by Germany.

The Germans told the world that vom Rath's killing was the reason for the depredations, which they described as spontaneous. Today it is known what then was not: Kristallnacht was the beginning of Hitler's planned, systematic genocidal war against the Jews, surpassing by far the various persecutions unleashed during earlier Nazi years.

Kristallnacht increased my family's urgency to leave Germany. My parents had had an emigration application on file at the American Embassy since 1934. At that time, Daddy was told he could go to America and send for us to join him once he earned a living. He declined that offer because he would have had to leave his wife and children behind in a Germany where the situation for Jews worsened by the day. Our family's application remained on file, and we did not stop trying to get out. In anticipation of emigration, Mother hired a tutor to teach me to write in the form of penmanship used in America, which differed somewhat from the German. During the weeks and months following Kristallnacht we most anxiously waited for our quota number to come up. The quota system was the key for acquiring visas to enter the United States. Our quota number became a consuming obsession; it was our only way to safety. Mother frequently sent Resi, who had learned English in school, to the American consulate to inquire where matters stood. My sister would queue up along with other Jews and wait for hours to hear whether their number had come up. Poland was allotted very few openings for emigrants, because of a law enacted by the United States Congress in the 1920s that was designed to limit the number of East Europeans and South Europeans, because of ethnic and religious prejudice. At the same time, American authorities opened the gates wide for the more desirable English and non-Jewish German immigrants. Jews living in Germany were targeted by a cabal of rabid anti-Semites in the State Department. These high-placed bigots were determined in their efforts to keep the Jews from coming to America even as the Jews in Germany were being excluded from normal civic life, rounded up for concentration camps, and killed.

With Daddy in Warsaw and no quota number in hand, Mother thought that it might be best if we joined him in Poland to wait there for our emigration permits. An official at the American consulate in Berlin warned us against such a move, advising that it would complicate our application. By offering us his honest assessment, the official did us a lifesaving favor, because, as it turned out, the odds were against us making it out of Poland to the United States before the outbreak of the war.

While we were waiting and Mother was considering what was best to do, she continued to operate the business with the help of Gentile employees. Ironically, business was good. With the store's front shuttered, loyal German customers came through the rear court-yard door. Business was so strong Mother purchased bundles of furs from other Jewish furriers who were not doing well. I remember accompanying Mother on a garment delivery, which may have been during this time. We went to the residence of a mistress of a very high-ranking Wehrmacht general. I remember her more clearly than I might otherwise because she met us in her sitting room attired in a flimsy negligee, which revealed more of the female form than I had ever seen. Being well brought up, I immediately averted my eyes.

Finally, the day came when our quota number was granted, in March but formally issued by the Department of State on April 11, 1939. My immigration number was 6064, and the card is a cherished possession. The back of my immigration identity card documented our arrival date in America, on May 16, 1939. After so much fearful waiting, our long-sought departure from the Third Reich was bureau-cratically mundane. Daddy was permitted to return to Germany and did so on March 30, so that he could accompany his family to the United States. Stacks of forms had to be authenticated before the bureaucratic wheels would turn. Birth and marriage dates along with other data had to be validated. A number of official documents in Polish were translated into German, from which I drew many of the details used in this account.

With Daddy still in Poland, the three of us trooped to the con-sulate to stand in a long slow-moving line. After a long time, we reached the desk of a bureaucrat. I just had a tooth pulled, and my face was distorted by swelling. In our anxiety we feared that since my swollen face looked different from the photo in our official papers, it might interfere with receiving our visas. The consulate official was a young fellow, who greeted us with his feet propped on the desk in an obvious gesture of contempt and total indifference to the grave situ-ation out of which we were trying to extricate ourselves. His outer office was managed by a young German woman, who was viewed by the desperate would-be immigrants as a dispenser of fateful power. Years later, my parents ran across her in New York. They spoke to her and learned that she was Jewish. Her life in New York was not going well. She was poorly dressed and living in a rooming house, a powerless and bereft figure.

After our formal papers were in hand, Mother sold her precious furniture to a young German couple for a pittance. Under normal circumstances they probably could not have been able to afford such fine furniture. By the time Daddy returned to us in Berlin, we had moved out of our apartment and had taken rooms in an apartment building across the street. The rooms were on an upper floor and we looked down at our closed storefront. My sister remembers Daddy being depressed, sitting at the window for long periods, silent and staring.

The apartment in which we rented two rooms was the residence of an elderly Gentile woman. Her late husband had been Jewish, and she had a son who was a musician. The son might have been in his twenties or thirties. In desperation, the widow implored my parents to permit her son to marry Resi so that he could leave Germany with us. But that scheme had no chance of succeeding, given the bureaucratic obstacles.

In addition to selling off what we could, we were allowed to ship a number of very large duffel bags that were stuffed with goods. Each of us was limited to taking ten Marks out of the country. So Mother ordered feather comforters and linens, and she got me a custom-made bathrobe, blue with large red dots. In the duffels we shipped valuable crystal and other fineries, including one large Persian rug and oil paintings from our apartment. Again, Resi was given the task of getting these duffels to the train station. A Gentile girl-friend accompanied her. They waited for hours as the paperwork was processed and a Gestapo officer looked the goods over and allowed the shipment to go on to New York. Resi was a brave and obedient daughter, and I idolized her for the care she always took of me.

I said goodbye to my friends and acquaintances, some of them not all that friendly. I could not resist deploying my storytelling talents, admittedly to irritate them and arouse envy. I said we were moving to the American West where an (imaginary) uncle owned a ranch. Not to overdo it, I said I did not know for sure whether I would encounter any Indians when I got there.

3

Coming to America

In April 1939, my family left Berlin and took a train to Hamburg. We put up in a Hamburg hotel before departing for England the next day. We spent our last day in Germany waiting to board a ship to carry us across the North Sea to Hull, a port on the northeast coast of England. For lunch that day, we bought cold cuts and bread and sat on a park bench eating sandwiches. It was April 16, 1939, as we prepared to board the small ship. At that point I almost made a critical error. I was asked by a German functionary how it felt to leave Germany. I momentarily dropped my guard and began to answer more honestly than I should have. Luckily, my father stopped me in mid-sentence before I could blurt out my true feelings and perhaps endanger our departure.

The North Sea crossing was so rough that every passenger except me, my sister, and a male passenger became seasick. By the next day, before we landed in Hull, I remained the only one not under the weather. We had permission to remain in England until May 10, and in London we stayed with the family of my great-aunt, who had a house in Clapham. My father's depression disappeared with his arrival in England. One evening, everyone listened to a shortwave broadcast of a speech by Adolf Hitler. Resi became so agitated by his rant that she urged us to leave immediately and catch an earlier ship.

When our scheduled sojourn ended, we moved to a hotel on our last night in England as part of our embarkation process. I developed a severe rash all over my body, probably from coarse bedsheets. For some hours it appeared that Mother and I might have to remain in England, because of fears that the authorities would not permit me to board in that condition. By morning, the spots had cleared up as mysteriously as they had appeared and we boarded the Cunard liner *SS Aquitania.* She was one of the major luxury liners making regular Atlantic crossings from 1914 through the 1940s, a very luxurious ship in her public spaces. Our second-class cabins were cramped and had pipework running along the ceiling. It was exciting to roam freely around the ship and its several tiers of decks. There was a swimming pool that I admired only from a distance. I had not yet learned to swim.

We chose to be served in the kosher dining room, a decision my parents made not because we observed kashruth, but because we simply preferred to be with Jewish people more than anyone else, given our recent experience. On this voyage, we had a good time, all except Daddy, who was the only one of us who continued to suffer from seasickness. Six days after leaving Southampton, *Aquitania* sailed into New York Harbor. I got my first and most meaningful look at the Statue of Liberty, understanding as a boy the symbolism of her standing at the gateway to America. My appreciation of what she stood for deepened over the years as I learned of her history and of the ideals she represents.

In New York, our immigration papers were processed aboard the ship, and so we missed the experience, shared by so many immigrants, of setting foot in America on Ellis Island. *Aquitania* docked at the Cunard pier on the West Side of Manhattan and we stood at the rail and waved to relatives waiting on the pier below. Daddy's brothers Wolf and Charlie were there, as was his sister, Frieda, and their families. Mother pointed out an uncle here and a cousin there. They had no trouble recognizing each other despite a gap of many years since they were last together. After we collected our baggage, we took a taxi to the Bronx, which would be my first home in America and where Uncle Wolf's family lived.

With that taxi ride the Americanization of Harry Rosenfeld began. From the first moment, I instinctively and wholeheartedly searched for ways to become part of the new life that was opening for me in my new homeland.

Uncle Wolf, known as Willie in America, was Daddy's youngest brother, who had emigrated from Poland many years earlier. His family's apartment was decorated with red, white, and blue paper streamers and a welcoming sign. I was fascinated that my cousin, Alvin, had a collection of books that were new to me. There were squarish children's books, which were smaller than regular books, with a hard cover. He also had many comic books, which to me at first seemed far less interesting and important since they lacked hard covers. I spent my first days in America while Alvin was in school rearranging his books, and I totally disregarded the comics. In time, I, too became an avid reader of comics, my favorites being Submariner, a man who had pointed ears and could breathe under water, along with a character who could transform his body into a flame.

We stayed with Uncle Willie on 184th Street for one week. Daddy was uneasy about imposing on his brother so he went out and, without speaking any English, rented an apartment a few blocks away from Willie's place. He did this without consulting Mother, perhaps for the first and only time in his married life. She never forgave him. Our first apartment in America was at 2363 Valentine Avenue at the corner of 184th Street. It was two blocks east of the Grand Concourse, the prime shopping district in the Bronx in those days. Uncle Willie took Daddy with him to the downtown wholesale fur factory where he worked. My father didn't last long there, not because he couldn't do the work but because he wouldn't. The craftsmanship that went into the making of garments was not up to his standards. In short order, my parents rented a store on the western side of the Grand Concourse, on the same block where the Alexander department store, a Bronx institution, anchored the corner. My parents' business consisted of a showroom in front and a workroom in the back. It was a comedown from Ansbacherstrasse, but it was where Sam and Esther Rosenfeld made their living in America. It was called the Rosenfeld Fur Shoppe.

In those early days, our family was materially better off than our American relatives, thanks to my parents' London bank account. From the outset, Daddy co-signed notes for his brother and Mother's cousin to help them out. When we got around to unpacking the duffels sent from Germany, our relatives were amazed to see the crystal and other fineries, much of which my parents shared with them.

In our first months in America my English was rudimentary, but I was acquiring it quickly. I made a conscious decision not to speak German, and in a short time largely had shed it and my accent for practical purposes. In those early days, I was intrigued by many mysteries about America. Passing an urban garage, I noticed that the brick wall featured a large painted sign: No Smoking. I could not fathom why a garage had to forbid either their customers or their workers from wearing tuxedos. To me and my German background, a "smoking" was, of course, a dinner jacket. Similarly, I would come across signs proclaiming: Post No Bills. Why would anyone place dollar bills on some nondescript wall?

All my playmates in the first few months in America lived on or near the block where the store was located. The leader of the group, which included some girls, was Buddy Flanigan. Another kid, a bit younger than the others, was a tall and skinny boy named Jack Molinas. When it came to choosing sides for games, Jack was the last one picked. I was next to last. Jack lived with his widowed mother and a sister. He became an All-American basketball player at Columbia University before turning pro, bringing hope to his poor family. It was a pity that his grasp on fame and fortune was fleeting. Investigations revealed that he had arranged to fix college games on which he had bet. He was barred from pro basketball, remained involved in organized crime, and was killed by mobsters in 1973.

The first movie I saw in America was *Stagecoach,* and I think I remember it being shown through a greenish filter. Another early film I saw was *The Wizard of Oz,* and moviegoing became a weekly habit. We lived very close to the premier movie house in the Bronx, perhaps the finest in all of New York City. Loew's Paradise was decked out in rococo style and was a movie palace, with goldfish swimming in pools in the lobby. Inside the theater, clouds moved against a dark blue background upon which the lights of stars twinkled. As a kid, I would arrive as soon as the Paradise opened its doors on Saturday morning, sit through serials and cartoons, newsreels and coming attractions, in addition to the double feature. A matron, dressed in a white uniform and brandishing a flashlight, was all the authority needed, most times, to keep the rambunctious kids more or less in line in the assigned children's section. Too often I would sit through two showings of the double feature, emerging in the afternoon with a throbbing headache after so many hours in the flickering darkness.

My first day in an American school was in September 1939 just as World War II started. My sister Resi, at the insistence of an uncle, Americanized her name to Ray. She enrolled me in P.S. 115, more elegantly Elizabeth Barrett Browning, which was just down the block on Valentine Avenue from our apartment. Considering my meager English, the school authorities decided I should begin my studies in class 2B, which placed me a few years behind other ten-year-olds.

As a result, when we lined up in the school yard before class, I was the tallest in the group, a rare occurrence for me.

During my elementary school years I was moved up a grade on a couple of occasions, which indicated that the teachers and administrators paid attention to my particular needs and rewarded my progress. When I got to Creston Junior High, I qualified for inclusion in an accelerated class, picking up another half year. There were no special programs for non-English-speaking students, and I believe I was the only one at P.S. 115 for whom English was a second language. Full language immersion worked for me, no doubt because of the innate decency and professionalism of the teachers who took in stride the challenge I posed for their teaching and the curriculum. I never quite caught up, and graduated from high school at age eighteen, behind most of my peers.

Growing fluency in English in elementary school was only one manifestation of my rapid assimilation. I became part of the P.S. 115 school patrol before being appointed to command the Valentine Avenue squad. We got to wear official seals as armbands as well as a version of Sam Browne belts. It was a responsible position and my teachers deemed me worthy of it. I quickly settled into an American boyhood, including becoming a devoted New York Yankees fan for life, which, like marriage, is for better or worse. In my many visits to Yankee Stadium, only a mile from where I lived, I saw two no-hitters. The first was thrown by Cleveland's Bob Feller, a game for which I had cut high school; the second, years later, was Don Larsen's storied perfect World Series game.

Learning English was not the only challenge I faced. My near-sightedness and astigmatism were diagnosed in those early school years because I could not read the blackboard from my seat toward the rear of the classroom. When moving up front did not solve the problem, I was outfitted with prescription glasses by an optometrist—going to an ophthalmologist was unheard of in those days. I have worn eyeglasses ever since.

It was in elementary school that I learned a bitter lesson. The class was discussing Sherlock Holmes, and I ventured that he was a real person, as my mother had told me. I was hooted down by my classmates and felt great embarrassment. I could not imagine how she could have been so wrong. Many, many years later, steeped in the lore of newspapering, I came across the advice that supposedly was given to reporters about the need to remain skeptical: "If your mother says she loves you, check it out"—a vainglorious admonition surely more honored in the breach than the observance.

The most lasting impact the elementary school years had on me was that during that time I discovered our local public library. At school, we were encouraged to read as a matter of course. Our teachers made a competition of it to spur us on. A poster recorded how many books each kid in class had read. Our public library branch was on Bainbridge Avenue, off Fordham Road, and I became a regular patron. I started checking out history books that I had no possibility of comprehending. Soon enough, I found my own level and began a reading campaign that including devouring the Bomba the Jungle Boy adventure books, among others. My favorite books in those days were the Civil War novels for young readers by Joseph Altscheler.

After P.S. 115, girls and boys moved on to junior high, going to single-sex schools, thus ending co-ed education for me in the New York City public school system. I went to seventh grade at P.S. 79, also known as Creston Junior High, which was several blocks farther removed from my immediate neighborhood. As a consequence, I got to mingle with a much wider universe of boys from the upper reaches of the borough. The sons of the largely lower-middle and middle-middle class that lived in the northwest Bronx in the 1940s were taught at P.S. 79. Comprised of a mix of Irish, Italian, and Jewish youngsters, the school produced a generation of strivers. In my eighth grade classroom, that striving found expression in an unusual way—the establishment of a weekly newspaper, produced entirely by students, its pages run off on a mimeograph machine and distributed to the entire school. Our fellow students were not nearly as impressed as our teachers. My job on this enterprise was to act as the foreign editor (a foreshadowing if ever there was one). Each week I closely read the newspapers, mostly the tabloid *Daily Mirror* and *Daily News*, listened nightly to radio broadcasts, and gathered the information I needed for my articles. It was natural for me to want to keep up with events throughout the war-torn world, and in those days most kids were familiar with the names and locations of far-removed battle fronts.

One issue of our newspaper was devoted to a symposium on where the Second Front, the invasion of continental Europe by the Allies, should take place. My pick was Norway, on the compellingly logical grounds that invasion there would be accomplished with smaller loss of life. This scenario also would bring Sweden into the war on the Allied side and provide a base from which the final attack on the Third Reich could be staged directly, instead of having to battle through France and the Lowlands. Had Eisenhower adopted my plan, the war would have been shortened and casualties reduced. But nobody listens to a kid in junior high. My interest in newspapering grew from this beginning.

As a now nearly regular American kid, I was taught to swim at sleepover summer camp. I played baseball, softball, and football, became a Boy Scout and learned Morse code, semaphore signaling, and how to tie knots. We hiked and camped out in all but the most extreme winter days. At Scout camp I qualified for lifesaving accreditation by becoming proficient in skills that included swamping a canoe, righting it, climbing back in, and bailing it out. I collected stamps, and wrapped my best stamps in cellophane from empty cigarette packs to preserve them. I built model airplanes, without developing an addiction to the glue used to construct the models that dangled from the ceiling in my room.

In my later teens, my friend Al Bernstein and I occasionally spent the day on the beach at Coney Island. We had one scare. The surf was rough. It must have been in morning or late afternoon, because there were few people on the beach. No one was in the water besides ourselves and two little kids. Suddenly, both of them were overcome by a tidal pull and were on the verge of getting into trouble from the undertow. Al and I quickly realized what was happening and each of us grabbed a kid to drag back onto the beach. For me it was a sort of payback for the time a bystander rescued me from drowning.

My family's life was changing as much as mine. My sister was married shortly before my bar mitzvah in 1942. I held my emotions in check throughout the long and elaborate buffet reception, parrying questions about how it felt to have my only sister marry. It was during the ceremony that my composed façade crumbled and I could no longer hold back tears. She was marrying Leo Damski, whom I really liked. But an enormous milestone was being passed, a sign that we were leaving behind the close relationship of our younger years. In 1948, the summer before I left home for college, Ray and Leo bought a house in Roslyn, Long Island, the first privately owned home in our family in America (or likely elsewhere).

At Hebrew school I received the minimal instruction to get me through the bar mitzvah ceremony. The Hebrew school teachers were marked by their lack of qualification, coarseness, and ill-temper. I was made to learn the blessings only, and the rabbi would read from the Torah, the Five Books of Moses, and the Haftorah, a selection from the Book of the Prophets. I also had to memorize a speech written for me. Even this small task proved difficult. In the middle of delivering the speech, I lost track of my place and had to pull a copy out of my pocket to pick up someone else's train of thought. The only lasting impact of Hebrew school for me was that I learned to read and pronounce Hebrew, though not to actually understand the words.

My bar mitzvah celebration was modest, even by the standards of that less ostentatious era. My bar mitzvah suit was the double-breasted dark suit I wore for my sister's wedding the preceding March. The party involved a small gathering for dinner in our home for family and friends. No kids were invited. My presents were customary. I received a gold ring with my initials and a fine fountain pen. I also received a book I came to value. It was by an explorer named Richard Halliburton. It recounted his adventures as he sought places and people off the beaten track around the world.

Sometime during the years of my early teens I began to take on part-time jobs. For a short time, I sold the *Saturday Evening Post,* by going door to door, mainly to stores. I never made enough to keep up my interest. I worked briefly as a delivery boy for a grocery store, but abandoned the job when I found that tips in this lower-middle-class neighborhood were skimpy for hauling heavy boxes up several flights of stairs. Long before high school, I began to work in the family business. I picked up and delivered fur coats for winter storage in a Harlem warehouse. I was also sent downtown to pick up needed supplies. I regularly went to the embroiderers, who like us, were a family of refugees. They produced elegant initials in needlework, in whatever color and design was ordered by the customer. The initials were incorporated into the silky lining of the finished garment. The staple garment for the rising Jewish middle class in the Bronx was a Persian lamb coat. A less costly version was the Persian paw coat. There were also Hudson seals and silver foxes. But the people who were emerging from the Great Depression were still a long way from being able to afford to wear mink.

Whether working or not, I spent much of my time in the store, where both my parents stayed until well into the night, frequently until about 10 or 10:30 p.m., six days a week, much of the year. It was a hard life for them. My father thrived on work and by his example in this and many other things he shaped my behavior. He had strong arms, hands, and fingers. To make a coat, a furrier wetted the pelts and stretched them. Then he placed them on large wooden boards and nailed them down so they would dry at their most expandable size. In one hand, Daddy held a flat-headed hammer, somewhat like tongs with flattened ends. He hammered the nails at neat, regular intervals, one hit to a nail. They were so evenly spaced that any variance was too small to notice. With one side of the pelt nailed, he would stretch the other side, grasping it with the hammer head. Stretching it to its utmost required strength in the wrist as well as the hand.

When one side of the large wooden board was filled with pelts, he picked it up, one hand on the left side and the other on the right. With his arms fully stretched he lifted the board, turned it over and placed it on two wooden sawhorses with the unused side facing up. These everyday manual labors testified to his dexterity and strength.

Daddy designed the coat, cut the pelts with a razor-sharp knife, and also sewed the skins together. As business picked up he hired part-time finishers (his sister Frieda was one; another was a cousin by marriage) and an operator to work the fur sewing machine. I remember one operator clearly. I used to watch him work and listen to him talk. He told me his dream had been to become an auto worker for Ford. As Ford would not hire Jews, he found his life's work in the fur trade, a traditional Jewish occupation. He was a member of the fur workers' union but his work for Daddy was not done with the approval of the union. Daddy's was not a union shop, nor would he stand for one. The union was not only communist but also corrupt.

From time to time, union inspectors swooped down on the fur stores on the Grand Concourse to check whether their members were moonlighting in nonunion shops. The shop owners contrived an alarm system. At the first indication of a union raid, the first owner to get a sense of it phoned another, who was obliged to alert the next one and so on. On those occasions when the union apparatchiks caught Daddy in the act, there was a payoff, in the form of a subscription to the Yiddish Communist paper, *Die Freiheit*, which was never delivered. No serious loss there.

I came to enjoy the rituals and rhythms of the store. On Saturday afternoons, Daddy without fail had the radio in the workroom set to the *Texaco Opera of the Air*. There are times when I find myself listening to the *Opera of the Air*, still being broadcast so many years later, or playing opera recordings, when it all comes back to me and I am swept up by the memory of my father at his work.

During the war, when I was fourteen or so, I became a messenger in the Air Raid Warden System for our neighborhood. When the alarm sounded and people turned off their lights, I would put on my dark blue garrison cap and armband, and run downstairs to meet my Air Raid Warden, shouting at violators to put out their lights. My job was to be a runner and to help with the logistics. I continued to do this until the air raid warning system was disbanded.

During those wartime years all outside lights were turned down and when darkness fell we lived in a constant state of brownout. Many lighted store signs were extinguished for the duration of the war, others were dimmed. Car headlights were blacked out except for a narrow horizontal strip across their middle. We listened intently to the news of the war on the radio. The most riveting of all radio broadcasts were, without question, President Roosevelt's. When he took to the air, customarily at night around nine o'clock, the streets in the Bronx's business section, busy until then, cleared entirely. Immediately after the president finished, activity resumed on the streets. It was in this neighborhood of the Grand Concourse and Fordham Road that on a cold, rainy October day in 1944, I glimpsed my first president. FDR was campaigning for his fourth term and toured the Bronx that day, despite the rain, in an open car, waving to the crowds massed on the sidewalks.

One summer, Daddy arranged through a relative for a job for me as a floor boy with a wholesale fur manufacturer downtown. My pay was about twenty dollars a week, maybe less. The owners were Novick and Moss. Moss was an English Jew who also lived in the Bronx. Partnerships in the fur trade were often short-lived arrangements. Two operators would scratch up a handful of capital, rent a loft, install the machinery, and set up shop. Often they had at least one pretty large customer who kept them going. When their short string ran out, they broke up and went back to being workmen, or found themselves a new partner and a fresh source of start-up capital.

Novick and Moss didn't know what they were getting when they hired me. Not only did I do all that was required of me—I wetted the leopard-dyed rabbit skins before the cutter worked on them, hauled the mouton pelts from the stacks, and so forth. When I was not so occupied, on my own initiative I set about cleaning the place up. Not merely sweeping up the surface dirt, I cleaned behind and underneath the machinery, attacking dirt that had never been disturbed.

I earned a reputation as a good worker who did not need to be told how to keep busy. Every day I piloted a Jewish "jet" through the side streets of the Fur District in the twenties and thirties between Seventh and Eighth Avenues, making deliveries to various coat manufacturers, dropping off fur collars and cuffs to adorn their garments. The Jewish jet was a rectangular wooden cart set on four small wheels, with a built-in rack on which to hang the clothing items. The cart was about three feet high on all four sides.

I worked hard, sweated profusely, and never considered myself too good for the menial tasks I was doing. Nevertheless, if Daddy expected this exposure to help prepare me to join him in his business—as I believe he did—it failed. While I was glad to have the work and paycheck, I did not see it as a prelude to a career.

The decision to go to a high school outside of the neighborhood was entirely mine. My parents had no grasp of the American educational system. I had decided to avoid going to the designated high school in the Bronx for Creston graduates, who completed ninth grade there. Without any encouragement or discouragement, I took the competitive entrance exam for Stuyvesant High, a selective science school. I was one of a small handful of boys from Creston to apply. Two of my close friends, Al Bernstein and Joe McClintock, made the cut along with me. Others elected to go to the Bronx High School of Science, which at the time was located exactly three and one-half blocks from my house. I sought broader horizons so I chose Stuyvesant, which meant that I either walked less than a mile to a station of the Woodlawn-Jerome Avenue elevated train or I walked three blocks to the 183rd Street subway station. There I took the D local to the 161st Street stop, where I got off the train, obtained a paper transfer, climbed out of the subway, and walked up other stairs to connect with the Jerome Avenue El. The whole trip to Union Square took the better part of an hour, not a big deal for a true New Yorker.

Stuyvesant was then located on Fifteenth Street between First and Second Avenues. The school was small and crowded, requiring double sessions. In my first year at Stuyvesant, which I entered as a tenth grader, classes began at about 12:40 p.m. and lasted until 6 p.m. There was no lunch break, and because of our full schedule, the standard gym requirement was cut in half.

I was an indifferent student in high school, although I did well in some subjects. Geometry, chemistry, and physics interested me, and it showed in my marks. I memorized chemistry tables while commuting to school. I carried a geometry workbook in my back pocket and would solve problems while riding the subway doing chores for my father. I liked English and Social Studies and history also, but my marks dropped in those subjects because I did not study nearly enough. English classes interested me more when the lectures moved beyond the rules of grammar, which had been difficult for me since elementary school.

In my junior year, classes began very early and concluded before 1 p.m. It was only then that extracurricular activities became feasible. I made an attempt to join the school newspaper, *The Spectator*. I submitted one article, which was rejected. Instead of persisting against the elitist clique that ran the paper, I turned my interest to sports. A lot of my time was invested in the soccer team. Mostly I played center half, a fairly key position. During the two years I was on the team, Stuyvesant was a championship contender. My best buddy, Joe McClintock, joined the team as well, becoming manager. My friends in high school were largely from the soccer squad, a grab bag of the various ethnic, religious, and national strains that comprised the city of New York. Most of the Stuyvesant students came from all over the city. High school was stimulating and interesting. The instruction was excellent.

In 1947, I won a current affairs contest sponsored by *Time* magazine. First prize was a book selection, and I chose *Gentlemen's Agreement*, by Laura Hobson, the story of anti-Semitism in the corporate world immediately following World War II. But I received a much bigger prize that year. I officially became what it seemed I had become the minute I stepped off the *Aquitania* gangplank: an American.

Everything I had learned and absorbed from that moment onward shaped my new nationality. I never considered myself Polish, although as the son of Polish parents that was my legal status. I certainly never considered myself German—and neither did the German state—although it was the land of my birth. Still, formalities had to be observed. I legally became a U.S. citizen on April 28, 1947, based on my parents' earlier naturalization. In 1952, in the 176th year of U.S. independence, I took the oath of allegiance and received my own document of citizenship at federal offices in Columbus Circle.

Stuyvesant was not free from occasional anti-Semitism, intentional or unintentional. One incident occurred when a cranky teacher irritated by the oafish behavior of his class commented, "Strange what seems funny to the Jewish mind." There were indeed a lot of Jewish kids in the high school at that time, as many as Asians today, but not all those acting up were Jews.

In Spanish class another incident occurred. The teacher was an elegant Hispanic man, with a trim mustache, always attired in well-pressed suits (not the habit of all my male teachers). The class was reading a passage about Torquemada, the Grand Inquisitor, and the teacher, expounding on the text, provided the traditional Roman Catholic interpretation. He hailed the cardinal as a Defender of the Faith, rooting out the Marranos (swine), Jews who had been coerced to convert to Christianity but secretly continued to practice Judaism. One of the Jewish kids, who knew more than the rest of us, got up and asked the teacher a series of Socratic questions, which resulted in the emergence of a far different picture of Torquemada. It was an instructive incident as I looked on as my classmate, staying calm but with a good deal of knowledge about the matter, managed to expose the class to a fuller depiction of Torquemada.

In an English class, taught by Dr. Kelley, a tall and distinguished gentleman, Izaak Walton was up for discussion. I had not heard of the great writer and fisherman. Speaking out loud rather than to myself, as I should have done, I said something along the lines of, "If he's so famous, how come I never heard of him?" Whereupon Dr. Kelley looked down at me over his spectacles and archly pointed out that there were a good many things of value in the world of which I had yet to have the first inkling. That's how one acquires essential life lessons in high school.

My germinating political views were largely based on the liberal assumptions of the time and place. In that universe, politics meant that you didn't cross picket lines and that you put your nickels or dimes into cans being shaken by volunteer collectors in front of Alexander's department store during a long strike by the United Auto Workers against General Motors. Everyone we knew voted for Franklin Delano Roosevelt; the only Republican exception was the father of a playmate in my preteen years. The man was a postal worker who was disgruntled with F.D.R. for not having delivered a promised pay raise during the Depression.

With the end of World War II, I became convinced that the surest way to prevent a recurrence was through a world government to which all nations would subject their sovereignty. I don't remember whether I actually joined the World Federalist organization, but at a minimum I was a believer.

Over time, my views evolved. In high school we were encouraged in our homeroom to subscribe to a newspaper. Teacher preference and peer pressure was clearly to select *The New York Times*. It was my contempt for intellectual bullying that encouraged me to choose *The New York Herald Tribune,* a politically moderate Republican paper I became fond of long before I thought of working there. For reasons that were unclear at the time, I was developing somewhat conservative views, more so in foreign affairs than in domestic ones. Crossing a picket line remained anathema to me, but when it came to what was happening overseas my views hardened.

As a high school senior I participated in a schoolwide debate about the shape of the postwar world. I was the only speaker to take an anti-Soviet line. It was not a popular position to take at Stuyvesant, where the faculty and students were almost uniformly Left-liberals. Discussion of the Truman Doctrine focused on the Greek Civil War then in full force, with the British backing the government and the Soviets the Red Guerrillas. I was being pressed on how I could support historic British imperialism. My response was that even as we condemned British imperialism we must not shirk from condemning the imperialism of the Bolsheviks. Not to do so would not only be hypocritical but immoral. "Two wrongs still don't make a right," I intoned to the strong applause of a school assembly that for a moment abandoned its conventional proclivities. My argument was intellectually feeble, perhaps, but it worked. I left the assembly hall with my debating skin intact.

As my high school years approached their end, it was time to plan for college. My father was not taken with the idea. If I insisted on going to college, my parents preferred one in New York City, which I resisted because it would keep me living at home. I wanted to get away, but my father still hoped that I would join and eventually take over his fur business.

The discussion about college naturally involved what was to become of me. Mommy favored dentistry. I was committed to journalism, but Mommy and Daddy were opposed. The anti-journalism bloc was large. During an extended family confab, involving my parents, my sister and brother-in-law, as well as my sister's in-laws, the debate about my career aspirations grew quite heated. I resented the tribal process of discussing my personal life in the living room. Only my sister took my side. She argued that she was sure that as a newspaperman I would be able to make as much as five thousand dollars a year. I thought she was hallucinating.

4

Annie

Don Horowitz and I had been friends since childhood, living across the street from each other and going to school together until high school, when he opted for Bronx Science. We spent a lot of time in each other's company, including the Boy Scouts.

In September 1947, we agreed to go the Friday dance given regularly at nearby Walton High School. In previous visits the routine at those dances had been firmly fixed. You would dress up in your one and only suit, and, once in the gymnasium, stand back against the wall, too timid to ask a girl to dance.

Weary of this disappointing pattern, I was hell-bent on ending it that evening. Self-conscious about my appearance, I removed my glasses, which meant I could only dimly make people out. Thus hampered, I managed to spot a girl with dark hair falling down below her shoulders, tall and slender. I went over to her and asked whether she would like to dance. She said she would. And with that my life pivoted.

We began to lindy and kept on with fox trots, and continued to dance with each other. I asked her name while we were lindying and she told me as I was spinning her out. I did not hear her name. and I did not want to appear foolish by asking her again. After a number of dances, I asked the young lady whether she would like to go for an ice cream soda, assuring her that afterward I would escort her home. She told her sister and the friend who had invited them to the dance (neither sister had ever been there before) that she was going, and off we went.

As we walked south from Walton High, down Jerome Avenue, farther east and south, past Fordham Road, we talked easily. For me, this was a rare experience, finding the words to keep the conversation going with a girl. We walked toward our destination, J. S. Krum, a massive ice cream emporium with a huge sign on its roof on which its name was spelled out in lights. There was an entrance on the Grand Concourse and another one on the side street. Inside, it was all bright colors, with long counters and tables, at which were served an extensive variety of sodas, sundaes, and dishes of ice cream. We each ordered a soda.

Afterward, we walked a block to Fordham Road and rode the trolley, open on the sides to the warm night air, all the way to upper Manhattan. At 207th Street we transferred to a bus that took us down to 174th Street, where this attractive girl resided. I accompanied her into the lobby of her apartment building, got her telephone number, and had the pleasure of one goodnight kiss.

No more than a couple of weeks later, Don and I decided that we would ask the young lady and her sister out on a double date. I called the number I had not written down but remembered, and an older woman answered. Not knowing who to ask for by name, I said who I was and could I talk to—and then ran my fingers over my mouth as I mumbled a sound. Without hesitation, the woman put on the line her older daughter, Anne, as she told me when she picked up the phone. Mostly, she was called Annie.

Annie and her younger sister Doris agreed to go out with us, and we set the date. On the way to pick up the girls, Don and I promised ourselves that under no circumstances would we take them to a downtown movie, as that was a major commitment in money and something you did only after becoming much better acquainted. As we stood outside the girls' apartment house deciding where to go, Don and I kept on mentioning films featured at local movie houses, and the girls kept insisting that they had seen what was playing there. The only movies they hadn't yet seen, they maintained, were playing downtown. We saw no alternative and so we headed downtown, the second of countless evenings I have spent in the company of the former Annie Hahn.

Annie and her family—her father Sol (or Sally), mother Martha, and sister Doris—had also emigrated from Germany. Unlike the Rosenfelds, they were German for as long as could be traced, having lived in towns and villages in the state of Hesse for hundreds of years. Annie's mother was born a Strauss and her mother's maiden name was Lehmann. They resided in the town of Reinheim, although perhaps village would be a more accurate description. When the Hahns and their forbearers lived there it was a little world unto itself.

Martha Strauss was born in Reinheim on April 13, 1897, in the family's house. The family was in the cattle trade and ran a slaughterhouse and a kosher butcher retail shop that was also patronized by Gentiles. Martha and her siblings had a comfortable middle-class upbringing, with a full-time maid, and part-time help from a laundress and a seamstress. The children were educated beyond public school, attending Gymnasium, a high school that prepared students for university. The Strausses were observantly Orthodox, celebrating the holidays in prescribed fashion.

As a young woman, Martha commuted by rail to Frankfurt and worked as a saleswoman and seamstress at Rothschild's department store. She was introduced to her husband-to-be, Sally Hahn, by relatives. Sally was a butcher, born on November 26, 1893, and raised in Kuelsheim.

Sally served in the Imperial German Army during World War I on both the Western and Eastern fronts. This means that each of our families had a relative fighting on each side of the Russian front, conceivably at the same time. Sol (as he called himself in America) told how in the final year of the war the soldiers on the front became dispirited when the United States joined the fight, bringing fresh troops and weaponry to the battle. The German cannon had been worn out during the three years of fighting, as had the soldiers who had been in the trenches all that time.

Sally and Martha were married in 1928, or perhaps 1927—the date is hazy—and they settled in Reinheim, where Sally joined the family business. Their first child, a daughter named Inge, died at the age of five or six months. Their second child, Anny, was born on April 19, 1931. Anny came into the world in the same house in which her mother was born. (Anny formally became Anne in America). Anny's sister Doris came along fourteen months later and somewhere in that time frame the Hahns moved in with the Strausses. The anti-Jewish boycott forced that business to decline and the Strauss and Hahn families had to reduce their living costs.

If anything, the Nazis were more militant in towns like Reinheim, with its six hundred Jews, than in larger cities such as Berlin. They had wide support from the country people and held early and popular demonstrations and marches in Reinheim's streets and squares. As Anny was being born, her mother heard the marching throng in the streets. Anti-Semitism was all around Anny and Doris as they grew up. They tell the story of a hayride they went on with neighbor children. Doris had a nosebleed, and the other children taunted her with cries of *"Judenblut."*

While the Nazis had many fervent followers, there were those among the Germans in Reinheim who behaved decently. One, a baker, paid a crushing price for it. Nazi thugs took the baker's teenage son, forced his hands onto a live electric power line, and electrocuted the youth.

Official records show that Moritz Strauss, Martha's father, and his son-in-law Sally Hahn stood up to the Nazis even in these grim and dangerous times. A municipal history cites a letter they sent protesting the stationing of an SS man in front of their business, which discouraged customers. According to the document, the SS man was removed. By 1934, the business was forced to close by the Nazis.

As things were going from worse to intolerable, Anny's relatives began to emigrate in the early 1930s. Some went to South Africa, where they prospered. One couple went first to Turkey, then Switzerland, before coming to the United States in 1940. On Sally's side of the family, a sister and a brother had immigrated to America in the 1920s and another sibling got out in 1938.

Sally and Martha Hahn decided that they and their children could no longer remain in Germany. They applied for visas with the help of their American relatives. The process was not easy. Twice they had to travel to Stuttgart to apply at the American consulate. Each time, they were rejected on specious grounds. Once it was because Doris had a pimple and the consular officials chose to suspect that as smallpox. The second time, Martha had a cough, and they were rejected because she might have tuberculosis. These were diagnoses that no Aryan would have received. The third time, no objection interfered.

Martha was devastated by having to leave her elderly parents behind. The Hahns had neither visas nor funds to purchase her parents' passage. The Hahn family departed on November 3, 1936, and sailed on the *USS George Washington* from Hamburg. They arrived in New York a week later. Of those who remained in Germany, all but one were lost in the Holocaust. Martha's oldest sister and her husband were deported to a concentration camp. Recha had some medical training, and the Nazis forced her to inject air into Jewish inmates to kill them. Rather than carry out her dreadful assignment, she injected herself and died. Others were deported and were not heard from again.

The sole survivor among the Hahn family was Sally's brother Hermann Hahn who remained in Germany, went into hiding, and survived. He was a Hebrew teacher and married a well-to-do Christian woman. He lived with her in Stuttgart throughout the war and emerged unharmed at the end of it. Anny's grandmother was diabetic and died in Frankfurt from complications of the disease. Her grandparents had been forced to give up their Reinheim home and move into the city.

Moritz Strauss, her grandfather, born in 1865, was deported to Theresienstadt on September 18, 1942, where he succumbed on February 3, 1943. He was the last Jew to receive a religious burial in the concentration camp, which was Hitler's "model" camp and was used in propaganda materials to show how good the Jews had it in captivity. After that, burials were proscribed and the dead were consigned to the crematorium. A stone commemorating Moritz Strauss was erected in the 1990s by his great-grandson, Jonathan Cobb, the son of Annie's first cousin. Annie and I paid our respects to her grandfather's memorial stone (for the location of his grave remains unknown) when we visited the camp grounds in October 2009. We said Kaddish and placed stones on his marker. As we left, Annie spoke to him: "We will never forget you, Opa." Indeed, before us his great-grandchildren and great-great-grandchildren had come to pay him honor, leaving stones to mark their commemoration.

When he arrived in America with his family, Sol Hahn had eighteen dollars in his pocket. His siblings set them up in a small apartment, sparsely outfitted with secondhand furniture, because this was the middle of the Depression. He found work right away, as a wholesale butcher in the Meatpacking District at West 14th Street in Manhattan. That's where he spent most of the rest of his working life, toiling in a meat locker for many hours each day. It exacted a heavy toll on his health.

Annie's mother worked as a cleaning woman in people's homes. She became a piece goods worker and crocheted hats and scarves before she became a sales clerk at B. Altman's downtown. With two incomes they made do. They took in a boarder at their 174th St. apartment for several years. Some time after the boarder left, their cousin Anneliese came to live with the Hahns. Martha had managed to scrape together the money, either from her small earnings or her in-laws, that was needed to qualify Annaliese for entry to the United States. Annaliese was Martha's only success in rescuing relatives from Nazi Germany. While also helping to earn a livelihood, Martha went hat in hand to her more distant and well-to-do relatives (she was, after all, a Strauss and a Lehmann) to implore them to lend money to get visas for the old parents and for siblings and nieces remaining in Germany. Their modest loans would be repaid once the relatives had made it to America. They turned her down.

Annie and I saw each other several times over the next months, enough to encourage me to ask her to be my date for New Year's Eve. In the winter of 1947, a major storm dumped heavy snow on the Eastern Seaboard. While the storm hit, Annie was visiting her aunt and uncle in Belmont, Massachusetts. She made them shovel the driveway clear so that she could make it to the train station and back to New York for the holiday, a sign that our relationship had prospects.

I took my college boards and turned my attention to picking a school. My first application was to New York University to appease my parents, though I did not want to go there because it would mean continuing to live at home. I was admitted for the spring term that followed my high school graduation in January 1948. To select an out-of-town college I went to the neighborhood library where I pored over a thick college reference guide. Since I wanted to study journalism, the choices were limited. Northeastern University was appealing because its five-year program combined study with relevant work. But I applied to Syracuse University and was accepted. My father posed no objection and paid for my entire education without complaint. I convinced Don Horowitz to come along, and we roomed together in dormitories and off-campus rentals for our entire four years.

5

The Trib

Between the end of high school and the beginning of college there was a seven-month hiatus, so I looked for a job. Since I was focused on journalism as my major, any temp job would not do. I wanted to work for a newspaper, any newspaper, but my first choice was the *Herald Tribune,* because I had read it in high school. I went to the offices of the paper, which were on 41st Street between Seventh and Eighth Avenues. Over the years, I had noticed the façade of the Trib from time to time. The Trib was located across the street from the bus depot where we caught the bus to Union City, New Jersey. The reason for nocturnal trips to Union City was to see the burlesque shows, which were then permitted to be performed there but nowhere else in the region. While not a habitué of these shows, when the time came for me to seek a job at the *Herald Tribune* I knew exactly where to go.

The Trib's personnel department had no openings in the newsroom for copy boys, and I was sent to the syndicate department, where a shipping clerk's job was available. Although it was not what I wanted, it was a foot in the door. In the syndicate office, the manager, John Dema, liked my application. Dema was a tall, balding man with a heartiness partially expressed by his bow ties and by smoking not very good cigars. His main concern was whether I was reliable and would stick around for a while. He was satisfied with my high school credentials, and since my Syracuse acceptance had not yet arrived I must have told him that my college plans were not set.

I did not hear from the Trib right away. One day John Dema called and said I got the job. He had actually phoned earlier and reached my dad. Dema explained who he was, but thinking it was a joke my dad abruptly hung up. Something about the conversation troubled Dema. He realized that my father, who spoke heavily accented English, might not have exactly understood. So he took the trouble to phone again, bless him.

I began my career in journalism as a shipping clerk in the syndicate department. I worked at the *Herald Tribune* until it ended its distinguished run in 1966. During those first months I began to learn about the newspaper business in boundless detail, an introduction for which I always have been grateful. The shipping clerk duties were varied and touched on many of the paper's operations. I got to know the infrastructure of the Trib from top to bottom and inside and out. It was a priceless experience.

Arnold Kinsella was in charge of the shipping room. He was short and bespectacled. Without fail, he wore a starched white shirt, the knot of his necktie always cinched tightly to the top. His appearance was a clue to his personality. He was on top of every problem, dealing efficiently with them as they arose. At the end of the workday he was as neat as at the beginning. He had served in the Civilian Conservation Corps, or CCC, during the Depression and his work ethic did not suffer from the experience.

The syndicate was the mechanism through which the Trib sold its work to other newspapers across the country, as well as internationally in Canada, Australia, Greece, and wherever an opportunity presented itself. It sold comic strips; the columnists Walter Lippmann, Joseph and Stewart Alsop, Mark Sullivan, Roscoe Drummond, Art Buchwald, John Crosby, Red Smith; the editorial cartoonist Dan Dowling; the bridge column; the crossword puzzle; fashion and food coverage; fine arts criticism and photographs; the Sunday supplement magazine *This Week*—whatever other newspapers were willing to buy.

The shipping clerks gathered these materials, processed, and packaged them. They collected the zinc plates of the comic strips and other features and stored them in bins in the syndicate shipping room on the twelfth floor. The larger newspapers received the columns, articles, and specials over a wire from the *Herald Tribune* News Service, which was a subordinate part of the syndicate. The smaller papers got the material by mail.

Getting to see firsthand the tempo and flow of the composing room operation was a special treat. The foreman was Willie Manlove, a man in his seventies. In the days of hot type and ink he performed his job attired in white duck pants, white shirt, and a black bow tie. He also wore a white apron and black-rimmed round glasses attached to a tether. In his slightly stooped manner, he walked swiftly over the rough wooden floor permeated with years of ink, supervising the composing room's multitude of tasks. I trailed him attentively, awed by the range of his skills and his ability to keep himself unstained by the inky surroundings.

My instructors ranged from white-haired Willie to the young apprentices who spent years before they attained fully qualified membership in their powerful union. I learned about newspapers on the ground where they were made and put together by craftsmen. One of the most important lessons was derived from witnessing the procedural relationships initiated by a story typed on foolscap on a reporter's typewriter and reviewed at the copy editor's desk, before its transformation into sticks of type on a Linotype machine. The rows of type were then proofread. Once they passed that careful examination, the type was placed artfully into the chases (forms) of each page. The compositor often adjusted the prescribed layout (design) to accommodate unforeseen problems. Type and headlines and the zinc plates of photos had to be shifted and made to fit, with balance and style. It was a daily tour de force, done on deadline.

When ready, the chases were transported on heavy metal tables with rollers and pushed to the stereotyper. There, they were centered on a flat bed, covered with a thick pink papier maché sheet called a matrix (mat). Next, the mat-covered chase was pushed through a heavy steel roller under great pressure, which made a perfect impression of the once-hot type into the mat—if everything had gone right. These mats were cast into curved lead plates to be affixed to the press.

The men who constituted the stereo department at the Trib in my time were named Nick and Lester. Nick was a short, portly man with a full, round face and slicked-down black hair. He smoked cigars. Lester was taller and leaner, a cigarette smoker with a neck that was permanently bent to one side by some arthritic condition. Both directed teasing good humor at me, giving the new kid the hard time prescribed by back shop tradition. That was part of the initiation, a rite of passage that welcomed me into the tribal camaraderie of the composing room.

My job was to gather the mats made of various comic strips, editorial cartoons, and the illustration that accompanied the bridge column. Both Nick and Lester had to be convinced that the syndicate's turn had finally come and it was time to press the mats we needed. This was a dicey business, because they had a lot to do and they shifted priorities in order to accommodate to various pressures and preferences. I quickly learned the necessity of being on good terms with everyone. I needed to be seen as part of their universe, ready to shoot the bull about sports or celebrities, as well as to discuss the weightier issues of the day. Badinage was essential to good relations in the composing room, much more than in other segments of the newspaper business that I encountered over the years. The composing room had its own rules, its own etiquette, formalities, and courtesies, the factory ambience notwithstanding. Those who did not observe the customs, or displayed condescension, quickly discovered what it was like to be frozen out and thus not able to get work done when it was needed.

After Nick and Lester had "pulled" the mats for me in the requisite quantities, my function was to chop off the excess material that resulted from the mats being squeezed through the stereo rollers. This was accomplished at a cutting table in the stereo department. The result of my labor was a batch of comic strips or cartoons trimmed roughly to the same size.

I followed a similar routine to convince the proof boys to pull the proofs of printed features that would be mailed to syndicate clients. These younger men also required jollying to get your stuff. These proofs also had to be trimmed at the chopper, which required me to use its heavy and keenly sharpened blade, which was curved like a scimitar.

One day, while I was busy at these tasks, the larger implications of what I was doing struck me. A group of thirty or so students from Columbia University's Graduate School of Journalism were taking a tour through the composing room and getting a lecture about its activities. I spoke to a few graduate students several years older than me, and I was able to answer some of the questions they asked. It occurred to me that here I was being paid to do this work and to learn whatever there was to be absorbed; and here they were, visitors for an hour or so, learning the same lessons in a more superficial way. For this privilege they paid tuition.

My duties in the shipping room amounted to a lesson that could not be purchased. Never again would I come to understand the inner workings of a newspaper operation as thoroughly. I knew the key players in the various departments intimately. I knew about their families and their prejudices. I knew how good they were at their jobs. I knew what motivated them and what turned them off. I knew how the different departments related to each other.

The most fascinating aspect of the job was the chance to enter the city room, where the reporters and editors worked. My job included getting hold of the original copy from the distinguished columnists who wrote there, as well as the articles and columns transmitted by teletype from the Washington bureau. Then I cajoled a news service editor to read them, took them to a typist, and looked over her shoulder as she cut the blue stencil. Then I returned to the shipping room to run the stories off on the mimeograph machine. The pages were then collated and the separate airmail and first-class envelopes were stuffed with the copy before being run down to the General Post Office at 34th Street in order to make the earliest possible trains, planes, and buses for speedy delivery. Since we were frequently late, run was the exact word.

Operation of the mimeograph machine required adroitness because the infernal device was temperamental, causing difficulties at the most pressing times. Mimeo protocol was demanding. First, the stencil was attached to the drum and smoothed down. The hard paper back was ripped off and the drum was rotated to expose the hollow interior, into which just the right amount of ink was poured and evenly distributed. If all that was flawlessly executed, then it was almost a given that the stack of single sheets that were fed through the machine would clog at least once and often many more times. Various deft maneuvers were required, including extracting bits of jammed paper out of hard-to-reach areas. All this effort was carried out for mail clients, some of whom paid a pittance for the service.

Simultaneously, the clients who subscribed to the wire service received this material instantaneously as soon as a teletypist cut a tape that was fed through a machine for transmission at the rate of sixty words per minute—when everything and everyone was operating as intended. Among the fascinations of the job for me was the chance to stand over the incoming teletype machine as a Walter Lippmann or Joseph Alsop column was transmitted from Washington or elsewhere. I read the piece as it was printed out line by line on the ticker. My first exposure to editing occurred at this juncture. It was a rudimentary form of copy editing as I scrutinized the incoming copy for any typos or obvious errors.

The copy for clients was handled by editors of the news service. Their operation was located at the edge of the city room, next to the Western Union office, the telephone recording room, and the machines of the great wire services: Associated Press, United Press, and the International News Service. Nearby, other machines transmitted messages overseas, to and from foreign correspondents and the Washington bureau. There was equipment dedicated to the needs of the Paris edition of the *Herald Tribune*, which was distributed throughout Europe, North Africa, the Middle East, and other parts of the world.

The news service editors first took care of the demands of the wire (they were called wire-filers). They mirrored some of the work done by traditional copy editors—checking spelling, grammar, and looking for holes in the narrative, but they did not write headlines. To a degree, wire-filers also performed some city desk duties such as making judgments about the quality and length of stories. After that was done, they attended to the needs of our mail clients by editing stories to eliminate time references to make them suitable for later publication. Breaking news stories were almost always not appropriate for mailing. Analyses, features, and articles from specialists such as science and health, economics, education, fashion, and the lively arts held up well when sent by mail.

During my first stint in the shipping room, I joined the New York Newspaper Guild. At the time I was making twenty-four dollars a week. I held on to my Guild membership through years of disillusionment with the union until the *Herald Tribune* folded. At one point during my years at the Trib, three of us decided to run for the unit's steering committee as a protest. We were the only ones to challenge the union's slate. Eager to prevent any possibility that our opposition could evolve into a movement, the union leadership declared the three of us elected and canceled the vote.

Because I dressed slightly better than the other clerks and sometimes wore a sport jacket or a suit, I was frequently chosen for out-of-office chores. One day I was tasked to carry a message to Joseph Alsop, who was that afternoon at his club, the Lynx, on Manhattan's East Side. I was awed by the prospect of my first sighting of the great man, wondering what I would say when the moment came to speak to him. At the club's front lobby, I was taken in hand by a functionary in knee breeches who escorted me up a couple of flights of wide, carpeted stairs, the walls paneled in rich, dark wood. The wall hangings and paintings smelled of old money well spent. We halted at a landing where four or five men sat around a low table having drinks and conversation. The attendant whispered to Alsop, whom I saw in partial profile. He moved his head a trifle toward me, never turning fully to look at me, held out his hand, accepted the envelope I carried and continued talking while reading. He dismissed me without a word.

Many years later, as an editor at *The Washington Post,* I found myself occasionally at table with him, once at an intimate Christmas Eve dinner at Katharine Graham's. His blanket indifference to anything or anyone not immediately on his mind still characterized his demeanor. As talented as he surely was, as courageous in print as he sometimes was, he remained a consummate snob, a bit of a well-dressed shit, as far as I was concerned. While Alsop and I shared little conversation, it turned out we did share a secretary, Dagmar Miller. She worked for Alsop first and later became my secretary when I was Foreign Editor at *The Washington Post.* She was a first-rate aide. She had cultivated manners and a sense of order and control, knowing which calls to allow through to me and which to fob off pleasantly. Dagmar told me that I was better to work with than Alsop, which was consoling in a certain sense but not surprising given Alsop's highly developed narcissism. Working for anyone other than Alsop had to be an improvement.

I worked at the Trib during that first tour between February and September 1948, and made good friends with the guys in the shipping room as well as in the front office. That fall, I began my studies at Syracuse University. My grades were helped by my having the good luck to concentrate all my classes on Mondays, Wednesdays, and Fridays, making for very long days but leaving Tuesdays and Thursdays free for study. The result was that I made the Dean's List in my freshmen year.

Before classes began that fall there was time for horseplay. The freshman dorms were a distance from campus, requiring shuttle bus service. The dorms were called Skytop, because they were on top of a hill. Skytop consisted of a series of prefabricated barracks, divided into the individual rooms, each housing two students. They were brand new, and the Class of '52 was the first to occupy them.

One night there was a major water fight. At one point, I stole into the room of one of my adversaries and donned his best suit before confronting him. I dared him to dump his bucket on me, which he was too sensible to do, while I had a free shot at him. It was that kind of night.

When the frivolities had calmed down a bit and we were back in our own rooms, there was a knock on the door. Outside were two guys from the other end of the dorm. The spokesman of the two complained that the noise had interfered with their attempts to concentrate on their studies. My roommate Don Horowitz and I had difficulty suppressing our laughter as no classes had met yet. The spokesman made his way into our room. On my dresser was a photo portrait of my new girlfriend. He looked at it and said, "I know that girl." Indeed, he did. He was Joe Abelson and he had attended George Washington High School with Annie, and they had known each other since seventh grade. Joe and I quickly overcame our first testy encounter to become good friends and, in time, we married sisters.

It was during the freshman convocation that the chancellor of the university, William Pearson Tolley, encouraged us to take our studies seriously as he prophesied that during our time at Syracuse another war would involve the United States. We considered his words excessively pessimistic. Less than two years later, in the summer of 1950, the Korean War broke out. I was working during the break from college in the syndicate shipping room. After my shift one night, I went to a Times Square movie house to see a timely revival of the famed antiwar film set in World War I, *All Quiet on the Western Front*. It depicts the war as it affected German soldiers worn out physically and mentally by trench warfare. At one point in the film the sergeant, a father figure to the young men in the platoon, says that the next war should be fought not by common soldiers but by the generals, politicians, and bankers from both sides in a huge boxing ring, and they should be made to settle their differences with gloves on. At this point, the audience broke out into strong applause, reflecting the disheartenment of another war so soon after the conclusion of the bloody Second World War.

Probably my most successful class was freshman English, taught that first semester by an instructor named Dan Curley. He was a budding writer and in later years developed a distinguished reputation as a short story writer, novelist, and professor. He was a discerning teacher who overcame the difficulties of having too many students crammed into his classroom. He once read aloud a passage from one of my essays and commented in its margin, "For an illiterate you write amazingly well." The paper earned an A-/B. You can see how little his comment meant to me. I turned to him for advice long after that first semester. In the summer before my senior year I wrote him asking for help, as I was not having success with the first-person approach he had recommended. He responded in a full-page typed letter that said: "I suggested that you try it so that you could in that way get closer to the material. Stiffness, as you know, has always been one of your vices." He concluded with the cogent judgment: "You know as well as I do that there is nothing anyone can do for you." This was long before I had experienced neither enough of life to tackle fiction nor the scars and scabs or time in the trenches to aspire to autobiography.

In the second semester, I again had good fortune in my English instructor. Her name was Mrs. Dorsi, a young woman with whom I unintentionally got off on the wrong foot. I apparently exuded too much of what she perceived as the persona of a New York City wise guy. If I did, I was playing against type, for that was not like me. Before the term ended our relationship changed for the better. In the late spring, she called me in for a conference and we spent a long time discussing my future.

She wanted to know what I had in mind, and I told her journalism. She prompted me to think of public service, perhaps in diplomacy. From that meeting I returned to the dorm elated by her interest and her confidence in my future. It was the most explicit encouragement I had received that I might some day develop the intellectual capacity to contribute to the real world I would enter after graduation.

During summer breaks from college I was rehired by the *Herald Tribune* in the same job, and each of these years my knowledge of how the paper operated continued to expand. I had dealings with the mailroom, the photographers, the composing room, and the circulation department. My efforts to become a copy boy in the newsroom failed. One of the summers, the fun increased for me. A co-worker of mine was Seymour "Whitey" Silverman, and we shared the ambition to become newspapermen. In the course of the incessant conversations around the shipping room's massive rectangular steel table, upon which the work of the shipping room was done, we plotted projects that would take us out of the shipping room and into the newsroom.

We decided to collaborate on a story that we hoped would be published in *This Week* magazine, the Sunday supplement of the

Herald Tribune. The subject was Union Square, the park that was the setting for the quintessential free speech forum in the country, the Hyde Park of the United States. After work ended around eight o'clock we took the subway downtown to 14th Street. In the square on hot summer nights there was always a crowd. Mostly they were Bolsheviks or Trotskyites, along with other left-wing splinter factions, who ferociously disputed policies, politics, and personalities. Their arguments mostly derived from internecine historical conflicts about how to make a revolution. Only the participants could comprehend the often recondite reasons for their entrenched disagreements.

On occasion, I went to Union Square without Whitey. However, instead of merely listening and observing, I sometimes got caught up in the arguments. This exposed me to the rigors of heated debate, where you had better never ever be at a loss for a single word. To hesitate was to give the other fellow the opening he was waiting to pounce on to keep you from reclaiming the floor. I faltered often. I saw how the communists served as each other's claques in order to gang up on an outsider fool enough to try to have his say, when the night before they had been bitter enemies.

In the end, Whitey and I never wrote anything beyond a first draft, which we didn't deem good enough.

As I was about to enter my sophomore year, I sought to sell the *Herald Tribune* on the Syracuse campus. *The New York Times* claimed the franchise of newspaper readership among students and faculty and this offended the loyalty that I had come to feel to the Trib. The *Times* was required reading for political science courses because it was the basis for weekly current affairs quizzes. First, I lobbied the circulation bosses in New York, whom I had come to know through my clerkship. Against their strong advice I got their approval to peddle the Trib at the university. They told me that this would be a fool's undertaking because the *Times* was too entrenched. I insisted on going ahead.

Next, I confronted the chairs of the academic departments and argued that requiring the *Times,* and accrediting no other newspaper, did not accord with academic ethics. I said the Trib's news in review section was just as thorough and authoritative as the *Times*'s and I won their grudging agreement. After that, the real work began. Selling the Trib turned out to be daunting. I visited dormitories and cottages that housed students in whatever free time I could find in the afternoons and evenings. Selling one subscription to a coed in a cottage counted as a major success. In the mornings I delivered the papers and walked great distances between drop-offs. In places where I had a single customer there were multiple copies of the *Times* stacked on the porches, more on Sundays.

Because subscription sales were so poor, on Sundays I peddled the Trib in the dining halls, picking up a modest amount of sales. I could not do this on my own. I enlisted my housemates. Sy Strongin, who owned a car, picked up the papers from the distributor downtown. Then Sy, Einar Lindholm, and Don Horowitz all participated in hawking the paper. We kept up the enterprise on campus for a full year before conceding that there was nothing rewarding in it despite our best efforts. The experience was instructive nevertheless, and contributed to my preparation for my later work on newspapers.

By the start of my second year at Syracuse, I had become disillusioned with the journalism dual major. I was disappointed to discover that I did not connect with the journalism faculty. I found the classes boring, a dreary recital of rules and formulas whose origins and purposes remained obscure. Classes lacked energy and enthusiasm. With two outstanding exceptions, the instructors were not good teachers. I continued to take a few classes in the Journalism School and began to work on the campus paper, the *Daily Orange*, but I changed my major to American Studies.

In my sophomore year I was compelled to choose between taking advanced mathematics or a foreign language. Given my trouble with trigonometry in high school, it was Hobson's choice: I took German. It made sense because as a nine-year-old in Berlin I had not learned much German grammar, nor retained much else from my brief and vexed German school years. I thought this would be an opportunity to correct that deficiency. I was booted out of first-year German class when my teacher quickly discerned my background from how well I pronounced German. I was moved into an advanced course where we studied the writers Lessing and Goethe in German. It was a more appropriate level for me; at the same time, I lost a good chance to expand my knowledge of German grammar. In the event, in 1951 I was elected to the German language honorary society, Delta Phi Alpha, an odd denouement for one who as a protest against Hitler had deliberately discarded his German language skills.

Another standout course was writing, conducted by Norman J. Whitney, a superb teacher. Mr. Whitney assigned us to analyze good and bad writing. We were made to count the number of syllables in a Hemingway sentence. In each class we were given an assignment to complete overnight that had to be placed into a mailbox on the front of his office door, punctually by 9 a.m. the following day. Our assignments had to be one page long and no longer. He would give us a series of words and tell us to incorporate them into a theme. He required us to write an essay using root words without their commonly accompanied prefixes. Vincible, for example, instead of invincible; defatigable, instead of indefatigable and so on.

He was an exacting reader, precise and helpful in his criticisms. He read and critiqued our themes quickly. His wit was sharp and it was rewarding to listen to him attentively. We could not help but learn, and while his assignments were sometimes viewed as an unreasonable imposition, I came to value Mr. Whitney's classes above most others.

Mr. Whitney was a bachelor gentleman and a devoted Quaker activist. As a result of his Quaker affiliation, he hosted a group of German academics at Syracuse, and arranged an afternoon tea to which he invited his students. I had no intention of going, because I was concerned that my reaction at meeting the Germans face to face would lead me either, by silence, to accord them redemption so soon after the war's end, or to challenge them and thereby violate the etiquette a guest is owed. Mr. Whitney pressed me to come, though I explained that I didn't feel right about doing so. Finally, I pleaded that I had failed to shave that morning and that I was not in form to meet visitors. Mr. Whitney persisted, and I finally relented and listened to the Germans make their case about the hardships that their country endured in the postwar world. They praised the faith and commitment of the Quakers for their relief work in Germany.

Despite my reservations about speaking out, I did not resist questioning whether the Germans' admiration for Quaker ways was a true conversion or rather more an appreciation of the material help the Quakers provided. The lead German listened and studied my face for a bit and then said that he could understand how Jews could not so quickly forgive the Germans as had the Quakers and other non-Jews. His response confirmed that my instinct had been correct and that I should have avoided the meeting. The German deftly managed to separate the interests and behavior of Jews from the rest of the universe.

The literature establishment at Syracuse hosted distinguished guests every so often. One was W. H. Auden. We had read his superb poetry in freshman English, and it was a gift to be in his presence. His face was bloated from overindulgence in food, drink, and tobacco. He spoke in a gravelly voice and smoked incessantly, the ashes falling over his jacket and shirt, and he drank steadily. He was quite tolerant of the English major kinds of questions that were put to him, and said one line that will live with me forever: "A poem is never finished; only abandoned."

The other part of the curriculum, political science, was no less fascinating.

My most memorable professor in the poli sci field was T. V. Smith, a tall, soft-spoken Texan who had served in the Congress, and who taught political philosophy and was held in high esteem by his colleagues. In his seminar, into which I was fortunate enough to be accepted, he inculcated what he called the essential clichés of democracy, concepts that shaped my thoughts about our government. One was "Compromise exists for the sake of the uncompromisable." Another one was the superiority of the property of privacy over the privacy of property. We studied Locke and Hobbes and John Stuart Mill, among others.

My extracurricular activities remained largely focused on the campus *Daily Orange,* where I became a junior editor. I also covered a variety of sports, including soccer and lacrosse. Part of the job was working the night shift once a week at a rickety printshop owned by the university. There, the daily paper was put together by a union printer. We learned to write headlines and produce them on a Ludlow typesetter, altering them not so often for clarity as to make them fit the available column widths. The printer shifted type around the pages to make everything fit the page.

Another extracurricular role I had was as co-publicity chair for the campus fund drive. The mission of the drive was to raise money from the student body, faculty, and staff for a bundle of good causes. I remember we were sitting around a table at a planning session and were asked to come up with a slogan. I scribbled my suggestion on a sheet from my looseleaf notebook but did not write my name on it. When the submitted ideas were read aloud, mine was greeted with derision, so I did not acknowledge authorship. Lacking a better one, it was adopted. Since then, I have often seen it used by other fund drives, but I had never seen it before I wrote it down. The slogan was "Give once—and for all."

In my junior year, I received the notice from my draft board that I was required to take a medical exam for induction. I was classified

1-A, which meant that I qualified for Army service, but I received a college deferral.

The longer I spent in school, the better student I became. As the coursework grew more challenging, my marks went up. In the final semester of my senior year I earned straight As except in one course, where I received a B+. Looking back I increasingly realize how much Syracuse University broadened my knowledge and appreciation and opened new worlds for my contemplation and enjoyment.

After graduating in June 1952, I returned once more to work at the *Herald Tribune*. I no longer toiled in the shipping room but worked as an editorial assistant in the news service, which was the first editorial job I held at the Trib. During this time I signed a memo with my initials, HR. Keith Spalding, editor of the news service, saw it and was upset. HR was the sign-off for Helen (Rogers) Reid, the widow of Ogden Reid and the publisher-owner of the *Herald Tribune*. It would not do for a lowly editorial assistant to be signing himself in the same way as the publisher. As a remedy, I picked up my middle initial M for Morris, and kept using it throughout my working life, although not for all bylines.

Just before I departed for my Army service, I published my first important newspaper story. It was an interview with the widow of "Gentleman Jim" Corbett, the world champion boxer. The occasion was the sixtieth anniversary of his famous victory as an unknown over the mighty John L. Sullivan. *The Boston Globe,* a news service client, had asked for a story and I went out to Queens to meet with the elegant and by then elderly Mrs. Corbett. It was a successful interview and the *Globe* ran it. I offered it to the *Herald Tribune* sports department. The Sports Editor accepted it readily enough. It was published it on September 7, 1952, but only after an editor clumsily reworked the lead and removed my byline. Even so, I was happy, so happy, in fact, that I sent flowers to Mrs. Corbett to thank her for having been such a good talker. The Trib paid me $9.50 for the story.

6

In the Army

On September 25, I went downtown to the then-famous Church Street Induction Center, had my physical, and was shipped off in that day's last bus to Camp Kilmer, in New Jersey, for processing. After a brief stay at Camp Kilmer, I was assigned to eight weeks' basic training in nearby Fort Dix, followed by eight weeks of training in a Military Occupational Specialty. There was nothing especially grueling about basic. It toughened the body, notably the hikes with a full field pack on a trail of soft sand. I quickly learned how not to arouse the interest of the drill sergeant. Each trainee had to paste his last name across the front of his helmet liner, which we wore almost always without the steel pot meant to cover it. Only on firing ranges did we wear the steel. Many of the trainees made works of art out of their name tapes, boldly drawing every letter. My own strategy was to print my name as faintly as I could with a ballpoint pen. Officer instructors and NCOs would have trouble reading my name at a short distance. As they could not easily call on me by name, I was spared their attention.

I scored well enough on the firing range with the 30-caliber M-1 to be awarded sharpshooter status. This sounds grander than it was, since it ranked next to the lowest category. Except for some difficulty with a plantar callus on my left foot, which eventually had to be removed, and stomach cramps every time we were fed C rations, which was once a week, and a severe bout of bronchitis, I came through basic training well enough.

One of the fundamental lessons I learned during basic was that when you returned to the barracks after a long day in the field, dirty, sweaty, bone-tired, and hungry, the first thing you did was not rest, or clean yourself up, or find something to eat. The first thing you did was clean your rifle so that it would be ready for use. The second thing you did was clean your other equipment—mess kit, canteen, boots. After these were put in shape for inspection, you took care of yourself.

There were more than a handful of Jews in my company, because so many of us came from New York or other Northeastern states. One Friday night, there was a football game in which our battalion team played. When most of the Jews in our platoon said they wanted to go to Friday night services instead of the not very appealing game, the sergeant reluctantly approved the request after he couldn't talk us out of it. While the rest of our company marched off to the field, the Jews who remained behind were assigned to swab down the barracks. We wielded the mops in Class A dress uniforms.

There was one black soldier in our platoon, a likeable and affable man. Most everyone took some interest in him, to try to cushion him as much as we were able from the racist traditions that lingered in the Army, especially among some noncommissioned officers. There were Southerners in our training company to whom serving alongside Negroes (as they were then called) was a new and trying experience. Taking orders from the occasional black officer or NCO was hard for them. At lunch in the mess hall one day, one Southerner summed it up for me. "At home, they move; in the Army, I move," to avoid any black person.

Our training took place during the late fall, in weather invariably cold and often rainy. Keeping the World War II barracks heated was perpetually difficult. The temperamental 1940s vintage furnaces were no longer up to the job, if they ever had been. They needed constant tending or they died. The barracks would turn uncomfortably frigid and troops coming in off the training field would gripe to their annoyed NCOs and officers.

Our company commander concluded that rotating different recruits through furnace-tending duties, the way KP was assigned, was not working. He solved his problem by taking four soldiers out of their basic rotation, training them in the art of furnace management, and assigning them for an unstated period of time to the job. I was one of the first batch of four. We were excused from military training and worked four days on and three days off. During the off time, we had a permanent pass to leave the base. I used mine to visit Annie in New York and became a regular commuter.

The captain's plan solved the problem of the underperforming furnaces, and the four of us were content. Although the work was dirty, the time off was a bonus. It was too good to last. The enterprise came to a screeching halt when battalion got wind of it. The captain was upbraided for taking the four enlisted men out of the training cycle and we were returned to our previous assignments.

The personal questionnaire I had filled out on being processed at Fort Dix covered all pertinent information about my pre-Army background. This included that I had done editorial work at the *Herald Tribune*. The Army, in its own bureaucratic obtuseness, translated that into assigning me to wire man school after basic. Wire men laid communications wires wherever they were needed. This kind of work is not what one learns on the editorial side of a newspaper. I did not relish the assignment and so I took myself off to the personnel section, Classification & Assignment, where a fellow Syracusan had a cushy job. I explained the incongruity of the wire man assignment. He agreed, and asked what I would rather do. I answered that more fitting to my newspaper experience would be the public information school at Fort Slocum in New York State. That was a highly coveted assignment and far beyond the reach of a casual college acquaintanceship. Instead, I accepted an assignment to clerk-typist school.

Before I got that far, Annie decided she had waited long enough and confronted me one day while I was visiting at her parents' apartment. Annie wanted to discuss setting the date for our wedding. We had decided while I was in college that we would marry. A wedding date was put off as I began my Army service. I did not think that getting married while in the Army was a prudent idea, with the prospect of overseas service during the Korean War and its uncertainties. Annie brushed these concerns aside and pointed to the special allotment paid to married soldiers. She presented me with a calendar and instructed me to pick the date. I did. February 28, 1953.

As our wedding date drew near, I took up the issue of a pass with the first sergeant, who in turn discussed it with the captain. An answer was long delayed, and when it came it was not reassuring. The captain explained he had no way of knowing where I would be on February 28. I responded that if I were overseas he wouldn't be obliged to honor my weekend pass. To support my appeal, we called on the rabbi who was going to marry us, G. Herbert Fedder. He wrote my commanding officer to tell him how much he appreciated Pvt. Harry M. Rosenfeld being able to show up for his own wedding. He signed the letter with his title as a chaplain in the U.S. Army Inactive Reserve with the rank of captain. My captain managed to eke out a weekend pass for me without imperiling the war effort.

Annie and Doris made all the arrangements for the wedding: hiring the hall (the Park Royal Hotel, on West 74th Street) and the caterer, the band, the photographer. Fifty-eight people were in attendance. The cost came to $674.00, and we retain the bill to prove it. For our honeymoon I had withdrawn my life's savings, $82.03, from the Bronx Dollar Savings Bank. That helped pay for our two-night stay at the Waldorf-Astoria Hotel, which cost $50.16, and for a celebratory dinner at the Russian Tea Room, located next to Carnegie Hall. Subsidized by cash presents, we saw a Broadway play. On Tuesday, Annie went back to work as a secretary at Goldstein-Gerson Jewelers at 126 W. 46th Street and I resumed my job as a private at Fort Dix. Our war-shortened honeymoon was over.

At the Army base, I was in clerk-typist school from January through April 1953. I was one of a small group to be kept on after the training cycle to serve as an aide and instructor. Weekend passes became regular, and I joined Annie in New York. But there were not many weekends together, because I soon received orders for the Far East. On Mother's Day, I took my first airplane ride, a flight to Fort Lewis in Washington State and the embarkation port of Seattle. It was a small plane and I could stand in the aisle and almost touch the cabin wall on either side. It had to make a refueling stop in Chicago.

Three of us from basic training flew out together. We got to Seattle before we had to report to Fort Lewis and so had a little bit of time in the city. When we asked the cabbie for suggestions about where to stay, he made a remark about whites of course wanting to put up in a white hotel and not any run by Japs. Not the most fitting words for three young American soldiers on the way to doing our duty for American democracy abroad.

As we boarded our troop transport on May 22, a cruise ship docked at an adjacent pier was receiving passengers for a pleasure trip to Alaska. A band played and passengers were showered with party streamers and confetti. On the Army pier, an MP band dully performed marches. The Red Cross presented us with a pack of cigarettes, a cup of coffee, and two cookies. The stark juxtaposition of the two ships and their missions reflected the nation's attitude toward the Korean War.

Accommodations were basic aboard the troopship, the *General Robert Lee Howze*, loaded to capacity and bound for Sasebo, Japan. Bunks were stacked four deep in cavernous compartments. We received no sheets and one blanket apiece. There was just enough room to fit a stretched-out body with a few inches to spare between the tip of the nose and the bottom of the soldier's taut tarp above. The heat and closeness were oppressive.

A fierce desire to avoid KP (a permanent kitchen detail aboard ship) encouraged me to seek other assignments at the troop office, on the premise that in the Army typists were always in demand. On the second day at sea, I was designated as the editor of the ship's paper. It was my first job as an editor, such as it was. The paper was called *The Howzette* and came out every day except Sunday. It usually consisted of two or three pages, mimeographed on both sides to make up a four- or six-page paper. The pages were stapled together. National and international news as well as sports scores came to us in extremely terse bulletins from the radio room. Each morning I went up to the radio room and collected whatever news had been received, took it back to the paper's office, and wrote up the items with my staff of a few fellow newsmen.

During our voyage, the truce talks were played big on Page 1. Our first edition of *The Howzette* was a one-sheeter, issued on May 23. Two days later, we had only short items in our second edition. Among them, portentously, was one datelined Hanoi telling of high casualties inflicted by French and Vietnamese troops on four Communist companies.

Every issue contained information important to the troops: shower, bingo, and movie schedules. A message from the chaplain and times for Catholic and Protestant services were standard. Sports were emphasized, as well as an occasional editorial and frequent cartoons drawn by staff artists. It was a useful publication that crammed into its few pages all the news we could lay our hands on while confined to a troopship in the middle of the Pacific Ocean.

The editor's job not only gave me something to do, it also provided a workspace where I had a bit of privacy to hang out and read and write letters. It surely was a better place to sleep than the cramped bunk. Stretching out on top of a long steel desk, using a life vest as a pillow, was far preferable to sacking out below decks. The *Howzette* staff had special passes for chow, the movies, and access to off-limit areas of the ship. We also could shower more often than the other troops.

We docked at Sasebo, a large naval installation in southern Japan in the first week of June 1953. On our truck ride from the ship to the processing center, we saw people living in caves, their laundry hanging outside to dry. It was the most desperately poor sight I had ever seen, and I supposed then that I would never see worse. Soon enough I would, and in the years to come see yet worse again. In Sasebo we were issued M-1 rifles and sent to the range to zero them in. Of the three of us who left Fort Dix together, I was the only one to get orders for Korea. The others remained in Japan.

I boarded the ship again, and as we reached the western coast of South Korea, we were ordered to break down our rifles and pack them in our duffle bags. We transferred to an LCI (Landing Craft Infantry) and sailed toward shore. Because I was among the last to board, I stood at the back of the craft on a ledge as the boat came into Inchon, where two and one-half years before General Douglas MacArthur had landed his forces in a maneuver that outflanked the triumphant North Korean Army and instantly reversed the course of the war.

We made our landing on June 16. An officer who received our contingent was outraged that our rifles were packed in duffels. He ordered us to assemble our weapons, and we boarded a troop train for the ride to a Repo-Depo (Replacement Depot). It had been thirteen hours since we had eaten our early morning chow and we were issued C rations for our meal on the train. The windows were covered with metal screens to guard against stones or other projectiles. As the train rolled, we began to eat. We passed a throng of children who ran toward our train, many of them stark naked, shouting, "Hello, Joe," desperately begging for food. It had taken a very short time to be exposed to even worse poverty than I had seen outside of Sasebo. Almost in unison, the soldiers unhinged the metal screens and tossed rations out the windows for the kids, among whom the bigger and stronger ones wrestled away more than their fair share from the smaller kids.

Although we had hoped to land in a Korea at truce, South Korean opposition had delayed it. The troop train taking us to spend our first night in Korea came briefly to a stop alongside another train going the other way, carrying Korean students. We struck up a conversation with a young Korean and asked about the truce. "We don't want truce," he replied. We blew our stacks and cursed him. One of the GIs offered him his rifle and told him to go fight.

That night we wound up at the Yongdongpo Repo-Depo. The next morning, we rode a train to Taegu, the best station in Korea, where we had hot showers, a steak dinner, and a haircut that cost twenty-five cents. Afterward, we were informed that we had been taken off the train by mistake. The following morning, we continued on a train to Pusan. So I landed in the North, visited the center, and wound up in the South.

At Pusan, I received my permanent station assignment, which sent me back to Taegu, the headquarters of the Korean Communications Zone, a major command center. I was assigned as a clerk-typist to the Military History Section where Lt. Col. Francis W. Haskell, a West Pointer and an officer not of the stereotypical infantry cut, was in command. He managed to look the other way when an enlisted man approached so he did not have to exchange salutes. He had a round face and a round body and a trim mustache. Mostly he smiled. He had taught Spanish at the Point and was an intellectual, a person of refinement. His grandfather had been governor of Oklahoma. He had a law degree from the University of Michigan.

The Military History Section under the colonel consisted of First Lt. David Conrad, ROTC, who wanted to be a teacher when he returned to civilian life. The top NCO was a Regular Army sergeant first class who had served across much of the world. Although he made a favorable first impression, he turned out to be a hack, blaming everyone but himself when things went wrong. After he rotated to a new assignment in Japan, efficiency and morale in the office rose noticeably.

There was also Pvt. Dave Cohen, from San Francisco, who loved his city and everything about it. His mother regularly sent him clips of the Baghdad by the Sea column written by Herb Caen, the prototypical hometown columnist. Cohen and I began a friendship that was to last for many years beyond our Army service, mostly through an exchange of letters.

The work of the section involved gathering information from all the support commands: intelligence, transportation, prisoner of war, medical, food, and other operations. This information came to us in written reports and was compiled into monthly Command Reports.

These eventually made their way to the Pentagon Military History Division, where, in years to come, they provided the data for the official histories of the war that would be written.

When I arrived in the office they gave me a typing test. I took my time and passed. It took me a while to build up my speed and accuracy. In fact, my erasing improved more rapidly than my typing. Soon enough, I was so bored by the job that I thought of getting myself transferred to the Public Information Office. I began to grow my first mustache for the lack of having something more interesting to do.

In the course of work, I lobbied to do more than type reports. About one month into my assignment, I was entrusted with writing up some of the minor sections of the report. For this sort of work I had to be cleared to handle material classified as Secret. I began to rewrite the reports as they came to us so that they would convey a more comprehensible picture of what had happened. Sometimes I would backtrack and ask additional questions to gather more facts from the reporting units than they had supplied us.

In the first week of my arrival at the post, South Korean president Syngman Rhee opened the prison camp gates to allow the escape of certain North Korean prisoners. Those released did not wish to be repatriated, but might be forced to do so by the United States in fulfillment of its commitments under the terms of the truce then being negotiated. It was a crisis with ramifications for the cease-fire and peace talks. Immediately, we were restricted to post and ordered to carry our carbines at all times. Then we were relieved of our regular duties and assigned to guard duty at a local prisoner of war compound, which meant sleeping in the open on cots. It was a challenging assignment, because we were not permitted to fire at any South Koreans, soldiers or civilians, who might try to set free more of the North Korean prisoners, some of whom had already managed to escape. Only if we were fired on first did we have clearance to return fire.

I was assigned with two other GIs to a post that was surrounded by sandbags topped with barbed wire. Our position faced a barley field that was worked all day by farmers. It became a neighborhood gathering point as we handed out cigarettes, crackers, and whatever candy we had to the kids and adults who lined up for our treats. I tried to strike up conversation with a North Korean POW to find out about life in his country. He kept repeating a single phrase:

"I anti-Communist." After two days and one night, infantry units moved in to take over guard duty.

At the KComZ we were quartered in Quonset huts that were quite comfortable. Two houseboys, for which we each chipped in $1.50 a month, did all the household chores: sweeping up, making beds, shining boots. We played touch football in the wide space between the Quonsets. In August 1953, I received orders for temporary duty in Munsan-ni. It was in the north of the country, a U.S. base not far from Panmunjom. This was a break in routine I had been hoping to get. The assignment became mine only because the colonel was on Rest & Recuperation leave and Lt. Conrad, who would otherwise have been sent, felt he had to remain in charge in Taegu. But he was kind enough to go up north with me for a couple of days to help me settle in.

The farther north we traveled the more war destruction we saw. Bridges over the Han River had been destroyed, buildings were in ruins or pocked by shells and rifle fire. In Seoul we were picked up by a driver in a Jeep. The driver needed to get something at the main Army Post Exchange, where all manner of goods were available for purchase. So we saw a bit of the city. While Lt. Conrad and I waited in the Jeep, we were surrounded by begging kids. One boy who was about seven wore nothing more than a fatigue cap.

A Provisional Command, a tent city, was set up in Munsan-ni. My job was to gather information of possible historical value on Operation SWAP, the POW exchange. On the morning of August 5, Lt. Conrad and I drove to the Freedom Village, a cluster of structures built to receive the repatriated Allied troops. The area was loaded with U.S. brass, including the Secretary of the Army, Robert T. Stevens, Army General Maxwell Taylor, a four-star Air Force general, and many lower-ranking generals. A Marine band played in the background. The international press corps was there in numbers, as well as their military counterparts from the Signal Corps and Public Information Office.

The first female nurses I had seen in Korea were present, evidently to help and cheer the returning soldiers. Helicopters transported the first arrivals, the more severely sick and wounded soldiers. After them, many ambulances unloaded more animated newly freed prisoners of war. In the afternoon, I was among a group of forty Americans who traveled behind enemy lines in two buses. We drove past the United Nations receiving area where we had been in the morning and saw strung barbed wire, bunkers, and mined areas. We crossed a bridge where a North Korean sentry was stationed. The buses parked near the "Peace Pagoda," where the truce was signed, where we were supposed to pick up a North Korean escort. He was delayed because his Russian-made Jeep had mechanical difficulties.

The Communist reception area featured a large red arch. As a group of Chinese prisoners arrived from United Nations captivity, they ostentatiously discarded the new clothes they had been issued. They proceeded to the processing lines wearing only their underwear and military caps. Once the generals and the media had departed, I watched as Chinese soldiers harvested each article of the cast-off clothing.

The showy stripping routine continued the next day as ambulatory North Koreans unloaded at a train siding. The road from the rail point to the exchange was littered with their discards. Communist soldiers loaded up a truck with the clothes. In addition to demonstrating by their act of stripping, the prisoners being swapped tried to provoke the guards by spitting at them.

The most obnoxious repatriates were the women, accompanied by twenty-three children dressed in Communist uniforms. The women were not only the loudest, they smashed the ambulance windows and were as aggressive as they could get away with. I photographed many of these events with a reflex camera that I had acquired at the PX shortly after I arrived in Taegu. Cameras were known as the KComZ sidearm.

After Lt. Conrad returned to headquarters, I continued to have access to a Jeep and driver. I also was authorized to attend General's Call, which was a daily afternoon briefing given by a general. I was the only enlisted man present. At the time, I was a private. As such, I was not authorized to wear any stripes or other insignia of rank. As a result, I was generally considered by others around me, officers and enlisted men alike, to be a Central Intelligence Agency operative, with some of sort of important officer rank equivalent. CIA operatives were known to move about Korea without any identifying markings. The fact that I commanded the services of a Jeep and driver and attended General's Call fit the bill of a stealth CIA mission. In all circumstances, I remained circumspect and had fun with it. What they didn't know wouldn't hurt me.

Col. Haskell, back in Taegu from his R & R, instructed me to focus on writing a narrative of the prisoner exchange. I conducted many interviews with officers and enlisted men and took pictures. I went along on the first ambulance convoy to the Communist receiving area where sick and wounded as well as able-bodied POWs were handed over. As they arrived, they openly wept until an officer from their national army, either North Korean or Chinese, spoke a few words, and the crying stopped instantly. They, too, tore off their clothes, and were applauded by a double row of soldiers through which they passed.

Afterward, we drove to the United Nations receiving area to watch the return of Allied troops. In contrast to what was happening not far away among the Communist personnel, the Allied soldiers were stoic. Their clothing remained intact and they did not damage the vehicles that brought them to the exchange point. A U.S. corporal spotted his brother among the wounded who arrived.

During this assignment I ran across a French correspondent for Agence France-Presse who was covering the exchange. He told me he just finished working in Indo-China, which he said was a hell hole compared to Korea. I spent my twenty-fourth birthday in 1953 on a one-day pass in Seoul, enjoying a steak and potatoes dinner (for $2.00), and shortly afterward returned to Taegu. The Command Report for August covered the exchange, and it included six of my photographs. My day as an assumed CIA operative was forever behind me; my journalistic work had been given a boost.

Col. Haskell was a teacher and mentor in many ways. One day he overheard me being chewed out by the first sergeant for some transgression. I launched into an explanation. Col. Haskell took immediate umbrage and said, "That's the wrong answer." What I learned is that I should have said, "No excuse, sergeant. The reason is . . . etcetera." In other words, I must first own up to my responsibilities before explaining or alibing. I adopted the colonel's formula for people who reported to me during my career as a newspaper editor—with mixed results.

Col. Haskell regularly spoke to me about the value of graduate school. He thought journalism was not a suitable career. He diligently pored through a catalogue of universities to find a course of study that would arouse my interest. As far as I was concerned, I had had enough of school and had no thought of further study. Yet, he planted a seed.

The colonel was a Christian Scientist, but once when his stomach was stressed we saw him taking milk of magnesia. He was in all respects a good soul. Apparently through a previous officer, he was put into contact with a group of Christian Korean academics in Taegu. He became the conduit for books and clothes that were shipped through the colonel's military mail for use by the Koreans. In September 1953, the colonel was invited to dinner by Mr. Kim, an academician. Col. Haskell asked Dave and me to accompany him and arranged for a sedan and driver. The occasion was Ancestors' Day and a thanksgiving ritual for the rice harvest, which was the best in fifteen years, we were told.

We arrived at the Kim house, a drab concrete structure that was a perk of being a university professor. Following custom, we removed our boots in the vestibule. We were ushered into a communal room that served multiple purposes and where a low table had been set, covered with a white tablecloth. Mr. Kim wore his usual Western suit. Mrs. Kim appeared in Korean garb, with a high Empire waist and a bolero jacket, all in white.

The all-purpose room had sliding glass doors that opened onto a garden. The garden and the tidy and austere Kim household was a sharp contrast to the general squalor and disorder that typified Taegu. The walls of the Kims' house were decorated with several not very good paintings of Korean scenes. There was also a picture of the South Korean flag and several depictions of Jesus Christ.

It was a very rare treat for Americans to be invited into a Korean's home in that era. Entertaining typically was done away from the home in a restaurant. Only the more Westernized Koreans opened their homes to foreign guests. As we dined with Mr. Kim and his medical school colleague Dr. Lee, the Kims' four children, their teacher, and assorted female relatives sat at a separate table in a far corner on a bare floor, while our table was located on a matted floor. We were served rice, soup, chicken with heavy noodles, omelets filled with meat, several varieties of fish, and Korean sweets, which resembled hardened molasses. The ample dinner surely taxed the resources of the Kim household. We brought along a variety of food, cocoa, and candy to help offset at least some of their sharing a limited food supply with their visitors.

After dinner, we all played a board game that involved moving objects around a circle track. It was made more interesting since the rules of the game provided openings for a player's piece, or horse, to take shortcuts and knock a competitor off the board.

When the colonel rotated home, he asked me to serve as the conduit to the Kims, which I did until it was my time to leave. When Col. Haskell's tour neared its end, and since Lt. Conrad was already gone, Cohen and I decided to write up the colonel for a decoration, which customarily accompanied a successful tour of duty. For an officer of Haskell's rank, Cohen and I thought a Legion of Merit was appropriate. Although we understood that this was a bit of a reach for such a small command, we decided to go for it. Our doing so elicited favorable comment and support from the chain of command, who were pleased to see two enlisted men making this effort on behalf of their commanding officer. Dave and I had the pleasure of being the first to tell him that he had been awarded the Bronze Star.

Somewhat later, I wrote up my company, HQ & HQ Co., KComZ, for the Meritorious Unit Award, which was approved without amendment by higher headquarters. It was a well-earned honor and there was satisfaction in applying my writing skills on behalf of such a good cause.

Cohen and I were extremely fond of the colonel. When he departed in October 1953 on the first leg of his rotation home, Cohen accompanied him to Pusan to help him out in whatever way possible. I followed the next day with a couple of items the colonel had left behind. Dave and I chipped in to buy the colonel a silver cigarette case and a silver casing for his lighter, inscribed with his initials. In that same month, I was made a private first class, which meant I had earned my first stripe.

Col. Haskell was replaced by Lt. Col. Ben A. Falzgraf, an officer in the Military Police Corps who did not have the benefit of Col. Haskell's family or educational background. The contrast between the two men was total. Haskell was stocky and given to smiling, while Falzgraf was thin and tall, with an upright bearing and a serious mien. In time, we found out that he suffered badly from arthritis, but we did not hear him complain.

Col. Falzgraf was a man of the rulebook. Unlike Col. Haskell, who edited and revised our work regularly, our new commanding officer took no active part in preparing the reports. He left that to Cohen and me, which we liked. Col. Falzgraf's deputy was not a first lieutenant but a fellow lieutenant colonel, named Russell, who was a military historian. The Army obviously was winding down its Korean mission and there was an abundance of officers; otherwise,

Col. Falzgraf would have found another assignment with the military police.

In December 1953, it was my turn to go on R & R in Tokyo. Four of us from our Quonset hut went on leave together. We did some sightseeing, enjoyed nightclubbing, and I made time for shopping. Annie had instructed me to purchase a certain set of china. I went to the biggest department store and asked for a pattern called Dormant Tree. I could not make myself understood very well, but I finally elicited a response from the salesman, who said that they did have something called Dead Tree. I said, "That's it." The last set of this china on the premises was on display. So they obligingly gathered the plates and cups together and wrapped and crated them for overseas shipment. I picked up some very old Japanese prints for us and as gifts, and managed to ship home keepsakes for all our extended family.

I got to the see the emperor's palace and the Dai Ichi building, where General MacArthur had his headquarters. Tokyo was an even more splendid city to visit after the long months spent in Korea. The department stores were stuffed with merchandise. All the modern attributes of a city—subway, streets, impressive architecture—contrasted starkly with the war-shattered cities in Korea. In all, I had eight days in Tokyo, in addition to several days of travel and processing time.

At the start of 1954, our work consisted of putting together a chronology of the command, and we wrote quarterly Command Reports instead of monthly ones. In February 1954 I made corporal, which meant an increase in my pay that went home and a little more in my pocket. About the same time, Col. Russell received the news that he was being let go, Riffed, as the jargon had it—which meant Reduction in Force. The Army was thinning out its officer corps. With so much time invested, he felt he had to protect the fifteen years he had earned toward his pension. To do so, he had to sign up as a master sergeant. He received orders to join a different unit in Taegu, off our post, where he would begin to serve the five years he needed to be able to retire with his pension. None of us was happy about it.

We were, generally, happy about the reduction of the enlisted ranks that was also beginning. If you were accepted for college courses you could have as much as three months lopped off your two-year tour. At first, I paid little attention to this early release incentive because I thought it meant undertaking several years of study for either an undergraduate or graduate degree. The way I calculated it, the program might result in ten days' reduction in my tour of duty. That was not worth the trouble, I thought, especially since Col. Haskell's indoctrination had not taken the hold it later would.

Only when I discovered in late March 1954 that enrolling in summer school would meet the requirement for early discharge did I get excited, because that meant I could return home three months early. I phoned Annie, which was difficult because the circuits were down more then they were up and running. A long process began, which fell entirely on Annie, who spent many hours trying to get me admitted into a college. Annie went from university to university to university and pressed admissions officials to overcome their innate bureaucratic listlessness and move my application along in light of a tight deadline. She worked tirelessly in her effort despite coming down with a suspected bout of rheumatic fever. Her doctor instructed her to retreat to bed rest for six weeks. Annie recalled that she didn't feel too bad, although she did run a low-grade fever. Instead of following the doctor's order, she undertook the mission to get me released early from the Army. Annie being Annie, she shared none of her medical diagnosis as it was happening. Instead, she soldiered on so that our life together, interrupted soon after our marriage, might at long last be resumed.

Despite all the roadblocks that my inattention and wrong-headedness helped to create, the paperwork came through, literally at the last minute. I received a radiogram from Annie on April 23, followed by acceptances from New York University and Columbia. I chose NYU because its acceptance letter was stronger. I got official Army clearance on May 1.

The same day that the college acceptance arrived, papers were prepared to get me what I had long sought: an appropriate MOS—Military Occupational Specialty. Except for my earliest days in the military history section, I had never limited my work to clerking and typing. I was being put in for Historical Research Analyst, a rare and prestigious MOS. To cap the eventful day, special orders arrived awarding me the Commendation Ribbon with Medal Pendant—known as the Green Hornet—an award given to enlisted men "for meritorious service." About a week later, Col. Falzgraf pinned the medal on me. I appreciated his generous comments about my work and me personally.

My relationship with Col. Falzgraf had evolved from initial hostility through a functional but uneasy state to these final touching words he offered about me. A few days before I shipped out, he presented me and two others in our section who were also heading home with cigarette lighters embossed with the KComZ emblem. I had not heard of such a gesture from a commanding officer to his men in my time in the Army. Along with our NCO, I took the colonel out for farewell drinks and presented him with the Scrabble set my sister had sent me.

Just before wrapping up my duty in Taegu, I shaved off the mustache I had been growing since I arrived in Korea. The official order for my release from active duty was issued on May 4, 1954, and my final day would be June 26. On May 12, I said my farewells to the men remaining in our hut. It was difficult. There were seven of us shipping out and although we were happy to head home, we were sad about severing deep ties with good men. We had gotten on each other's nerves at times, but living together in tight quarters we had become friends.

Our departure aboard the transport ship *USS Black* was delayed. The *Black* had arrived in Pusan behind schedule, and the turnaround was interrupted when a loading crane broke down. Finally, at 8 p.m. on May 19, 1954, she steamed into a calm but foggy sea. The next morning, the seas were still calm and despite the heavy fog, the ship was cruising at full speed, probably to make up for lost time. At 10 a.m. I was squatting with a buddy at the stern of the ship when we felt a sudden sharp jolt, as if the ship had struck something large.

Alarms sounded and immediately the *Black* began to list to starboard. Someone said we had collided with a whale, which sounded plausible. The loudspeaker ordered all troops amidships. Sailors were running around in a state of panic. The GIs remained phlegmatic and moved to their stations in an orderly manner. It turned out that no whale was involved. We had been rammed on our port side by another ship. The other vessel, a Nationalist Chinese LST (Landing Ship, Tank), had emerged from the fog and by the time the two vessels sighted each other it was too late for evasive maneuvers. Later that morning we learned that the Chinese craft was carrying munitions.

The *Black* shut down engines as damage was assessed. We waited a stressful ten minutes. The time crawled, we were worried, and hardly anyone spoke. The civilian crew, for its part, had donned lifejackets and gathered around the lifeboats. This was no drill. Only a few of the GIs had lifejackets. I decided not to go below decks to retrieve my lifejacket. I calculated that if the situation got worse it was better to be topside in order to abandon ship. The damage turned out to be a hole about twelve feet long and four feet wide at the widest part, and luckily all above the water line. An order was broadcast to return lifejackets. Then the *Black* circled the Chinese LST, which was more heavily damaged. We lowered two small boats and dispatched medical personnel to the Chinese craft, whose front, called the moat door, flapped in the gentle roll of the sea. Once our boats returned, our captain abandoned our homeward voyage, changed course, and headed to nearby Sasebo. In Sasebo, we lived aboard ship while the *Black* was repaired. This was a disheartening setback as all were eager to get home, but it could have been catastrophic had the ammunition on the Chinese boat exploded.

Before departing Pusan, I was told that all special jobs aboard ship had been filled ashore. Nevertheless, while on board, I applied at the newspaper anyway and was assigned the editor's job. The immediate benefit was that I got out of a cleanup detail. While we were not yet publishing a paper, at least I had a place in which to sit down. In port, we enjoyed freshwater showers and were issued sheets and pillowcases. After a day or so, day passes began to be issued, with half the troops going the first day, and the rest the next. At that point, I had a total of nine dollars, and that wouldn't take me far. We received a special payment, and I spent it getting a haircut, swimming at a pool in an Army installation, and treating myself to a steak dinner in the company of a college chum I had encountered shaving in the base washroom in Pusan.

The repairs finished, the *Black* once again headed to open sea and set a course for home, at long last. Debarking in San Francisco, we were lined up in preparation for boarding a troop train to the East Coast that night, which was downright frigid. We weren't prepared for the cold night clad in our summer khaki uniforms. The sleepers turned out to be more comfortable than I would have guessed. We traveled for three days, and passed through Southern California and Arizona and back up to the flatlands of the Midwest, and then came down through northern New York to Camp Kilmer, where my Army tour had begun. After processing a few days at Kilmer, I was separated from the Army.

7

Fighting to Save the Trib

The day my active duty ended, I took the bus from camp to Midtown Manhattan and rode the subway up to Washington Heights, where Annie had sublet a studio apartment that had a narrow but clear view of the Hudson River. At the very beginning, the small premises were filled for days with welcoming relatives. As none of my pre-Army clothes were large enough (I had put on about ten pounds in the Army and weighed 160), we went downtown to Klein's Union Square department store to buy the first of the on-sale civilian suits that it would be my lot to wear for many years.

Annie and I had never lived together before, and there was that period when a couple begins their lifelong effort to mesh with each other, day in, day out. We pressured ourselves to find our own apartment and were frustrated by our lack of quick success. When I wanted to read, she wanted to sleep, given that she had a full-time job. I had no job and could sleep in. It was nothing more serious than that.

My requirement was to attend NYU to fulfill the terms for my early release. The summer graduate course I took was Romantic Poetry, because that built on my undergraduate work in literature. My remaining obligation to the Army was to serve in the Reserves for six years. I was lucky to be given my preference for the Inactive Reserves, and was not troubled further by the Army. I received an Honorable Discharge in 1960, a formality and an anticlimax.

As I was going to class, I applied for a job at the *Herald Tribune*. The paper had no legal obligation to rehire me, and at first I thought they would not. But an opening turned up for a typist with the news service, and I was glad for the paycheck. The job involved typing stencils of columns and articles. The stencils were run off by someone doing my old job in the syndicate shipping room. Typing skills honed in the Army came in handy. The subject matter was interesting because I was working on pieces by eminent columnists and writers. My favorite columnist was Red Smith, unquestionably the greatest sportswriter of all time. What made him special for me was that he wrote many of his columns in a nearby office.

For all his fame, he was modest and courteous, especially to people like me who were far below him in the pecking order. Deadlines were always a problem, but Red Smith was the most cooperative. He customarily wrote three pages, double-spaced, sometimes with a few lines running over to a fourth page. He would walk from his desk to mine, carrying each page over as soon as he pulled it out of his typewriter. There was never a strikeover, reflecting his extraordinary concentration in producing columns that were nothing less than polished, insightful essays that often rose to the level of literary gems.

Meanwhile, Annie and I had moved to a one-bedroom apartment in Forest Hills in Queens, which Annie's mother found for us. We lived on Burns Street alongside the tracks of the Long Island Railroad. Our apartment was on the second floor in the rear. Our windows were level with the raised rail bed. We became used to the din of rail traffic and eventually paid it no mind. With both of us working full-time, we had evenings and weekends together. As I sat there typing day after day, the same sort of frustration came over me that I'd experienced in Korea when I toiled as a clerk-typist. I couldn't stand the boredom of the routine, so I volunteered to help with editing. In time, they let me handle copy from *The Observer* that arrived in mail packets from Britain. The *Herald Tribune* News Service was the distributor of *Observer* copy in North America. Its stories from around the world were stylishly written and sophisticated. However, they tended to be too wordy for American tastes. I would edit them tightly and convert the British spellings to American usage. I did this in my free time when I had no stencils to type. On occasion, I stayed late on my own to edit the copy. I was out to prove myself worthy of promotion.

Keith Spalding, the editor of the news service, fell sick with hepatitis. He was out for many weeks recuperating. He could easily claim that he was the hardest worker in any operation with which he was associated. He became a role model for me. Despite his serious illness, for which he was supposed to log a lot of bed rest, he called relentlessly with suggestions and questions. During his absence, his assistant, Bill Miller, ran the news service. On his return, Keith moved into a supervisory role on the Trib's city desk. Bill took over as news service editor, and Nat Kingsley (who had been the Paris *Herald Tribune*'s man in New York) was moved to Managing Editor, which created a vacancy. I was offered the job in June 1955 on probationary status for eighteen months. I was overjoyed. This was an honest-to-goodness professional newspaper job, and I was determined to make a success of it.

Since I was low man on the roster, I was assigned the least desirable shift. I started at 6 p.m. and finished at 2 a.m. I could not have both Saturday and Sunday off. To get a weekend day, I had to split my days off. I then worked for a considerable time with Thursdays and Saturdays off. This meant that on Mondays, Tuesdays, Wednesdays, and Fridays Annie's schedule and mine did not coincide. We saw each other on rare occasions in the Continental Avenue subway station or across the platforms as she was coming home from work and I was leaving for it.

On the other hand, the job came with a raise. I was lucky that I had known almost all of the staff at the news service for the years when I was a clerk, editorial assistant, or typist. My challenge was to overcome the fact of my youth and inexperience with veteran newspeople. I directed two staff teletype operators: Vinnie Borelli, conscientious and helpful, and another operator less inclined to work hard. He loved nothing so much as the downtime that came to him when he had to run a tape again for a client who had missed it because of a transmission problem or machine malfunctions. This meant that he would have to work that much less on his shift. Coaxing him to be productive was a constant chore. I managed to get on with him, even though I'm sure he regarded me as a young, overly ambitious, hard-charging wire filer.

A benefit of the Sunday shift was that I handled the desk by myself. To gird for the challenge, I thoroughly read the Trib and the *Times* at home before going to work. In the first weeks, I frequently had to overcome a queasy stomach.

By the time the tryout period was up, my boss described me as "the most conscientious wire filer on the staff" in the memo recommending me for permanent status. I didn't attain the pay level my sister had predicted for me until the beginning of my second year on the job, when I phoned Annie at her office to tell her I was now a five thousand dollars a year man.

Before long, after a trip to Bermuda, Annie was pregnant. We needed to find a larger apartment, this time without a railway soundtrack. We found a two-bedroom apartment farther out on the Queens subway line, in Flushing. Shortly after we moved, we headed off to Mt. Sinai Hospital for the arrival of our first child. I left Annie in the care of her obstetrician, who was inducing labor. Annie had reached her due date and the doctor was scheduled for vacation. I could not bear it when I watched Annie in her discomfort as he examined her, and had to leave the room. The doctor told me it would be a long day.

As I walked down Fifth Avenue from 100th Street to the Trib in Midtown, I realized that it would be the longest day of my life, filled with a mix of intense anticipation and anxiety. It was March 18, 1957. At the office, I sat at my desk in a daze or walked aimlessly around the city room. Toward evening, I went back to Mt. Sinai and waited as Annie's labor continued. After a while, my sister Ray and her husband Leo arrived and shortly thereafter, so did our baby, Susan. In that moment, our world changed forever, and forever for the better.

Although we now were a real family, my schedule at work did not change for the better. One time I had to work fourteen hours through the night. The reason for this double shift was the collision at sea between the Swedish liner *Stockholm* and the Italian liner *Andrea Doria*. While the *Herald Tribune* itself marshaled its staff to report this big story, the news service focused on chronicling the accounts of survivors from cities around the country where we had client newspapers.

The news service's Nat Kingsley was vacationing on Cape Cod, and I learned that a Coast Guard cutter was departing that night from the Cape bound for the collision site and would take reporters along. I wanted to get Nat on the cutter but I did not know where in the Cape township he was putting up, and this was long before cell phones. In the middle of the night, I called close friends of his on the staff to see if anyone knew precisely where the Kingsleys were staying. Among those I roused from sleep was Herb Kupferberg, an editorial writer. Having no luck, I looked up the name of the Cape Cod paper in the *Editor & Publisher* Year Book and called the *Cape Cod Times*. I spoke with a staffer and explained the situation. I asked him to get the local cops or state troopers to go from motel to hotel on the main road of the township where the Kingsleys were vacationing to see if they might not, in the English phrase, "knock Nat up." That too failed. Later the next morning, Kupferberg upon waking told his wife he had had the strangest dream about Kingsley being in a disaster at sea.

Still unable to contact Kingsley, I took whatever copy was available from the *Herald Tribune* staff and kept the wire going well past its customary shut down at 2 a.m. By the time I wrapped it up, everyone else had left the office because the final edition, updated, had long since been put to bed and circulated. I was the last one out of the building. I looked up at the clock jutting out from the Trib building. It was 8 a.m. It had been a marathon shift, but I was thrilled to have worked on a major breaking news story. It was the first of many strenuous nights in the newsroom overseeing major stories until they were fit to print. In a crisis, nothing matters as much as the hard work of sticking with it and getting the details right until the package is wrapped up.

Many years later, on an election night when I was at *The Washington Post,* I was having dinner with a group that included Tom O'Toole, our science reporter. The table talk got around to the good old days in our business. I reminisced about the *Herald Tribune,* and Tom remembered that when he was a young reporter at the *Cape Cod Times* he got an early morning phone call from some idiot at the Trib who asked him to enlist in a fool's errand the night that the two great ocean liners collided. When he concluded his anecdote, I wadded my napkin as tightly as I could and took dead aim at Tom's face.

News service work wasn't all editing for me. Once a week I had the chance to do some writing in response to requests from the fifty or so newspapers that were our wire service clients. This did not expose me much to actual reporting, as writing features would require more than a day's work. I did a number of backgrounders and profiles, for which I relied on the clips in the library, augmented with occasional phone interviews. During a period of racial strife in Mississippi in May 1959, I wrote a piece about Governor James P. Coleman and his efforts to reconcile his segregationist convictions with his efforts to modernize his state's economy. It was published by more than one newspaper client. A year earlier, I wrote a profile of Dr. Robert Goheen, at thirty-nine the youngest president of Princeton University.

Another time, following up on a client newspaper's request, I checked out a feature done by a Trib staffer about a family that claimed it had a seventh son of a seventh son. The story seemed too good to be true, and likely was. When I called, the family was not able to trace their lineage that far back. Interviews with genealogists at Columbia University made clear that the family's claim was extremely implausible. The cherry on top was that one family member was a skilled publicist. I welcomed these opportunities, for I still yearned to be a reporter.

Bill Miller and Nat Kingsley were good bosses, and I enjoyed working for them. It was a happy time for me as a young newspaperman. I had a warm professional and social relationship with both men. At our supper break, Nat and I often ate together at Dubrow's on Seventh Avenue, a wonderful cafeteria in the nearby Garment District. We regaled each other with stories about our work, journalism in general, and the larger world. We laughed a lot.

A newspaper, just as other enterprises, is always in motion. Change is constant, and not always for the better. In time, Keith Spalding left newspaper work to become the assistant to Milton Eisenhower, the president's brother, first when he headed Penn State and then at Johns Hopkins. At the time of Keith's second move, Bill Miller decided to team up with Keith again and left (both were from Iowa) to join him at Johns Hopkins. He was replaced as editor by Thomas B. Dorsey, who was basically a traveling salesman. With his arrival, the mood of the operation changed drastically. He made things extremely unpleasant. He was a braggart and devious, seeking scapegoats when things went wrong. His behavior reminded me very much of my first sergeant in Korea. I seriously did not like him. The feeling was mutual. When the Trib was struck, the news service kept operating, at first with only Dorsey doing the editing. The workload was too much for him to handle, so gradually he got management's permission to call back to work one after another of the news service staffers. The only two who never got that call were Nat and I.

I reached my limit with Dorsey, and began weighing other options. I updated my resume and tested the job market. Nat and I were interviewed for two different level jobs with the Rockefeller Brothers Fund, a major arm of the family's philanthropy. Neither of us received an offer, so for the time being I did not have to face the anguish of a career move that could end my days as a newspaperman. I angled for a job with the *Herald Tribune* newsroom staff. Luke Carroll, the City Editor, for all his gruffness was approachable. I asked him for a reporter's job. In dismissing my bid, he said something I have never forgotten: "Reporters are a dime a dozen; good editors are hard to find." My consolation was to be lumped with good editors, which kept me going.

About eighteen months after Susan was born, Amy arrived, on October 8, 1958. We put her crib in our bedroom, and it quickly became evident that the two-bedroom apartment was no longer big enough for the four of us. Much house hunting ensued. Considering the absence of any savings, after a frustrating search we came across a new development of single-family houses being built in then far-off south New Jersey, in a community named Sayre Woods South. There we bought our first house in 1960 for $17,100, with one hundred dollars down and a 5 percent G.I. mortgage. In a sprawling two thousand–home development in Old Bridge, New Jersey, we selected the split-level model. It offered three bedrooms, one and one-half baths, a living room, dining room, family room, and a commodious eat-in kitchen. It also featured a large entry hall and an unfinished half basement. The lot was 65' x 100' and barren. There was not a blade of grass or a shrub, and only one young, scrawny tree on the entire expanse. Still, it was a welcome step up in our lifestyle.

Although our investment was modest, our resources were no better. Annie was amazingly creative. Our apartment furniture fit right in. She covered the large living room picture window with white bedsheets that did duty as drapes, suspended from brass rings and a brass curtain rod. She did the same with the smaller window in the dining room, which connected with the living room and formed an L shape. Our new dining room set was purchased at an outlet store and paid for by Annie's work as a babysitter for the children of a neighbor. Since we couldn't afford a credenza, we improvised and attached handsome brackets to the dining room wall on which we stacked the three inserts of the dining room table. It looked like an elegant piece of furniture. All the decorating was totally Annie's work; I hammered nails where I was told.

Annie's mother sewed the kitchen curtains and the curtains for the girls' room. Annie covered the kitchen chairs with a designer fabric. I became a happy homeowner and gardener, cultivating a lawn, planting shrubs and flowers and even trees, which flourished in the six years we lived there. I was handy around the house, up to a point, but was extremely lucky to be living next door to a jewelry craftsman who helped me out with work in the house on many occasions, including paneling our entrance hall, building a bookcase and a door to separate it from the playroom.

The house was a fifty-minute commute to the main bus terminal in New York City. The *Herald Tribune* was down the block from the terminal on 40th Street, so I had it better than many commuters to Manhattan who either drove and battled traffic or had to endure much longer daily trips. I was able to use the bus ride to catch up on reading or more often, coming home, on nap time.

My buddy Nat Kingsley finally got his big break, a job he really wanted in Paris as a high-ranking editor with the Paris *Herald Tribune*. I made my life more bearable by finally heeding the advice of Col. Haskell. I enrolled in graduate studies at the Faculty of Public Law and Government at Columbia University. I took afternoon classes before my work shift started at 6 p.m. At the time, big changes were underway at the *Herald Tribune*. During Dorsey's stewardship, the Reid family, having run a losing operation for years, sold the paper in 1958 to John Hay Whitney, who was then ambassador to the Court of St. James's. He was, as were the Reids, prominent in moderate Republican circles. He enlarged his inherited fortune through good investments, and Whitney's pile of money was bigger than the Reids'.

Whitney structured a holding company into which he placed the *Herald Tribune* along with magazine, radio, and other communications properties. This strategy was intended to offset the other media profits with the *Herald Tribune*'s perennial losses. At the same time, the gods were finally just and Dorsey left. He was replaced by Justin Faherty, who had held a high-level job on the *St. Louis Globe-Democrat*. Dorsey's departure from the *Herald Tribune* improved my morale. It soared when Faherty surveyed the staff and decided to name me Managing Editor of the new service, his lieutenant. It was exactly four years after I started as a wire filer. Faherty concentrated on the business side. He handled the budget, dealt with client contracts, and traveled to sign up more clients. Running the news operation of the news service was left to me. After a while, I wrote Nat Kingsley in Paris that "the best thing about the new job is that I can make up my own hours to work on my day off." Work now was so consuming that I ended my graduate studies after completing course work and the required language exam for my master's degree. But I abandoned my stalled effort to write the master's thesis that was the one missing piece to earn the advanced degree. I came to regret this misstep.

The same time that I was named Managing Editor of the news service, Richard C. Wald, a cityside reporter I'd known in high school, got his big break. He was named London correspondent, which at the *Herald Tribune* meant he would also do a lot of traveling around Europe.

Mr. Whitney shook the place up, and a number of new, high-ranking people were brought on board. John Denson, a former editor at *Newsweek*, became Editor. He was innovative and iconoclastic, at least within the context of the *Herald Tribune* at the time. He hired Jim Bellows as his Executive Editor for news operations early in 1961, because Denson understood he was better at concepts than execution.

Seymour Freidin, a former *Herald Tribune* war correspondent and writer, rejoined the paper as a top editor to oversee the paper's foreign coverage. Already at the paper was Murray Michael "Buddy" Weiss, the City Editor. I had become friendly with Weiss. This was not hard to do, as he was smart, funny, and the best company. Before reaching the heights at the newspaper, Weiss had started as a lowly gofer. Night after night, Weiss was dispatched by an editor to get a Danish and coffee from the cafeteria. Whatever Weiss selected was inevitably regarded with grumbling dissatisfaction by the editor. One night, Buddy was determined to show him. He brought back a tray full of different pastries and shoved them under the editor's critical nose. Without saying a word, the editor rummaged around the offerings, selected one, and tossed the rest into the trash.

It was a new age for the reviving newspaper. Typography was jazzed up and headlines became more provocative, often employing a question mark. A front-page summary ran down columns one and two. Precedes to front-page stories tersely presented the significance of the articles that followed. Soon the joke was that the precedes were longer than the stories.

At the news service, the copy produced by the local staff still had limited appeal to other newspapers far away. Of course, there was always something going on in the Big Apple worthy of national attention. But the bulk of the copy moved by wire or mail consisted of sports features and commentary, other general features, the reportage of a highly respected Washington bureau, the work of our small staff of foreign correspondents, and coverage from our one-man United Nations bureau. I was accustomed to working closely with the correspondents in the Washington bureau. Their coverage was much sought after by news service clients because they were first-rate reporters. I routinely discussed story ideas with them and called them when I had a question about their copy. My new position expanded my duties and with it my sphere of influence.

One night, a national crisis broke in Washington, the particulars of which have long since escaped me. It was shaping up as the lead story for the paper. As I read the copy, it struck me that it had fundamental inconsistencies. I called the Washington bureau and convinced the writer to reconcile the contradictions. I informed Denson so that he could alter the copy that would appear in the paper. This threw me into Denson's orbit that night, and for the first time he became personally aware of my work.

It turned out to be a long night. In the end, the story earned its prominent display. As Denson was leaving with one of his protégés to dine and drink at Bleecks' next door, he walked up to the news service desk. He was stooped and given to grinding his teeth. He tended to the taciturn. He proffered a cigar as a way of saying thanks. Although the cigar had seen better days, it was as if I had been awarded a medal.

During Denson's editorship, Si Freidin and his colleagues were not satisfied with the way the foreign operation was being handled in New York. I never learned the details, but when Si wanted to make a change Buddy advised him to consider me for the job. Freidin chose me, and after so many years I left the news service and the syndicate behind in June 1962 to finally become part of the daily newspaper. That is where I had wanted to be from the first time I walked into the *Herald Tribune* lobby in 1948.

My job as Cable Editor was to run the foreign desk in New York and oversee staff correspondents and free-lance contributors. Si became my boss, mentor, and lifelong friend. We worked together in New York and later reconnected in Washington while I was at the *Post* and he was working for a senator. We again found ourselves on the same payroll when he signed up with Hearst headquarters in New York City after I had joined the corporation.

At the Trib, we never had more than a handful of full-time foreign correspondents. At times there was a correspondent in Buenos Aires. London had a bureau, as did Paris. We also staffed Moscow, Bonn, and Rome. We had contract contributors in Israel, Canada, and Vietnam. We staffed the United Nations in New York. We were up against *The New York Times*, which boasted the largest foreign reporting staff of any American newspaper. Yet the *Times,* and not the other dailies in New York (the *World-Telegram & Sun;* the *Journal-American,* the *New York Post,* the *Daily Mirror,* and the *Daily News*), was our competition, because we appealed to the same reader demographic.

We faced a formidable challenge. I worked more closely than ever with the Washington bureau, especially with our correspondents covering the Pentagon and the State Department. Along with our UN correspondent, they helped by contributing full stories or inserts to flesh out articles generated by the Associated Press and United Press International. The paper also received a weekly mailed packet of articles from *The Observer* in London. To compensate for our small staff of correspondents, we developed a most important tool, resorted to especially for Vietnam coverage. We compiled reports from a number of sources and labeled them "from cable dispatches." These were written by the desk in New York, drawing on whatever sources we were able to harness: the news agencies, background memos, or material with Washington or UN angles from the bureaus, as well as library files and reference books. Essentially, it was an operation combining editing and rewriting.

The news agency managers naturally objected to their reportage being subsumed in cable dispatches, and they complained to Bellows. On one occasion, they charged that by melding the AP and UPI reports out of Saigon about the same event, accounts that were similar but not identical, we managed to paint a fuller picture than actually existed. One technique that I insisted on came into play in reporting ground or air attacks in Vietnam. When the news agencies reported that an attack occurred nine miles from Saigon, we inserted what nine miles represented in terms New Yorkers could quickly grasp, such as from Battery Park to Central Park. Years later, I used the same device at *The Washington Post,* for example describing a Communist strike very close to Saigon as the distance from National Airport to the White House.

I do not claim that we invented cable dispatches but I am sure we resorted to them more extensively than other newspapers. In time, we were widely copied. The technique was adapted from *Time* and *Newsweek.* They collected their information by having correspondents filing long memos that a writer in New York would pull together to produce a whole greater than its parts, thus creating a much-admired format.

The Trib's top editors, including Bellows and Weiss, occasionally thought we were overdoing the cable dispatches. In my opinion, that was at least in part because they believed that if we did less writing on the desk we could spare some slots for other needy operations. Despite their opposition and our occasional misfires, we stuck with the technique. There was also the challenge of how our correspondents' copy was edited. Once, Bellows decided that a story by our Rome correspondent had been insufficiently edited. The following day I gave the correspondent's copy a thorough going over, and Bellows complained about meddling. I stood over him as he sat at his work desk in the wide-open city room, held the subject copy in my hand, and said, "What you're telling me is I'm damned if I do and damned if I don't." Looking up at me, he calmly replied, "That's right." Getting it just right is what a good newspaper is about.

It was a heady time for news, the exciting years of the Kennedy presidency and the events of a world that was then, and for a long time afterward, generally running amok. The result was that I was spending even more time in the office, but loving every moment and each big story. In the foreign news area, these were years of intense activity and high interest in world affairs, which often contained the seeds of dire threats to the nation's security.

During the early days of American involvement in Vietnam, relatively few U.S. military personnel were in the country, as advisers and trainers. Their numbers slowly grew, and as they got closer to the fighting, by 1962, they began to take casualties. There were a handful of combat deaths, and the *Herald Tribune* printed the names of the fallen. From time to time, a soldier from our New York circulation area appeared on the list. When that happened, we contacted the family to get personal details for our story. It was a burden to anyone assigned to do it.

One day, I handed a rewrite man the name and hometown of a captain killed in action in Vietnam. A short time later, he came to my desk, his face strained and white with anger. He was furious because the family had not received notification of their relative's fate. Our phone call conveying the heartbreaking news was the first to reach the family. I understood the rewrite man's feelings and we regretted that we had intruded for a newspaper story. I wrote the uncle of the slain officer to apologize for our unintentional blunder and to express condolences. Not long afterward I received a letter from him thanking us for having written the apology, which eased my conscience.

During the Cuban missile crisis in 1962 it looked like the world was on the brink of a nuclear war. When Annie dropped me off at the bus stop to go to work, we did not know whether we would see each other that night. The threat that hung over our lives was that palpable. On a Saturday in October of that year, Soviet ships carrying missiles appeared that they would challenge the American blockade and possibly unleash nuclear war. I sat at my desk reading the copy coming in from Moscow reporting the truculent words being uttered by Nikita Khrushchev, the Soviet leader. Our man in Moscow, David Miller, filed a dispatch that noted that amid the crisis the blustering Khrushchev had attended an arts performance, which David pointed out was not the behavior of a leader about to take his nation into war.

Trying to make out what was happening, I closely reread the text of the Soviet statement. I went over it for a third time to confirm my reaction. There was more than enough bellicose verbiage, but nowhere did the Soviets say they would run the blockade. When that became clear to me, I jumped up and shouted the news to anyone within listening range. It was not to be Armageddon.

Denson's innovative editorship resulted in much commentary in the media world, in New York and elsewhere. Yet both his perfectionism and his indecision, depending on one's point of view, impeded production and ran up costs. There were huge conflicts with the front office, headed by Whitney's man, Walter Thayer. Despite a marked increase in circulation, matters came to a head. In one of his last acts, Denson fired Dick Wald, who was in New York on home leave. Because of his posting in London, Wald had become tight with Ambassador Whitney and his wife Betsy. So the sudden and unwarranted firing was a final defiant gesture on Denson's part. The next day, October 11, 1962, Denson was fired. Although I thought that taking his frustration out on Wald was a pathetic and irrational lashing out, I wrote Denson expressing my admiration for his editorship.

Bellows took over, soon getting the title of Editor. Looking around for a national editor, he gave the job to Dick Wald, who would indeed be ending his overseas assignment but trading it for a much bigger one in New York. The way Bellows structured his management team, Weiss became the Executive Managing Editor for local news, Wald for national, and Freidin for foreign. The week before, Wald had reported to me; now I was looking up at him. He'd been a better student than me in high school, too.

During the Vietnam War, the *Herald Tribune* did not have a staff correspondent stationed in country. For the most part we relied on freelancers. From time to time, one or another of the Washington staff or foreign correspondents spent weeks or months there on special assignment. One of these was Marguerite Higgins, winner of a Pulitzer for her coverage of the Korean War. She was a celebrity among correspondents, because of her long tenure as a war correspondent as well as a record of exposing herself to danger to get the story. She was talented and ambitious. Her extended tour in Vietnam resulted in a series of articles. To our extreme disappointment, when her copy arrived in New York it was a mishmash of impressions and loose writing. There was no way the paper could run it the way it was submitted. Although she was deservedly esteemed in the trade, we had to straighten out her language to muster the coherence that it lacked. That required an extensive rewrite. As an aside, her insights were partial to the company line, endorsing the U.S. government's Strategic Hamlet program in which people were removed from their homes and concentrated in government-erected compounds. That turned out to be a major blunder. Instead of separating the population from the Viet Cong, this policy made friends for them and enemies for our side.

Higgins objected to the scope of the rewrite. "This series," she wired me, "certainly is as personal as a column." She went on to say that if her byline was on it the text should basically reflect the way she wrote it. She had a point. Yet removing her byline was not feasible, as her series had been heavily promoted and doing so most likely would offend her even more. The choice was stark: use her series as written with its host of problems or use it with substantial reworking.

Rewriting a star correspondent is unusual, but it happens, and not just at newspapers struggling for survival. During my years on the foreign desk I became acquainted with the *New York Times* editor in charge of its foreign copy desk. We were attending a meeting of the American Press Institute at Columbia University where the question of rewriting was discussed. The *Times* editor told the group that he had permission to rewrite only one correspondent in their very large stable. That was David Halberstam, then a young reporter establishing his reputation covering the Vietnam War. Good as he was, in time winning a Pulitzer, his writing at one stage was deemed not up to the *Times*'s standard.

Of the freelancers, special correspondents, or contract writers we used in Vietnam, the most memorable was Beverly Deepe, who had a firm grasp on events there. She communicated with us mostly by mail to save transmission costs. Expenditures were constantly being tightened. Stringency was in the office air. Still, I insisted on signing my cables to foreign correspondents "regards rosenfeld." To the guardians of the budget, this was an extravagance, as each word bore a cost. I believed this small gesture of civility was warranted, especially because of the time differential between the cables' dispatch and arrival. When Wald, then the London bureau chief, got around to congratulating me on being named Cable Editor, he also alerted me to how angry a spouse could become when awakened by query cables arriving in the dead of night.

The small group of foreign correspondents broke roughly into two parts, I came to learn. The first comprised the younger ones: better educated, better writers, and ambitious. Some of the veterans—the second part of the group—could hold their own with them or were smart enough and retained the capacity to respond with vigor on occasion. But a noticeable portion of their copy had unacceptable holes. It wasn't that they were not able to meet reporting standards; they just thought they no longer had to do so. It was much easier to regurgitate whatever the most authoritative newspapers in their assigned country were printing. And the indifferent supervision in New York did not challenge them to do better. Then there were reporters with awkward writing skills. Covering unrest in French North Africa, one correspondent, wanting to represent the points of view of ordinary people, repeatedly described them as "the spaghetti eaters in the streets of Algiers."

8

The Long Battle Rages On

The year 1963 began with a strike that closed all of New York City's newspapers. Because I was still not exempt from Newspaper Guild jurisdiction, I was furloughed for the duration. Si looked after me, lining up a job for me at CBS News through his connections with news executive Les Midgley, an old newspaper comrade-in-arms. Midgley was absorbed in setting up a special strike unit and wouldn't take my phone calls but sent word that he would get back to me. A weekly paycheck of some kind was imperative. I phoned Midgley repeatedly. Finally, I got through to him and was told to come in. The special unit to which I was assigned was still in its organizational phase. Executive Producer Bill Leonard was in charge. He would go on to head CBS News. I was assigned a desk, but not given anything to do. I was not able to volunteer myself, because the operation was totally new to me. That first day I sat at my desk and did not do one bit of work. It was the worst day of my working life. I came home that night and told Annie that I didn't think I could take any more complete uselessness.

Fortunately, on the second day I was assigned to the newscast of Douglas Edwards. I wrote feature items for him and felt that at least I was earning my salary, reduced though it was. I edited copy for Robert Trout and Harry Reasoner for their nightly broadcasts. In time, the producers finalized their plans for a weekly, hour-long television program intended to plug a bit of the gap created by the absence of all New York newspapers. It was called *The Sunday News* and was telecast from 9 to 10 a.m. for the duration of the strike. There were seventeen broadcasts to cover a strike that lasted several weeks longer.

Bill Porter was named the producer under Leonard, and I became Porter's associate producer. The concept was to integrate writers from the shut-down print publications and others, along with CBS staff, to report on subjects in their areas of expertise. The challenge was to overcome the static presentation of a talking head by augmenting the presentations with images. Inventive schemes were worked up. Once, with the talented Vern Diamond directing, we staged a fashion show that also included striking models in swimsuits. Another feature was a piece put together on the release of a new recording from Swing Street, a block on 52nd Street where the great jazz musicians played in a cluster of small clubs. All these had been torn down, to make way for a new headquarters for CBS. We used the music from the record as a background soundtrack and Diamond then slowly panned the camera over the slipcover of the recording, which featured a picture of 52nd Street of long ago. Diamond did it so skillfully that viewers might well have believed that they were watching a film rather than looking at a still photo.

Among other chores, I helped recruit newspaper reporters to appear on camera. One was my friend Stuart Loory, a *Herald Tribune* science writer, who did some fine pieces over several weeks. Another was Terry Smith, the son of Red Smith, the columnist who had so awed me when I was a news service typist. Terry had reported for work at the Trib the week the strike began. Because Terry was a totally unknown quantity to me as well as the CBS guys, there was a question about how good he would be. I said, "Let's see if he's a chip off the old block." He got the assignment and did well.

I got to know other newspaper people who were on board: Herb Mitgang, Arthur Gelb, and Stanley Levey, all of *The New York Times*. They were outstanding professionals as well as warm people. Top CBS correspondents were available to our program, including Charles Collingwood, Charles Kuralt, and Dan Rather.

The Sunday program was broadcast from Studio 42, which was located in the upper reaches of the old Grand Central Station. The daily programs were broadcast from offices and studios in buildings nearby. I learned to respect the people in television for their skills. The editors and producers were extremely quick on their feet. Having a phenomenally accurate memory helped enormously, because they had nothing more than incomplete old newspapers stacked in piles for research backup. Anyway, there was precious little time for research. I enjoyed working with people that I liked almost without exception. As the strike was ending, Bill Leonard offered me a job at CBS News. I was gratified by his interest, but decided to return to the *Herald Tribune* when the strike finally was over. But it was another omen of the Trib's fragility.

In addition to the escalating war in Vietnam and the Cuban missile crisis, big news was made by the reign of Pope John XXIII, a new kind of pontiff who reached out to non-Catholic Christians and to non-Christians. Pope John updated and revolutionized his ancient church by convening the Second Vatican Council in 1962. Sanche de Gramont, our Rome correspondent, provided insightful coverage. In April 1963, two months before his death, the pope issued his most famous encyclical. His *Pacem in Terris* was addressed not only to Catholics, as was his custom, but to "all men of goodwill." I persuaded Bellows that this was a bigger story than he was prepared to make it in the pages of the paper. With de Gramont's fine reporting and the dedication of a large amount of costly space and handsome art, the Trib outdid itself. Bellows wrote me: "That was certainly great work on the encyclical."

In May, Bellows assigned me to come up with a plan to consolidate the cable and telegraph operations, the latter a synonym for national news. The purpose was to make better use of space and end the occasional jurisdictional disputes of who had ownership over a story that legitimately could have been claimed by either operation. Mostly, it was a move to squeeze more production out of fewer staffers. Bellows accepted the plan, but for reasons not known to me did not implement it. These were troubled days for the *Herald Tribune*, as labor strikes threatened the survival of the paper. The Trib was not able to work its way to prosperity and depended for its existence on the willingness of its owner to continue to underwrite considerable losses. An attribute of this parlous state of affairs was that resources were slender and we were compelled to make do and to muster whatever creativity we could.

Matters improved when David Laventhol joined the staff in 1963. He was hired by Bellows and had previously worked for the *St. Petersburg Times* and briefly at *The Washington Post*. To break him in, he was temporarily assigned to the foreign desk. It did not take long to see what a consummate newspaperman he was. He fell right in with our way of working and proved especially adept at putting together cable dispatches. David and I hit it off personally and we began a lifelong friendship. Soon enough, he advanced to more important roles at the Trib, first on the night desk and then as City Editor. After the Trib folded and I joined *The Washington Post*, I urged Ben Bradlee to hire Dave, which he did.

The Profumo Scandal, as it became known, followed in June when a long-hidden romantic affair burst into the news as a public spectacle. Contrary to his usual instincts, Bellows was going to play it relatively modestly, relying on the rather staid coverage of our London correspondent, Tom Lambert, who was of the old school and whom I admired and liked. He was giving the story the traditional treatment, glancing over the reckless personal behavior of upper-crust politicians. I told Bellows he was about to underplay the story. He reconsidered, and we used our resources on the desk to flesh out in greater detail what happened in the scandal. It didn't hurt that the principal players were a member of the British cabinet, Secretary of State for War John Profumo, and a couple of young beauties, one of whom was comforting Profumo while also romantically involved with a Soviet naval attaché who was a spy. It was a great story that merited dramatic treatment.

While on the foreign desk at the Trib, I twice was sent overseas. The first time was for more than two weeks, from mid-October to early November in 1963, when Si and his cohorts decided I had earned a special reward. Annie's mother looked after the kids so she could accompany me on visits to our European bureaus. It was a nice perk, especially in light of of our perpetually tight budgets. We traveled to France, Germany, Italy, and Britain. In Paris, I spent much of my time with Don Cook. His title, Chief Correspondent, was bestowed on him long before Denson took over, in an era when the cable operation in New York did not have a strong editor-in-charge. Times had changed and new relationships had to be forged, which was not easy for Cook.

While in Paris, we had the chance to visit relatives I had not seen since childhood. Our cousins, the Lottenbergs, had managed to get out of Nazi Germany before us. Instead of finding safety somewhere more distant, they settled in France. They survived the Occupation by quick-wittedness and luck, along with the help of French people and even one Wehrmacht officer. More than once they evaded capture and deportation to the death camps. They basically remained in hiding, paying people to conceal them, because they could not pass as French. Their daughter, Elfie, on the other hand, was blonde and blue-eyed and spoke unaccented French. She was able to move about and work. Toward the end of the war they were hiding in a village in the south of France. A German officer was quartered in a nearby house. German soldiers came to search the village. They were not hunting for Jews; they were looking for Italian soldiers who had deserted the Fascists after Mussolini's fall. When the German soldiers were about to search the Lottenbergs' hiding place, the German officer living in the village waved them off and said no Italians were there. Obviously, the German officer was aware that Jews were in hiding and intervened to save their lives.

In West Germany, our correspondent Myron Kandel and I interviewed Konrad Adenauer, who had just stepped down as chancellor. When Adenauer entered his office I greeted him in my best remembered German: *"Es freud mich sehr, Herr Bundeskanzler."* He commented that I spoke excellent German. I demurred and said, *"Aber leider, nicht,"* which means "but regretfully not." Though just out of the office he had held and the government he had dominated for fourteen years, Der Alte, as he was known, opened a manila folder, extracted briefing papers, and for forty-five minutes launched into vigorous critiques of what was happening in relations between the U.S. and West Germany. That evening, Mike and I met for more than an hour with Gerhard Schroeder, the foreign minister. He spoke of his relationship with Adenauer and described it in father and son terms, with all the pluses and minuses that analogy implied. He was, unsurprisingly, optimistic about how the new chancellor Ludwig Erhard would do. At the conclusion of our interview he asked me to write him my impressions when I would revisit Berlin a quarter of a century after we had fled Germany. He said that period in German history was a sad time. Both he and Adenauer deftly handled the potentially touchy subject of my life in Nazi Germany, saying neither too much nor too little.

While we were in Bonn, I rented a Mercedes and we drove to Reinheim to visit Annie's birthplace. I had heard much about Reinheim over the years from Annie, who described the large house in which she grew up. When we found the old house still intact, it wasn't as large as it loomed in her memory. As we stood in the street outside of the house, a woman wearing high rubber boots came up to speak to us. She remembered the Strauss and Hahn families and Annie and Doris. Annie recognized her as a friendly neighbor whose daughter played with Annie and her sister. The woman continued to live nearby and the rubber boots were for tramping through her barnyard. In that moment, seeing again the home she lived in as a child, Annie could not put out of her mind the fate that had claimed the lives of her grandparents and her aunts, uncles, and cousins.

When we got to Berlin, Don Cook was there to meet us. Our few correspondents traveled often to other countries to cover important developments. Because Berlin was a recurring flashpoint in the Cold War, our reporters from London or Paris would also swing through as needed. Don drove us into East Berlin and got into an argument with a Vopo (Volkspolizei) who noted a traffic violation committed by Don. I urged Don to stop arguing with the police officer and simply say he was sorry, which he finally did, ending the flap, much to Annie's and my relief.

In East Berlin, we visited the huge Soviet cemetery and saw the massive commemorative sculpture erected as a tribute to the enormous casualties the Soviets suffered in taking the city during World War II. The cemetery and the sculpture underscored the Soviets' rationale for maintaining a tight grip on a nation that had wreaked devastation on their land and people.

We toured the Berlin Wall on the Western side, the Bernauerstrasse, and Cook trenchantly remarked that "'it took Germans to do this to Germans." While in Berlin I wanted to see the apartment house where I grew up. At night we drove through the neighborhood which had changed over the years and left me discombobulated. Nothing coincided with my recollections. At first we could not locate Ansbacherstrasse 56 and I ran ahead of Annie and Don as I searched for the address. But there was no apartment house on the site. There was only a gaping hole.

We visited the Fasanenstrasse Temple, where I had attended the Jewish Community School after Hitler threw Jewish children out of the public schools. This was the temple I saw burning on Kristallnacht. Now only a portion of one wall of the original building remained and the property had been converted into the Jewish Community Center for Berlin.

David Miller, our Moscow correspondent, joined us in Berlin, since my travel plan did not include the Soviet Union. There were a number of housekeeping matters to handle to furnish David's office and residence, and Berlin was a better place than most to buy what was needed. Suitable office equipment was not available in the Soviet Union. We were mindful that we were three Jews in Berlin. What our fate in that setting would have been in an earlier time did not escape our mordant reflections.

After a full day of work and sightseeing, Annie and I rested in our room in the Kempinski Hotel. In the late evening, we didn't feel up to dinner at a restaurant. We hailed a cab and asked the driver to suggest a place where we could get a simple meal. He drove us to a Bierstube, where delicious German cold cuts and sausages were on the menu and Berliner Weisse beer was on tap. We had started to eat when out of a backroom of the establishment, curtained off from the main dining area, we heard loud singing of martial tunes that reminded Annie and me all too much of the rousing songs of Nazi times. We quickly left that Bierstube because the experience stirred painful memories in us both.

In Rome, our host was our correspondent Sanche de Gramont. There were the usual interviews with fractious Italian politicians. An oft-repeated remark making the rounds among Americans was probably inspired by the Marx Brothers: "Italy would be a lovely country if they ever finished it." Telephones worked occasionally. Late at night, when some of New York's cables required responses, Sanche had to lower a message attached to a long rope to a courier waiting on the ground because the elevators were not operating. During our visit, the Second Vatican Council was underway, and that was the most fascinating thing about our visit to Rome. Sanche and his wife introduced us to several priests who were advisers to the bishops meeting in the Council. As in the United States Congress, the priests, who were the clerical equivalent of high-level congressional aides, played an important role shaping the revolution that was taking place within the Roman Catholic Church. One of the issues that upset the adviser-priests I encountered was the bishops' faction that stressed Mariology, which they deemed a distraction from the intended reforms of the Council.

Sanche, who descended from famous French nobility and who had won a Pulitzer Prize for local reporting at the Trib before being assigned overseas, went on to a notable career writing both fiction and nonfiction under the name of Ted Morgan, an anagram of his family's surname. When he and his wife were on home leave, we invited them to dinner at our home in Old Bridge. Looking over our art collection, he spotted my father's dowry, which was two 500-denominated Czarist rubles framed along with a gold watch, displayed in a gilded frame. He remarked that he had a trunk full of those bills, all in mint condition, from his family's coffers, and made us a gift of a couple.

In London, we had the chance to visit the family that we had stayed with when we left Germany for America. This was my mother's aunt's brood. It was heartwarming to be reunited with people who were kind and supportive of us and to note how the young people had settled so well into grownup life. On the working side, Charlie Portis, a talented cityside reporter, was in London on his first days as a foreign correspondent. He did not have the conventional background for this assignment, and tended to play up his country boy Arkansas upbringing. It was more pose than was required because he was smart, a quick study, and a superb writer. In time he authored noteworthy novels, two of which were made into successful films, including *True Grit*, starring John Wayne.

Annie was pregnant during our European tour and our third child, Stefanie, was born in St. Peter's Hospital, in New Brunswick, New Jersey, on April 11, 1964. On the day she was born, a Saturday, I went to the hospital to see Annie and our baby, phoned my mother and other relatives, bought a box of cigars, and went to work. My mother-in-law was at home taking care of the older girls. Going to work even on such an occasion demonstrated how deeply involved I was in my job and how important the Sunday edition was to the success of a newspaper struggling to maintain its quality while trying hard to lose less money.

On my return to the office from Europe, I wrote a report that Bellows liked. Not long thereafter, Si Freidin transferred to London. He left me with the impression that he wanted to get back into the field. Richard Kluger's definitive history of the *Herald Tribune*, *The Paper*, described it differently. Kluger depicted Freidin's move as an exile. According to that version, Bellows convinced him to go abroad because Jim had come to regard Si as a hindrance in New York. From London, Si traveled to wherever he might find a story that he thought worthy. Later, he wrote me that he had had enough of the constant and fruitless struggle he waged to bolster the foreign operation at home and abroad. His frustration focused on Denson, who had enticed him to rejoin the paper by making promises he could not keep. If anything, Bellows had more money restraints placed on him. Si had an insider's knowledge of the budgetary difficulties and recognized how vulnerable his particular turf would remain.

My work was not limited to the foreign desk. I was put to use on election night to shepherd all political copy into the paper, which in the time of hot lead and linotypes was a daunting challenge. After the assassination of President John F. Kennedy, the Warren Commission issued its report on September 27, 1964. It was of course an extremely important story for all Americans. Bellows put me in charge of the Trib's coverage. I organized it, made the assignments, and oversaw the editing.

At this juncture, I was asked for a second time to come up with a plan to combine the cable and telegraph desks, which I would run. I remained ready to challenge Bellows when it appeared to me that he was gradually pulling back on provocative stories to accommodate the commonplace. This was totally in conflict with his stated battle plan. To me this was especially wrongheaded for the Sunday paper. I urged Bellows to emphasize more enterprise stories that would set the Trib apart from the competition.

In January 1965, after Si had been abroad for a year and had grown more detached from administrative responsibilities, Bellows decided that a title change was appropriate for me. He wanted to make clear that as Cable Editor I was doing the heavy lifting. To underscore that point for the benefit of readers, newsmakers, and the industry, he named me Foreign Editor, with the Cable Editor title going to my assistant. It was also intended as a signal to Si to concentrate on his writing.

This staff restructuring was more important than ever because budget cuts had shuttered our bureaus in Rome, London, and Bonn. We had to be more selective in assigning our remaining correspondents. The deployment of U.S. staffers to cover breaking news around the world meant that swift decisions had to be made in New York. We applied the new approach to our coverage when Winston Churchill died in January 1965. For the state funeral we dispatched two people from New York. Si was there at his London base. Because it was Shabbat, the Israeli delegation, including David Ben-Gurion, walked to Westminster Abbey from their hotel. Si walked with them and got a good story. Jimmy Breslin, by this time a celebrity columnist of the common man, was there. So was John Crosby, the famed radio and TV columnist of the *Herald Tribune*. It was decided by Bellows that Jimmy would write the lead story encompassing the day's ceremonies and activities. When the copy came in over the cable for publication in our Sunday paper, it turned out that Jimmy was up to his old habits. He had not done as he was asked. Instead of writing a comprehensive overview, he went off to one of his favorite sites, an Irish bar, for a unique perspective on the old Empire builder. It made for authentic Breslin and a fine sidebar, but we could not lead the paper with it. I was upset as I contemplated having to put together the main story on this historic occasion from cable dispatches, exposing the sparseness of the *Herald Tribune* staff.

As I was getting my mind accustomed to the idea of cobbling together a lead story, which would earn the paper no high marks, I read Crosby's copy. Crosby's piece was detailed and fully captured the day's grand occasion. By eliminating the column-like introduction, it was fairly easy to edit it into an impressive lead story. John Crosby saved our skins that day, as I told him in a note of appreciation. Jimmy was contrite. I could tell because he didn't raise hell with me upon return. Also, he departed the Sceptred Isle having left luggage behind.

The occasion led Si to reminisce about Winnie in a letter recollecting his war correspondence. "I won't ever forget peeing with him from the Rhine River bridge after we crossed it" in the closing weeks of WWII. What the great man said on that auspicious occasion was, "I've been meaning to do this a long time."

By the summer of 1965, rumors were rife about the *Herald Tribune* seeking a merger, which did not do a thing for morale. Toward the end of the summer I went overseas again, this time alone. The Israeli government underwrote a press junket for the opening of the Hilton Hotel in Tel Aviv. The trip was offered to me by my bosses and it gave me an opportunity to visit our Israel correspondent, Richard Chesnoff. He was a freelancer working on retainer.

In Tel Aviv, Chesnoff set up an interview with David Ben-Gurion, who had just stepped down as prime minister. When Richard and I sat down with a founding father of Israel in his study, he turned to us and said, "Rosenfeld I know, but explain Chesnoff to me." He meant he could tell from my name what my Jewish origins were but could not place Chesnoff, which Richard clarified for him. I also met Golda Meir, who was then foreign minister, and other leaders of Israeli political and cultural life.

While in Tel Aviv I went to the home of my uncle Henyek Sherman, my mother's brother, who had emigrated from Poland during the thirties. He had tried farming but was not successful and moved to the city. I also sought to contact my uncle Leo Neumann, the widower of my mother's youngest sister Margot. While in Tel Aviv I tried looking him up in the phone book. I found a handful of Neumanns, but no Leo. In Haifa, there was an Aryeh Neumann, whose first name means lion (Leo) in Hebrew. I did not call right away because I was not sure that it was the right family.

The government had assigned a car and a driver to me. As he drove me around the country, I was exposed to sights that I would not have seen otherwise. We visited a kibbutz in the Galilee where a cousin of a family friend lived. The kibbutz was in the plain below the Golan Heights and consequently under frequent fire from the Syrians, who then held the Heights. For protection, a series of trenches, some roofed with sturdy steel sheets, ran throughout the farm. Kibbutzniks were able to move from their living quarters to their dining rooms to their work places in these protective trenches when the situation required. It illustrated how the Israelis were living under the gun, quite literally.

In Jerusalem, I visited a city divided. The Israelis had erected high, thick concrete barriers to deflect sniper fire coming from Jordanians in the Old City. Like many others before me, I stuck my head around a barrier to take a peek and then quickly ducked back before I drew gunfire. In Bethlehem I bought some vials of holy water to present to Catholic friends at the office. There were visits to the Negev, where I acquired a Bedouin knife and could clearly see the line of demarcation between the desert and the deep green fields that had been brought to life through irrigation using recycled wastewater.

The most striking contrast I encountered was during a Friday afternoon when I saw a Chassid, an ultra-Orthodox Jew, walking along a dusty country road. It was uncomfortably hot, and yet he wore a long black caftan that reached nearly to his ankles, over his trousers tucked into white socks. He wore a streimel, a round wide hat made of gorgeous mink, despite the oppressive heat.

We arrived in Haifa by car that evening. I resumed my search for my uncle, going to the apartment house address in the phone book for Aryeh Neumann and ringing the bell. A man looked out over the balcony and I shouted up to him, *"Ich bin Harry Rosenfeld."* Leo Neumann was now an old man, with a halo of white hair; and he was short, which was not the way I remembered him from Berlin. He had been widowed many years earlier, and he and his second wife graciously invited me to stay for Shabbat dinner. My two cousins also came by for a short visit.

After dinner, Leo and I went for a walk and then sat down at a table at an outdoor café. We had a lot of catching up to do. As we talked, we were distracted by a rising sound. Suddenly, a mass of young people appeared in the street in front of the café. Most of the boys wore white shortsleeved shirts and dark trousers, and the girls wore white blouses and dark skirts. They were talking animatedly. Uncle Leo swept his hand toward the oncoming crowd, turned to me and said in Yiddish, *"Siehts, Harry, alle insere Yiddishe Kinder?"* ("Do you see, Harry, all our Jewish children?") It was a moment infused with deep feelings, seeing the large number of handsome and pretty young people, real and alive. We could not avoid remembering the Jews' fate in Europe. Watching these youngsters that Shabbat eve in Haifa, we were witnessing the resurrection of our people in Israel, and joy mingled with inner sorrow.

Toward the end of the trip, I stopped at an upscale boutique in Tel Aviv to buy clothes for Susie, Amy, and Stefanie. I selected stylish, knitted outfits, for which the Israelis were known. At that point, Chesnoff joined me in the store and handed me a cable from Dick Wald in New York. It informed me that *The New York Times* had been struck and that the Trib, along with other papers in the Publishers' Association, had suspended their operations in solidarity. Most people were told not to come to work. I would remain on the payroll until my scheduled return. I suddenly felt economically vulnerable. I hesitated for a moment before going ahead with the purchase of the fairly pricey garments. On the way home, I stopped off in Rome as planned and met with several candidates for a stringer opening and hired one. From then on we had a person in place we could call on as needed to cover breaking news and other stories.

The *Herald Tribune* resumed publishing in about a week. The management decided that the *Times*'s troubles were not theirs. The stoppage was neither the first nor the last of the strikes that roiled the newspaper business in New York. In those years, the *Daily Mirror* stopped publishing and the *Sun* merged with the *World-Telegram.* Other papers, the *Herald Tribune* among them, held on by their fingernails. During a strike, the management tactic at the *Herald Tribune* was to lay off all but a handful of exempt managers. Although I had been named Foreign Editor in January 1965, I was not exempt under the contract with the Newspaper Guild. Indeed, the monetary reward of becoming Foreign Editor amounted to $1.15 a week. I was also owed what I had been promised as merit increases but had not yet received. Whether this was because of an administrative screw-up or budgeting gimmicks, or both, I don't know. Eleven months after the promotion, I complained again to Bellows. It brought me some relief.

Labor disruptions were nothing new. During one strike, around the Christmas holidays before we had kids, the Guild got me a city job as a temporary postal carrier to help out with the holiday rush. I woke up very early, dressed in a warm jacket, and took the subway into Manhattan to deliver the mail. I did a very good job, so much so that a mailman that I was working alongside suggested I take it easy. He was accustomed to working at a slower pace. Sure enough, with all the temporary help available to the Postal Service, the backlog was cleared up in about a week. They laid us off.

The *Herald Tribune* faced its last crisis in 1966. In a last-ditch effort to save their hides, the Trib, Hearst's *Journal-American,* and Scripps-Howard's *World Telegram & Sun* announced a merger. There were ups and downs in negotiations with the unions before the merger of the three publications into one. With Si's insider information to guide me, I had begun looking for another job since the previous fall. I did not see a future for me or the *Herald Tribune* after a merger, whatever form it might take. I sent *The New York Times* my resume.

As the merger was taking shape, the *Herald Tribune*'s last work day was April 23, 1966, a Saturday, for the final edition dated Sunday, April 24. I tried my best to make the last day as normal as possible, going through the usual motions. Most every one in the newsroom had pretty much stopped work and started drinking. Nonetheless, I continued to run down the flight of stairs to the composing room, making fixes. As a result, I was not in the newsroom when a photographer snapped a final picture of the staff. The most doleful moment that day came when the night desk sent down a revised headline on a story and the word came back that the type already had been packed away. After a valiant battle, waged with flashes of brilliance, it was over. The Trib was no more.

Our correspondents overseas cabled their thoughts. The Washington bureau kept the telegraph machine chattering with pithy observations and apropos quotations. The bureau transmitted at 5 p.m., close to the end, the following verse from Addison, directed at me:

Should the whole frame of nature round him break
In ruin and confusion hurled,
He, unconcerned, would hear the mighty crack,
And stand secure amidst a falling world.

Before I left the building that day, I wrote a long memo to Dick Wald, enumerating the status and requirements of our overseas staff, mostly stringers. The next day I received a form letter from the *World Journal Tribune* Inc.—the name of the merged paper—advising me "that your employment will be continued by the successor enterprise" when publication resumed.

The *Herald Tribune* was where I learned my trade, from the ground up, step by laborious step. In a perfect world in which the paper would have flourished because of its saving qualities of imagination and enterprise, I would never have looked for another place to work. I loved it for its feistiness, for its innovative schemes to discover a niche. I loved it for the quality and competitiveness of many of its people, for its ability to unnerve the staid, overstaffed, overmoneyed *New York Times*. I loved it for the distinct voice it was among the newspapers that had survived as long and as ably as it did under relentless economic pressures. The people who put the paper together each day imbued it with spirit and wit. At its best, it was the paper of which aspiring ink-stained wretches wanted a piece.

Rajca Ruchla (Waksdryker) and Hersz Szerman, Harry's maternal grandparents, in Warsaw. Harry was named for him. They wear stylish secular apparel.

Harry's paternal grandparents Jochweta (Rudel) and Judka Rozenfeld, in Warsaw circa 1930s. She wears the sheitel (wig), worn by Orthodox Jewish women. His head is covered and he is clothed in the manner of Orthodox men. The surname was spelled with a "z" in Polish.

Engagement photo of Esther Szerman and Solomon Rozenfeld, circa 1918, in Warsaw a year before they married.

Left: Resi Rosenfeld, Harry's sister, taken in Berlin, about 1936. She used many variations of her name, starting with Rosa, then Roeschen, followed by Resi, Ray and finally Rachel.

Right: Harry's sister, Ray Damski (her married name), at age 32. In her 90s, she was known as GeeGee to her 11 great-grandchildren. She was always stylish. She lives near her daughter in Palm Springs.

Left: Harry in the courtyard of the Jewish Community School in the Fasanenstrasse Temple, Berlin, around 1937.

Right: Gustav Lowenstein, Harry's boyhood friend in Berlin, who was killed by the Germans in a work camp in Estonia.

Harry at about age 4 (left). Years later, he would recognize himself in the iconic photograph (right) of an unnamed young Jewish boy in the Warsaw Ghetto holding his hands up in surrender to the Wehrmacht, dressed in a coat and cap strikingly similar to the kind he wore as a young child.

Harry's first day of school in Berlin. He wears a rigid leather book pack strapped on his back and holds the traditional cardboard cone, filled with candy, given a child on this occasion.

The synagogue on Fasanenstrasse, Berlin (top), as it appeared circa 1916, and the interior (below) after it was set on fire during Kristallnacht on November 9, 1938, by the order of Joseph Goebbels. Photo credits: (top) Waldemar Titzenthaler (1869–1937); (bottom) bpk, Berlin / Bildarchiv Preussischer Kulturbesitz / Abraham Pisarek (1901–1983), photographer / Art Resource, NY.

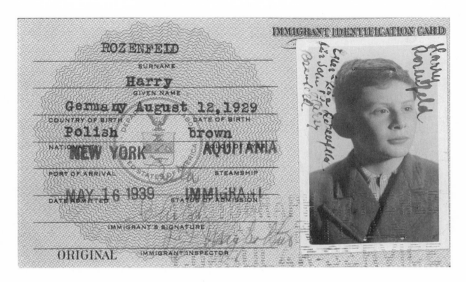

On arrival in New York on May 16, 1939, Harry received his official United States identification card, issued by the Department of State aboard the Cunard liner Aquitania, docked on Manhattan's West Side.

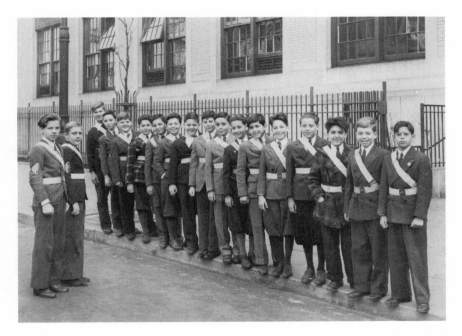

The P.S. 115 School Patrol in the Bronx. Harry, a fifth grader, is the eighth from the left. Other lifelong friends on the squad are Stanley Wolk, tenth from left, Harold Schwartz, 14th from left, and Al Bernstein, at far right.

Harry as a high school student with his parents, Esther and Sam Rosenfeld.

Korean Communications Zone, Taegu, in 1953. Private Harry M Rosenfeld US51178256, at work in the Military History Section. A bug out sheet is attached to the wall on the right. Updated each morning, it recorded the number of days each member of the outfit still had to serve in Korea.

Special Correspondent Beverly Deepe, on home leave from South Vietnam assignment, meets with Harry, her editor, at *The New York Herald Tribune* in the early 1960s. She was a talented and insightful reporter. Photo credit: Whitney Communications.

Daily news conference held by editors at the *Herald Tribune* circa 1965. From left, David Laventhol, City Editor, Richard C. Wald, Managing Editor, Roy Yerger, Night Desk Editor, Harry Rosenfeld, Foreign Editor and James Bellows, Editor. That's where Page 1 stories were touted. Photo credit: Whitney Communications.

During a 1963 tour of *Herald Tribune* news bureaus in Europe, Harry meets with Konrad Adenauer, who had just stepped down as West German Chancellor, at his office in Bonn. The paper's European Economics correspondent Myron (Mike) Kandel is at right, across from an interpreter.

Running the foreign desk, Harry confers with colleague Lee Lescaze, to his far right. The photo shows *The Washington Post's* crowded newsroom before it expanded to upscale quarters. The news, national and local desks are in the background. Pneumatic tubes on desks moved copy to composing room. Photo credit: *The Washington Post.*

Harry interviews President Nguyen Van Thieu at the Presidential Palace in Saigon, South Vietnam on March 17, 1969. He was the last President before the Communists took over. Thieu labored to keep his country independent.

Golda Meir, soon after she was elected Prime Minister of Israel, gave a personal interview to *Post* Foreign Editor Harry Rosenfeld, during her visit to Washington D.C. in 1969. They met in Israel when she was the Foreign Minister. Photo credit: *The Washington Post.*

A bearded AME/Metro, Harry talks it over with his Deputy Metro Editor, Andrew Barnes (on the left) and Maryland editor, Thomas Lipmann. Photo credit: Dennis Brack.

A *Washington Post* table at the White House Correspondents' Dinner, Washington, D.C., April 14, 1973. From left, Harry, style writer Donnie Radcliffe, Bob Woodward, Carl Bernstein, Ben Bradlee, and Edward Bennett Williams, a close Bradlee friend and the *Post's* attorney. Photo credit: *The Washington Post*.

President Gerald Ford interviewed by *Washington Post* National staffers in the Oval Office, January 1975. From left, Carroll Kilpatrick, White House Correspondent; Haynes Johnson; President Ford; political writer, Lou Cannon; and Harry Rosenfeld, then Assistant Managing Editor at the *Post*.

9

The Washington Post

I had been at the *Herald Tribune,* boy and man, for eighteen years, roughly half my life, interrupted only by college and army duty. Now it was time to face reality and find another job. I contacted ABC, CBS (where I got an encouraging note saying they were interested), and *Newsweek* (where interest was also expressed). At *Time* I got a brushoff. A tryout was arranged for me on the *Times* foreign desk as a copy editor. I had never done copy editing as such and I did not like it. But I knew the *Times*'s chief of the foreign copy desk. I also knew the Foreign Editor, against whom I had competed. I worked there for a week. I made suggestions about the *Times*'s reportage that I was editing, criticisms that went beyond what was expected or desired from a *Times* copy editor. I was paid for the week's work and after a considerable delay, I was back at the *Times* to hear the verdict. I did not fear the interview because the job did not interest me. With some embarrassment, the Foreign Editor told me that the *Times* would not hire me because they deemed me overqualified. He was right. The *Times* was wrong in not bringing me on board and grooming me for a job better suited to my experience.

There was a postscript to my failed *Times* tryout. Years later when I was at *The Washington Post,* my first boss there, Phil Foisie, was at the *Times* dealing with some business. My name and what I was doing came up. Foisie told me that the *Times*'s Executive Editor, Abe Rosenthal, wondered aloud, "How did we let that guy get away from us?"

With my wife and three children at home to support, along with a mortgage, I needed to find work soon. Jim Bellows arranged for me to get a temporary job in the Public Information Office at Columbia

University. It paid much less than what I had been making at the Trib, but it was enough to cover most immediate bills. What was left of our negligible savings was spent, including emptying our kids' small savings accounts. Nat Kingsley, now the director of news for Radio Free Europe, wrote of his distress on learning I was not on salary during the hiatus and offered to help out with cash. Think of that. I never had to take him up on his generous offer.

During this stressful period, I received a phone call at home from an editor at *Newsday*. He offered me a job on its copy desk, sight unseen, based on my reputation. The offer moved me deeply, but I declined because I wanted something better. Annie had always stood by me, but with no savings left to fall back on, her concerns were growing. Even a small purchase such as a new pair of stockings had to be put off.

My work at Columbia differed fundamentally from what I was accustomed to doing. Instead of covering news, I was trying to stimulate news coverage about good things happening at the university. It also meant that, every day, I reported and wrote more than I had at my newspaper job. My press releases were often picked up by newspapers around the country.

One of the chores that the office had to perform was to help enhance the image of Columbia in the community. There was constant tension between town and gown because Columbia carried a lot of weight in the Morningside Heights neighborhood. To offset criticism from the community as the university took over more apartment houses, the administration created a small park out of a smidgen of property that was not otherwise developable and presented it as a gift to the neighborhood. In my release I dubbed it a "vest pocket" park. That descriptive was later used by others, and may have been my creation.

I kept searching for a newspaper job that fit my skills and experience level. In the first week of May, 1966, I flew to Washington and met with Phil Foisie, who was the Foreign Editor of *The Washington Post*. He sized me up for a job. I did not apply for a specific position but left it to the paper to decide. Phil and I talked at length and found that we had similar views about the nature of news coverage and editing. A follow-up visit included a meeting with Ben Bradlee, then Managing Editor. We talked for a while and he offered me the job of night foreign editor. His salary proposal was a little bit less than I was making at the Trib at the end—and still less than I would have been if the *Herald Tribune* resumed publication. In that event, I was slated to become the general editor-in-charge of both foreign and national news.

I told Bradlee that I very much wanted to join the *Post* but that I couldn't do it on the salary he had in mind. "I don't even have enough money to pay for the move down here," I said. Bradlee wouldn't budge on the paycheck but would pick up moving expenses, which turned out to be about eight hundred dollars. At home, I discussed the offer with Annie. We decided it was best to accept those terms. I phoned Bradlee and he was enthusiastic about my decision. We left my starting date undecided because, among other things, we would have to sell our house in New Jersey. I did not share with Ben my hope to go back to the Trib after the strike and help it resume publication.

One day at Columbia I received a phone call from Bill Leonard at CBS. He had found a position for me as Managing Editor at CBS News. This offer posed a dilemma. Television news would be a radical change for me, but I had enjoyed my time working in it. Also, the position was much more prestigious than night foreign editor at the *Post*. The pay would have far surpassed the *Post* salary, too. But I had given my word to Bradlee and my inner gyro told me to stay in newspapering, so I declined Leonard's tempting offer.

I was still hemming and hawing about my starting date at the *Post*, when Bradlee called and insisted I get off the dime. My starting date was set for September 1966. Jim Bellows and Dick Wald took me to lunch and supported my decision to join the *Post*. They cautioned me to tone down my natural exuberance. They thought Bradlee and Co. probably would not take kindly to it. Bellows wrote me a warm sendoff letter: "I just wanted to thank you for the joy and pleasure of working with you. Believe me, it was all that and more. You kept the place on its toes, and worried about it—you showed your heart." He ended with a summation that spoke for everyone at the paper during those challenging and yet exciting years: "And it was great sport and work at the Trib while it lasted."

We put our house on the market and quickly sold it to the one person who showed interest. Our profit was infinitesimal. Then Annie and I left the kids in her mother's care and drove down to Washington, where we met Bradlee at Duke Zeibert's for lunch. Annie had also cautioned me about curbing my outspoken behavior. The three of us hit it off from the first, so much so that after lunch Annie told me I could be myself with Bradlee. We looked at a number of rental houses that day. Toward the end of a long day we saw a raised ranch in Kensington, Maryland, that seemed the best of a not very good lot. We rented the Kensington house from a naval officer who was on duty elsewhere, and we lived there for about a year.

I joined the *Post* in its early stages of remaking itself. Foisie had wanted me for the foreign desk for good reason. His plan was to upgrade and expand the foreign staff and he judged that I would be useful in that undertaking, especially as we subscribed to the same professional standards. Foisie was implementing Bradlee's and Katharine Graham's vision for the *Post* to make it among the most important newspapers in the country. The demise of the *Herald Tribune* helped greatly. Until then, the customary iteration of the best papers was the *Times* and the Trib. Now a vacancy existed at the top that the *Post* was preparing to fill.

Mrs. Graham had taken over as publisher after the death of her husband, Philip Graham, who had occupied that seat at the behest of her father, the financier Eugene E. Meyer. Prior to Phil Graham's death, she had held minor positions in the family business while she raised their children. Many years later, in 1999, when she was doing research for her memoir, she and I talked for hours, and she kindly provided me with a transcript of our conversation. In the course of the session she recalled those days: "You know I'd arrived in '63, knowing nothing, nothing, nothing." Except that she did know something, from being at Phil's side and from being close to her father. She had had an inside look at the challenges that confronted the paper in the early years of the Meyer ownership from 1933 to 1954, when the *Post* bought the *Times Herald* and secured the *Post*'s survival in a highly competitive market. When it fell to her to assume leadership of the paper, she remembered in our extended conversation, "I had that indirect knowledge, and only that. And then I stumbled around trying to learn. And I didn't know much. Except instinctively."

At first, she said, "I kept making horrible mistakes . . . but when I went to work, I thought, well, I own this control now. And people say, 'How did you have the courage to go to work?' I didn't. I thought I was just going to learn what I needed to know in case I had to make some decision of an ultimate kind. And of course what I didn't realize that things don't stand still . . . Things happen to you. You have to participate."

"So, by '66 when you arrived, I'm still pretty new. I mean I'd put Ben there," she told me. She did this because she "knew there was dreck underneath me. I didn't know what to do about it. I loved Al [Friendly]. And then Walter Lippmann did this thing of kind of pushing and more than I'd thought. He kind of fired Al for me. I didn't mean him to but he did. So then Ben was pushing to come in . . . I wanted it but I didn't know how to bring it about and then it came about. . . ."

She continued, "When you inherit editors who have known you . . . they condescend without knowing they're condescending. Because here you are, you don't know anything, they know you don't know anything. You're a woman, which of course in those days was not terrific. When I put in Ben I discovered that when you put somebody there, there's a whole new relationship between you and him. And this surprised and thrilled me. Because Ben knew that I had put him there. And our relationship was entirely different than mine had been with Al whom I'd known forever. And Russ [Wiggins] whom I'd known a long time. Ben was very strong. If he didn't want to do what you thought ought to be done, he never did it. And in a way our relationship was very good . . . I knew I needed somebody who was very strong and who would listen to me, but not particularly do whatever it was I was talking about, but at least listen. I must say, sometimes Ben didn't and at that point I devised a new method. Which was to go around him . . ." She wasn't certain she handled that well. She summed up their relationship as "partly luck but it was a terrific team." This judgment surely has to be one of the most self-evident to anyone who has a feeling for the creativity, the energy, the commitment, and the resources that Bradlee and Mrs. Graham deployed to make the *Post* the distinguished newspaper it came to be.

Seeking my opinion of her stewardship, she noted that " 'I very much related to you. I mean I sort of knew you.' " I responded that the key decision a publisher makes is in picking the right person as editor and then backing him or her.

I was brought on board about a year after Bradlee returned to the *Post,* where he had worked as a young reporter. I was among a significant number of reporters and editors who joined at the time and in the years to come as the staff continued to grow. These new faces included the political writer David Broder, Haynes Johnson,

Lou Cannon, William Greider, and Richard Harwood, among many others.

Almost immediately upon arriving in the *Post* city room, I began to advocate for the hiring of those who I knew would fit into the evolving mission of the paper. I succeeded with Dave Laventhol but failed with Stuart Loory, who landed a job with the *Los Angeles Times* Washington bureau.

The *Post*'s foreign staff was small but destined for growth. The habits of the staff correspondents were casual when it came to inserting their opinions into their copy. They were not accustomed to having their work reviewed and commented on by the foreign desk in Washington. As night foreign editor, I began to partake in asserting the role of the desk by stressing basic journalistic standards. This irritated the correspondents, some of them to distraction. There were head-to-head confrontations, and I was beginning to be resented by some as a hardass, demanding to know the identity of the ubiquitous unnamed observer who often delivered the trenchant insight. We insisted on providing attribution for our readers to strengthen the credibility of our foreign coverage. This required that the correspondents work harder and with greater care.

On the other hand, my strong editing and administrative skills were valued by Bradlee, who early on gave me out-of-grade assignments. I was picked to plan and organize the flow of copy from the newsroom to the composing room on the night of the November 1966 election. As the copy controller for national news that night, any changes in deadlines had to be cleared with me. I monitored bulletins and changes in story lengths. It was the night that Spiro Agnew, the "liberal" candidate, was elected governor of Maryland, defeating a racist opponent. That victory set him up to become Richard Nixon's vice president.

Election night in the time of hot type was always harrowing. The backup, predictably, occurred in the composing room, because it could not keep pace as the newsroom fed it new leads one after the other. Deadlines were routinely stretched way beyond reason and a lot of good effort went for naught because of the composing room logjam, with the latest information winding up on the composing room floor rather than in the pages of the newspaper. It was frustrating all around.

My role was to help plan the copy flow with the national editors. It is one thing to lay out such a plan; it is another to make it happen. In my hand I held a sheaf of papers listing all the details. Throughout the night I moved between the national operation and news desk editors, who funnel all copy to the composing room, to keep everyone on track. If changes were urgently needed to be made in the face of unexpected developments, which were as certain as certain can be, I was charged with being, as presidential words much later were to have it, "the decider."

The complex challenge went more smoothly that election night than anyone could have hoped for, and my standing with Bradlee was strengthened. I was beginning to feel at home at the *Post* and had regular access to Bradlee, as did others on the staff. If a matter came up outside the purview of the foreign operation, I felt at ease approaching Bradlee. When Vice President Spiro Agnew gave his famous speech denouncing the media it of course was going to be a front-page story. But I thought the paper should do more. I suggested to Bradlee that we publish the full text of Agnew's remarks. My reasoning was that we would gain credibility with our readers if we demonstrated our willingness to cover objectively such a stinging criticism of the media.

Bradlee assured me, "We are going to print the text, but on Sunday. We don't have the space to do it tomorrow." I countered, "Sunday isn't good enough. Others, *The New York Times* almost certainly, will steal our thunder. The moment is now. Make the space." Bradlee hurried to his office to make arrangements to shift ads and create the space necessary to publish the entire text immediately. The next morning Bradlee thanked me. It was another boost to my standing.

In that first year I threw myself into the job, working the night shift. At that time I was a heavy smoker (typically three or sometimes as many as four packs a day) and often drank my supper. It wasn't long before I began feeling chronic pain centered in my back. It got so bad I would stretch myself out flat on a metal desk in the office to seek relief.

Bradlee recommended a specialist who put me on an aspirin-based painkiller, Darvon. One night, I awakened and had a scary black bowel movement. In the morning I called the doctor. When I finally was able to get through to him, he told me to consult my personal physician and showed no further interest. We did not know where to turn, since I had not yet chosen a personal doctor. Stu Loory, our friend, had previously recommended Annie to his doctor. In desperation we phoned Annie's doctor's office and made contact with his partner, Dr. Arnold Lear. Unlike the Darvon-prescribing physician, he instantly grasped what was happening and instructed us to take ourselves immediately to the Washington Hospital Center, where he would meet us. I arrived and was directly placed in a semi-private room. Dr. Lear met me for the first time as I was lying in my hospital bed, smoking a cigarette. He looked at me and said, "You might as well enjoy it because it's your last one." Arnold Lear remained my doctor until we left for Albany.

My problem was that I had a bleeding ulcer and had lost a dangerous amount of blood. I received so many transfusions that most of the blood in my body was replaced. For the second time in my life, I had come close to dying. Bradlee sent over some books on foreign affairs, taken from the ample stack of books sent to the *Post* for review. His note said, "I always knew you were a bleeder."

Following my hospitalization and lengthy recovery, we searched energetically for a house to buy, which at first seemed beyond our means. Fortunately, that changed. When the *Herald Tribune* resumed publication, in the very week that I began at the *Post,* it had been merged into the *World Journal Tribune.* When that misalliance soon collapsed, severance pay was awarded to qualifying staffers. Bellows and Wald saw to it that I was among those who got a check. Courtesy of the Trib's Jock Whitney and the *Journal-American's* William Randolph Hearst Jr., as well as the owners of the WT&S, I received $13,000 as compensation for my last twelve years of service at the *Herald Tribune.* Unfortunately, the earlier six years of interrupted employment between 1948 and 1953 did not count. Still, the severance pay was a windfall that paid for the purchase of our first new automobile, a Pontiac, which we needed because our over-the-hill Dodge was required for my commute to work. The substantial remainder was available for a down payment on a house, without which we couldn't buy a hut.

When the day foreign editor under Foisie—in effect, the No. 2 man on the desk—got his wish to report from overseas, I took over his position. This gave me added responsibility for dealing with assignments as they were being made rather than mainly contributing my views after they had already been carried out. With the promotion, I finally traded in the night shift for daytime hours, making home life that much better.

When I got there, and for a long a time afterward, the foreign desk editing staff consisted of too many past-their-prime Washington reporters and copy editors. Some of them were not all that good in their prime but had been kept after their natural expiration date by an indulgent management content with things as they were, which I considered mediocre. Correspondents and freelancers were added to a staff that was larger than the Trib's. Foisie was indefatigable in making alliances with news organizations abroad so that we were able to cherry-pick the best and most relevant of their work to suit our needs.

One afternoon as I was preparing the news budget, I was logging a follow-up story to the Profumo scandal, which involved the beautiful call girls. In my enthusiasm, I blurted out that if we had their photos on file we could sell out the next day's paper. Bradlee, walking by, overheard and laughed, pointing out that the *Post* sold out everyday (with 85 percent of its circulation home delivered). Bradlee had been rather quickly elevated to Executive Editor and he had hired Gene Patterson as his Managing Editor. Ben was showing Gene around the newsroom and as they walked past the foreign desk, Foisie and I heard Bradlee say, "This is the foreign desk. This one you don't have to worry about."

Meanwhile, on the home front, after an arduous search with the help of several realtors and disappointment that we could not afford a grander house, we settled on a ranch in Kensington. It had five bedrooms, two of them in the finished basement into which Susan and Amy happily moved. It had three full bathrooms, one downstairs. There was a large living room and off it a dining room. One of the ground-level bedrooms was turned into a family room and the remaining two were occupied by Stefanie and Annie and me.

We lived in that house all the remaining years that I worked in Washington. We loved its large stone patio and screened back porch, the ample grounds, and the gracious neighborhood. After we moved in, we read in the original deed that the house was not permitted to be sold to Syrians or Hebrews, which made us feel warm all over about our new neighbors. In fact, many were fine people, including one older couple across the street who turned out to be heavily camouflaged Jews. Their cover was blown after their married son became a regular at our synagogue.

Back at the paper, work in the foreign operation was going along smoothly. The foreign staff was growing, and its work gradually became more professional as most reporters and editors adjusted to stricter standards. Resentment at times ran high. Our correspondent in France wrote a long letter of complaint stating that virtually all the reporters in the field shared his unhappiness with the desk. I hoped he was exaggerating. In any event, we weren't competing in a popularity contest. We were striving to make our work first-rate.

All this time, the Vietnam War was raging, and it absorbed my attention although other parts of the world also erupted into crises. For example, in 1967 there was the war between Israel and the Arab nations. Al Friendly, the long-tenured Managing Editor whom Bradlee had replaced, was thrown into that assignment as the prospect for war materialized. After Friendly lost his management job he gracefully returned to his roots as a foreign correspondent. He owned a home in Turkey that he often visited and so in many ways he was knowledgeable about the politics of the Middle East.

In covering the war, Friendly frequently filed his dispatches at the last minute by telephone. On the foreign desk we took his dictation. On one occasion, while I was talking to him about an important story, he advised me that an Israeli censor was listening in and that the information he provided was all he could share. He could not respond to questions, so we were not to ask any, for that would violate the clearance he had received.

He worked hard to cover the epic war between the Arabs and the Israelis that was to determine the fate of the Middle East for decades to come. Two days before fighting broke out, he wrote an article that stated the Israelis had decided on waging war. He was the first American correspondent to provide eyewitness coverage from the ferocious fighting on the Golan Heights, where the Israelis came close to being overwhelmed by Syrian forces.

When nominations for that year's Pulitzer Prize were submitted by the foreign desk, Friendly's work was not included. When the list okayed by Bradlee reached the desk of J. Russell Wiggins, the editor (nominally of the paper as well as the editorial page) persuaded Bradlee to add Friendly's work to the paper's Pulitzer entries. Friendly won. Whether this was a result of the Pulitzer Board valuing his work more than the *Post* editors, or whether it was an example of the kind of insider machinations that are occasionally suspected in the awarding of journalism's highest accolade, I do not know. This is not to detract from Friendly's reporting from Israel. It was praiseworthy and prize worthy.

With the 1967 war quickly settled, Iraq erupted in a coup the next year, which facilitated Saddam Hussein's subsequent accession to power. History has taught how that turned out.

Bradlee encouraged competition among editors in charge of the various news departments. It was labeled "creative tension." The technique was intended to keep a sharp edge to the paper and its coverage. Creative tension was not benign or problem-free and indeed Bradlee always denied its very existence. A major component of this tension was to move newsroom managers around in three-bank billiard shots, which unsettled newsroom equanimity but also resulted in some excellent improvements, especially if they were audacious and totally unexpected. A moderate version of that occurred when Bradlee decided to name Foisie an Assistant Managing Editor, elevating me to the Foreign Editor title, No. 2 to Phil with expanded responsibilities.

Foisie basically concentrated on the bluer sky administrative side of the operation, including developing relationships with foreign publications for use of their reportage. He was a member of the board of the news service, which was a partnership of the *Post* and the *Los Angeles Times*. He had other such interests, which focused on the long-range challenges. I handled the news side, overseeing the correspondents' work and the desk editors in Washington. Foisie and I would consult on major decisions affecting the foreign desk, including hiring. For all his virtues as an editor, and he had many, he tended to delay making decisions as he pondered the future course of the operation. Over the years, I came to discover from the *sotto voce* complaints of several correspondents that Foisie's deliberateness engendered frustration. From the beginning of the new arrangement, tension built between Foisie and me. When I required access to certain administrative documents under Foisie's control, he said he was prepared to share them, but he never did manage to get around to it. This was just one of my frustrations with Phil. His hesitancy to implement the intentions of our new roles affected me, as my first important assignment was to travel around the world to visit our correspondents. In a memo before my departure, Foisie alluded to the difficulties we were having. He wrote of the need "to resolve our evident misunderstandings on our relative roles." He clearly was unhappy with the new setup.

Managing Editor Gene Patterson decided to assign me to the world trip for several purposes. First, it was a means to get acquainted in my new role with the staff correspondents stationed throughout Europe and Asia. I also would help select stringers and freelancers in areas where our correspondents could not regularly report. At the same time, I would be able to resolve some administrative problems in India and Thailand and in effect visit every major foreign bureau except those in Africa and Latin America.

Patterson also wanted me to fill in as a correspondent in South Vietnam for two months. This opportunity presented itself in the time between one of our reporters finishing his tour and the arrival of his replacement. The experience would provide me with the reporting credentials I lacked. I had done some feature writing at the *Herald Tribune* and as Foreign Editor at the Trib I had written several page-one analyses and op-ed commentaries, but I had never been a reporter. Our correspondents knew that full well, and this deficiency raised the issue of my credibility with the writers whose work I was handling (or mishandling, according to some). A tour in Vietnam would help fill the gap in my resume.

Because our Saigon bureau used VW bugs, I had to learn to drive a manual shift car. Colleague Lee Lescaze's wife, Becky, was good enough not only to "volunteer" to teach me to drive a stick shift car but also to allow me to use the Lescaze family car to learn how. I shuddered each time I grinded gears, which I did a couple of times before I got the hang of it, more or less, without stalling the car or burning out the clutch.

I approached the newsroom administrator and struck a deal with him. Nothing was to interfere with my family receiving my regular salary, since we were living from paycheck to paycheck. Questions that might arise over accounting of expense advances would be resolved between me and the business office or held in abeyance until my return. I left confident that we had a solid agreement, one that was almost immediately disregarded, as happens in bureaucracies. Annie was troubled a couple of times during my absence by a diminished paycheck or some other financial shortfall, and Foisie was of no help.

During my preparations for the trip, I was taken to lunch by Phil Geyelin, editor of the editorial page, and Ward Just, a foreign correspondent who was wounded in Vietnam and returned after his tours to the home office to join the editorial page. He departed soon enough to take up a successful career as a novelist. Both Geyelin and Just had reported from Vietnam during the war and they shared their valuable knowledge of the place with me. They offered advice about hotels, official modalities in place for correspondents, and the relationship with the Army public information bureaucracy. It was a pleasant meal and I appreciated their thoughtfulness. During the lunch it became evident that beyond cluing me in to the logistics of working in Saigon they had another purpose in mind. Both stressed that the Vietnam story had developed from a war story to a political and diplomatic one. They meant that I should focus on what was happening in Saigon rather than going into the field. I listened attentively.

10

Assignment Vietnam

My world tour began when Annie and the girls took me to the Baltimore International Airport and I flew in the middle of January 1969 to San Francisco. There I spent a day with my Korean War buddy Dave Cohen, who was working in public relations for the Pacific Gas & Electric Co. The next morning I flew to Hawaii and stayed at the Royal Hawaiian, which in its prime had been Oahu's premier hotel. By the time I checked in, it was an aging beauty whose best times were long past. Its strong point remained its location on Waikiki Beach. I bought cheap swimming trunks and went swimming in the placid water, savoring the sight of Diamond Head. The next day, a high-level briefing had been set up for me with CINCPAC (Commander in Chief, Pacific) at Camp Smith, the command center for the Vietnam War. I met with a lieutenant general for a personal talk, an acknowledgment of the status of *The Washington Post*. In the briefing room, high-backed leather chairs were arrayed before a lectern with a screen behind it. My name had been affixed to the back of the chair in which I was invited to sit.

The briefing was detailed, and I was told certain particulars much the same as had been given to the commander in charge an hour earlier. From the structured form of my notes and the legibility of the handwriting, it was obvious that they had been written immediately afterward rather than during the session. According to these notes, the briefers repeatedly stressed that "now was wrong time to withdraw troops . . . for first time equipped to handle war . . . enemy is hurting."

The notes indicate the following points were stressed:

"The one message he wanted to get across is that now is not the time to pull out. We now have a solid position of strength from which to negotiate and there is no military reason why concessions should be made."

"They tend to put things almost entirely in military terms until asked a question about political aspects, when they answer optimistically, almost glowingly, about the increasing efficiency of the Thieu regime."

"They feel that the press can lose the war for us and they have a fatalistic fear of American public opinion."

"As they wanted me to get this message across to American people (they really misunderstand the role of the press in a profound way) I attempted a bit to straighten them out . . . I told them that I could not carry any message—that was not my role—but that I would like to report their views, that this was big news."

"I sensed that my remark was bringing the briefer to go on the record when the Col. Information officer (we should all dress so neatly) made his one intervention to point out that at this juncture with the Paris talks about to open, they should not say anything that might affect the talks. But they transparently wanted me to . . . I was several times enjoined not to connect it in any way with Hawaii."

My notes continue thusly:

"Asked what had happened to the conventional military wisdom that said you didn't put American troops into Asia to fight a land war, he said he was a good soldier and that his President, who obviously has more facts available than he, must have a good reason for doing it; and that was good enough for him."

My notes added:

"It was my impression that despite sincere efforts to see this war in its political implications, they are not up to it. They are more at home in tonnages of supplies moved, enemy killed, weapons captured etc. and never, unless asked, speak about political fallouts of operations, the problem of the Saigon govt. in relation to the people etc."

Afterward, I was escorted on a tour of the naval facilities at Pearl Harbor, where ships of all sizes were docked. Included was a visit to the aircraft carrier *Enterprise*, the Navy's largest ship. Over the years I had seen many depictions of carriers in newsreels and other films. They had not prepared me for this vessel's immensity. She was, in every sense of the words, stunningly impressive, with a forty-two-acre flight deck. *Enterprise* was then under repair because planes had recently exploded while she was at sea. The captain, a skilled sailor, had headed the stricken vessel into the wind and kept the raging fires from damaging the nuclear reactor that powered her.

From Pearl Harbor, I was driven to the airport to catch a flight to Tokyo so that I could meet with our resident correspondent there, Selig "Sig" Harrison. Sig not only had field experience (having served in India and Pakistan) but he had more academic background for his assignment than most correspondents. He brought a great deal of intellectual vigor to his reporting, which sometimes made for less exciting but more insightful copy. In short, he was not Ben Bradlee's kind of guy. He had joined the *Post*'s staff before Bradlee's return, and lacked the panache that Bradlee admired. I landed in Tokyo at 11 p.m. the next day, Saturday, having crossed the International Date Line during the flight. Sig and his car and driver met me and we went straight to the Okura Hotel, where we talked shop while I unpacked. Years earlier, on leave in Tokyo as a PFC during my Korean service, I had viewed the big luxury hotels from the outside looking in. Now, I was on the elegant inside.

We had agreed to lunch at 11 a.m. on Sunday at his residence. Despite my long day preceding my arrival, I was up at 6:30. After breakfast, I decided to take a cab to Tokyo University, where rioting students had occupied the main administration building. Police were all around the campus. As the taxi let me out across the street from the main gate, three helicopters flew over dangling large canisters containing tear gas, which they dropped on a besieged building. Everyone around me was holding handkerchiefs to their eyes or mouths, although I was unaffected. Students were hanging out of windows and papers were strewn all around. I began to walk the perimeter of the large campus. Soon a young student approached me and asked whether he could accompany me. I was delighted. His English was sufficient for our needs, and we talked as we walked for the next hour or so. Our discussion ranged over many topics, including Okinawa, the large U.S. military base which then as later was the center of contention between Washington and Tokyo. We also talked about President Nixon and Vietnam. At one point we passed what looked like a graveyard. Students in very neat uniforms were standing by, apparently attending the funeral of one of their classmates killed in the riots.

After lunch, Sig and I went to the office for a few hours of work, and then we toured Tokyo. The Ginza on a Sunday afternoon was a sight to behold. It was crowded, and the big department stores were open. Family Day drew many people from the suburbs downtown. I took the opportunity to buy gifts for the girls, which I did at every stop on my journey. That night, Sig entertained at dinner the editors of *Asahi Shimbun*, Japan's most respected newspaper. A Japanese meal was served at a teahouse. I ate raw seafood, including crab and other foods that were not customary for me, accompanied by sake. We were so absorbed in our discussion that we overstayed by an hour the time for which the room had been reserved.

Monday morning began with an interview with the foreign minister, followed by a lunch hosted by the ministry. Just before we were to leave for lunch, Sig reminded me that it would be in a Japanese restaurant, meaning that we would remove our shoes upon entering. I remembered then that I had a hole in one sock. So we looked around the city trying to buy a pair of socks that would fit me. The closest we could come was a half-size smaller than I wore, but that had to suffice. My expense account listed a "purchase of emergency equipment" at a cost of nine hundred Yen, or less than three dollars U.S. While I do not recall the substance of the talk at lunch, I do remember that we were served meat. That was very unusual for a Japanese meal that almost always made fish the main course. To entertain a visiting foreign editor, the foreign ministry staff thoughtfully provided a beef dish.

Luncheon was followed by a briefing at the American Embassy and a cocktail party that evening at the Foreign Correspondents Club, an event that was well attended by the Japanese and foreign press. At one point in the talk, my Japanese colleagues asked for my impressions of Tokyo and Japan. My response was that everything I was able to see I found admirable. I was struck by the modernity of Tokyo, which I had not anticipated.

They considered my comments and then, one after the other, said this picture I had in my mind was highly misleading. They said that Tokyo's principal streets indeed equaled those of the most modern European or American metropolises. But, they said, off those main arteries of commerce and government there were unpaved side streets, some with open sewers. In short, what I had seen and expressed so much admiration for was little more than a façade. The exchange underlined the limitations inherent in personal observation. It was a most useful reminder for a journalist.

It was a busy and hectic visit and it gave me a close-up look at Sig, and I liked what I saw and also noted that the *Post* seemed to enjoy a good name in Tokyo. Tired out by the whirlwind but pleased, I was off to Hong Kong. Stan Karnow was stationed in that city but traveled to Vietnam regularly for extended coverage, in addition to roaming the region while keeping an eye on what was happening in China next door. He was among the most traveled and experienced correspondents on our staff. (In the years after he left the *Post* he had a distinguished career as an author and historian, including winning the Pulitzer Prize in History for his book *In Our Image: America's Empire in the Philippines.*)

Stan and his wife one night convened a dinner (one might better say feast) at the Golden City Restaurant, which served Cantonese cuisine. I kept a copy of the menu, because along with fried prawns, roasted suckling pig, barbecued chicken, fried rice, and the like, there were "five snakes soup with mixed meat" and "baked and stuffed snail." Luckily, the exotic food did not distress my usually sensitive stomach. The Karnows could not have been more generous hosts. They entertained me at dinner in their home and took me to a cocktail party at their club. Stan and I got along easily, which was a good omen.

Before I left Hong Kong, *Wall Street Journal* correspondent Peter Kann and his fiancée Francine took me along on an overnight visit to nearby Macao, which we reached by hydrofoil in about ninety minutes. The main attraction of the place was the casino. When we got there after dinner, it was a lackluster place, with an old Chinese woman here or there playing games of chance. I played some blackjack and roulette and contributed thirty dollars to the Macanese economy. In the early morning, the three of us went for a walk while it was still dark. A multitude of Chinese gracefully performed tai chi exercises as they walked. When daylight broke, the Communist Chinese, across the adjacent border, assaulted the ears by activating loudspeakers that blared martial music and Maoist slogans.

I arrived at Tansonnhut Airport in Saigon in the last week of January 1969. Peter Braestrup, the bureau chief, and Dave Hoffman, our other correspondent, were there to greet me. It took forty minutes to be allowed to get off the plane and another two hours to be cleared through customs. Some Chinese on the plane with us managed to make deals with the officials on the other side of the barrier, who made arrangements that hastened the procedures for them. Peter Kann, who was also on the flight, remarked that it was the very best way to be introduced to Vietnam, where nothing worked the way it was supposed to and a well-placed bribe eased life's daily challenges.

As exotic as Vietnam was, there was an aura of homecoming in the air for me, as many people I had worked with at the *Herald Tribune* were in country. Besides Peter and Dave, there was Dave Miller, the Trib's Moscow correspondent, now heading the CBS bureau, and Woody Dickerman, who worked on the cable desk, now *Newsday*'s man in Vietnam.

At the bureau I met Joyce Bolo, who was the office manager in every sense of the word. She was an American married to Felix Bolo, a French correspondent for Agence France-Presse, and a long-time resident in Vietnam. The first night, Peter Braestrup hosted a dinner party where I met an articulate colonel involved in the pacification program, as well as a number of American newsmen. Peter and I stayed for a few hours and then went to the office to work before adjourning to my room for a long briefing. I was taken by what Braestrup, who had a reputation as a bit of a war lover, had to say about the situation in Vietnam. Peter would be returning to Washington quite soon, and I was taking his place in the interim prior to Bob Kaiser's arrival.

I was issued equipment for my work in the field. I acquired two sets of fatigues with my name in Vietnamese and English over the left front pocket and my profession, Journalist, or *Bao Chi*, over the right. I was also given a steel helmet, boots, a ground cloth, and an air mattress for sleeping in the field.

From the outset, the *Post* connection gained me access to the highest officials, including a luncheon in the first week with the commanding general of U.S. Forces, Creighton Abrams, an honor because he didn't often do that kind of thing. He was subtle in his views and perceptive, as many officers turned out to be. Top-level meetings continued with Ambassador Ellsworth Bunker at his elegant residence. We agreed to compare notes before I left. Get-togethers followed with several other high-ranking generals, including the commanders of the 1st Cavalry and the 101st Airborne, along with important U.S. diplomats.

My room at the Continental Hotel was large, with a balcony that overlooked the plaza and the canopy of a lovely flowering tree at my second-story window. There was a sitting area and an enormous bed. Service was provided at any hour by hotel attendants always at hand outside the door. The Continental was renowned for its wraparound veranda, where it was customary at night to sit with friends to have drinks and to share scuttlebutt.

In an effort to follow the advice I had been given, at first I attended the daily late-afternoon briefing by the military command. A large room was crowded with reporters. The official, obviously limited information the press received from the military briefer caused the enterprise to be labeled "The Five O'Clock Follies." Under the ground rules, reporters were obliged to regard the provided information as definitive unless they had firsthand experience of the action being described. Then it was okay to write from the eyewitness perspective. Attending the Follies was often a waste of time. I rarely went to these briefings except when it served my reporting purposes or if some interesting person was being trotted out for questioning.

Instead, with the consent and help of Peter and Dave, I quickly found an opportunity during the first week to go out into the battle zone to see for myself. For two days I joined the 1st Cavalry flying in by helicopter and staying in the field at the headquarters of the 2nd Brigade. I slept on a cot outside, next to the troops. Coping with primitive hygienic facilities in the field was not a problem for me. I was not in the least discomfited using a one-holer latrine, in the Army parlance. My Army service had prepared me for roughing it but so had my experience as a Boy Scout. My sojourn in the field produced three stories. There could have been more, except I was soon on the move again, this time to visit Hue in the north for several days.

In the following weeks, my desk diary recorded I visited these places: Can Tho, Soc Tran, Tam Chau, Danang, An Quong, Long An, Long Binh, Hue, and Tam Ky as well was many nameless hamlets. I spent nearly a week traveling through the Mekong Delta.

Beginning with my briefing at Pearl Harbor, the military's attempts to control the news were constant. It had become clear after the 1968 Tet Offensive, if not before, that American public opinion was in play. This was brought home to me after my visit to Hue, which resulted in a long, reflective piece intended to be published in the Sunday Outlook section. The military's media policy included selecting for republication articles filed from Vietnam in the regional edition of *Stars & Stripes* as long as they served the party line. Hue was South Vietnam's major provincial capital, and it was nearly over-run by the Viet Cong during the 1968 Tet Offensive. It had been the last South Vietnamese city cleared of Viet Cong by the U.S. Marines. A year later, I was part of a press tour that visited the city to see how it had been brought back to life.

My article recounted the eager-beaver provincial chief's accomplishments. At roughly the midpoint of my lengthy takeout article, I detailed the camouflage covering some of these achievements, along with the less positive aspects of the reality of the city's current status. In reprinting this piece, *Stars & Stripes* kept the first part and discarded the more critical portion. As a result, my piece, as it appeared, read as a complete endorsement, which the original was not.

Not long afterward, Peter Kann and I made a five-day trip to the Mekong Delta, where most of the South Vietnamese population lived. We stopped at different towns, villages, and U.S. outposts. It was a chance to see how the people managed in wartime. Many memories remain from that trip, but none more lasting than the almost tangible serenity as we drove along dirt roads and looked into open-sided huts constructed on raised platforms. In one, there was a full-sized pool table. At another site, there was a modern Shell gas station catering mainly to motorbike riders. Civilians were pursuing their everyday tasks. Juxtaposed with the quietude was the muffled sound of distant battle that could be heard from time to time.

Amid this tranquility I witnessed the aftereffects of a concentrated bombardment by high-flying B-52s. They dropped their bombs from great altitude in a rectangular pattern. From miles away, a massive plume of debris, dust, and smoke rose from the bombed earth and could be seen clearly. Nothing within the target area appeared to have any chance of escaping destruction, or at least heavy damage. The exercise, called Arc Light, was a standard tactic.

My main purpose for spending time in the Mekong Delta was to assess the progress of a government-sponsored plan to resettle refugees in their former hamlets. The strongest impression was that the striking disparities in South Vietnamese life—the contrasts between the haves and have-nots—applied equally in the rural areas as in the cities. The main difference was that in the countryside most of the haves did not have all that much. This observation encompassed both personal wealth and the status that accompanied political power.

Overall, it was a somber but not totally negative assessment of how the political side—the key side—of the war was going. Although it was considered late in the game at the time, we did not know how many more years the bloodletting would continue.

At a Vietnamese hospital we visited, conditions were shocking. Often, two patients shared one cot, without sheets. Viet Cong prisoners being treated were chained to their cots. There were children with legs and arms shot off. Relatives cared for their kin because nurses were scarce and doctors even scarcer. There was no real effort at sterilization in the facility. What there was in plenty, I was told, was a cultural resignation to death. As a result, many died who need not have. It was an experience not easily forgotten.

One night Peter and I bunked with a U.S. Army advisory group. Within its heavily sandbagged quarters, besides the usual workspaces and bunkrooms, there was—I am not exaggerating—a well-equipped bar with a neon sign, where liquor was plentiful and cheap. After a long day in the field, it did not take much to get me feeling little pain. As we drank, we played poker with the noncoms. In me they thought they had found a pigeon at the table. By rights, I should have been an easy mark. In an absurdity that surely unsettled them, I made far shrewder decisions and took more risks playing my cards boozed up than ever I could do sober. I won a good deal of money, my one and only success at passing for a card shark.

The next morning, I suffered a hangover as we accompanied a sergeant who made his way among the Vietnamese villagers. His idea of winning hearts and minds was to ogle and insult the women and point his carbine here and there as he made his rounds. Having cleaned him out at the poker table was a twofold pleasure for me.

In contrast to the Ugly American sergeant, we encountered young and effective Americans who worked on the civil aid projects. They clearly understood the necessity of gaining the people's support and had imaginative yet practical ideas of how to go about it. Some could speak conversational Vietnamese. Their efforts obviously did not suffice to halt the declining success of American initiatives in Vietnam. The concept made sense, but it was overwhelmed by the overpowering and destructive military effort.

At one point, Peter and I were in the company of an escort officer and the three of us went to an airstrip to welcome another American visitor, Pat O'Brien. In his time, in the 1930s and '40s, he had been a ranking film star. Because of my age, of the three of us

I was the only one who knew what a major celebrity he had been. The other two had no memory of O'Brien and his memorable roles as a steadfast World War I officer, the hardnosed and yet compassionate cop or prison warden, the stand-up Catholic priest, the best pal who didn't get the girl. He mostly played stereotypical Irish characters in his one hundred films. One exception was his portrayal of Knute Rockne, coach of Notre Dame's Fighting Irish (of course). In Vietnam, O'Brien was nearly in his eighth decade, paunchy and ashen-faced and seriously perspiring in the Mekong Delta swelter. He had come to entertain troops who didn't have the slightest idea of who he was. Peter and I did not hang around to find out how O'Brien connected with the troops.

Peter vividly demonstrated his people skills during our trip. When we came to an open-air market, he fearlessly sampled different kinds of food—which I wouldn't dare touch. Throughout much of my Vietnam tour I suffered bouts of diarrhea which I controlled by taking Lomotil and carefully watching what I ate. Peter had no such problems. Sad to say, in time he did pay for this behavior, contracting an intestinal disease.

Our Mekong Delta sojourn ended at an airstrip where we waited for an aircraft to take us to Saigon. The transport plane approached the field several times, only to veer off because the pilot suspected that his craft was vulnerable to enemy fire during landing. His repeated attempts probably consumed the better part of two hours. I passed the time pressing the field's operators about alternative transportation options to get to Saigon. Peter, on the other hand, did not look on the delay unkindly. He sacked out on the tarmac, unperturbed that he was being kept from productive work. I recount this story because Peter, who was awarded a Pulitzer Prize in 1972 for his reporting on the India-Pakistan War the year before, in time became chairman of Dow Jones. In later years, when Peter threatened to reveal my attempts to throw my weight around to get us back to Saigon, I would counter that I would then tell his reporters how he was perfectly content to pass the time napping, head propped on his gear, when another in his party was anxious to get back to work.

By the second week in February 1969, I had been able to take the measure of Dave Hoffman, whom I had known but had not worked with at the *Herald Tribune*. We were getting on fine although he had a short temper that occasionally led to his being a pain in the ass. When that happened I told him that he was losing it, and that settled him down. He was more energetic and hard-working than his reputation in the States suggested. He was well versed about what was happening on his beat. I thought that, given time, he would rank high among our reporters in Saigon.

I was getting acclimated in a hurry. My efforts at driving the stick shift car, however, were not admirable. I tended to stall out. This ticked Dave off, but he was such a reckless driver that one colleague almost bailed out of the car while Dave was brushing against barriers and other impediments on or near the road. One night I was behind the wheel of the VW bug, loaded with other reporters, including Terry Smith, by then of *The New York Times*. We were heading to a restaurant. As I turned down a street, all of a sudden in front loomed an Army of the Republic of Vietnam soldier firing his rifle into the air. Despite my status as an inept beginner driving a shift car, I neatly executed a broken U-turn and sped us away to safety. Nothing like being thrown into deep end of the pool to teach you how to swim. In the blink of an eye and some gunshots, I had earned my spurs as a VW driver with my nifty evasive maneuver.

Other former *Herald Tribune* connections appeared on the scene to help me in my Vietnam assignment. Bob Shaplen, a respected Asia correspondent for the *New Yorker*, came to town and looked me up. He was an old *Herald Tribune* hand and introduced me to many of his contacts, a generous gesture that certainly gave me a leg up on competing reporters. I also met with a South Vietnamese journalist, Pham Xuan An, who worked for *Time* magazine, first on a part-time basis and later as a full correspondent. There was a *Herald Tribune* connection with An also: he had been my occasional stringer during my foreign editorship at the *Herald Tribune*. We had a friendly meeting and arranged to see each other again. Many years later, he was revealed to have been a North Vietnamese agent assigned to infiltrate the American press corps.

I met Jack Foisie, Phil's brother, who was with the *Los Angeles Times* stationed in Bangkok. He came to Saigon every so often for extended stays. Jack had been a stringer in San Francisco for the *Herald Tribune* News Service. Physically he little resembled Phil, and he had a more outgoing personality. I liked him immediately and the better I got to know him, the more I liked him.

George Syvertsen came to Saigon to join the CBS bureau on a rotating assignment. He had been the Moscow correspondent for the Associated Press when we became friends in the early 1960s. His wife Gusta accompanied him to Vietnam. She generously offered to help me shop for my family, and she knew the shops to patronize where I wouldn't get fleeced.

During Tet, the Vietnamese New Year holiday, Saigon was quiet and more boring than usual. I accompanied a two-Jeep night patrol of the city that was uneventful. It did provide a look at sections of the city I had not seen. Outside the built-up downtown area, with its modern structures and fine homes, there was little else besides shacks. The GIs on patrol reflected their distaste, sometimes hatred, of all things Vietnamese—including the people.

With nothing more interesting on the agenda, I decided to visit my old division, the 9th Infantry, with whom I'd done basic training at Fort Dix. It was stationed near the Cambodian border. At one firebase in the heart of VC country the GIs, who routinely sustained mortar fire, had erected an outdoor shower. One GI was showering in full view of everyone, including the Vietnamese women filling sandbags, and, of course, the general and me, who were visiting.

Later on, I ran into General Abrams at a division ceremony and briefly chatted with him. He said he did not recognize me at first because he did not expect a foreign editor to be wearing fatigues. I said that maybe the time was long overdue for foreign editors to be in the field wearing fatigues.

More than once, I got a close-up look at combat and sampled the boredom and the life-threatening perils that the troops faced in the field. While with the 9th Division in the Mekong Delta, I was a passenger in a Command and Control helicopter. The commanding colonel sat on a rubber doughnut cushion because of a rectal problem. His aide held gridded tactical maps covered in plastic. The chopper circled over the battlefield, where an American force of three companies was inserted into hostile territory seeking to engage a VC battalion.

As the hours passed, the three companies were pinned down by unexpectedly heavy fire and lost track of each other. With dusk coming on, one unit was in particular trouble, with its commanding officer wounded. The soldiers had run out of water hours before and now were low on ammo. In the confusion, the company fired over the positions of the other two, not knowing where they were located. As the fighting intensified, artillery and airpower support were called in. Now the operation required reinforcements as well as resupply of the engaged troops and the evacuation of the wounded and dead. The colonel, clearly upset and frustrated, shouted orders at his aide, a captain. He gave what struck me as an extraordinary order that his helicopter should pick up one company commander in the middle of the battle for a briefing.

In the dark of night, after a long time circling, the C&C copter came under fire from fifty-caliber machine guns. They were mounted so that four fired simultaneously, two on top, two on the bottom—a sophisticated field weapon known as a quad fifty. The American force was surprised that the VC had such a gun. Tracers were bursting in the night sky around the chopper when the pilot suddenly seemed to stop in midair and pulled the craft into a steep climb to evade the gunfire. The colonel remarked afterward that "we obviously orbited too long and they suddenly realized who we were." I felt very lucky to have had such a cool and skilled pilot under fire.

Troop reinforcements and heavy air and artillery power helped salvage the operation. When the high body count of enemy dead confirmed that an important Viet Cong battalion had been engaged, the operation evolved from near failure to significant success. The next morning I accompanied the assistant division commander on his helicopter as it flew over the battlefield. Not far away, a South Vietnamese Army aircraft dive-bombed Communist positions. As we watched from the helicopter, we saw the pilot make one attack after another. His dives were rather shallow and he released his bombs from fairly high up. The general turned to me and said, "He must be the father of many children." The mocking aside was meant to suggest the pilot was not prepared to risk his life by making steeper dives.

The generational gap between me at thirty-nine and the teen-agers in combat had become evident to me on one of my earliest ventures into the field. I was flown by helicopter into a battle site shortly after an engagement in which several GIs had been killed. Upon landing, I looked into the surviving soldiers' very young faces, taut with grief at the loss of their buddies. The soldiers were fierce in their anger and wanted me to tell the world that they hated gooks and how happy they were to kill them. The emotional burden men so young were forced to bear was achingly poignant.

After one sojourn in the field I was asked by the 9th Division chief of staff about my impressions. I answered that it appeared to me that the U.S. was swatting mosquitoes with a sledgehammer. He said that as long as we owned the sledgehammer, why not use it?

One weekend, I accompanied William Colby, head of the pacification program under the aegis of the Agency for International Development, on a trip into the field. Colby was the deputy ambassador (and a high-ranking CIA operative). The Saturday and Sunday I spent with Ambassador Colby turned out to be more eventful than expected. Colby was one of the most insightful among the American leadership, a low-key and effective official. Occasionally he invited a reporter to accompany him on weekend trips into the hinterlands. These were undertaken in a small aircraft, and the rules were that the journalist got a close look at how a top official operated—off the record. You could not write about it.

We flew north to Tam Ky and were met by the province chief, a colonel in the South Vietnamese Army, and his U.S. adviser, also a colonel. The province chief decided to entertain Colby at a hamlet near the beach. As we landed at about six in the evening, it usually would have been too late to motor to the hamlet, for most Vietnamese roads were not secure at that hour. But we were well guarded by many troops stationed along the road. The drive was probably meant to be a demonstration of how secure the province had become. Later, I learned that an American unit had been deployed to augment the South Vietnamese in order to make sure that nothing would happen to the ambassador.

When we arrived at the hamlet, Colby inspected a unit of the Popular Forces militia, smartly turned out, paid his respects at a memorial for the fallen, and sat down to a tasty and bountiful Vietnamese meal of soups, chicken, and salads. It was served by the mother of a family whose husband had been killed by the Viet Cong and whose sons were politically active in the government. The meal was followed by an intriguing discussion about the issues confronting the nation among Colby, the province chief, and the American adviser. I had a fine time listening. After midnight we retired. Colby went off to sleep in a house by himself. The American colonel and I slept on cots in a shrine with a floor and a roof but no walls. I had trouble falling asleep and I took a sleeping pill. Still awake a half-hour later, I took another. And that is how I slept through the beginning of the second Tet General Offensive staged by the communists. A sergeant finally kicked my cot to rouse me. The hamlet was under attack. All the top officials sat around two radios, one tuned to a Vietnamese broadcast and the other to an American station to try to find out what was going on elsewhere. At first light, a helicopter came to take Colby and me to Tam Ky. It was imperative that such a high-ranking U.S. official as Colby be promptly removed so that the Communists could not score a big propaganda victory. I got to accompany him, as I was his guest. The American forces remained to help defend the hamlet. A plane coming to Tam Ky to return us to Saigon could not land because its landing gear had been damaged by enemy fire. As we waited for a backup aircraft, only one of us got the chance to shave. Of course, it had to be Colby. We got back to Saigon not much later than planned.

To top off the unexpectedly exciting excursion, Colby invited me to lunch at the General's Mess. I tried to beg off because of my unshaven and generally grubby appearance. Colby insisted, so we sat down in fine surroundings to eat with General Abrams and Ambassador Bunker at a nearby table. This juxtaposition, the proximity of great danger to the commonplace aspects of life, was prevalent in this nation at war with itself.

It was the Tet attacks the year before that doomed the hopes of optimistic Americans who believed there actually was light at the end of the tunnel for U.S. involvement. Although the communists were defeated on the battlefield after bloody fights, the scope of their attacks seriously eroded already waning support for the war among the American public. That affected politics in America. In the months since those attacks, the military had tallied more progress as peace talks began in Paris. The second Tet campaign had been anticipated. Before it was over and the enemy was beaten back again, U.S. troops suffered high casualties.

A more vivid contrast between the war on one hand and normal affairs on the other came on a morning at the end of February when I interviewed the president of South Vietnam, Nguyen Van Thieu. Dave Hoffman and I met with the head of state in the Presidential Palace. Thieu was assisted by an aide, and Dave took notes as I asked questions. We ended up being given a full hour with the president and covered a lot of ground.

The Paris peace negotiations were on the agenda, with Saigon suspected of opposing any deal that would reward the Viet Cong. To counter those suspicions and demonstrate Saigon's openness to a deal, President Thieu cited the Greek experience after World War II as a model for compromise—the communists would be able to participate in any election, but not as a party. As a backdrop to the interview, officials were assessing a surprise attack on a hamlet near Bien Hoa, the huge American airbase about forty kilometers northeast of the capital. That attack was too close for comfort and had been repelled a few hours before. When the interview ended, I headed back to the Continental Hotel to change out of my dark blue suit, white shirt, and tie into fatigues. I begged off a luncheon with Deputy Ambassador Samuel Berger. I pointed the office VW bug toward Bien Hoa. I drove on a four-lane highway that resembled the northern portion of the New Jersey Turnpike, including factories and smokestacks spewing filthy discharges into the air. The traffic was heavy, and it took about an hour to get there. The hamlet that was the scene of the action was a short distance past Bien Hoa. The attack on the hamlet had been blunted, but it took bombs and napalm to fight off Viet Cong equipped only with rifles and small arms. Following the night attack, the bodies of two dozen VC were putrefying in the blazing afternoon sun. Carcasses of pigs and water buffalo killed in the bombing or charred by napalm rotted nearby. The beasts lay where they fell. The human bodies had been collected and lined up along the outside walls of a Roman Catholic Church that had been shot up. Other bodies were stretched out behind some small houses. The Vietnamese civilians, having suffered through these kinds of assaults for a generation, went on with their lives. Adjacent to the devastated hamlet the buildings were not damaged. The striking paradox of utter devastation alongside ordinary life was characteristic of this war.

The number of enemy dead, which was a metric for who won or lost in Vietnam, did not add up to the body count claimed by the South Vietnamese Army. The official explanation of why the communists targeted Bien Hoa was that they could not penetrate the defenses of Saigon. Still, the attack demonstrated the reach of the insurgency. That evening, I returned to my hotel from Bien Hoa and had a drink with Jack Foisie. I was so wound up I bummed a cigarette from him. It calmed me, and a bad old habit was revived.

In Saigon itself, the contrasts of war amid quotidian life was on view. One night I dined with Flora Lewis. She was formerly at the *Post* and had become a *Newsday* columnist, and was briefly in Vietnam to write about the war. We ate at an Algerian rooftop restaurant. The night was balmy and the sangria was satisfying. As we enjoyed our food and drink, with a darkened sky as the backdrop, we saw the flashes of exploding tracer bullets in the distance. The fighting did not keep daytime hours.

Correspondents frequently found themselves on the fringes if not the middle of combat operations. Despite the risks involved, observing basic rules such as keeping your head down at the right moment helped increase the chances of avoiding harm. Under fire, prudence improved one's chances. That was not as much an option for soldiers as it was for the press. My friend George Syvertsen did not always observe caution. While reporting for CBS, he had leaned out over a barrier holding his microphone during a firefight. His cameraman managed to capture dramatic footage for the evening news. After one such incident, I dined with George and his wife. His behavior was also on the menu. I scolded him, and Gusta Syvertsen heartily concurred. I told George that covering combat was part of the job, but courting danger was foolish and reckless. Thirteen months after my return to Washington, a story came across the wires that George and four colleagues had been killed at a roadblock while they were driving to cover a major battle in neighboring Cambodia. The executioners were Khmer Rouge, allied with the Viet Cong. According to a colleague, George had insisted that the newsmen pursue the story in hostile territory.

In March, the Viet Cong began firing rockets on Saigon, and targeted civilians rather than military or governmental installations. The transparent purpose was to influence the peace talks in Paris by unsettling American public opinion. After one such barrage, I went to take a look at three targets, which were the modest shacks of very poor civilians, the sort of folks the communists said they championed. The people victimized by the rockets possessed little to begin with and now were deprived of their meager shelter. Repeated efforts by a Japanese reporter colleague to get them to denounce the Viet Cong were met by silence.

In the first week of March, Dave Hoffman got to take long-delayed R&R in Taipei and Hong Kong. While he was gone, the big story was the visit of Defense Secretary Melvin Laird, who met with American and Vietnamese leaders, civilian and military. It was an important visit with implications for future American policy. At an off-the-record backgrounder for the Saigon press corps, the secretary said he wanted to hear the correspondents' views about the state of the war effort. To me it appeared to be a ploy on his part to butter up the reporters. I was not there to tell him what I thought, but to hear what he had to say. Many colleagues, including some prominent journalists, couldn't resist proffering their opinions. I followed Laird closely during his visit and listened carefully. I asked a lot of questions and got good background information from American diplomatic contacts. Many of these stories, unsurprisingly, made Page 1 even though for the most part they did not go beyond the recitation of events.

After Laird's departure, I reflected on his visit and put various elements together. I then wrote an analysis whose main thrust was that Laird had not come to listen and learn, as advertised, but to lay down the rules for the future. He would ask for more funding from Congress only to speed up the training of the South Vietnamese Army. The reason was the clear need to begin withdrawing American troops and to turn over their combat mission to the Vietnamese and not let it become Nixon's war.

Lee Lescaze, who ran the desk in Washington in my absence, spiked my article. He did so in part because elements had been touched on in a previous piece by Braestrup, written in Washington, of which I was unaware. Lee also decided I was wrong in my conclusions. The analysis piece was one of my better efforts and I was disappointed. Lee was a truth-teller, untroubled by hidden agendas. He had previously done splendid work in Vietnam, especially during the challenging time of the first Tet Offensive. He was a knowledgeable and thoughtful editor and his decisions merited respect, even in the face of disagreement. Others besides me differed with Lee's decision. In a letter to me after I had been named Metro Editor, Bob Kaiser wrote: "Do you remember John Margison of the British Embassy here? He came up to me at a party the other night and said 'How is that very clever foreign editor of yours?' I replied innocently 'Rosenfeld?' 'Yes,' he said. 'I saw Mr. Rosenfeld last March, when Sec. Laird was here. He told me Laird had come to tell the American generals to get ready for Vietnamization, that the U.S. was pulling out. I didn't believe your Mr. Rosenfeld. But he certainly was right, wasn't he.'"

The Bolos gave a party one night, at which a topic previously under discussion took shape. Through the intervention of Madame Bolo and her husband, it was arranged for me to spend a weekend at a French rubber plantation within Viet Cong territory. I was not aware of any firsthand coverage about these enterprises, which continued to operate long after the French withdrawal. With Dave back from his leave and just days before I was to depart, I was working in the office at 2 a.m. when I received a cable from Washington to call. With the help of a *New York Times* colleague whose office was down the hall, I got a military line to Washington in about five minutes. I reached Lescaze who told me Bradlee had received a hot tip about a story involving the U.S. Air Force. The details of what it concerned long ago are no longer clear in my mind, but pursuing the story entailed either Dave or me going to Bangkok. From experience I knew better than to try to negotiate with Bradlee, who in such circumstances expected unquestioning acquiescence. It was decided that since I was winding up my tour, Dave Hoffman would chase the story in Thailand. I remained in Saigon to keep the bureau covered. That meant canceling the plantation visit. Bradlee's tip turned out to be a false lead. As a result, the paper lost out on what could have been a unique insight into the relationship between the once-colonial French and the communists under the umbrella of the now dominant influence of the U.S.

There was a final piece of important business to do in Saigon. I wrote Bradlee that Hoffman complained about having to exchange his dollars for piasters on what was euphemistically called the free market. All news outfits did this, because the official exchange rate was absurdly low. I suggested we explore the purchase of blocked piaster accounts with dollars in the U.S. for delivery in Saigon. That would get us a rate better than the official one but less than the black market. But it would be kosher. I wrote: "I feel it is necessary that we in Washington make the decision and accept the responsibility. I think it is unfair that the responsibility repose on the correspondent alone." Bradlee endorsed the request with the front office.

Well before Bob Kaiser came to Vietnam to replace me, I wrote him: "Let me also say to you what Dave Hoffman was good enough to say to me before I got here: prepare for the worst, the heat, the stench, the annoyances, and then you will be able to take it in stride. Great patience is required here." When Bob and his wife Hannah arrived in the last days before my departure, I squired them around town to acquaint them with the PX, the post office, and the like, locations that would be useful to them during their tour.

As we walked, a couple of urchins, a girl and boy, came up to us begging for money, which was common. Before I could even make an attempt to find them some piasters, the skinny little boy's hand was in and out of my pocket, taking with it a wad of bills. It could not have been more instructive for the Kaisers if it had been staged.

On one of my last nights in Vietnam, I hosted the Bolos, the Kaisers, and Dave at Maxim's, the priciest restaurant cabaret revue in war-torn Saigon, a final paradox. In the field the fare was different. My enduring memories of Vietnam include the trenchant motto painted on the hull of a two-man Cobra helicopter. It read: "Happiness Is a Blind VC."

11

World Tour

My tour in Vietnam was over, and I was much better for it. The reporting lacuna in my resume had been diminished if not eliminated. I had had the opportunity to report for more than two months and to do it during wartime, competing against the best in the American press corps. Because of what colleagues joked was my Jewish guilt, I may have filed too many stories. My days were filled with purposeful work, and the opportunities to learn were limitless. In hallowed foreign correspondent style, I argued with the desk for more space. I gained insight into how a correspondent in the field feels when his copy is edited (from the viewpoint of the desk) or tampered with (in the viewpoint of the writer). That had to be in Patterson's mind when he gave me the assignment in the expectation that it would stand me in good stead with the foreign staff on my return to Washington.

Uppermost in my mind throughout was how well I did a job that for years I had supervised from afar. Lee Lescaze, filling in for me in Washington, had written to Annie that he "admires enormously" my Vietnam reporting. In a letter filling me in on staffing changes on the desk, he was more measured in his praise. "Your stories," he wrote, "have been very good. Despite our disagreement over two of them, it has been a pleasure having you out there—speaking as a deskman who picks up copy and is glad when it is complete, clear and answers all the questions." Actually, there were more disagreements than that. Foisie never said one word one way or the other. He also delayed informing me of staff changes and hirings he made without consulting me. Those shifty acts reflected his unhappiness with the changes that had made me Foreign Editor. It was clear to me that large problems between the two of us remained.

While I was having one of the most striking experiences of my professional life, things were not going well at home. Almost from the day I left Washington, Annie had to cope with serial strep throat infections passed among Amy, the most susceptible, Susan, and Steffie. Annie herself underwent periodontal treatment that involved painful gum surgery. It was frustrating to be half a world away and in no position to help Annie. She had her hands full and despite her own health issues saw the kids through their illnesses.

The original plan was for me to leave Saigon for Laos, but Stan Karnow intervened and urged me to return to Hong Kong for additional discussions. As I had no particular business set up in Laos, I agreed. It was also an opportunity to decompress and avail myself of one of Hong Kong's miracles. At ridiculously low prices, I acquired a bespoke suit tailored overnight, along with two made-to-measure shirts. I selected the fabrics for suit and shirts. That was a first (also a last) for me.

Peter Kann took me sailing on a junk one afternoon in Hong Kong. We were joined by Peter's wife-to-be and a young Chinese woman who was dating an American reporter whom I knew from the *Herald Tribune*. It was a pleasant afternoon. Many years later, it was reported that the reporter's girlfriend was a Chinese Communist agent assigned to befriend American journalists. She made no attempt to wangle secrets out of me; she could at least have tried.

Elegantly outfitted, I proceeded on the journey around the world to visit the *Post*'s bureaus. The next stop was Bangkok, where I met with the ambassador and also with Sig Harrison, who was on his way back to Tokyo from an assignment in Dacca, East Pakistan. While there, part of my mission was to give two hundred dollars to the wife of our Vientiane stringer, who had been hospitalized. Jack Foisie, whom I met at his base in Bangkok, was of special assistance in accompanying me to the meeting with the woman, Mrs. Than Hue.

In India, my next stop, the *Post* still held the lease on its New Delhi residence, in which our correspondent lived until the bureau was closed for financial reasons. The house was impressive and came with a large garden and a staff that continued to be paid their pittance. They kept the residence in good shape inside and out. Again, I was struck by the sharp contrast between the beauty and the squalor in India. In New Delhi's teeming streets, an up-close look revealed people casually squatting to defecate while pedestrians continued on their way unconcerned. That was a new level of destitution, magnified by societal ambivalences that even a short-time visitor could not miss. I got a good look at the other end of Indian society, lunching at the home of Frank Moraes, editor of the *Indian Express,* whom I had met in Washington. His guests included his Jewish-American mistress, a White Russian painter, and a Bengali who was in her time India's most beautiful film star. During my visit, I set up a stringer relationship after meeting with several candidates.

From New Delhi, I flew to Moscow, where our correspondent Anatole Shub had booked me into a recently opened hotel on the Moscow River. It was a massive, sprawling concrete structure devoid of charm inside and out. Its interior floors were covered with thin carpeting that provided no cushioning. The room was small, with Danish modern furniture downscaled to fit into it.

Huge dining facilities were available on the ground floor, but they were the size of an armory set up to cater to large groups of tourists. Unappetizing, to say the least. On each floor there was a food kiosk serviced by a couple of women who provided sandwiches, tea, and snacks. The queue in the morning reached far down the very long hallway. Many of the guests were from the hinterlands, in Moscow on business. The service at the corner booth on my floor was achingly slow, leading some in line to give up and go off annoyed and unfed in order to keep their appointments. It demonstrated the Soviet Union's inherent contradictions. It was a superpower capable of being first in manned space travel and world-class in manufacturing intercontinental ballistic missiles. These achievements disguised the fact that the Soviet Union remained strikingly backward in ordinary quality of life functions compared to other industrialized nations that were not close to being superpowers.

Moscow offered compelling sightseeing opportunities, including a visit to Lenin's Tomb and a performance of the world-renowned Moiseyev Dance Company, and afterward a brief meeting with its founder, Igor Moiseyev. Prominent Soviet people were not encouraged to publicly mingle with foreigners, especially journalists. I also had business to attend to. Tony was not trouble-free to his editors, because of his expense account profligacy. It was a steady job to rein him in. Tony thought his editors were petty and picky; his editors thought his expense accounts ranked with his most imaginative writing.

Shub was an effective foreign correspondent, intelligent and steeped in the backstories in the countries on his beat. His coverage of the intellectual and political dissidents was bold and shed much-needed light despite the efforts of the Soviet authorities to keep them shrouded from public view at home and abroad. It was his focus on the dissidents that the foreign ministry placed on the top of its agenda when Shub took me there for an arranged meet and greet. The officials did not bother with niceties, and got right into it. Why, they demanded, was Shub permitted by his newspaper to write such untrue propaganda about the Soviet Union? They went on and on with their complaints about his stories.

At last I responded. I told them we each had our own view of the work of the other country's journalists. Soviet correspondents routinely wrote scurrilously about U.S. government leaders and American society. We did not like it, but did not hassle the Soviet correspondents, because they had a right to do it. I told the officials that they knew this full well. I added that we could never accept their censorship of our reporters. The one thing that I was not going to do was to beg the Soviet officials to let our correspondent stay.

Furthermore, I argued, Tony's multiple applications to have the two of us cleared for a visit to Leningrad had not been granted. I told them that was no way to treat a guest and not in keeping with well-known Russian hospitality. After all, both my parents had been born and raised in Russian Poland. I said I wanted to visit Leningrad to see the historical sites of the tumultuous period leading up to the Bolshevik Revolution.

Remarkably, on the spot we received permission for the Leningrad trip. And they did not order Shub's expulsion, as it had appeared they might use my visit to do. I had made up my mind that if Shub was going to be expelled that it was just as well while I was in Moscow and could help him pack. It turned out that his expulsion came weeks later. He had been scheduled for reassignment to Paris by us anyway. In the middle of May, with Tony traveling on assignment, his wife Joyce wrote me: "I have been under constant harassment for the last few days . . . I feel like a trapped animal." She asked for help to ensure that the Shubs' personal property would get out of Russia when they left. The Shubs' departure was not interfered with.

Tony and I flew to Leningrad on an Aeroflot plane, and the shabbiness of the craft was another signpost of Soviet deficiencies. The flight attendant, a bit older than was customary in the West at the time, was a no-nonsense woman. A passenger boarded who was very drunk and on the spot she kicked him off the plane, over his muddled protests.

Leningrad was the site of a group of active dissidents, which is likely why the authorities were inclined to bar Shub from the city. While Tony was connecting with dissidents, it was arranged for me to tour the Hermitage and other sites. The city tour was conducted by an official guide from Intourist who at my request took me to the Smolny Institute, which figured prominently in the early days of the October Revolution. There was less time available for the Hermitage as a result. Fortunately, my guide there was a young curator, fluent in English and of high enough rank to be authorized to associate with foreigners. Soviet officialdom was justly proud of the nation's collection of art treasures.

That evening it was arranged that Tony and I would entertain the curator at dinner, an invitation she was cleared to accept. We took a taxi to her apartment building, which looked nice from the outside. Inside the courtyard and corridors, decay was all too evident. Her apartment was half the size it had been in pre-Revolutionary days. She and her husband, their child, and her mother were crammed into the small space. He was a nuclear physicist who was not allowed to associate with foreigners, so he could not join us at dinner.

For what was supposed to have been a few minutes, we sat in the family's very narrow living room, which was actually half of the original hallway. The talk was so absorbing that dinner was forgotten. The husband, a Jew, wanted to know how Israel fared after the Six-Day War of 1967. Official Soviet accounts were deemed unreliable. The couple spoke about the difficulties in the aftermath of the recent Soviet invasion of Czechoslovakia. They moved in a circle of friends demoralized by the invasion, in which Soviet tanks abruptly ended the Prague Spring. The crackdown underscored for the Soviet Union's liberal intelligentsia that hardliners controlled the government, and killed hopes for internal liberalization. They could not complain publicly so they brooded about these developments among their friends. They took care not to speak of their discontent in front of their children, lest they unwittingly betray their parents to their playmates. Being forced to hide their authentic feelings from their children reminded me of my parents' discretion, for the same reason, when as a young boy in Nazi Germany they worried that I might overhear what they could not express openly and repeat it to playmates.

Later that night, Tony and I went to a bar established for the purpose of reaping foreign currency. It was not Westerners who were the intended customers, but young people from neighboring Finland. They flocked to Leningrad to buy cheap booze, and they totally overdid it. Since the better hotels like the Europa and Astoria were full, we found so-called deluxe rooms in a new hotel. The elevators ran, at most, once every fifteen minutes. The next day, we took the overnight train for the return trip to Moscow. Each of us was assigned his own cabin. As far as we could see, Tony and I were the only passengers in that railroad car. This could have been the strangest of coincidences—or it could have been the KGB isolating us.

One morning in Moscow, while waiting for Tony to pick me up, I decided to take a short walk. I went to the nearby riverfront and looked around before walking back to the hotel. As I approached the main entrance I saw a number of men frantically running around in search of something. One of them spotted me and called out to the others. They immediately halted their search. It was apparent to me, and confirmed later by Tony, that unintentionally I had eluded the KGB operatives assigned to track me. Come to think of it, it was also a commentary on the quality of the KGB's performance.

Each floor of the hotel had a babushka, a grandmotherly matron, who saw to the needs of the guests. The day before I was to leave Moscow, I had placed my dirty laundry in a sack hung on the back of the door that the babushka was supposed to pick up for laundering. Tony and I stopped by my room that evening before continuing with that night's program. I noticed that the sack was still hanging there. Tony suggested that we enlist the hotel to do a rush job, but I said, "No reason to bother. I can have it done in Prague." The Czechoslovak capital was my next stop and a bête noir of Soviet officialdom. Almost instantly, there was a knock on my door. It was the babushka, who had come to pick up my laundry. She assured me it would be quite ready by morning. It was circumstantial, but it was evidence that my room was bugged. For the Soviet system, the bright side was that this time its surveillance system worked.

Prague was still in the unsettled aftermath of the Soviet invasion when I arrived. The *Post* had covered the story by occasionally moving a reporter from a nearby assignment, augmented by a stringer, Ken Ames, who also worked for *The Economist* and traveled to Prague frequently. One of my main purposes in Prague was to meet with Ames, on whom we relied heavily during these tumultuous times.

Dan Morgan joined me there. He was the *Post*'s correspondent stationed in Bonn, but his beat included Czechoslovakia.

I had an intense conversation with a Czech journalist. He did not speak English and I spoke no Czech. So we resorted to German, which he spoke well and I could make out sufficiently. He sought reassurance that the United States would intervene to help oust the Soviets. I disagreed. Informed by my experience in Vietnam and the drawdown of American troops I believed was coming, my opinion was that the U.S. did not have the stomach for a major confrontation. Still, he held to his hopes. Although my visit was brief, Dan and I toured the Old City and visited the famed Jewish cemetery there. It was a reminder of how long Jews had dwelled in Europe and how often over the centuries they had been oppressed before the cataclysm of Nazism. In that cemetery since 1609 rests rabbi Judah Loew in a grave still identifiable. He is said to have magically fashioned a Golem, a superman, out of clay, to protect the Jews of his day.

After three days, I met Shub at the airport and together we flew to Belgrade. The highlight of that visit was the dinner meeting that we—Shub, David Binder of *The New York Times*, and I—had with Milovan Djilas. He had been a principal founder of the Yugoslav Communist Party, a hero of the Partisan resistance. Years later, when he was in power and on the verge of becoming president, Djilas's increasingly critical writings distanced him from Tito and the Party. He became a famous dissident, imprisoned by the regime he had devotedly served.

Djilas had only recently been released from his latest incarceration when he accepted our invitation. We picked him up at his apartment, took him to a fine restaurant, and listened to his discourse on the Yugoslav state of affairs. The encounter was immeasurably enhanced because both Shub and Binder brought to the conversation deep experience working as journalists in Yugoslavia.

After Djilas returned home (his driver had followed our car to the restaurant), the three of us went to a different café for a nightcap. A strolling musician moved among the tables. When he approached our table, Binder or Shub asked him to play an old Partisan marching song. The musician recoiled and said he would not, because it would cause a riot right then and there. As aware of Yugoslav history as the correspondent was, he did not appreciate how volatile the passions still were among factions and ethnic communities. They continue even long after Yugoslavia sundered as a nation.

Belgrade reminded me of the Berlin of my boyhood, particularly the facades of the apartment buildings. Before I left, I asked a bank clerk to exchange the Indian rupees I had not had time to spend before leaving New Delhi. The rupee at the time was one of the world's least desirable currencies, and the clerk declined with a smile. I pointed out that India was a close ally of Yugoslavia in the Non-Aligned Bloc. He answered, "Allies we are; crazy we're not."

I reached Israel by flying first to Zurich and then to Tel Aviv. Israel was a country that we staffed for years with stringers (as at the *Herald Tribune*). So our relationship with the stringer was unusually critical since news regularly emanated from Israel. We were fortunate to have Yuval Elizur as our freelancer, and we had a lot to discuss. He and his wife accompanied me in Jerusalem, where I stayed at the King David Hotel. On a nighttime visit to the Western Wall, I did not know the appropriate prayer to offer at Judaism's holiest shrine. I said the Shema (Hear O Israel . . .), which sums it up anyway. This was two years after the Six Day War in which the Israelis ousted the Jordanians from the Old City, which included sections revered in Judaism. The streets around the Temple Mount at night were empty and peaceful. Yuval maintained that one was safer walking at night in Jerusalem than in New York. I toured the Dome of the Rock with a Palestinian guide and also revisited the areas I had seen on my first trip to Israel, when a tense and heavily armed border separated the parts of the city. Now the physical barriers had been removed even as the religious, cultural, political, and all too human ones remained.

I visited the Israel Museum where the Dead Sea Scrolls were displayed in secure cases. I asked our guide if she could read the ancient script. Without hesitation, she read a parchment page as if it had been printed yesterday. Her ability to do this, along with the Wall, is testament to the connection between the Jewish people and its Eretz, its Land.

With the help of my driver, the day before my departure I managed to squeeze in visits to Jaffa, Haifa, the West Bank, and the Golan Heights. On my previous trip to Israel I also had seen the Heights, looking up at them towering over the kibbutz below, where the workers were under sporadic Syrian fire. Now I was on top looking down, confirmed in my views that in unfriendly hands this vantage would have deadly consequences for Israel.

After brief stopovers in Bonn and Berlin, including a visit, accompanying Dan Morgan and his wife, with an intellectual residing in East Berlin, I proceeded to London, where Foisie and I were scheduled to meet to discuss the foreign operation. As I approached the end of my tour, he was at the start of his. London was the station of a staff correspondent, Karl E. Meyer. It was also the communications hub for transmittal of our European, Middle Eastern, and African correspondents' copy, under the direction of an editor—but the two were not getting along. This conflict distressed Foisie, and he was going to confront Meyer once and for all because he considered Karl the culprit. Meyer, for his part, had made known to a colleague (who alerted me) of the seriousness of the estrangement between the correspondent and Foisie. Karl thought, I was told, that "things would be better with you in the foreign editorship, because you were a good guy, smart and much easier to deal with than PF." Foisie tended to be intense, at times to a fault. He could be seen at the urinal, triple-tasking, a cigarette dangling from his lips, studying some paper he held in one hand while attending to his personal needs with the other.

I checked in at the Savoy and that night Foisie I dined and talked over the managerial problems that had accumulated during my absence, including the shifts in assignment. Almost all of these had been made with scant consultation with me—because of time pressures, Foisie explained. Foisie had arranged for us to meet with an up-and-coming newspaper executive who was working on a redesign for one of his recently acquired publications. He was Rupert Murdoch, and he walked us through his plans before entertaining us at lunch at the Savoy. (Many years later I would break bread with him again.)

In between meetings and other obligations there was more than enough to keep me entertained. I visited my cousins. Karl accompanied me to interview the soon-to-be prime minister Edward Heath at Albany, his prestigious residence. Karl and his wife took me to see a daring new interpretation of *Hamlet* that was the talk of London. It was performed in what once had been a warehouse, and the seats were bleachers arranged in a square.

Bob Kaiser's parents were also in London. Phil Kaiser was the minister in the U.S. delegation, making him the No. 2 in the Embassy. They invited me to dinner, an elegant affair with many distinguished guests. I rented a black tie outfit at Moss Bros. Since I had just returned from a Vietnam assignment, during the cocktail hour people pressed me with questions about the war. At dinner

I was lucky to be seated next to Mrs. Edward R. Murrow. When the evening drew to a close, I was given the honor of escorting the widow of the eminent broadcaster to her home.

After nearly a week, Foisie and I left for Paris, meeting with Murrey Marder. He was National's diplomatic correspondent who was reporting on the Vietnam peace talks under way there. David Miller, of CBS, whom I had last seen in Saigon, was also in town. He and I got together with Murray Weiss, our old comrade from the Trib, who was editor of what was now titled the *International Herald Tribune*, which had continued publication after the demise of its New York parent. Foisie received an invitation from French news executives to dine at Tour d'Argent. The meal was surely as fine as the restaurant's stellar reputation. More than the food, I remember the stunning view, from the upper dining salon, of the illuminated Notre Dame Cathedral.

I arrived home in May and was greeted by my family at the airport. It had been a long separation and although there had been much to entrance and distract me during the journey, I had sorely missed them. While I was away, Annie had written that she would never permit us to be separated for such a long time again. For all the range of exceptional experiences I had amassed—they were priceless in countless ways—it was a sentiment I fully shared and which we managed to uphold through the following decades. Two extensive separations were more than enough.

The array of sights and sounds, the exposure to different cultures and peoples, and the personal contact with impressive, even historic personalities was an unmatchable savoring of what the world has to offer. I returned a better newspaperman. My reappearance in the newsroom was greeted with applause.

12

Back in Washington

Coming back to the office, regrettably, meant immersion in the endless bureaucratic haggling about my expense accounts. It was a dispute in which I had to navigate a maze of financial procedures that defied the simple arithmetic that should have sufficed. It lasted for more than a year. My adversaries were good people but we dwelled in separate realms. It burned up more company money paying for the time spent by business-side executives than in the end was saved. From the corporate point of view, I guess, a principle had to be maintained and damn the cost. From my point of view, real money was at stake.

Part of the job on the foreign desk was to present its Page 1 candidates for the next day's paper at the late afternoon news meeting at which departments offered their best stories. As day foreign editor I had begun to do this, relieving Foisie of the chore when he had a reason for not wanting to do it himself. Now, as Foreign Editor, I attended the news meeting almost all of the time. At the *Post*, the national news had a lock on Page 1. This was natural enough, given that Washington was first and foremost a government town and the paper maintained its chops by being in the vanguard of reporting on all aspects of the government. At Ben Bradlee's *Post* the disposition was intensified. National news was his baby, since he had been Washington bureau chief at *Newsweek* before rejoining the paper as Deputy Managing Editor. Bradlee was particularly engrossed by the human connections in government and politics. He relished most the reportage that recorded frailties and defects of persons in their official or public positions—or policies. Knowing who was in and who was out—or, especially, on the way in either direction—was his favorite dish.

Page 1 was National's space unless one of the other departments—Foreign, Metro, Business, Features, or Sports—could manage to claw its way onto it. So the more persuasive I could make a particular offering, for example linking the weightier context of a daily story to future consequences, the better its chance to appear on Page 1. Aside from some occasional hype, mine was an attempt to assure a story's merited presence on Page 1 that would have appeared there except for the built-in bias against it. Foreign news was especially vulnerable in the news meeting because by definition it was so far from Main Street.

It was not only a matter of pushing Foreign; it was nearly as much about calling attention to the clay feet of the other presentations. Humor and sarcasm helped. This good-natured though often pointed banter had been the mode at the *Herald Tribune*. Being challenged was part of the game.

In Washington, it struck me that the editorial conferences and discussions tended to the solemn, with editors overdosing on their own presumed gravitas. My style was so different that rather quickly I developed a reputation as an amusing character, with the emphasis on character. One outside writer, in a weighty article analyzing what was happening at and to the *Post*, and not admiring it, commented on my Seventh Avenue humor. (Whatever could he have meant?) As for my colleagues, some laughed; others not so much, but in time the performance attracted a following.

Several years later, when I headed National, William Goldman, novelist and screenwriter, who wrote the first script for the film *All the President's Men*, had a look at this news meeting. Writing *Adventures in the Screen Trade* in 1983, he described what happened to him in the summer of 1974 when the film was in preparation.

Attending his first news meetings, he found them fascinating:

> But afterward, the top editors came up and told me that they weren't as funny as they usually are. Because one of the editors—Harry Rosenfeld, the part played by Jack Warden in the movie—was out that day. . . .
>
> The next day Rosenfeld was back and was, as advertised, hysterical. In these meetings the various editors—metropolitan, national, foreign—all argue with each other about the importance of their stories and the prominence their stories should receive.

And every time one of these guys would tout a story, Rosenfeld would zap him. Funny, funny jokes. And sitting in a corner of the room, I copied down Rosenfeld's lines in my notebook.

And in my screenplay, when I wrote the budget meeting scenes, I used Rosenfeld's lines.

The reaction of the editors, he wrote, was that "they hated all the jokes I'd put into their budget meetings."

On one occasion Gene Patterson and I made a bet. The wager was an ice cream soda. When the results were in, Gene had won. I arranged with the owner of Chez Camille, a French restaurant that we patronized, to make an elegant presentation. A waiter dressed in a yellow bolero jacket, dark trousers, white shirt, and black bow tie, with a serviette draped over his arm, served Patterson his ice cream soda winnings in the middle of a regular editorial meeting. It made a big hit and Gene kept the empty glass, straw and napkin included, on a shelf in his office.

Before I met Carl Bernstein I encountered his parents more than once at a friend's house. We had nice chats and our talks revealed their concern about their son's status and future at the *Post*. What little I knew about Carl came through office gossip, and I would not burden his parents with the unflattering portrait this idle talk painted of their son. It was on the foreign desk that I first had direct contact with Carl. I was informed that Carl had been assigned, not by the foreign desk, to a story with a foreign connection. It was proposed to Bradlee by Steve Isaacs, the Metro Editor, surely at the urging of Carl who always tried to break into the bigger time of anything but local coverage. The idea was for Carl to go to Canada to interview Americans, presumably some from the Washington metropolitan area, who had fled the U.S. to avoid Army duty in Vietnam. The foreign desk was tasked with editing it for publication, for reasons I could only speculate about.

It had also been decided by others than the foreign desk that Carl would spend time in Canada, do the leg work, and return to Washington to write. That is not uncommon, but it made me nervous. Drawbacks are that the writer is far removed in time and distance from the scene of the reporting, risking its spontaneity. It did not help that Carl was known in the newsroom as dilatory and as an objector to the war and the Nixon administration's policies. To some editors, such a committed antiwar person might not be the ideal reporter for such an assignment. On the other hand, it probably was felt that Carl would have rapport with war opponents so that they would frankly share with him the details of their fateful decisions.

Carl went off and returned. Some time elapsed. I began to ask where the series stood. More time passed; more conversations about its whereabouts, more assurances that it was in the works. It became an absurd minuet. For long stretches I forgot about the whole thing, as it was not in the forefront of my concerns. Then something would remind me and I would press for it yet again.

At long last, a stack of copy books was plopped on my desk. The series was a disappointment. After such a long delay, the articles were not good enough to print. Much later, I found out that the reason I got anything at all from Bernstein was because Isaacs and perhaps Richard Cohen and others interceded to finally take Carl literally by the hand

Periodically, the *Post*'s news department managers would convene at what was tagged Pugwash conferences to reflect on how the paper was doing and how to improve it. Pugwash was the name of a famous international conference, and I'm sure it was appropriated for our get-togethers by Howard Simons. One was in Bermuda, another in Sanibel Island, Florida. When the budget was tight, one was in nearby Fort Deposit, Maryland. At one of these, after a long time spent threatening each other, Bradlee and I played our first tennis. His offense was classic. He followed his serve swiftly to the net, prepared to put my return away. I frustrated him by frequently winning points with passing shots. He was pissed and wrote it off to luck. There was no doubt that he had better style. When he was a young kid he learned to play; when I was a young kid I dodged Nazis. The first encounter ended before the set was completed, at 5-3, Bradlee on top. We followed up and reached the score of 7-5. When I pushed to go on, Bradlee said, "You don't get it Rosenfeld. Our lifetime score is 7-5 and that's where it's going to remain."

Actually, we played one more time, doubles, at another Pugwash. It matched Bradlee and Dick Harwood against George Solomon, the Sports Editor, and me. They squeaked out a win and made a point that their combined ages outnumbered ours, supposedly to increase the severity of our loss. George and I didn't care all that much; earlier we had chatted at length with Virginia Wade, the hotel's tennis pro, and she was a hell of a lot better looking on a court than Bradlee-Harwood.

In 1969, there was a Pugwash in Puerto Rico. During a break, a number of us gathered around the swimming pool. I was standing on the topmost diving board, hesitating. I had never been that high and was timid about diving, as others encouraged me to go for it. Finally, I said I would do it if Patterson, who was stretched out on a chaise, agreed to reopen the New Delhi bureau. He said yes; I jumped and hurt my back (nothing serious at the time; the chickens came to roost later on). The New Delhi bureau remained closed despite my valiant leap.

It must have been sometime after I was named Foreign Editor that Bradlee talked to me about moving across the city room to take over the local news operation. He and Patterson continued to be disturbed by its underperformance. It remained the factious, unprofessional mishmash it historically was, untouched by Bradlee's reforms since his arrival in 1965. It was not a firm offer on Bradlee's part and still less an order. It was Bradlee turning matters over in his mind and feeling me out. After my trip abroad, and given my expanded responsibilities, I was fully absorbed with the foreign news operation. Moreover, I did not have any burning interest in local news.

One day Bradlee asked me to accompany him to the office of Paul Ignatius, who as president was the highest-ranking non-family business executive on the premises. I was handed ten thousand dollars in restricted private stock as a reward for my work. Bradlee waxed enthusiastically, saying the stock's value over the years until my retirement would grow to hundreds of thousand dollars. I did not allow myself to speculate about the reality of such a bonanza. There could have been an additional reason for the *Post*'s largesse. Dave Laventhol, my colleague from the *Herald Tribune*, who created the successful and much emulated Style section, had left the *Post* to become editor of *Newsday*. Perhaps I was given the stock also to help keep me at the paper. In 1991, during our extended conversation, Mrs.Graham recounted how she would occasionally go around Bradlee when he did not carry out her wishes, intervening in what rightly was Bradlee's business. She told me she regretted having done so in one instance especially, when she lobbied to soften the then-radical and salacious tone of Style after it supplanted the conventional Women's section. She said she thought that intervention was the reason Laventhol left for New York.

When I discussed this with Dave two decades later, in 2010, he told me that it was Bradlee who had put into Kay's head that reason for Dave's departure. Dave told me he also had been offered *Post* stock to stay, but he declined. He said he left not because of anything Mrs. Graham had done but because *Newsday* offered a better job.

The understanding about the stock was that you kept quiet about it and that you could only cash it in with the corporation. Still, it could be used to leverage money. We put it up as collateral for a bank loan at low interest, at the *Post*'s bank, to pay all four years of Susan's tuition at Boston University up front, sparing us annual increases. That was a major component of our ability to have Susan at B.U. and Amy at Duke at overlapping times.

As the months passed, continued implementation of the reforms supported by both Foisie and me kept the foreign desk assignment interesting. Perhaps in part as a result of our success, it began to occur to me that I could ratchet up my aspirations. Until that point, Foreign Editor was all I had ever wanted to be and I had attained the position at two metropolitan newspapers. Now I thought I might become a plausible aspirant for a managing editor position or higher. To have a realistic chance at those upper-level positions, I felt I needed to demonstrate that I could run a larger operation. The Metro staff had more slots than any other department (more than one hundred at the time, compared to Style, the second largest, with fifty). Although I did not have an intense interest in local news or the background—most of my experience was in foreign news—doing well as the chief Metro Editor would certainly punch my ticket toward upward mobility.

Spurring me to make a change was that it had become plain that my relations with Foisie were not going to improve, though I believe we earnestly liked each other and on important matters shared each other's values. We got along. But it got to be a grind, as much for Phil as for me.

At this juncture, I no longer remember whether Bradlee approached me or I him. I do recall that there came a time that I turned to Bradlee and said I was ready to shift to local news. Bradlee jumped at the opening since the disparity in professionalism between Metro and the much-improved National, Foreign, and Style operations continued to widen. He was more than ready to implement a grand restructuring so dear to his managerial heart. Bradlee's drastic personnel moves appealed to something inside of him and he craved the public notoriety that would come to him because of the audacity of the move. Kay Graham, on the basis of her experience, certainly believed that periodic staff shakeups energized an ambitious newspaper.

In preparation for the new assignment, Bradlee had us meet for breakfast downstairs at the Sheraton Hotel. As we entered the restaurant, Ben Bagdikian, recently arrived at the *Post* to take over the National operation, hailed Bradlee and invited us to join him, which under the circumstances we couldn't. Bagdikian, who was nobody's fool, surely suspected that something was up. Bradlee just as surely figured that out, no doubt motivating him to speed up the proposed arrangements. He hated to be scooped.

When we were seated, Bradlee opened his tan leather attaché case and drew out a roster of the local staff. He went down the list of reporters and editors one by one as he nibbled on his burnt bacon strips and eggs, recounting their strengths and drawbacks as well as their potentialities.

The editor-in-charge at Metro, Steve Isaacs, was physically tall and bulky, aggressive and bright, with a reputation as a manipulator and in-house politician. His father, Norman Isaacs, was a respected newspaper editor. Under Steve's leadership the local staff was a pot of stewing cliques and rivalries that resulted in personal antagonisms.

The plan was for John Anderson, as City Editor under Isaacs, to take my job on the foreign desk while I took his on Metro, leaving Isaacs in place if not entirely in charge. I argued that it wouldn't work, given the scope of the reforms that were desired. It was necessary for me to take charge of the entire operation. Taking on the City Editor's job did not interest me and I said so. On reflection, Bradlee and Patterson agreed. Anderson made a seamless transition to Foreign Editor. This was a perfect fit for John because of the breadth of his knowledge and the likelihood that his personality would better mesh with Foisie's. Isaacs became editor of the Sunday magazine *Potomac* before joining the National staff.

The weekend before I was actually to move from foreign to local, there was an office party at Jack Lemmon's house to which Annie and I were invited. Jack was the News Desk Editor. As conversation flowed it soon settled onto a particularly disturbing matter. There was a great deal of scuttlebutt about the entangled personal relationship among the local reporters. As the evening progressed, I heard that several of them were dating each other's wives and some of the marriages were headed for divorce court. One reporter's marriage was in particularly poor shape. His wife was going out with another reporter at the *Post*, who was black, and his friends on the staff were making threats to exact some form of vengeance from the black reporter. It was an extremely volatile situation.

I was stunned. Nothing like this had ever confronted me as an editor. I spent the balance of the weekend pondering what to do to keep the staff from blowing up in a melee with racial overtones. I spoke privately to several staffers who had been vocal at the party or who had been identified to me as being the more active stirrers of the cauldron. I invited one reporter to go outside for a walk. As we circled the blocks around the paper, I spelled out for him the implications to his career at the *Post* of any actions he might be contemplating. I assured him he would be fired if he beat anybody up or otherwise caused harm. I spoke to others at the office. One potential troublemaker was dispatched for a week on an out-of-town assignment. Fortunately, nothing came of the threats. No one was beaten up. Perhaps the threats were nothing more than bluster. Since I couldn't be sure, it was wise to intervene quickly and decisively to avert a potentially ugly blowup.

In these early, unexpectedly challenging opening days, Isaacs and I were talking in my new office, likely about this mess. He handed me a slip of paper with the name of a psychiatrist he recommended on occasion for staffers with problems. I crumpled the paper and threw it in the trash. I told Steve that I would not be interfering in the private affairs of the staffers. What concerned me was their behavior at work. I said something along the lines that he had been too paternalistic. I did not intend to put up with the personal bickering that characterized the staff. It wasn't that they were not capable of adult behavior as much as they hadn't been held accountable and so too often acted childishly. Over the years I had occasion to repeat, "This is not a nursery, this is a place of work." I also found myself reminding my colleagues that I was not their mother, I was their boss.

My departure from the foreign desk brought congratulations from the staff on the new assignment and regrets that I was leaving. Al Friendly wrote, "I'll miss you, Buster. It's been good working with you: a pleasure to have had someone at the other end that cared about what was happening abroad and was determined to have it properly reported. Inject Anderson with some of your passion."

To Dan Morgan the news of my move "came as quite a shock . . . you will be sorely missed." Tony Shub wrote, "Things have just not been the same . . . since you renounced auslandskorrespondenz." Others also wrote from overseas. Whatever problems had existed at the beginning, real or imagined, these messages confirmed they had been overcome.

My insistence on taking complete charge of Metro was neither a ploy nor a matter of ego gratification. I had been reflecting on the nature of the assignment and how to fulfill Bradlee's expectations. It was clear to me that the old approach to covering local news was passé. The world had changed and with it America's cities. People were abandoning the core city in large numbers to satisfy other life-style requirements in the suburbs and in time in the exurbs. Washington, D.C., like so many other cities, had sprawled and become a metropolitan region.

While these demographic and geographic shifts were substantially under way, the structure of the newspaper's local coverage remained too much devoted to the core city, shortchanging the suburbs that were steadily increasing in population. My battle plan as Metropolitan Editor was first to articulate a theory of coverage and then to refocus assignments. We needed to concentrate not only on the District of Columbia but also on the adjacent Maryland and Virginia counties—as well as their respective statehouses and politics. I abolished the titles of City Editor and Suburban Editor and in their place created three assigning editors. The editor directing the coverage of the core city was the District of Columbia Editor. This position was joined by the existing Virginia and Maryland editors, but from then onward they were considered co-equals. All reported to me along with the editor in charge of a weekly community news section. A Deputy Metropolitan Editor would be my right hand in running the operation.

In this departmental structure, form reflected function. You cannot successfully run a complicated metropolitan news operation without having settled on an articulated mission under whose canopy a host of everyday decisions would be made.

My being named Metropolitan Editor disappointed Tom Kendrick, one of Isaacs's heirs apparent. It stood to reason that he could not see why he shouldn't have been given the job. He welcomed me with understandable reserve, perhaps in part because, adding insult to injury, he needed to stay with me for a transitional period to acquaint me with the routines of the operation. Despite his obvious letdown, he produced for my benefit a detailed analysis of the local reporters and editors.

Obviously, I wanted to judge for myself. I was determined to meet every staffer face to face in my office to begin the long process of getting to know each one so that I could make my own judgments. I began by calling each reporter and editor into my office to get acquainted and to talk about what they were doing and what they hoped to do. It took some time to accomplish this. Finally, it came down to one person on the roster whom I had not met and for a time could not find. It took a while but we finally discovered the missing reporter ensconced in a cubicle next to my office. He made police checks through the night and arrived at work as others wrapped up their day. Invariably, he carried a paper bag holding a malted drink and a sandwich. He sat down in his tight space and made his cop calls. He almost never emerged from his cubby to mingle with the other staffers who worked nightside. It was unclear how much of his work actually wound up in the paper. He was a nice fellow, more well-mannered than most, but his self-confidence was as painfully underdeveloped as his ambition. At some point he left the paper. The next time I became aware of him was many years later. He appeared in a series of television ads and gave convincing performances. He apparently had found his calling.

The one-on-one meetings were going over well. That was the feedback that my secretary Maureen Joyce was picking up in the newsroom. While I mostly listened during these sessions, if I wished to convey a message I was direct. One of these meetings was of particular significance because of its later consequence. Len Downie, a talented investigative reporter, was known to be close to Isaacs in the political factionalism that characterized the local staff. I assured him that the past was the past and my concerns focused on the future. I remember saying, "We begin with a new slate."

A couple of weeks into my new editorship, as I was struggling to energize the local staff and accustom it to meeting higher standards, a murder occurred that served as a catalyst to further those aims. Debra Mattingly, known as Muffin, was a fourteen-year-old runaway, the despair of her widowed father, a civil service employee of the District of Columbia. She had been adopted and her adoptive mother died when she was eleven.

She took up with notorious bikers, a local version of the Hell's Angels. As her father continued to complain about her lifestyle, eventually Muffin and her bearded biker boyfriend decided to take extreme measures. They wanted to remove her sixty-three-year-old father from their lives once and for all.

The fatal attack began when the boyfriend knocked the older man down in the Mattingly house in suburban Arlington, Virginia. He placed a crowbar across Mattingly's throat, and with his feet straddled both ends while applying his full weight. It was a crime that encompassed many elements of contemporary social pathologies. There was the rebellious hippie culture, the underage sex, the outlaw biker, and the drug connections as well as binge drinking. There was the fact that a single parent was trying to cope with raising a defiant teenager. Furthermore, the father was a government worker in a town where government was the dominant industry.

Obviously, the story was a big one for the local press. Our reporters were on it. As I read their stories I noticed holes in our reporting. I read the competing *Washington Star* coverage line by line, with Kendrick looking over my shoulder. I underlined the elements that the *Star* had and we lacked. There were many. I told Kendrick we needed to get serious about how we covered Muffin. Then and there, I decided to make Muffin the make-or-break story for the local staff. We assigned as many reporters to Muffin as it would take to put us in front of our competitors and keep us there.

I pressed the reporters to get earnest about their work, especially by making contact with their relevant sources. My insistence on hard, quick reporting disturbed many on the staff, including some good writers. Too often, reporters were inclined to remain at their desks, using the telephone to search out facts. Only under some circumstances did this technique suffice. One incident involved Peter Osnos, then a young reporter and among my favorite people in the business. I had worked with him earlier when he was an assistant in our London bureau before the foreign desk helped get him a place on the staff in Washington. On this particular evening we wanted coverage out of the DuPont Circle area, where bikers congregated. Osnos was assigned. He began to work the phone. I told him no, I wanted him to go to the scene to see for himself and talk to people.

Phil Carter, a handsome Southerner and scion of a renowned newspaper family, was assigned to write one of the early lead stories on Muffin. That day he had trouble gathering and assembling facts in order to write a complicated major story on deadline. He had been given the assignment because he was a better writer than most. Around seven o'clock that evening I wandered past his desk and saw that the paper in his typewriter had only a few first-draft paragraphs on it. He argued that he didn't have the time to produce the story that night. He assured me that tomorrow he would have an excellent account well in hand.

I pointed out the obvious to him: we were a daily newspaper and he had been given a daily assignment. I instructed him to put words on paper and that his story was to be ready for the first edition. He complained, but he managed to stitch together a story. Another small triumph stemming from Muffin came out of an assignment I gave to Carl Bernstein. While Carl had a troubled history at the paper, one very important factor in his favor was that he was born and raised in Washington and its suburbs. Most reporters at the paper came from somewhere else; Washington was not their hometown and they didn't have the intimate knowledge of places and people that Carl had as a matter of course. He didn't need a map to get around town.

Carl also had a reputation as a writer, and I directed him to find out everything about Muffin "from the time she left her mother's breast until today." He did it so well that when he and I both had moved on, he wrote me a note: "In cleaning out my desk, I found the attached and decided that you should have it. Think of it as a baptismal certificate." It was a carbon copy of his Muffin profile that was twelve pages long.

Our coverage quickly caught up to the competing Washington dailies and then began to beat them with regularity. Every day, we produced several stories, as we stuck to my game plan and stayed focused. As a result of these and other efforts, the local staff began to produce articles that broke new ground. Muffin was a big story, the talk of the town. It was uncharacteristic for the *Post* to pursue a murder in such fashion. There were those who deemed the coverage unseemly and inappropriate, bordering on tabloid journalism. But Bradlee and especially Patterson were encouraging and supportive throughout.

One day, a *Post* reporter at the District of Columbia Government Building, which in all other places would be called City Hall, found himself in what had been Richard Mattingly's office. Looking around the dead man's empty office, he casually pulled open the desk's drawer. Inside, he found a letter that had been written by the father to the daughter. Either it had not been mailed or it was a copy. It was a poignant appeal from a father to his child. In Bradlee's office we engaged in a furious argument over whether the paper should use it. Some editors, including Howard Simons, were outraged by what they saw as a gratuitous invasion of privacy. Besides me, others, including Patterson, considered it a gripping and pertinent development in a big story. In the end, we used the letter in our story, Patterson's argument winning out. I stuck to my core belief that the central role of a newspaper was to publish rather than withhold, the latter being the right choice in limited circumstances. In addition, with our Muffin coverage we succeeded, setting the pattern for aggressive local coverage that we continued in the years ahead.

It was my custom to receive a copy of the first edition delivered to my home by a special messenger. Bradlee, Mrs. Graham, and key editors received the paper that way. The first edition arrived at my home between 11 p.m. and midnight and I scrutinized the local coverage. If there were problems I phoned the originating desk or the copy desk or news desk, whichever was appropriate. One night during the Muffin run I turned to the editorial page and saw an editorial decrying Metro's coverage of Muffin for its sensationalism. I had never heard of an editorial page taking on the work of its own staff. I was furious and angrily phoned Bradlee. I told him that I had had it and was resigning. The editorial was too much. I had been breaking my back, working excessively long, demanding hours, trying to shape up the staff, with no thanks (I was feeling sorry for myself) and now came this conspicuous insult. If that was all that the top echelon at the newspaper cared, then I didn't have to go on. Bradlee calmed me and reassured me that those editorial sentiments were not his and that I would feel a lot better in the morning.

From my later and less emotional analysis the editorial page's objections were genuine. That sentiment was at the least encouraged by one staffer who had been a local editor some years before, when such coverage was apparently more subdued. And there was an invisible yet persistent divide between the old-timers who were there before Bradlee and those he hired. Moreover, the *Post* editorial page had taken on the *Los Angeles Times* over its coverage of the Manson murders that had occurred about six months earlier. Leveling that criticism was tricky, because the *Post* and the L.A. *Times* were partners in a News Service. In addition, the L.A. *Times*, then a distinguished and well-resourced newspaper, had an inferiority complex because its excellent work did not receive the acclaim that the *Post* regularly got simply by publishing in Washington.

Given these elements, I could understand that the editorial page writers might have felt obliged to criticize their own paper in order to project a sense of fairness. It might go a long way to smooth out hurt feelings in L.A., I figured.

The morning after the editorial appeared Bradlee sent the following note: "Harry baby: You getting mad at me is like the guy who beats a dog for not giving milk. If that editorial is aimed at anyone it is aimed at me. I think it's a horseshit editorial, and I intend to move on to serious problems." It was signed " 'B."

The note actually defused my anger. It was important for me to see that he had my back. Soon I received a two-page, single-spaced memo from Phil Geyelin. He not only had been helpful when I became Foreign Editor, he also reminded me that he had supported my move to Metro. He wrote that the editorial was not aimed at our Muffin coverage. The editorial that appeared was the fifth version, the previous ones having been rejected by Phil. The fourth was killed when it was already in type. The point he was trying to make in the editorial was "that over concentration on the Mattingly case, with its hippie content, suggested a social significance which is not valid, or, rather, which leads us away from the real problems and the real solutions." His staff thought he had gone into the tank for Bradlee and the news side and were upset with him. It was a touching and eloquent explanation of the editorial board's processes. It opened a window onto Geyelin's role in balancing the pressure from his staff against his own more moderate but still critical assessment of our coverage. In the end, I had to conclude that although I still resented it, the editorial demonstrated the strength of the *Post* rather than a shabby commercial weakness that I, in my knee-jerk reaction late at night, had at first deemed it to be. Even at the time, with my feelings sorely bruised, my relationship with Geyelin mattered to me. I could not really remain angry with Phil Geyelin because he was a class act. The gulf between us was easily bridged. It may have been before or after Muffin that Geyelin shared with me his opinion of where I stood with Bradlee. Using a naval term that he and Bradlee learned while serving in the Navy in World War II, Geyelin said to me: "Bradlee divides the world into two types: those who can be trusted to take the con and those who can't. Bradlee can see you taking the con." The con refers to the ability to steer a ship facing trouble.

The Muffin label was to remain mine, all mine. Eight years later, when I left the *Post*, the banner headline on the celebratory mock front page that is newspaper tradition when someone leaves, read: "Rosenfeld, Muffin Go to Albany."

Once Kendrick had moved to head up the Style section, Peter Jay, Metro's chief political writer, became Deputy Metro Editor. He was a well-educated and respected reporter, with a recognized ability to handle complicated stories. During the six months he held the assignment his astuteness and reserve—in contrast to my assertive manner—was critical in this time of transition. He went on to a career as a Nieman fellow, a foreign correspondent, and later a columnist for the *Baltimore Sun*. He had a family resemblance to the portrait of his ancestor, John Jay, a Founding Father and the first Chief Justice of the United States.

Peter Jay was succeeded by Andy Barnes, highly intelligent and not concerned with disguising it. He was savvy and helpful to me throughout his tenure. I considered him a man for all seasons, making functional decisions that helped smooth our operations. He had put his own ambitions on hold to help me as I secured my footing. I was grateful for his help. After he left the *Post*, he became editor of the *St. Petersburg Times* of Florida on his way to becoming publisher and then head of the Poynter Foundation, a journalistic think tank and conference center. He was the son of Joe Barnes, who many years earlier had been the last person to hold the title of Foreign Editor of *The New York Herald Tribune* before I assumed it many years later.

My next, and final, deputy at Metro was Len Downie. He was admired for his ability to vet all sorts of official records. He was considered to have concentrated too narrowly on this work with documents and leaving his writing underdeveloped. By the time of my arrival at Metro, there were questions about his productivity. After I took over he won a year-long fellowship from the Alicia Patterson Foundation—one of journalism's notable awards. On his return I took that into account as well as his intelligence and evident ability, despite his close association with Isaacs, who might have resented my appearance on the scene. I viewed him as the kind of person I would be happy with as a deputy. My expectations were more than fulfilled and in time he succeeded me, at my insistence, and then progressed through several steps to take over from Bradlee as Executive Editor. Under his direction, the *Post* won a passel of Pulitzers. Long before all this came to pass, when Downie was still a young reporter, Bradlee told of an encounter he had with Len. They had lunched and from their conversation Bradlee concluded that Downie was too obviously full of himself. Given Len's career achievements his early self-confidence was well founded.

13

Shaping Up Metro

With my deputies' invaluable assistance, and the help of the assignment editors and their assistants, the local staff increasingly displayed its professionalism. Time and again they showed that they could rise to the occasion when the goals were clearly stated and their performances fairly evaluated. It began with Muffin but resonated throughout my time in Metro. Their success demonstrated that past deficiencies in performance were not as much a lack of ability as they were a lack of focus. Bad habits, unprofessional behavior, and perfunctory effort were overcome in the first place by getting underachievers to leave, and secondly by hiring better. The pressure of demanding but evenhanded leadership played a key role. Because I made it clear from the outset that I did not believe in favoritism and would not countenance factions, the staff settled down to more productive work. Just as importantly, I did not tolerate a political slant in the reportage. Throughout my editorships I have been described over and over again as tough. Almost always that description was twinned with fair. I am content with those judgments.

Getting the staff accustomed to higher standards was trying. One night at a party early in my tenure as Metro Editor, Mrs. Graham asked how it was going. I answered, "I had a good day today; nobody cried." When we looked over the changes in the staff since the beginning of 1970, we listed fifteen departures for whom no tears were shed; three who were hired and did not make it, eight who transferred out to bigger and better jobs, four who transferred in and four who, regretfully, left the paper. And nineteen were hired and succeeded. It is not an exaggeration to call this period a time of sea change, because the worst performers departed our premises. Most of their replacements made it feel as though we'd gained one and a half staff members.

Early on, after signs of improvement were manifest, I told the staff that from now on Bradlee and his management cadre would view Metro with the same respect as National, Foreign, or Style. It was hyperbole, of course, but my purpose was to instill confidence. I took pains to evaluate performances rigorously and fight for raises a long list of candidates. I ran across a copy of the *Des Moines Register*, whose front page I pinned on the corkboard behind my desk. It demonstrated the importance of local news. Its Page 1 banner headline read: "Des Moines Haircuts Go to $3.09." I told Bradlee, "If you were playing local news right, that's what you'd do."

Even in that first year, with the strong wind of Bradlee's mandate supposedly backing me, I had to fight off top management's predilection to raid Metro's roster, the longest in the newsroom, to solve personnel shortages in other departments. Strenuous objections, earnest lobbying, and forceful arguments that we had more inexperienced reporters than any other section did not keep the Metro roster from being cut by three slots. All the while I persisted in asking for a larger staff so that we could do more. I had learned early on in my career that losing a battle did not mean you stopped fighting.

Bradlee's favorite rejoinder when I pestered him generally about a difficult matter was, "Rosenfeld, you spend your time sticking your thumb in my eye." That was a compliment to be cherished until the day I discovered that I was not the only person so described.

In May 1970, there were widespread protests across the nation against the Vietnam War and the decision by President Nixon to expand the conflict into neighboring Cambodia. The demonstrators were fired up by the recent killings of four young people on the campus of Kent State by the Ohio National Guard, who were sent there to control campus unrest. In Washington this protest attracted an estimated sixty thousand to one hundred thousand people, both locals and out-of-towners. Violence was feared, and the White House was surrounded by a wall of buses parked bumper to bumper. There was little violence, as it turned out. It was National's story, and its lead writers handled the broader implications of the event. The local staff was deployed throughout the city to provide wall-to-wall coverage, which included a dozen articles for inside the paper. Metro also helped with a host of reporters who fed into National's overall story, known as a lede-all. It was a form of collaboration between Metro and National that soon had another occasion to flourish.

Independence Day in 1970 included a demonstration by supporters of the war and the Nixon administration to Honor America. This drew counterdemonstrators and was mostly a Metro project, with John Hanrahan sharing the byline on the main story with Bill Greider, National's first-rate writer. Most of Metro's coverage was, again, placed inside the paper.

In the Metro budget proposal for 1971, I asked for funds to establish a *Washington Post* Poll. The poll was envisioned as a continuing project to help shape our coverage by providing data about what subjects and issues most concerned the population of our circulation area. Although during my time at Metro we allocated some funds, a full-fledged poll did not come into existence. For one state election in 1972, we hired Peter Hart to do exit polls, the second one the respected pollster conducted. We also surveyed anti–Vietnam War demonstrators to find out how they fit into American society.

Toward the end of the first year, with many reforms well on the way or being gradually implemented, I proposed changing the name of the separate local section from City Life to Metro. Patterson was in favor of making a change, "But 'Metro' just doesn't turn my engine," he wrote. My proposal stalled for six weeks until Bradlee weighed in: "Rather uncomfortably, and without setting any precedents, I find myself agreeing with Harry that 'City Life' doesn't do it and 'Metro' does." The change was made early in the new year.

At the end of 1970, I announced a series of changes affecting desk editors. In addition to my deputy, assignment desk editors were shifted. Barry Sussman took over as District editor. He was a bright, creative editor. He was replaced on the Maryland desk by Tom Lippman, who in time went on to foreign assignments. Kevin Klose was the Virginia editor. Kevin went abroad as well and then on to a successful career with Radio Free Europe and National Public Radio. Tom Wilkinson became his assistant and in time Virginia editor. Tom had a long career at the *Post,* becoming Assistant Managing Editor/Administration. In addition to being an astute editor, and an alumnus of the *Albany Times Union,* he was a superb tennis player. Bart Barnes left the District editorship, having concluded a year in the tough job, and returned to reporting. Later, Irna Moore joined the editing pool as did Bill Curry and Herb Denton. In time, Irna married Peter Jay. Bill Curry, after a stint as Virginia editor and a National reporter, went to work for the *Los Angeles Times.*

These people had strong intellects and a passionate drive to do quality newspapering. They were zestful in their work and every day gave of themselves to improve the paper. To say that I grew fond of them would be to vastly understate it. It was a pleasure and an honor to be associated with such striving, energetic, thoughtful, and accomplished young editors. They were hard workers and intense competitors. They were my kind of people.

The cigarette smoking I had sporadically resumed in Vietnam grew into a habit on my return. When Patterson noticed it, he turned me in to Annie and I quit again. The pace of the work, and my overeating and smoking, finally began to have consequences. Our wedding anniversary in February 1971 fell on an unseasonably warm and sunny day. I spent the day off playing two sets of singles tennis and washing two cars before returning to the courts with the girls. All of a sudden, I felt ill. In fact, I felt so poorly that I asked Annie to drive me to the hospital. I was diagnosed with an irregular heartbeat, the first attack of atrial fibrillation that recurred over the years.

At first, the doctors tried shock therapy, thrusting my wrists into ice water. Several tries of the ice therapy did not work and I was admitted to the intensive care unit and given drugs intravenously. As I lay in bed, I contemplated my situation: past forty and flat on my back with a heart ailment. On top of the medical crisis, I piled depression, as I worried about what would become of my family if I died or became disabled.

The next morning, abed but awake, I suddenly noted the absence of the irregular beat. The episode was over and I was sent home, where I slept long stretches for days as I recuperated. I returned to the newsroom in about two weeks to be greeted by a round of spontaneous applause, the second time that had happened to me at the *Post.* As the designated Metro ogre—at least according to outside critics and commentators—I was touched by this show of affection. I began an earnest campaign to lose weight in which I was encouraged by Mrs. Graham. Within months, I dropped thirty-five pounds, I wrote Lee Lescaze, then based in Hong Kong.

Soon enough, I was back in the fray, literally no worse for wear. When I got into a pissing match with Richard Harwood, then the in-house ombudsman, I was not only protecting my people and our work, I was also objecting to his methodology. In order to overcome the all-too-natural self-defensiveness of department heads, Bradlee said the ombudsman's critiques would be discussed with the editor concerned before his memos would be published.

Bradlee's ground rules were not followed, which gave me a hook to object. Harwood could be very persuasive, not only because of his analytical skill fingering what was going amiss, but also because of his writing prowess. His criticism in this instance came down to the charge that our work had a liberal bias; my response was that his critique had a conservative one. My lengthy objections to the ombudsman's findings were addressed to Patterson and copied to Bradlee and Harwood.

An exasperated Patterson replied in a Dear Harry note: "It grieves me to receive a review of Ombudsman's memo style, which is his business, when all I wanted was a docile accord with *my* verdict on the single point that we have Pugwashed to death—I think it is necessary for the immortal soul of the *Washington Post* that we invariably think in terms of the Other Side in any story we write." I had seriously provoked Patterson. Beyond the validity of his response, what struck me forever afterward was the unfortunate construct "docile accord." A pain in the ass may seem more than anyone should have to bear, but it beats to bits an editor prone to docile accord.

There was an important point to my riposte to the ombudsman's memo that surmounts overdeveloped reflexive defensiveness. Even as I imposed demands on my reporters and editors to produce, I was obliged to be their advocate when their work was unfairly challenged. Sometimes the criticisms came from within the newspaper; more frequently they came from the outside. Journalism is prone to error, as so much of it done in a rush to meet a deadline. Mistakes need to be acknowledged and corrected promptly. But when charges of bias, bad faith, corrupt motivations are readily leveled by the persons or institutions whose shortcomings or worse had been revealed in print, the staff needs to know that the boss will not throw them over in order to cover himself. If that were to be written off as camouflage for the self-defensive crouch, so be it. What would fatally undermine morale would be—in the Nixonian expression—to leave your colleagues twisting slowly (or otherwise) in the wind. Furthermore, that support had to be applied across the board, including toward those downright hostile and/or dislikable.

All was not dreary. A Republican congressman from Iowa, who chaired a committee overseeing the District, said he got more information out of the *Post* about what was going on in the local government than he received in his official capacity from officials who testified before his committee.

From the beginning at Metro, my age, forty, if nothing else, distanced me from the staffers, who were generally in their twenties and thirties. In the context of the times, it amounted to a generational divide. Growing a beard became popular in the sixties and seventies. One young applicant, Sanford Ungar, concerned that his beard might interfere with his hiring, shaved it off before our interview. After he got the job, he grew it back. I thought about the beard phenomenon and while on Cape Cod decided to skip shaving for the duration of the vacation. When we got back to Washington I decided to keep it as a gesture of solidarity with my staff. It made a big hit at work, except with Bradlee, who thought I resembled a hairy old goat. I kept it, even though the constant itching annoyed me and had me scratching all the time. The beard also offended my mother-in-law. Together, the itching and her complaints led me to surrender the beard to the blade.

In 1971, there was a crucial departure. Patterson resigned, famously observing that "Bradlee needs a managing editor like a boar needs tits." He decompressed by taking a position as a professor of political science at Duke University. A newspaper warhorse like Patterson could not be stabled in academia for long, though. He took over as the top executive of the St. Petersburg operation, first as editor of the *Times,* and later as head of the Poynter Institute and the corporation. Kay Graham, in a 1991 interview, recalled it this way: "When Ben hired Gene he did it very quickly. There was a question I guess whether it was going to be Gene or Howie. And Ben decided to go outside. And Gene had just gotten fired from Atlanta. He came up here. Ben interviewed him for about an hour or two and hired him. And I was worried. And I said 'Ben, that's awful quick. You're sure?' I was worried it wasn't going to fly." It flew for less than three years, it turned out. I admired Patterson's traditional newspaper toughness and I understood that he lacked some attributes, a certain touch, that Bradlee required.

Patterson's exit resulted in the promotion of Howard Simons to Managing Editor from the Assistant Managing Editor he had been. In his new role, Howard did exceedingly well. He complemented Bradlee. Ben was famed for his short attention span and intuition and an ability to put his errors quickly behind him and move on to other matters. Howard's long suit was his extensive knowledge, his focus, and his analytical mind.

For long stretches during this year, we did not fill vacancies, in part because we took special care in hiring. Interviews with applicants were thorough and their clips were scrutinized. Partly it was because the top editors of newspapers everywhere did not fill openings, in order to keep their expenditures within budget or within reach. So it was that in 1971 we had a handful of vacancies to fill at one time. We had strung likely candidates along until we had clearance to hire. When it finally came, Karlyn Barker, Ron Taylor, Bill Bancroft and—oh yes—Bob Woodward joined the staff.

A very big story presented itself for Metro coverage in 1971. It was promoted by its organizers as a nationwide May Day protest against the Vietnam War, with Washington serving as the principal arena for the demonstration. The protesters' aim was to shut down government operations by tying up traffic on the Monday following the weekend protests. It came a little less than a year after the July 4th counterdemonstrations. A detailed order of battle assigned both reporters and editors to specific coverage. Given the well-known antipathy of the Nixon administration to dissenters and the law and order mantra of its policies, matched up with the demonstrators' left-wing contempt for the reigning establishment, the potential for violence from both sides was all too real.

We hired a helicopter to fly over the demonstrations around town. Bart Barnes, who was writing that story, and I were on that flight. Sussman, who would have been better employed on the ground overseeing the reporters that were being deployed, lobbied to go along for the ride. Flying over the sometimes rampaging protestors as they confronted or tried to evade the cops was something to see. Those arrested were held in makeshift camps cordoned off with barbed wire. It was not an everyday sight in America.

A reporter-intensive survey operation was set up to find out as much as we could about the demonstrators by polling three hundred of them. The coverage battle plan included assignments for the first three days and more general ones for the balance of the weeklong event.

Some seven thousand people were arrested—the largest number arrested in a single action in the nation's history—and that number was upped to twelve thousand on a recount. Many of them were taken into custody without having committed any illegal act. Over the duration, virtually the entire Metro staff was focused on reporting what was happening on the ground in Washington while National covered the march to the Pentagon, the Justice Department, and the president.

A couple of Sundays after the May Day demonstration ended, I assigned Sandy Ungar to write an overview of what had happened and what it might portend. It was a detail-rich and perceptive article, saliently focused on how civil strife had impacted the country. The basic question that emerged from the events, including the roundup of people who as yet committed no violation of laws, was "whether the government broke the law to preserve order." In other words, had the Constitution been set aside by the administration so that the peace might be kept. The police chief, Jerry Wilson, was bucking for the job as FBI chief at the time and amenable to the Nixon administration's desire to round up even potential troublemakers.

I presented Bradlee with Ungar's article, certain that such an accomplished piece of work was a natural for Page 1. Bradlee took a very long look but did not see it that way. Despite my repeated arguments, it was ordered inside the paper. I then placed it on the frontis of the Metro section, whose content and design was a Metro responsibility. As would later occur with some early Watergate stories that failed to make Page 1, the local section's frontis provided the best alternative.

It was in 1971 that *The Washington Post* and Mrs. Graham faced a test whose consequences reverberated in the future and helped shape it, both immediately and in the long term. *The New York Times* on June 13 began publishing an earthshaking series of articles that became known as the Pentagon Papers. It was a historic exclusive, and the National staff of the *Post* feverishly tried to obtain a copy of this top-secret study of the U.S. policy in the Vietnam War. In its entirety, the report made clear the duplicitous behavior of several administrations, most particularly Lyndon Johnson's barefaced lying to the American people about the origins and the escalations of the war.

A U.S. District Court judge in a temporary restraining order enjoined *The New York Times* from publishing stories from the seven thousand–page study after it had printed three days of articles. After the *Times* was stopped, Daniel Ellsberg, a former Pentagon analyst who had given the *Times* a copy of the study, released a portion of it to *The Washington Post* in response to maneuvering by Ben Bagdikian. Acquiring the Pentagon Papers confronted the *Post* with a dilemma. There was a furious and long argument in Ben Bradlee's Georgetown house, about whether to publish. The *Post*'s outside lawyers opposed publication because of the heightened legal exposure for the *Post* if it printed what a court had stopped the *Times* from doing. Senior editors, headed by Bradlee and urged on by Bagdikian and others, argued forcefully for the paper's obligation to inform the public about such crucial issues as well as to demonstrate the *Post*'s commitment to the highest journalistic values, specifically protected in the First Amendment.

What might have been at stake were the *Post*'s government-licensed and lucrative radio and television properties. In addition, the *Post* was then in the process of going public, and an adverse court ruling could interfere with the issuance of its public stock. Wall Street analysts certainly would not regard defiance of the federal government and courts as helpful to a public offering. The pressure bore down on Mrs. Graham, who listened attentively to all sides and then bravely concluded that her newspaper would take the fateful step to publish the Pentagon Papers.

The Nixon administration's Justice Department quickly got a court order blocking the *Post*. The government argued that what was being published revealed information that endangered national security in the midst of a war. At the *Post*, National reporters dug deep into the newspaper's files to show that the particulars of the government allegations had been published earlier. Therefore, the government's claim it was acting to protect national security was invalid.

Metro was out of it from beginning to end except to report on the court hearing. As court summonses to testify came down, a fever of "subpoena envy"—in the cogent observation of the editorial page's Meg Greenfield—afflicted those not on the list. Such covetousness would occur again during Watergate when Nixon's re-election committee subpoenas did not include Bradlee.

During one important court session, I went to the courthouse to hear the arguments. On a break in the testimony, I found myself in the hallway in the company of Kay Graham and Fritz Beebe, her much-respected financial adviser. I asked her, "Why did you do this, knowing the financial risks you personally were running?" For ink-stained wretches there was the joy of the hunt in addition to upholding journalistic honor, but we had no big money on the table.

Mrs. Graham replied—I can't quote her exact words—that she felt she had to do it to keep faith with the kind of enterprising paper the *Post* had become since she took over as publisher. She feared that were she not to publish the Pentagon Papers then the quality staff that the *Post* had amassed, old-timers and newcomers, would drift off, undermining the progress that had been made in the years since she took command. She had given Bradlee the go-ahead, understanding that her corporation's holdings were being put in peril.

As the Pentagon Papers case made its way through the federal court system, there came a point when the question was whether Nixon's Justice Department would try to have the Supreme Court reverse a favorable decision for the *Post* made by a lower-level appeals court. The *Post* editors wanted to know if and when the Justice Department approached Chief Justice Warren Burger with legal papers to that end. To find out, two Metro reporters were dispatched late on a Friday night to the home of the Chief Justice in nearby Arlington, Virginia. Burger's house was secluded at the end of a long driveway. The reporters drove in, past a No Trespassing sign and knocked twice on the Chief's front door. It was about 11:40 p.m.

After a brief time, Chief Justice Burger opened his door. He wore a bathrobe. In his right hand he held a long-barreled revolver. The gun was pointed at the ground. The Chief was upset, and chastised the reporters for not having phoned him (his number was unlisted but he said they could have reached him through a court staffer). His initial indignation soon vanished and the Chief, by this time the weapon concealed behind his back, said the reporters could wait at the foot of the driveway. After three hours, no messenger appeared and Burger never sent word, so the reporters went home.

It is not usual for an eminent person such as Burger to answer the door carrying a gun. Bradlee decided that it wasn't a story for the newspaper. It is likely Ben had in mind the overriding interests of the *Post* in winning the case in court and did not relish annoying the Chief Justice any more than we already had with our reporters' nocturnal visit to his house.

After the Supreme Court ruled in favor of the newspapers and against the government I wrote a note congratulating Mrs. Graham. Many years later, she told me that it was the first note she had received on that occasion. At the time, she wrote back on her Wedgwood blue notepaper an "Eyes Only" reply: "If there is one big credit due—& I think there is—it is to Ben whose tough & articulate determination—upheld though it was by all around him—was still the moving force."

In October 1971, I sent a memo to Bradlee to make a point: "Getting to talk to you at length without interruption is rarely possible." I pointed out the success Metro had ridding its staff of deadwood, unpleasant as it was, and hiring better replacements. The four-page, single-spaced memo argued that the we-they division between Metro and National persisted. Given its performance covering three large Vietnam demonstrations, Metro should be permitted to take the lead on large local stories of national significance. I wrote that management needed to recognize local news "as a major ingredient to the best job the *Post* seeks to do and that its role is held second to none in importance. (It also seems only prudent from the management viewpoint for a paper that is so quintessentially local in its readership, circulation and advertising and where . . . our future viability and economic success lies)." I said that Metro staffers worked under tougher journalistic standards than other departments and that Metro should not be used as a dumping ground for failed foreign correspondents. My screed was in response to Bradlee blowing off my earlier verbal arguments as "territorial." Soon the matter would be settled when Watergate occurred and Metro left National in its wake while it produced a story of national, indeed international, impact and significance.

Mrs. Graham and I had several memorable encounters during my time at the paper. Most of them occurred while I was Metro editor. She was particularly concerned that the *Post*—which had developed the quality of National and Foreign as well as Style, for the more sophisticated segment of our readership—must not seem condescending in its coverage of the local community. At her request, I arranged for the two of us to ride along in a police squad car as its officers made their nightly patrol. We accompanied the cops into homes where domestic disputes had reached the level for police intervention. We saw gunshot victims being rushed by ambulance to D. C. General Hospital, which cared primarily for the city's poor. At that point she said to me, "Harry, if anything ever happens to me I do not want to be taken there." Then she named a hospital known to have better medical resources as her preference.

Another time, Mrs. Graham and I toured Prince George's County, a suburb where many lower-middle- and middle-class people lived. We made the tour in her limousine with her chauffeur. Herb Denton was then the Prince George's County reporter. He had gone to Harvard University with Don Graham and served with him in Vietnam and was one of our up-and-coming staffers. Because Herb was black, Mrs. Graham did not want him to sit in the front passenger seat, as it might appear to others that Herb was a servant. She asked whether I minded sitting there. I did not mind.

Part of that tour was a visit to the home of the county commissioner, who was a man of the people and a diamond in the rough. We could not help but notice that his living room upholstered furniture was covered in plastic (as it was in my parents' home). We talked amiably if somewhat stiffly for a while, as the old pol sat on his couch, his knees spread far apart. It was not an engaging sight.

On the way out, Mrs. Graham spotted an object fixed on the front doorpost. When we were back in the limousine, she asked me what that was. Feigning astonishment, I teased her: "Katharine, I thought you would have known that it was a mezuzah," the slim, rectangular case that contains verses from the Torah, which is affixed to the doorpost of most Jewish homes. Her father was of Jewish background who married a Gentile and Katharine was raised as an Episcopalian. It was not surprising that Katharine did not have a clue about the mezuzah. The county official was not Jewish, but for whatever reasons had attached a mezuzah to his door, perhaps as a good luck charm or to play up to a particular constituency.

Mrs. Graham was frequently attacked by her more dedicated enemies for her Jewish connection, although mostly in private. I once asked Bradlee why she simply did not deny the Jewish tag publicly. He answered that she could not go around saying in so many words, "Hey, I'm not Jewish," as if being Jewish were shaming or having a Jewish connection was embarrassing. Throughout my years in Washington, I lunched every so often with Raymond K. Price Jr. We had been colleagues at the *Herald Tribune*, where he headed the editorial page. He attained that high position as a young man and quickly demonstrated his writing skill and depth of knowledge. After the demise of the *Herald Tribune*, he in time joined the Nixon staff and became dean of the president's speech writers. Although we lunched because of our friendship, topics of interest would come up especially when Watergate was breaking all around us. One time, Ray brought up Katharine Graham's Jewishness. It might have been in connection with the now well-known Nixon proclivity (and not only his) to blame Jewish-controlled media for his woes. I patiently explained to Ray that contrary to his assumption, she was not Jewish. She had been born to a Christian mother and a secular Jewish father. I could testify to her Christian credentials because I sat next to her and her son Don at a funeral service in an Episcopal church, where both of them knelt in prayer at the appropriate times as if to the manner born, which of course they had been.

Once, when Mrs. Graham and I were having lunch alone upstairs at the *Post*, she asked me to tell her just what an editor actually did. I kicked myself for not having anticipated that basic question and desperately searched my mind for an answer. What I came up with on the spot I have used many times since. An editor, I said, is analogous to a symphony conductor. The conductor doesn't compose the music and does not play an instrument. But by standing up in front of the orchestra and understanding the music and the functions of the instruments and waving the baton, he ensures that a pleasing sound is produced. As with the conductor, so with the editor, who doesn't go out to report, doesn't write the story, doesn't write the headline, or take or crop the pictures. But if the editor knows the job, overseeing all the constituent elements, what comes out in print is pretty good.

In our 1991 conversation, which was in preparation for what would become her Pulitzer Prize-winning autobiography *Personal History*, Mrs. Graham reminded me of what I had told her about investigative reporting. She wanted to discuss it in an upcoming speech. "And you said a really good thing. Which is that at the beginning, going into a story, you had to push and whip people on. And at some point when it was getting to the end, you had to do exactly the opposite. You had to pull them back and start saying 'How do you know and is it right.'" I told her then that the last part applied to Watergate especially.

As we continued the search for new talent, a couple of job seekers stood out for unusual reasons. When Eugene L. Meyer applied, I could not resist hiring him because he bore the same name, aside from the middle initial, as Katharine's father. Thankfully, Eugene Meyer had bona fide credentials and went on to perform as a reliable member of the staff. Word came down to me that Mrs. Graham was not overcome with glee, not appreciating the humor in it as much as I did.

Another applicant was a young, inexperienced man who walked into my office seeking a reporter's job. His outstanding accomplishment was that he had earned a PhD. I never had a PhD as a reporter.

The young man was diligent but did not manage to survive the tryout period. At that time, much to my regret, we agreed that there were more suitable careers for a PhD. He returned to Harvard to finish a book on East Asia. In May 1972, he wrote to ask for his old job at the *Post*: "I know that the academic thing is not what I want. I miss the excitement of the newsroom." It was not to be.

Later, a second PhD walked into my office seeking work. He seemed to be a viable candidate, but—like Mark Twain's cat that was scorched when it sat on a hot stove and thenceforth never sat on any stove, hot or cold—I could not bring myself to take a chance on another PhD. Big mistake. PhD No. 2 was Richard Bernstein, who went on to a brilliant journalistic career. He gently reminded me of my error when we walked across the Harvard Yard many years later during a Nieman conference on how American journalists covered Nazi Germany in the years leading up to World War II.

On the other hand, I was vindicated by resisting criticism when I hired a young, promising reporter who was a natural fit for Metro. Once the reporter was on board, Bradlee chided me and asked how I could have hired someone that homely. Bradlee wasn't joking; looks mattered to him. The reporter went on to a successful and long career at the *Post*.

One particular departure from Metro during my time running the department was especially disappointing. Aaron Latham was a fine writer who reported and wrote a telling four-part series on the mismanagement of Junior Village, where orphaned kids in Washington were sheltered. His investigation uncovered specific and systemic failures in the governance of the place, particularly its function as little more than a dumping ground. The first installment was the Page 1 off-lead, or the second most important story, of the January 17, 1971, paper, an edition that was reduced in size by a printer's union slowdown. Latham wrote:

> On their way to school one morning, two children, a small boy and a small girl, stopped and stared as if they thought they recognized one another but were not sure.
>
> "'Is she your friend?' the Head Start teacher asked the boy.
>
> "'I think she's my sister,' the boy answered, 'but I've forgotten her name.'"

Aaron's lead captured the human cost of a failing facility in vivid detail. Latham went on to a successful career in magazine and book writing. When he contacted me about some issues with his final employee timesheet, he took the occasion to commend us for sticking with the Junior Village story. He added a refrain I was to hear more than occasionally: "Once again, I enjoyed working with you. Or rather, I didn't enjoy it at first but by the end I enjoyed it a lot!"

Mrs. Graham, for her part, did not enjoy the Junior Village exposé. She told me that several of her friends served on the institution's board. They felt their operation was unfairly portrayed. I replied that we had made certain that our reporting was accurate. Latham's articles led to the city council first calling for a probe of Junior Village and then phasing it out entirely over two and a half years. Mrs. Graham never said another word to me about this matter, even though her newspaper's investigation might have strained relationships with her civic-minded friends.

These were times of challenge, as old habits were giving way, but much too slowly for the people directly affected. This was especially felt by women and blacks, whom we intensely recruited. There were black and women's caucuses protesting the scarcity of both on the paper's staff, among other complaints—which impacted Metro in the first instance as it was the gateway into the paper. The fact that the *Post* employed more black reporters than any other mainstream newspaper did not assuage their disappointment. Management over time tried many different approaches to increase minority representation throughout all levels and departments of the paper.

The results were lackluster. Once, I was assigned to attend a meeting in Boston convened by a newspaper consultant who was black. The meeting drew a handful of participants from metro newspapers. The upshot was that the consultant had a solution: hire his firm and he would work to deflect the rising tide of criticism. My proposal to management was that we pick up qualified young minority students in high school, put them on the payroll part-time during the school year, and set up training that would see them through college. Eventually, the individuals who successfully completed the program would be eligible for full-fledged jobs on the *Post*. That was just too ambitious a remedy. For all the real problems of disconnect between black and white viewpoints over what constituted racism, I received an award from the Black United Front of Washington.

The year 1972 stands out in the nation's history not only because of Watergate. In May, the month before those events began to unfold, during the presidential election campaign, Alabama's governor George Wallace was gunned down in a suburban Washington mall while campaigning. Although Wallace was a national figure, he was shot in a county covered by Metro. We jumped on the story. William Greider of the national desk was enlisted to write the main story. Metro reporters' leg work fed him details and quotes, and he was assisted by a senior Metro editor. Greider wrote with his characteristic distinctive grace and displayed steadiness under pressure. Haynes Johnson, another brilliant National writer, contributed a political analysis, while Metro quickly produced four additional front-page stories as well as three inside articles for the May 16 edition. It was a demonstration of applying the Muffin formula to a major story: commit the resources and the job gets done. More than thirty Metro staffers were thrown into the fray reporting the Wallace assassination attempt.

In the turmoil in the city room following the news of the attack on the governor, I assigned Bob Woodward to find out everything he could about the accused attacker, who was under arrest. Only later, during Watergate, did I learn that Bob turned to a special source for help. Woodward came up with information about Arthur Herman Bremer that no other news operation had early on. What he obtained came from his close personal source, a person who became known to us as Woodward's Friend, until Watergate. It was Howard Simons who then tagged the source Deep Throat, taken from the porno movie of that name playing in adult movie houses at the time.

The effectiveness and enthusiasm, bordering on possessiveness, of the local staffers in pursuing the Wallace story in the days ahead led Greider to joke that when Governor Wallace made his appearance at the Democratic National Convention, Metro reporters would wheel him onto the dais.

While the Wallace story and follow-ups continued their run in the pages of the newspaper, focusing most importantly on whether the governor would ever walk again—with his camp denouncing the *Post*'s eventually corroborated reports that he would not—another story broke that was to transform nothing so trivial as one ambitious metropolitan newspaper. It was Watergate, and it changed the culture of the nation. The *Post*'s investigative reporting came to stand throughout the world as a beacon of journalistic enterprise and achievement.

14

Inside Watergate

It is a tale told many times since its beginning in June 1972. As such, Watergate serves as an example of how personal perceptions and interests shape understanding. In Howard Simon's evocation, it was very much like *Rashomon,* a tale that differs when told from each participant's point of view. The version I value most is the straightforward narrative least impacted by the notoriety, celebrity, and claims to fame that enveloped Watergate after Richard Nixon became the first president to resign his office. To my mind, Bob Woodward and Carl Bernstein's first book, *All the President's Men,* is most useful because it is an account untainted by the contentions that inevitably arise in the wake of a historic event.

I don't see any added value in my going over the details of the investigative reporting as it, step by laborious step, uncovered the dimensions of the infamy that was the handiwork of the president's operatives. After all these years, my only valid contribution to elucidating the thoroughly worked-over ground is to relate what I remember witnessing and my interpretation of events as Watergate unfolded. What follows pretends to be no more, and it is no less, than my insider's view of that momentous story.

Early on Saturday morning, June 17, 1972, Managing Editor Howard Simons phoned me at home. He told me about two events that needed to be reported by Metro. One involved a car in a Virginia suburb that had crashed into a house. In doing so, it not only damaged the structure; it also dampened the ardor of a couple absorbed in making love. Talk about coitus interruptus. The second event had weightier implications but lacked the human interest appeal of the first.

Howard told me that burglars, wearing rubber gloves and carrying electronic gear, had been arrested overnight rummaging through the headquarters of the Democratic National Committee in the Watergate complex, a posh development along Washington's Potomac River that housed upscale apartments as well as business offices. Joseph Califano, the *Post*'s attorney who also was general counsel of the Democratic Party, had called Howard to inform him about the break-in.

From the first, it obviously was a big story for Metro, though its eventual consequences could not have been imagined initially. In turn, I called Barry Sussman, the District of Columbia editor, whose staff normally reported on a local crime in the city, including one with intriguing national attributes.

Barry and I agreed that we would put Al Lewis on the story, because he was our police reporter with long-standing sources in the police department. For all his contributions to police coverage, Al was not a probing reporter; he was a leg man. This story also called for additional staff. We agreed that Bob Woodward was the right choice. In his short time on staff, he had begun to make a reputation as a smart, hard worker who had the ability as well as the desire to root out hard-to-get information. Most Saturdays I went to the office to have a last look at our presentation for the Sunday paper, the *Post*'s showcase, and to catch up on paperwork left unattended during the pressing demands of a normal work week. This Saturday I dared not leave home. We were giving a dinner party for twelve. Annie insisted that at least this once I had to remain home to help, as I had frequently failed to do. I recall looking out our dining room window, on the one hand tempted to go to the office, on the other concerned about upsetting my wife by reneging on my promise to help her get ready. I stayed home.

Al Lewis had been a police reporter for so long that he was familiar to officers and even dressed like them in a blue cardigan. He liked cops and they liked him. He was dispatched to the crime scene, where he was able to sit down at a desk in the Democratic headquarters. From this vantage, he unobtrusively observed and listened to what was happening as the police investigated. Reporters from other news organization were held outside on the sidewalk, waiting to learn the details from an official spokesman. Carl Bernstein was volunteered by Tom Wilkinson, his Virginia editor, to work up profile material on those arrested. Woodward was in court and heard

James W. McCord Jr.—in an apparent effort to protect himself—tell the judge in a low voice that he had retired from the CIA. By the next day, McCord's direct connection to the Nixon campaign was established.

The first Watergate story appeared on Page 1, of course. It was bylined Alfred E. Lewis. The stories under Al Lewis's byline were distinguished by their diverse styles, which no other reporter matched. He had begun his newspaper career at a time when it was common, especially for reporters stationed at the cop shop, to phone in their notes to a rewrite bank. One of the staffers assigned to rewrite would take the notes and actually write the story that appeared in the newspaper. And the rewrite man—almost always a man, in the old newsrooms—would write it up in his own style. When Watergate broke, the traditional rewrite bank had virtually disappeared. At the *Post*, every reporter except Lewis was required to write his or her own story. In our operation, any reporter who was handy at the moment got the job of translating Al's reporting into prose. For the Sunday paper of June 18, 1972, Bart Barnes was assigned to pull the lead story together, including Al Lewis's contribution as well as those of other reporters.

The story was filled with details, including the background of the burglars and a diagram of the layout of the Democratic headquarters. Besides Lewis, Barnes, Woodward, and Bernstein, five other Metro reporters contributed to provide the information that distinguished our coverage, including the fact that the burglars carried a large amount of hundred dollar bills—their serial numbers in sequence.

That Sunday, Gene Bachinski, who also covered cops, was at work, and an officer let him look at an address book carried by one of the burglars. To Gene's everlasting credit, when going through it he encountered the name H. Hunt with W. House written next to it. He did not let that salient notation slip by him.

Gene also spotted among the papers carried by the burglars a Hunt check made out to his country club. To me that was even stronger evidence of a Hunt connection, because how else could such a personal item come to be in the possession of the burglar? Also on Sunday, Carroll Kilpatrick, National's White House correspondent, phoned a Metro editor to say that McCord was or had been connected to the CIA.

Monday's paper carried a front page follow-up, and the byline on it was Bob Woodward and Carl Bernstein. Their story focused on

McCord and the fact that he was in charge of security for Nixon's re-election committee. Here again, the writers of record were assisted by the contributions of six Metro staffers.

On Monday morning I called a staff meeting to organize for what already appeared to be a story with potential to last for days if not weeks to come. Many reporters would continue to be committed, and Woodward was asked to prepare a list of story possibilities. That first Monday Woodward made an important breakthrough by getting out of a White House telephone operator the fact that Howard Hunt had had an office in the White House and that he spent a lot of time with Charles Colson, President Nixon's special counsel. When we reported that Colson had hired Hunt, the White House immediately objected, firing one of its first salvos of non-denial denials. Their rebuttal said that Colson had not hired Hunt, he had merely recommended his employment to the personnel office. Oh, the Horror! We were on our way, and we didn't spare the horses. The spirit of Muffin governed again. One day in Superior Court for a bail bond hearing, we had three reporters there. A reporter from a competing paper asked, "What the hell is going on here?"

In the next day's paper, the byline was shared by Woodward and Bachinski and focused on Gene's discovery of Hunt's name and Bob's confirmation that he was a White House consultant. In that story, as in several to come, Hunt's name was rendered as Howard E. Hunt Jr. I questioned Woodward about the fact that other papers were reporting it as E. Howard Hunt Jr. At first, Bob insisted he was right, although he soon corrected his mistake. The story also made the connection between one of the burglars and the Young Republicans' organization in Florida. That same day, we got a tip that another one of the burglars, Frank Sturgis, had earlier come to Washington to beat up Daniel Ellsberg, of Pentagon Papers renown. We were not able to do more with it than run it as a brief paragraph within a long story. Ronald L. Ziegler, the White House Press Secretary, famously dismissed the Watergate break-in as "a third rate burglary" in the Nixon administration's efforts to control the damage and to try to discredit our aggressive coverage.

The weekend of the break-in, President Nixon was in Key Biscayne, Florida. Traveling with the president to his alternative White House frequently did not produce anything more than low-level news. When the National reporters who cover the president sensed this, the National desk sometimes offered the assignment to Metro.

For our people it was a treat, and we used the assignment to give a reporter a pat on the back. That's how the reporter whose regular beat was city hall found himself in Miami. He provided the news about the Young Republicans connection and was instructed to remain there to pursue the angle of the Cuban caper that was then gaining currency. In the days ahead, as the caper story still eluded us, I summoned back from his vacation my deputy, Peter Jay, who spoke Spanish, and dispatched him to Miami.

It was clear that Watergate was an extraordinarily important story, and I began to read all of the coverage before it was printed from the first Monday on, much as I had done with Muffin. The necessity for that focus intensified two weeks after the break-in, when the potential implications of Watergate emerged more distinctly. John Mitchell, the former attorney general, resigned his position as the head of the Committee to Re-Elect the President, known as CREEP. Mitchell said he did so to care for his wife Martha, who had an unfortunate reputation as an alcoholic who occasionally worked out her demons in a public way. At this time, the D.C. police chief, Jerry Wilson, invited me to his club in Virginia for lunch. We regularly dealt with each other because of our jobs. We had a good relationship. I admired his working style, for he had brought a refreshing change of attitude to a hidebound and too frequently racist police force.

At lunch, we talked about Mitchell. Coming from different perspectives—law enforcement and turn-over-the-rocks journalism—we readily agreed that the hard-shelled Mitchell was not the sort of man to walk away from such a politically critical role during an election campaign to care for his family and wife, as his public announcement stated. We both thought that what had happened at Watergate, and the connections between it and the Committee to Re-Elect the President that were being uncovered, was behind Mitchell stepping down. I shared my assessment with Woodward, who concurred.

From that point on, my oversight ratcheted up still more as I had an inkling of where this story might be going. That did not mean that I thought at that time it would reach all the way to the president, but I suspected that higher-ups working for his re-election might be implicated. This made it a story certain to endure strong counterattacks from the Nixon administration and the Republican Party. And we had better get it right.

Metro produced front-page Watergate stories that first week. After that, there was a pause. We still had groundbreaking stories but they were scheduled to be fitted into the national report in the A Section—overriding my best efforts to jimmy them onto Page 1. After a couple of times, I refused to hand our Watergate story over for A Section use. Instead, I put those stories on the front of the Metro's separate news section. As Metro Editor, I controlled that section, including the content and display of its cover. There were strenuous objections to my ploy, for the very good reason that by this time Watergate was certainly more than a local story. But if the senior editors and the news desk would not play the stories as they should have, I would give them as much prominence as was within my power rather than let them be underplayed inside the A Section. Between June 22 and August 1, six Watergate stories earned front page display. In that same span, we featured ten Watergate stories on the Metro frontis. From August onward, I did not have to resort to maneuvers for Watergate to receive regular front-page treatment. It is important to note that most if not all of the ten stories later on would have made the paper's front page because they were good enough, but not appreciated as such at the time. Those articles involved Bernstein and Woodward writing separately and sharing bylines both with each other, as would become standard, and with other Metro reporters, including Jim Mann, Peter Jay, Jon Katz, and Paul Valentine. It demonstrated Metro's group effort. While this pattern continued throughout Watergate—and especially when the story shifted into the courtroom and Congressional hearing rooms—from the first the investigative end of the enterprise placed Woodward and Bernstein in the vanguard, a position they maintained until there was no more to be said.

The next big breakthrough in Watergate was published in August. Reports came to us out of Miami from local investigators who suggested they had evidence about the burglars, but they did not follow through. Bernstein was dispatched by Sussman to Miami on a promise that Carl would be shown incriminating records. With ingenuity and persistence he found the check for twenty-five thousand dollars, which Woodward, working the phone in Washington, then confirmed as a political donation to the Republicans. The lead burglar, Bernard L. Barker, carried a hefty roll of hundred dollar bills on the job, while more than one hundred thousand dollars had been transferred into his bank account through a Mexican bank. The story, which was published August 1, brought into the spotlight one of Nixon's important fundraisers and Maurice Stans, the former commerce secretary, who had become the financial head of Nixon's re-election effort. In time he was revealed as the person who put the strong arm on American corporations to kick in to the Nixon campaign.

It was not in the least a coincidence that the donor of the twenty-five thousand dollars turned out to be Dwayne Andreas, a Minneapolis investor, who for decades continued to give freely on behalf of his private interests to both parties. In the midst of Watergate he was charged by the special prosecutor for consenting to an illegal hundred thousand dollar corporate donation—not to Nixon, but to Hubert Humphrey's 1968 campaign. In Washington, as Woodward was working the story, other reporters also hunted for information about Watergate. Sometimes that resulted in no more than a paragraph or two in a long story, but we thought it worthwhile. There was nothing as valuable as face-to-face interviewing whenever possible—or even if it seemed impossible. In Woodward and Bernstein's hands that became a major weapon to uncover the breadth of Watergate malfeasance and misfeasance. It led them to the Committee to Re-Elect the President and eventually the secret fund that underwrote the campaign of political dirty tricks. As a consequence of the *Post's* reporting connecting the "bugging incident to the campaign finance law," the General Accounting Office began an audit.

15

The Reporters Who
Became Woodstein

The two reporters we leaned on to spearhead the investigative part of the unfolding story—the combination of Woodward and Bernstein, known as Woodstein to us from then on—presented both opportunities and challenges.

Woodward came to the *Post* in 1970, looking for a job. Although he is inclined to romanticize it, he did not walk into my office off the street. He was recommended by Paul Ignatius, the former secretary of the navy, who at the time was president of the *Post*. Though Woodward did not have any newspaper experience, I was seeing him because of Ignatius. I quickly recognized that Woodward had a sober personality and was a solid adult—which had not been all that common an experience for me while interviewing aspiring young reporters. He had a Yale degree, which didn't hurt, yet was not that rare at the *Post*. More to the point, he had served five years as a naval officer, some of that time with top secret security clearance, in Washington. That made him stand out from other reporter candidates.

After the interview concluded and I considered how raw he was journalistically, I did something I had never done. I gave him a two-week tryout. This was not customary for the good reason that there is little to be learned about a novice cast as a reporter into an unfamiliar sea. I thought I owed it to Ignatius and to Bob's singular naval background to give him a shot.

I asked Andy Barnes, my deputy, to monitor Woodward's performance. When the two weeks were up, Andy described him as hardworking and willing to learn but inept at our craft. I decided that Woodward needed time to age in the barrel in order to soak up the practices of newspapering. To that end, we recommended him to the editor of the Montgomery County *Sentinel*, a weekly that hired him. As a courtesy, I told Woodward to keep in touch and that we would reevaluate him after a year or so.

Woodward went to work and soon reported newsworthy stories out of Montgomery County that were not typical of weekly coverage and indeed eluded our reporters assigned there. His articles gained attention more for their content than their writing flair. In March 1971, Woodward along with Bill Bancroft did a story evaluating the twenty-two principals of the county's high schools. One of the principals was rated "unsuited." He sued for $15 million.

Woodward began to call me regularly to see where he stood with us. I kept putting him off since I wanted him to continue to sand down his rough edges on somebody else's payroll. Our lead reporter in Montgomery Country became Woodward's strong advocate, recognizing the quality and depth of his reporting. Hiring him became a matter of time as there was a hiring freeze at the *Post*, as happened when economics impinged.

In the fall of 1971, my daughter Amy would become bat mitzvah, the Jewish rite of passage into religious adulthood for girls. The reception was to be in our home and Annie decided the catered luncheon would be served in our finished basement. It was more spacious than our living room and could accommodate our guests. As part of the preparation, Annie insisted that the basement needed a fresh coat of paint. In those days, our lifestyle did not encompass hiring a professional. Instead, Harry the Happy Homeowner became the designated painter.

There I was in a hot and humid Washington summer, painting the days away on what was supposed to be my vacation. I was not left to labor in peace. A young man who had worked for me in the foreign operation had suddenly disappeared, leaving behind his new wife and their even newer child. The man's wife understandably was distraught and frightened. So for reasons not clear to me, it became my job to try to help. I phoned the police to get them to undertake a missing person search. The police hesitated because in their experience many of these incidents were no more than a runaway problem not involving foul play. So I persisted, calling one level of command after another at the police department, pleading with them to do something. This meant climbing up and down the ladder in the basement to make and receive frequent phone calls each day. Any professional will tell you that's no way to handle a paint job. The repeated interruptions made the task of painting drag on as my patience diminished.

With my temper rapidly fraying, Woodward called me at home in one of his repetitive efforts over the months to get a job. Annie answered the phone and handed me the receiver. By this time I had more than had it and I curtly told him to get in touch with me when I returned to the office. Annie overhead my end of the conversation and asked what it was about. I told her how this young guy was pestering me for a job. She defused my distemper when she calmly asked, "Isn't this just the kind of reporter you always say you want to hire?" She could not have been more on point. When the hiring freeze was lifted, Woodward came to work, a year after he had first appeared in my office. Annie's observation was repeated in many accounts on Watergate that followed and wound up as a bonus question on an exam at American University.

The missing young man eventually turned up after causing his family anguish. The cops had been right, because he had tried to escape his marital responsibilities.

From the beginning of his employment Woodward displayed his mettle, setting an example with the intensity of his work habits. When it was suggested to Don Graham, Mrs. Graham's son and heir, that Woodward someday would become Managing Editor, Don disagreed. By that time, he thought, Woodward would have worked himself to death.

Woodward's earliest assignment was the police beat, a customary path for beginning reporters to learn to gather and write news. What was not customary was his attitude. At a time when most young reporters regarded cops as the enemy, Woodward displayed no such antagonism. He took to the police station copies of the *Post* and containers of coffee for the desk sergeant. He was accepted, and quickly developed a reputation for reliability. He was courteous and friendly with them, but not in the bag. When his reporting upset the police, he was not immune to their criticism.

One of his effective pre-Watergate projects was to review the hygienic conditions of public eating places, finding some alarming shortcomings among well-established restaurants. We insisted that as we assessed other eateries, in fairness we had to examine the *Post's* own. Applying the same standards, we discovered the failings in the company cafeteria and published them. In a major investigative piece, he took on Blue Cross and found that it was underpaying its claimants. His reporting was challenged, as it would continue to be by people whose misdeeds he exposed.

A foretaste of what Woodward might face in the future came in his early days at the *Post*, when he was deposed in a lawsuit filed by the Montgomery County principal who had been rated negatively. Bob declined to reveal the names of three sources involved—as did Bancroft and their editor Roger Farquhar—although in a previous ruling the judge had ordered the editor to do so. Woodward stuck to his position even after a *Post* attorney told him that he could face many problems. The *Post* was ready to support him and Bancroft with legal guidance as well as time off to fight the case, but would not go beyond that in event of liabilities being imposed on them.

By the time of Watergate, Woodward had established himself as a fully qualified reporter, sharper than most and more ambitious and hardworking than any. As good as he was, his not getting Hunt's name quite right at the start of Watergate showed that even the most conscientious reporters can lapse, which needed to be kept in mind as Watergate unfolded.

A couple of days after Watergate broke, Bernstein was returned to his Virginia assignment at the request of his editor. Bernstein was needed for political coverage during the time leading up to the state elections. His editor commented that Bernstein continued to display signs of laziness and a lack of interest in what Carl deemed mundane journalism. Carl hungered for the big story. He volunteered himself to the National desk to do traffic holiday or weather roundups, anything to get away from Metro assignments. Ben Bagdikian, the National editor, was a congenital body snatcher, who gladly obliged, resulting in an effective end run around Metro's assigning editors. This time, local was handling the bigger story and Carl wanted to be back on it. To make that happen, he wrote one of his lengthy memos outlining his theory that Murray Chotiner could be behind Watergate. Chotiner had the political chops for it and was serving in the White House as a Nixon adviser. This struck me as plausible enough—and demonstrated Carl's background knowledge—and so I told him to look into it. From then onward, that effectively put him on Watergate.

Up to that time, Carl had had what euphemistically used to be called a checkered career. Not long before my arrival at Metro, a news editor described Bernstein to Isaacs as "a bright young man with a lot of promise" citing in his favor that he was "a reasonably good writer and his enthusiasm." The news editor added, "However he needs his ass kicked for his carelessness and his inability to comprehend the importance of deadlines."

My encounters with Bernstein's capacity to backslide into unacceptable behavior went beyond his unsuccessful Canada episode when I was on the foreign desk. After I had become his boss, he reported on a plant in Saltville, Virginia. In his story, he managed to mislocate the town in question because he identified one Interstate with the number of another. There were other errors in the account, which Carl defended in a long response worthy of a jailhouse lawyer. Carl frequently felt compelled to write heartfelt rebuttals after he was chastised. To Bernstein's credit, in his time at the *Post* he demonstrated a superior sense of finding subjects that were not merely low-hanging fruit waiting to be plucked. One important undertaking was an exploration of the Brandywine People, a racial subgroup residing in D.C. and an adjacent suburb. They were especially enlightening because of their long history of racial amalgamation of white, black, and red and the challenges the mix posed sociologically in the present day. Another strong effort was a takeout on the hippie culture and the flourishing of heroin use. Being a Washington kid, he ably wrote about the bitter estrangement of whites living in a part of town that was quickly turning black.

Carl was getting fed up with his assignments. He lobbied Bradlee for a transfer to Style. "A move to Style would, I think, give me the opportunity to achieve a more satisfactory balance among the four things I am particularly interested in: daily reporting, travel and young people." He'd bothered to cite only three. Bradlee consulted his Managing Editor, who agreed that Bernstein had accurately described his strengths. Patterson said he had told Bradlee, "I'd rather leave it to Rosenfeld to use him for these things since you're looking for ventilation of your thick coverage."

Bernstein also managed to rack up provocative charges for overtime, much of it self-assigned, usually trumping all his colleagues. His explanations projected heartfelt hurt at having been accused of riding the gravy train. By April 1970, Carl had logged twice as much overtime as anyone else on the Metro staff. An indignant and sarcastic Gene Patterson queried me, "Don't you think you are overworking this man?" Efforts to restrain Carl fell short.

Part of Bernstein's high expense account numbers resulted from his renting cars to go on the roving assignments he loved and did well. Carl didn't own a car, perhaps out of ideological 1960s convictions, perhaps because reporters with cars were compensated only for their company-related expenses while having to pay out of pocket for their cars' purchase and upkeep. On more than one occasion, Carl left his rental car behind in a parking lot while his attention shifted elsewhere and the rental bill ran up. Again, he produced a plaintive account of how other people did not turn in the car as they had promised. It was remarkable how many people Carl encountered in life who failed him in some grievous way.

It finally hit the fan in May 1971, when Bernstein claimed to have cleared up his expense account advances by dropping them on the desk of an administrator dealing with editorial expenses. This long-suffering man said he had seen no expense account from Bernstein. An exasperated Bill Burton wrote: "I would have done handstands had he submitted an accounting."

Days later, I felt obliged to try to put a stop to Bernstein's abusive behavior. "Confirming in writing what has been the stated policy with you, and to remove any possibility of misunderstanding, I instruct you that you will not work any overtime unless you have the clearance of a responsible editor. . . . You will not clear a next day's overtime with the previous night's editors but with the principals. We will not pay for overtime that is not approved in this manner."

The next month, Bernstein failed to deliver a story on the port of Norfolk that he had promised several times. I sat in on a heart-to-heart session between Carl and his editor at the time, Kevin Klose. Kevin noted that Carl's work on another series required heavy editing. In a memo to my personnel file, I wrote, "The message was delivered to Bernstein that he either begins to be a productive reporter or he and the *Post* better go their separate ways and that if he cannot soon come to grips with his responsibilities to his job, that I would move against him on negligence of duty. . . .

"Bernstein said he realized he was at fault and that he was sorry. He did not want to say much more. He understood that if he could not become productive and that if he and his editors continued to be antagonistic all the time, it would be better for him to leave. He said that when I returned from vacation I would see a much changed man."

That new man clearly emerged in Watergate—a full year after his pledge. In the course of Watergate, the tiger changed his stripes, the leopard his spots, and Joshua commanded the sun not to set and the moon to stand still. The transformation was that epic. It is worth contemplating that Carl could have missed his historic role in Watergate had he succeeded in getting himself transferred to the alluring and less constrained by standards Style section. If he had persisted in his bad old ways on Metro, he almost surely would have been fired, for which the legal groundwork had been laid. Carl discovered his better self in Watergate. His talents of imagination and shrewdness flourished and did not fade; he never relented in pursuit of the story that he surely was smart enough to recognize as the most consequential for his career in journalism.

Woodward and Bernstein wound up as the mainstays of our coverage, breaking ground with their incisive, intensive, diligent reporting. They were emblematic of the outstanding overall staff effort. In the opening days, as Woodstein emerged as the lead reporters of our coverage, I was cognizant that Carl's journalistic weaknesses, including his '60s politics, had to be kept in mind. It was clearly my responsibility to be vigilant, the more so as the investigation that progressively connected the upper tiers of the Nixon administration to the expanding scandal. Everything could be at stake for the *Post*—its developing reputation as an outstanding newspaper, its federally licensed television and radio properties, and the value of its public stock.

Bob and Carl worked nights; they worked weekends. There was not a time for most of the rest of that year that they did not work. No editor could have asked that of them or driven them to it. It was their decision and they were deeply, personally motivated. My efforts from time to time to chase them out of the office to go home and get some rest achieved only so-so success.

As we unwound the skein of Watergate we began to realize that Metro had only modest understanding about the operations of the upper echelon of political Washington. No one, for example, knew much beyond the superficial about CREEP. Woodstein acquired a roster of CREEP personnel using the contacts of a news aide and worked the list. In repeatedly phoning the principals of the organization, they became acquainted with various secretaries and assistants. They reached an important conclusion: innocent bystanders can make good witnesses or at least good leads.

At one point Carl and Bob prepared a schematic of office layouts, plotting who sat next to whom. It took hours upon hours of work. By these tactics, Woodstein illustrated the great value of shoe-leather reporting, whose luster among journalists had waned. They reported to Sussman and all three reported to me. Barry was an excellent editor with strong conceptual skills. He directed much of the coverage that Woodstein did not initiate, especially in the early days. He was also good with his pencil and worked their copy over, making sure that illustrative background information was included in the narrative. The more intensely he was involved with Watergate, the clearer a potential problem began to emerge. Barry struck me at times as too much of an advocate and less skeptical than was necessary. It was natural for that to happen, given his role. That made it all the more important for me to assiduously scrutinize what they planned to write and to quiz them about what they were writing and how they acquired their information. Sussman said, on behalf of Woodstein and himself, that I "demanded proof with every paragraph."

Working with Woodward and under Sussman, Bernstein displayed the best side of himself—for the most part. There were still signs that within the New Bernstein there lurked vestiges of the Old. The head of the copy desk complained to me, for instance, that Bernstein had come to him the night before to have a look at the desk's Watergate story dupes "for a few minutes. Whereupon he disappeared with them. . . . In view of his lie and stealth, I will unless specifically ordered refuse any and all of Bernstein's requests in the future."

Another manifestation of the lingering Bad Bernstein emerged when still early in the Watergate days I was summoned to Bradlee's office. As soon as I walked in I knew that he and Simons were steamed. Bernstein was up to his old habits, having yet again rented a car and left it stranded in a parking lot for days, with costly rental fees mounting by the hour. The two editors were fed up. They wanted me to fire Bernstein. Where I had been on the verge of telling him to leave before Watergate, I said now it made no sense when "for once in his life, Carl is producing the goods."

Throughout my many years of editing at many levels of responsibility I grew uncomfortable with the often-expressed view that the only requirement for an editor to be safe and right was to have reporters working for him whom he could trust. That seemed to me courting trouble and shirking responsibility. It is not a question of trust, and it should not be framed in those terms. Of course, in a basic way you trust reporters working for you or else they shouldn't be on your staff. Trust gets them into the building. In practice, you might not know enough about each reporter to make valid decisions about their work all the time.

Furthermore, if you think you do, you might be mistaken. It is better to supplement trust. Nothing surpasses knowing as much as you can about the story, about its components and its dynamics: How did it originate, what are the motives and interests of the people sharing information, and what exactly was said? Reporters are not immune to the affliction of permitting the wish to be the father of the thought. The risk is that they would find what was desired by them and disregard what might be uncongenial to their personal, cultural, or political inclinations and beliefs.

In practice, such standards are applied to selected stories; most run-of-the-mill ones don't get that sort of scrutiny. Nor could they, for it would be impossible to put out a daily newspaper. As much as an editor can check, total backtracking is virtually impossible. Therein resides the need for trust, because those who violate trust—who don't tell you the truth—can all too easily get away with it.

Howard Simons also read every word of the Watergate coverage from early on. For a considerable period, he was more involved than Bradlee. Just as I was closely questioning Woodstein and Sussman, from the beginning Howard was monitoring me. When the story developed and became the talk of the town, Ben turned his mind to Watergate and also became a close reader and demanding questioner. Once he sent me a critical memo because a quote that had appeared in our paper was presented differently by one word in *The New York Times*. He thought that was material. This layered supervisory structure served the paper extremely well. In my experience in the trade, which ranges across fifty years, no other groundbreaking story running that long was as error-free.

In September, our investigative team uncovered the existence of a secret fund that Republicans used for clandestine intelligence operations against the Democrats. In that context, Deep Throat counseled Woodward to follow the money, although he did not use those words. Before he left the Justice Department, Mitchell was reported by Woodstein to have the authority to make disbursement from a fund (or funds, as was later discovered) that reached as high as seven hundred thousand dollars and was periodically replenished. There were four other figures that also could authorize the use of these monies for such purposes. One was Maurice Stans, the campaign's financial director. Another was Mitchell's deputy campaign manager, Jeb Stuart Magruder. Two others remained unknown to us, and the immediate future involved Woodstein's hunt for them. Late one night, after the story had developed sufficiently to be ready for publication, Bernstein phoned Mitchell at his home in New York seeking comment. When told what the story would report, he made a memorable outburst. "All that crap you're putting in the paper? It's all been denied," Mitchell was quoted as saying in the *Post*. "Katie Graham is going to get caught in a big fat wringer if that's published." That wasn't precisely what Mitchell had said, but the *Post* was too delicate to report that he said the wringer would mangle her "tit."

Beyond his indecency, Mitchell explicitly threatened the *Post*, saying "we're going to do a story on you." In the interim, House Republicans, with the help of some Democrats, managed to block a Banking and Currency Committee investigation of Watergate.

After the laurels of victory and vindication had settled on the brows of Woodstein, they presented Mrs. Graham with a gift recalling that incident. Bob had received a phone call alerting him that he could pick up an old-fashioned wringer at a particular garage sale. He forked over ten dollars for it, and Woodstein presented it to Mrs. Graham.

The National staff at first was amused, before becoming irritated by Metro's Watergate coverage. They thought we were out of our depth and risked embarrassing the newspaper, as the more foreboding the episodes of Watergate were revealed to be. Our reports of political sabotage were dismissed as old hat, and Democrats were not above doing it too, we were chided by National. The name of Dick Tuck was invoked. Tuck was known to insiders as a Democratic trickster. We did not know who he was. When we learned about his activities, we understood that his tricks were child's play compared to the organized campaign to subvert opponents waged by the Nixon administration's minions. As for the secret fund we had written about, one National staffer mimicked Republican efforts to belittle our reporting. He asked me, "If I have change in my pocket that no one can see, does that mean it's a secret fund?"

Skepticism began to wane and National lobbied hard to take over the story, with AME/National Richard Harwood making repeated efforts to do so, stressing the range of national issues experience his staffers had—in contrast to Metro's. When Bradlee broached the takeover proposal, I vigorously protested. I argued that one of Metro's advantages in breaking the Watergate story was the fresh and highly curious eye we brought to it. I stressed that the detailed and accurate reporting that Woodstein provided was an outgrowth of the hunger for success manifested by ambitious young reporters grasping for the brassiest ring that would ever come within their reach. The veterans on National already had made their mark, or else they wouldn't be on National.

It was to Woodstein's advantage that at the time of Watergate both Bob and Carl were single, without family obligations, and thus able to work ungodly hours and endless stretches without a day off. By contrast, the older though more experienced National staffers had families and the unavoidable obligations that go with a wife or children. I don't know how serious Bradlee was in raising the proposal with me, but for the time being Watergate remained a Metro responsibility under my purview.

As *The Washington Post's* Watergate work became known around the nation, people with knowledge of relevant information shared it with our reporters. Some of these claims were off the wall, while others seemed plausible but impossible to document. Lawyers who had been approached to participate in dirty political tricks led Woodstein to look intensively into the alleged organized campaign to sabotage the Democrats.

It was less than one month before the presidential election when the *Post* published Woodstein's exposé on October 10, 1972, that "FBI agents have established that the Watergate bugging incident stemmed from a massive campaign of political spying and sabotage. . . ." These efforts had been underway since 1971 and were a part of Nixon's strategy, we reported. Included in the Nixon effort was the Canuck letter that basically sank the campaign of Senator Ed Muskie, the Maine Democrat, and helped assure the nomination of the weakest candidate, Senator George McGovern. Related to the dirty tricks mentality of the Nixon administration were the secret slush funds amply filled and replenished by mostly illegal or questionable political contributions. These funds underwrote political espionage and sabotage, and after Watergate broke the funds were tapped for hush money to try to contain the metastasizing scandal that threatened the White House.

It was a time of unrelenting tension. One day while driving to work, mentally exhausted, I fell asleep briefly behind the wheel. I was lucky that I did not cause an accident. On another occasion the lot of us—Bradlee, Simons, myself, and Woodstein, perhaps others—gathered in the half-finished new building that the *Post* was constructing, which was connected to the old one. In one bare office, unfurnished and without electrical connections and thereby presumptively free of government-placed bugs, we heard from Woodstein that our phones likely were tapped and that lives might be in danger. It was a sobering moment. I had already asked a contact at the telephone company to sweep my personal and business lines to see if any had been bugged. He was glad to do it, but he warned that if the government had planted bugs, he could not alert me. So much for that. My daughters became accustomed to answering the office extension and our private phones in our home by saying, "Hello to anyone listening."

While these stressful factors piled up, I turned to a close friend to look after the safety of my family if I was arrested. I asked him to get them out of the country to Canada and told him that to do so he would have access to the couple of thousands of dollars we had in savings. I did not share this contingency plan with my wife until decades later. Looking back, it was an emergency plan born of weariness, paranoia, and the troubling memory of the vulnerability of our family in Nazi Germany and how narrowly we escaped that danger.

In follow-up stories, Woodstein tied the sabotage campaign to President Nixon's appointments secretary and the following day to Nixon's personal lawyer, Herbert Kalmbach. He also turned out to be the fourth person to control the slush fund. That left only the fifth man unidentified, who had for some time been said to be a high-ranking White House official.

The Republicans felt pushed to the wall by our latest stories, so much so that they trotted out Nixon's campaign manager, press secretary, and the chairman of the Republican National Committee to launch separate but coordinated counterattacks on the *Post* stories. They denounced our coverage as no more than "hearsay," "innuendo," and "unsubstantiated." After all our investigative reporting, I thought it was imperative to let the Republicans have their full say without any editorial quibbling. It would be a demonstration of integrity to our readers and the public. Even though the Republicans were by then famous for their "non-denial denials," as we called them, we could do our exegesis on another day. Bob and Carl who were writing the counterattack story, and Sussman who was editing it, resisted my guidance. When I insisted on my approach, Sussman went home in a huff and Woodstein reluctantly complied. Afterward, Sussman told me how unhappy Woodstein had been with me and my decision. The GOP charges were prominently displayed on Page 1. Their attacks, a harsher version of what had been said by them all along, in my opinion soon had an undesired impact on our coverage.

On October 25, the front page featured two Watergate stories. One reported that the Justice Department announced that there was "no credible evidence" that the alleged events of sabotage violated any federal laws. Above that story, leading the paper, was the *Post*'s identification of the "fifth man" who controlled the secret fund that underwrote clandestine political activity. It was Bob Haldeman, the president's chief of staff.

The worst mistake during the months we devoted to extensive coverage of the Watergate scandal had come on the preceding late afternoon. We were putting the final touches on the Haldeman story, which included rewriting. Several of us were summoned into Bradlee's office. To my mind, that story was the most important one up to that time that we could publish about Watergate. Haldeman was the highest-ranking figure to control the amply stocked clandestine fund. Implicating the president's chief of staff was another way of saying that the scandal had reached Nixon himself.

All manner of shifty operations could be paid for with this money without it being traced. The Nixon administration tried to distance itself from such funds, whose existence had been revealed by us fairly early on. The story we were about to publish would override the administration's cover stories.

The orchestrated Republican attacks only days earlier had gotten to Bradlee. He was particular sensitive to charges of our reliance on unnamed sources. If the *Post* had truthful information, critics charged, it would provide more specifics and name its sources so that their credibility, and actual existence, could be confirmed. More to the point, these charges were repeated by people in Bradlee's social circle. Ben was beginning to burn. Similar criticism was made by some reporters and editors on the National staff, the one that mattered most to Bradlee. Cumulatively, this produced an overwhelming effect that distressed Bradlee in a way that the analogous charges made earlier had not. Bradlee pressured us to put names and specific attributions in the paper. The Haldeman story would provide such an opportunity. For once, we would be able to share with our readers and the critics the authority underpinning the story beyond the phrase "according to informed sources" or some variant of that.

In pressing to get such information, Bob and Carl had extended interviews with one of their key sources, Hugh W. Sloan Jr., the former treasurer of the finance committee of CREEP. Sloan had resigned because he had become offended and frightened by the scope of the Watergate scandal, although earlier he went along with disbursing campaign funds for illegal campaign purposes, which he wrote off as politics as usual.

Despite his resignation, Sloan was reluctant to share what he knew because he remained a devoted follower of Richard Nixon, for whom he had worked in the White House before moving to CREEP. Carl and Bob needed his testimony, and what they got was extracted bit by painful bit. Sloan confirmed to Woodstein that Haldeman shared in controlling the fund and that he, Sloan, had told this to the grand jury investigating the scandal. At least that was what Bob and Carl were convinced Sloan had said. They were speaking in elliptical terms. Sloan was likely trying to avoid becoming an out and out snitch while wanting to remain an honorable man in the eyes of the two young reporters.

Bob and Carl came back from McLean, the Northern Virginia suburb where the Sloans resided, and wrote that Haldeman controlled the fund and that Sloan had so testified to the grand jury. That was manna for Bradlee because Sloan was the named source he craved. I was no less pleased when Woodstein finished the article and I went over the story after Sussman had done so. When I walked it across the newsroom to Bradlee's office where Simons was waiting, I felt we had finally delivered the goods to Bradlee. He and Simons remained uncertain and kept hammering away at how did we know this and how could we say that. This was extremely fateful business we were about to embark upon, connecting the scandal to the Oval Office. We had better be correct in all particulars or risk losing the *Post*'s credibility and possibly having the retributive powers of the federal government unleashed against our paper in its corporate guise. We were venturing the viability of the paper. If we were wrong, the public might swing into line behind the White House and support any punishment it might wish to impose on us.

To every question raised by Bradlee and Simons, Bob and Carl provided fuller specifics. Simons especially was uncertain. The clock was ticking toward deadline and the final go or no-go decision for the night. It was another manifestation of the air pocket—Bradlee's coinage—that we tended to hit just before deadline, with major questions still unresolved. No one wanted to hold the story for another day. We had worked on it so long that we wanted it in the paper. Great newspapers break big stories.

We were past deadline and Bob was back at his desk working into the article the latest revisions that had come out of the long-running meeting in Bradlee's office. All the questioning and the circular discussion had roused in me reservations that I had not had before. I looked over Woodward's shoulder and pressed him on whether he was totally comfortable that we had the attribution nailed down solidly enough to go with it. His answer was shakier than I found reassuring. He obviously retained some doubt himself in these stressful final minutes. Looking over his lead, a solution came to mind and I suggested a compromise. I wanted the information about Sloan's attributed grand jury testimony to be separated from the chief point: namely, that Haldeman was the highest of five presidential associates to control the slush fund, according to unnamed federal investigators. The second paragraph would then identify Sloan by name as the person who testified to that effect to the grand jury. What we had most solidly was Haldeman's connection to the fund. What we also had was a grand jury angle based, it turned out, on ambiguous testimony. Howard liked the revision I suggested. Bradlee did not. While I was standing next to Woodward's desk continuing the discussion on the rewrite, Bradlee came out of his office and crossed the newsroom until he was stopped by the mechanical track along which copy moved from the assignment editors to the copy editors. Rather than walking around the impediment, he called out across the room, "Thanks very much, Rosenfeld, but we will go with it. Just back off." His annoyance with me was clear.

The next morning, Dan Schorr of CBS News attempted to question Sloan as he appeared for a court session. Sloan did not say anything. His lawyer, however, did comment. He said that "we categorically deny that such a statement was made to the grand jury."

All hell broke loose. There was an urgent need to go over our story to see where we had gone wrong, to consider what to tell the media pressing us for comment, to decide what to tell our readers—and to try to pick up the pieces. By their account in *All the President's Men*, Woodstein began reexamining all their work. They could not reach Sloan. His lawyer was of some help, enough to indicate that the mistake might not have been substantive. They backtracked to their source in the FBI and confronted the agent in the hallway outside his office. Failing to get any explanation from him about how the mistake could have been made, they sought out the agent's superior and compromised their source's confidentiality and thereby ended any possibility of his remaining a confirming source.

My recollection differs from theirs. For much of that dark day, I did not know where Carl and Bob were. I was trying to find them to see how they were doing in their follow-up. It was very much later that I found out that they spent part of that day lunching with their publisher-to-be, Richard Snyder of Random House. They discussed the book they proposed to write about Watergate. Their meeting took place in the tony Hay-Adams Hotel, adjacent to Lafayette Park, on whose far side was the White House. It showed how self-possessed Carl and Bob were at a time of enormous pressure. Apparently, quite early they realized or were made to realize—some say by Robert Redford—what a valuable book and movie commodity they had within their grasp. It also may explain Bernstein's early habit of transcribing his interviews onto multipage copy books for his own immediate use and for distribution to appropriate colleagues. This procedure may also have been intended to provide fodder for whatever book might emerge from their coverage.

They told me not a word about how they spent their lunch hour on this trying day. Later in the afternoon, they finally phoned to fill me in about their unhappy encounter with the FBI agent. A third source, in the Justice Department, was next tested by a scheme that only someone with Carl's manipulative brain could have devised. Carl called this person, who insisted that he could not discuss any testimony about Haldeman before the grand jury. Carl proposed that he would ask the question and if the attorney did not hang up by the count of ten, the question was confirmed without a word being uttered. If it was false, the attorney should hang up immediately and the question would have been denied.

As deviously clever as it was in intending to make it possible for the attorney to claim deniability in the event he were asked by a superior if he had told Woodstein about the matter, this formulation proved too complicated. Much later, the attorney told Sussman that Carl had misunderstood his own ground rule. Whether it was Carl or the attorney who got it wrong is not important. Carl had outsmarted himself, his editors, and his paper in the bargain. He illustrated once more, just as with the interview with Sloan, how nebulous comprehension can be and the hazards of attempting to unravel complicated matters in anything less than clear language.

Late that afternoon, we gathered in Bradlee's office and pondered what to do next. Woodward advanced the proposition that confidentiality applied only as long as the source kept up his end of the bargain. If the source had deliberately lied (of which there was no certain evidence yet) then the obligation to protect the source's identity was lifted off the shoulders of the journalist. The FBI agent source had lied, according to Woodward, in that intensely anxious moment during the confrontation with him. Woodward recommended that we blame him in print for the mistake.

Dick Harwood disagreed. He thought the confidentiality bargain should remain intact even under these circumstances and that we could not throw in our FBI source without endangering our future ability to develop confidential informants. Not everyone would be patient enough to follow our reasoning and be convinced by its logic. Most would merely remember that the *Post* had sacrificed a source when the going got tough. Woodward's proposed remedy for a source deemed to have lied appears on the face of it to have been too self-serving, in my estimation. Woodstein's record honoring confidentiality was not perfect: They threw in their FBI source to his superior when it suited them to do it. In the same manner, in their book they threw in a White House source of mine who confidentially had given me information that I shared with Woodstein.

Not considered in the postmortem was how the controversy might have been diminished if we had separated the two thoughts. Simons said that day, "We wouldn't be in this fix if we had listened to Harry." Nevertheless, we still would have been in a fix.

Simons favored an immediate retraction. At my pleading, Bradlee agreed that for the time being our public posture would be, as he said in his statement, "We stand by our story." More than anything I wanted to avoid compounding our embarrassment if the follow-up showed, as we already suspected, that we had been basically right. The paper's credibility would only suffer further damage if a retraction itself had to be withdrawn.

Woodstein pressed that week to find where they had made the error. The following Sunday, Senator George McGovern, running against Nixon, used our Haldeman report in a TV interview to advance his candidacy. No sooner had he spoken (I was watching at home) than my office extension phone rang in my home. Simons was on the line and he had had enough. He ordered me to retract the story or explain that it was correct though partially flawed.

Fortunately, by that time Woodstein had gathered enough information to find the error. Sloan made clear in a subsequent interview that his lawyer's denial concerned only the fact of his having given testimony to the grand jury. He did not respond to the question of whether Haldeman had access to the fund. The other federal sources said the *Post* had been wrong on the grand jury, but right on Haldeman's access to the fund. With the help of Deep Throat's guidance in response to a worried Woodward's question, he replied that the fund was a Haldeman operation. What had gone wrong was a single, though important, detail, not the substance. Haldeman did have access to the fund. Sloan did not testify to that before the grand jury for one reason: he wasn't asked the question by the prosecutors. It is possible that the failure to do so might have partly motivated Woodstein's third source, the Justice Department attorney with whom Carl played his telephone game, I have to come surmise. The attorney might have been seeking to cover up his or a colleague's role in not questioning Sloan on the Haldeman connection to the fund.

The explanation of what had gone wrong was presented in the Monday, October 30, edition. It was included in an article by Woodstein citing a *Time* magazine report on Watergate. By this time, the magazine was coming up with its own Watergate scoops, as was *The New York Times*. In addition to that week's report about some critical testimony received by the FBI, the *Time* article stated that "no hard evidence could be developed to support" the *Post*'s Haldeman allegation. *Time* should have tried harder.

The *Post*'s major revelations were published within days of the 1972 election, as the paper's Watergate investigation gained traction with the public across the nation. The wider acceptance came about because Walter Cronkite, the respected TV anchor, devoted much more than the customary two minutes to tell the Watergate story. He broadcast a fourteen-minute report on the *CBS Evening News* and displayed the *Post*'s front page from that day on a screen behind him. Four days later, he followed up with an eight-minute segment, further familiarizing the American public with the Watergate scandal. His broadcasts elicited harsh threats from the White House against the network and caused top executives to buckle. No further reports of extraordinary dimension were aired by CBS.

The startling reports from the *Post* and other news outlets did not in the least affect the results of the election, in which President Nixon easily disposed of George McGovern. Shortly before the revelation about Haldeman, the *Post* published an article recalling that Nixon, in his 1962 bid to become governor of California, had financed a costly sabotage campaign against his opponent. That one did not succeed, and in 1964 a Superior Court in San Francisco issued an official judgment that found that Nixon and his campaign manager, H. R. Haldeman, had authorized and approved conduct that violated the state's election code. Tall oaks from little acorns grow.

In the campaign's concluding days the GOP gambit to undermine the *Post* by accusing it of acting on behalf of the Democrats intensified. Much to my dismay, following the blockbuster revelations of October, Woodstein's investigative reporting well had run dry. *Time* and *The New York Times* came up with incremental exclusive reports, but except for some modest contributions by the *Post*'s Justice Department reporter, nothing moved the ball very far down the field of inquiry. I pressed Woodstein for something, but nothing turned up. In the middle of November, Bob came up with a front-page story that at other times would have made me quite happy. It was about a probe of gambling payoffs to the D.C. cops. It didn't alter the appearance that after the election we had lost our interest in Watergate, as untrue as that was. Much later, a former high-ranking Republican official asked me how come our Watergate stories had stopped. I said that we printed all that we had when we had it. No other consideration mattered. His response to my answer was that we had been foolish and should have saved something for right after the election. The thought never occurred to me. In any event, a story of the caliber of Haldeman's role in the fund was not one that could or should have been kept in a desk drawer simply to disarm potential critics.

It wasn't until December 8 that Woodstein revealed more than had been known about the "White House Plumbers," a group of men assigned by the White House to track down leaks to the press. There had been a final paragraph in an earlier story in which sources said Hunt was part of the White House Plumbers, a cutesy name they bestowed on themselves because of their activities and their connections within the White House. Now Woodstein scored with an on-the-record interview with a former White House personal secretary who provided fuller information about the Plumbers. In fact, they were after much more than plugging leaks. Their first mission, "Hunt and Lilly Project #1," according to a 1974 indictment, was not to prevent leaks—too late for that—but to discredit the leaker of the Pentagon Papers, Daniel Ellsberg. They broke into the Beverly Hills office of Ellsberg's psychiatrist, Dr. Lewis J. Fielding, and scoured his files for anything they might be able to use against Ellsberg. It was Woodstein's final important Watergate story of the remarkable year of 1972. The Plumbers dispatched to California to do the deed on September 3, 1971, were the same ones that in June, 1972 broke into the Democratic National Headquarters. Some Plumbers.

Bob wound up the year with one additional front-page story, a strictly local one. On New Year's Eve he reported on a crackdown on the city's drug trade.

The mistakes and misadventures of the Sloan incident embodied the inherent dangers of confidential sources as well as the mythology that is part of the Watergate legacy: two sources were a guarantor of validity that one source was not. In the Sloan matter we had—or believed we had—three sources. Dealing with sources in the indirect language that is sometimes unavoidable in order to get anything out of them is a gamble because each person brings his or her attitude to the interview. From Sloan's point of view, he was answering truthfully. Woodstein heard what their reporting had prepped them to hear. They so much wanted to make the story work that they did not pin Sloan down out of fear of scaring him into silence. In all likelihood, if the conversation had been more direct, Sloan would not have gone along with it.

No doubt two sources are better than one—if both are sound. And three are better than two, et cetera. The reality is that two sources can be wrong. Three could be wrong. Any number could be wrong, including one source. The essence is the quality and integrity of the source, whether the source has direct knowledge or whether the source is influenced to the point of prevarication by a personal stake in the matter. A single source can be right and therefore sufficient. One danger lying in wait in the multiple source business is whether there actually are two (or more) sources. Did they learn the information directly or did they hear it from someone? Did the second source perhaps also hear it from that same someone? If so, that would bring it back to one source. Obviously, the most reliable source is a direct participant and his or her credibility is enormously buttressed by a document or a tape that backs up his or her contention.

The two source rule is useful but not a panacea. It becomes hazardous if elevated to holy writ. At the *Post* it began in the early days as Woodward and Bernstein, thrown together by circumstance and eyeing each other with suspicion, strived not to be outdone by each other. Plainly stated, they did not like or trust each other. When one landed a source, the other strained to match him. As they went along, they found they were overcoming their differences in temperament and perspective. Woodward was introverted and restrained in his judgments; Bernstein was flamboyant and ready to jump to conclusions. The result was the gradual evolution of a collaboration whose impact is hard to overstate. The two sources were cited with some regularity, and these sources proved sound. This is the acid test for reporters and their sources, as well as for newspapers: Are they vindicated in the end?

Bradlee picked up on the two sources formula and came to rely on it as a prophylactic against error. A nervous Katharine Graham put it to Bradlee: "How do we know we're right?" Ben invoked the two sources mantra to quiet her nerves. Years later, when I outlined to her the problems that even two sources could pose, she said, "Thank God I didn't know that." To which I responded, "We were right because we were right." Indeed, while she and other business executives were wondering why the *Post* pretty much had the story to itself so late in the game, I reveled in our competitive edge. I was happy the story remained ours for so long because I had total confidence in the accuracy of our reporting.

It also helped, though it was not conclusive, if the matter at hand was written down in the reporter's notebook. By way of example, Bernstein early on began to type up his notes, which of course are not a stenographic record of an interview. What we found on occasion when we needed to consult Bernstein's notes was that a key quote that became a subject of controversy and challenge appeared nowhere in them. Carl would justly say that the quote was firmly fixed in his memory, but it was not in a form that allayed an editor's concern. In actuality, note taking frequently covers the highlights enough to jog the memory later on. Furthermore, reporters have no more legible handwriting than anyone else. When we were being sued by Bebe Rebozo, Nixon's friend, we examined Ron Kessler's reporter notebook. He said he could read it, but I could not. His script resembled the EKG of a person about to expire—gentle waves with hardly any low or high points.

Confidential sources, while unnamed in print, are not entirely unknown. Editors know who they are, or would if they take pains to ask and insist. I did this with dreary regularity, and it led on occasion to Woodstein returning to the field to back up their reporting when their early source did not satisfy me as being sufficient. I should say I did this with one glaring exception. There came a time when I asked Woodward to name his friend, the source we called Deep Throat. The friend figured frequently in our talks, not so much as a person who revealed dark state secrets, but as one who was even more important to us, because we were inexperienced in covering the federal government. Deep Throat provided context and direction, encouraged and discouraged, issued warnings, and also was the crucial confirmer of information gleaned from others. I invited Woodward to join me in the cubicle that was my office. I shut the door. When I put the question to him, Woodward looked at me for a long, thoughtful moment and inclined his head slightly downward. He was solemn as he slowly spoke: "If you insist, I will tell you his name. I have promised never to do so." Bob made clear that naming Deep Throat would place him in the highest jeopardy as well as destroy the relationship between reporter and source.

I quickly considered what Woodward said and rationalized that in a practical way it was better for me to remain ignorant of the name. There was a real possibility of being pursued by Nixon's minions even into prison. It was not far-fetched that the time might come when one by one the reporters and editors working on the Watergate stories would be compelled to reveal sources to a grand jury or face the consequences. I was certain Woodward would never cooperate and likely would wind up jailed. I calculated that the more of us who could honestly say that Deep Throat's identity was not known to us, the more would remain at large to pursue the investigation. I did not anticipate perjuring myself to keep out of jail.

Another time, I raised the question with Woodward whether Watergate involved infighting at the FBI. I do not recall his exact response, but I was left with the impression that Woodward had said it did not. Decades later when Mark Felt, during Watergate the Acting Associate Director of the FBI, revealed himself as Deep Throat, the reality of such internal FBI conflict was at least a real possibility. It turned out that Felt was embittered over his failure to be promoted to the top job he felt he deserved after the death of J. Edgar Hoover. I need to emphasize that this was and remains only my impression because I cannot recall the actual words I used in posing the question to Woodward nor the exact words he used in assuring me (as I construed it) that it was not. After Felt went public as Deep Throat, I asked Bob about it and he said he did not recall our conversation. He was positive that he would not have said such a thing.

It was only a good deal later, after the conversation with Bob about Deep Throat's identity, that I recognized that not insisting on being told the name of his source was a major mistake. At least one editor, preferably more, needed to know the names of crucial sources to help assess their reliability—by which the newspaper might be judged in the end. To my certain knowledge, neither Simons nor Bradlee for a long time knew the identity of Deep Throat. Bradlee did not find out until after Nixon resigned. Years later, I asked Woodward why he had told Bradlee and not me. His answer was that Bradlee had insisted.

My error in not requiring to be told Deep Throat's identity had other implications. Had I been aware that it was at least in part a byproduct of internal FBI rivalry for succession to the directorship we would have had to consider whether we were obliged to pursue that line of inquiry. It is not certain that anything substantial would have changed, but it is possible that it could have—and that might have resulted in Deep Throat's retreating into silence or, worse, turning elsewhere to find another news outlet to offer his guidance. A pertinent angle would have explored whether such a conflict within the FBI was between one faction wanting to press ahead on the investigation of Watergate while the other wanted to protect the president from being entangled.

After the election, the Republicans were in a triumphal mood. Colson stated in a speech that forty-six million people had voted, 61 percent, which he boasted was the highest turnout in American history. It was obvious that even after the Watergate revelations Nixon remained a popular president. For all that, Colson and his cohorts were whistling past the graveyard.

At the end of 1972, I wrote Bradlee and Simons a two and a half page single-spaced memo in which I stated than in the three years I had been Metro Editor—a period which Bradlee had characterized as "Harry has the hardest job"—I had received small increases in salary. I was making modestly more than the highest-paid people I supervised and I was working far longer hours than they were. A comparison on an hourly rate would demonstrate the unfairness of the situation. I asked for considerably more money as I faced the need to pay two college tuitions and because I had damn well earned it. I did get an impressive bonus for Watergate; it was five thousand dollars, which was a record for me, but no more than was given to Nicholas von Hoffman, a columnist who hadn't had a particularly great year. So there.

16

Watergate Act Two

With the arrival of the new year of 1973, the *Post*'s Watergate investigation changed as the U.S. District Court prepared to try the arrested burglars and their handlers. At the same time, congressional committees took steps to hold hearings. When people say the *Post* brought down President Nixon, they are off the mark. He brought himself down. Our Watergate reporting finally stimulated the Congress to use its investigatory powers, including the issuance of subpoenas and the ability to demand sworn testimony, to take the nation into the inner workings of the Watergate scandal. House Republicans in 1972 outmaneuvered the Democratic majority to shut down one congressional committee hearing. Judges' rulings and practicalities of trial procedure as well as the appeals of defendants helped to prevent the trial of the Watergate burglars and their handlers from taking place before the election or soon afterward. Senator Edward Kennedy of Massachusetts had toyed with the idea of holding hearings in 1972. He did not, because as the target of GOP spying he decided he would not be the best person to conduct an investigation. By 1973 the stalling began to end.

In the first week of January, Mike Mansfield, the Democrat Senate Majority Leader, wrote of the necessity to investigate the Watergate bugging and "other insidious campaign practices," namely, the campaign of dirty tricks and political sabotage on which our reporting had focused. His letter was addressed to his colleague, Sam Ervin, Democrat of North Carolina, who ended up as chairman of the Select Special Watergate Committee established to conduct the official probe, which was unanimously approved by the Senate 77 to 0 on February 6.

From that time onward, much of the Watergate reporting focused on the formal hearings while our enterprise substantially but not entirely shifted to discovering what the investigators and prosecutors were looking into or learning from prospective witnesses. The trial of the Watergate burglars and their handlers opened the hunting season.

Woodstein expected that they would be assigned to cover the trial, though neither had experience doing that. Despite their wishes, and the strenuous objections of Sussman who insisted that I countermand my decision, Larry Meyer, our reporter in district court, was assigned to write the daily lead story. I did not want Woodstein tied down in court. They were of more use remaining free to investigate leads or write analyses coming out of court testimony. I doubted that Woodstein would thrive by giving up their mode of operation to sit patiently in the court day after day, focused entirely on what was unfolding before a judge and a multitude of media. The trial, for all Judge John Sirica's sometimes pointed if inconclusive questioning, did not get to the heart of the matter. Howard Hunt pleaded guilty and asserted that no Nixon administration higher-ups were involved. Except for G. Gordon Liddy and James McCord, the others pleaded guilty as well. All were convicted. The White House defense worked and kept the president from being implicated. The original prosecution concluded just about the way anyone interested in fostering a cover-up could have wished. Subsequently, the first prosecutors were criticized for not pursuing indications of criminal acts that would in time emerge, notably the dirty tricks campaign. No defendant talked until McCord, toward the end of March, sent a letter to Judge Sirica. McCord wrote that other people besides those convicted were involved in the Watergate conspiracy and that the defendants had been pressured to plead guilty. He spoke out as he was about to be sentenced, in an obvious attempt to gain leniency, and subsequently implicated two high White House aides. After Senate hearings had laid out much of the grand scheme of Watergate, the four actual burglars sought to withdraw their guilty pleas by claiming they had been coerced by Hunt. Hunt himself wanted to pull back his plea and argued that he had been misled by his superiors into believing the break-in was legal because it was approved by the government.

In the middle of March, the Democratic Party, in a suit against the Republican operatives and the Republican Party itself, went to court to obtain inside information from reporters who had exposed aspects of the Watergate scandal. Included were four reporters from the *Washington Evening Star-Daily News*, one reporter from *The New York Times*, and one from *Time* magazine. At the *Post*, those subpoenaed were Carl and Bob, publisher Katharine Graham, and Managing Editor Howard Simons, again arousing subpoena envy among those not on the list.

In the same month, L. Patrick Gray III's confirmation hearings to become permanent director of the FBI began to shed light publicly on the White House cover-up machinations through testimony before the Senate Judiciary Committee. Before the Ervin Select Committee heard witnesses in public, the wall shielding Nixon began to show its first fissures, and *Post* reporting was helping to tell America all about it. Compared to the early days when I had to fight to get Watergate stories on Page 1, for the rest of the year Watergate stories dominated the front page. Often, Watergate took up four or five of the ten or eleven articles displayed on Page 1.

Much of the heavy lifting was now done by other Metro reporters, in addition to Larry Meyer. Among them were Peter Osnos, Peter Jay, and John Hanrahan. Their participation grew although the investigatory aspects remained virtually in Woodstein's hands. A childhood friend of Woodward's, Scott Armstrong, was a staffer on the Ervin Committee. That did not impede our efforts. At the same time, because of several congressional hearings dealing with the operations of the federal government related to Watergate, National staffers in April became more heavily involved. During the month of April, National reporters came up with thirty-two front-page Watergate articles compared to Metro's twenty-seven—of which twenty-one were Woodstein's, a goodly number of them exclusives. The Senate Select Committee had outlined a work plan for itself to divide their inquiry into three phases: the Watergate break-in, the subsequent cover-up, and the espionage and sabotage. The committee began with hearings five days a week. When that became too grueling after the first two phases, it was reduced, as was the television coverage provided by the networks.

One of the best National contributions was written by Haynes Johnson and Jules Witcover. They interviewed one hundred voters from electoral districts that had given Nixon his recent sweeping majority. They found that Watergate was eroding Nixon's majority, as disenchantment piled on top of disillusionment. No doubt as a consequence of this dramatic reduction in his previously touted "New

Majority," and increasing pressure from congressional Republicans, Nixon all of a sudden perceived "major developments" that led to the reversal of his firm position forbidding his aides to testify before the committee investigating Watergate.

This was the season that the *Post* received accolades. The outpouring of praise included the George Polk Memorial Award, which cited Carl and Bob for outstanding national reporting. Other Polk winners for the *Post* were Ron Kessler for Community Service, for his series on conflicts of interest among trustees and administrators of local hospitals, and Sandy Ungar, who took leave from the *Post* to write a book titled *The Papers & The Papers*, about how the press handled the Pentagon Papers. He won in the Polk Book category.

When the Sidney Hillman Foundation Award was bestowed in New York, Howard Simons asked me to attend. At least that was what I understood him to want. What he actually intended was that I go to New York in place of Woodward. When that was cleared up, I declined to ask Woodward to remain in Washington. My inference was that Howard was concerned that cumulatively the awards might be going too much to Woodstein's heads. On the Eastern Airlines shuttle flight to New York that morning, Bob and I sat together. He was agitated and asked whether I knew what had been going on at the Pulitzers, which were in the process of being selected. He said that Bradlee, who was on the Pulitzer board, was lobbying to shift the Watergate entry from National reporting to the Gold Medal for Distinguished Meritorious Public Service category. The National award is given to individuals; Public Service meant the award would go to the *Post*. In my recommendation to Simons, I had put Woodstein's work into the National category and that is how Howard submitted our coverage. Although I had picked up some vague scuttlebutt about Bradlee's machinations, I had discounted it. What Bradlee was said to be doing was not all that unusual. The prizes, on which the board has the final say, are subject to the intrigues of the high-level journalists who are selected to serve on it.

At the Hillman Award luncheon, Woodward charmed an appreciative audience and introduced me and Sussman, who had come to New York at my suggestion. Bob coyly told the gathering that while he did not have a Jewish mother, like the absent Bernstein, he did have two Jewish editors, introducing us to a round of laughter. While in New York, I checked in with the office and learned that Mrs. Graham had invited Annie and me to dinner with the newspaper's board of directors that evening at her home. I called Annie to ask her to meet me at Mrs. Graham's Georgetown mansion. Her dining room was set up with several round tables. Bradlee and Simons were the only others invited from the newsroom. At dinner Annie was seated between Nicholas Katzenbach, a former U.S. Attorney General, and the financier Warren Buffett. She described them as very nice dinner companions.

A number of toasts were given. Bradlee's toast referred to my role in Watergate. He noted that I had joined the paper as a foreign editor and now had contributed so importantly to it, which the executives and board members in the room understood to be the crowning achievement for the *Post*. My toast centered on the paper as an institution. How Katharine Graham and Ben Bradlee had shaped the paper so that it was able to do groundbreaking and audacious work, unfettered by restrictions that might have been imposed to protect business interests. John Prescott, then president of the paper, said afterward that he thought mine was the toast of the evening because it said what needed saying. That dinner at Katharine's was not a prize, but for me it was important recognition from the people for whom I worked.

17

Nixon Gets a Wakeup Call

A few hours before the start of the annual White House Correspondents' Dinner on the evening of April 14, 1973, Carl Bernstein, Bob Woodward, and Barry Sussman crowded into my office, which was dominated by a white-topped rectangular desk. Behind my desk was a wall of bookshelves and a corkboard. Opposite my desk was a TV set and two chairs. Sussman rested against the TV and Woodward and Bernstein leaned forward from the chairs. Agitation marked their faces. Carl and Bob were distressed because they felt they were being robbed of their Pulitzers by Bradlee's actions. I tried to calm them before that night's festivities. I told them that in all but name it was their prize. Even though it was their prize, I said, it was also the *Post*'s. It was the persistent commitment of the *Post* that encouraged and supported their work and stuck with them despite the very real threat of economic retaliation by the government. I said they were worrying about nothing; no one but themselves would ever take note of the distinction between them as individual reporters and the paper. Never was I more prescient. Decades later, media references continue to cite Carl and Bob as winners of the Pulitzer Prize.

That night, Ray Price, the president's chief speechwriter, was at the correspondents' dinner as part of the Nixon entourage. The president usually gave the main speech at this occasion. I ran into Price as the event was breaking up. Watergate suffused the atmosphere at the dinner. Price asked me why the *Post* pursued Nixon relentlessly when the press had covered up for Jack Kennedy when he was president. This was an especially telling point because Bradlee had been an intimate friend of the slain president. I told Price that, as he well knew, I was still in New York during the JFK administration.

Had I been in Washington in those days, I said, I would not have looked the other way. I assured him that far from being partisan and irresponsible, we were holding out of the paper what we deemed solid information as we worked to make sure of its accuracy beyond the normal standards of proof. We were fully aware that we were writing about a sitting president and all that implied for the security and stability of the nation.

Ray Price paid attention and shared our talk with others in the White House. Our chance meeting led to eventful consequences following a conversation that took place a couple days later in the Oval Office, between the president and his press secretary, Ron Ziegler.

I had been aware since 1974, when some of the Nixon tapes were made public, that my name had come up in them. While preparing this memoir, I searched the 1,307-page document that President Nixon submitted under subpoena to the House Judiciary Committee a full year after the conversation with Ziegler. Not finding any reference to myself in the lengthy presidential submission, I turned to the National Archives in Washington, D.C. They mailed me a CD with an index of all the tapes. To obtain an audio copy, I was referred to the Nixon Library in Yorba Linda, California, where three Rosenfeld references were eventually found in the index. Two were attributed to Stephen Rosenfeld, then an editorial writer at the *Post*. One had no first name attached.

During our customary winter sojourn in the California desert in March, 2012, my wife and I visited the Nixon Library, where an archivist copied Nixon's April 16, 1973, conversation onto a CD. Although the index listed the April 16 conversation as involving Ray Price and Stephen Rosenfeld, this one was the most likely to actually have been with me. It was possible that Price talked to two Rosenfelds that night. But it was also possible that those who prepared the index had made an error on the first name.

According to National Archive records, no transcript of this tape had been made up to the time that I received it. The transcript of this tape was not submitted by the White House to the House Judiciary Committee. What attracts special attention to the Nixon-Ziegler tape is that four conversations the same day between Nixon and his top aides before Nixon-Ziegler, and five afterward, were given to the House Committee. This, then, is its first public revelation. It was evident that the conversation was between Price and me. I alerted the National Archives to correct the error.

When President Nixon submitted the voluminous—but incomplete—transcripts of White House tapes, his letter of transmittal cited his rights as president not to "participate in the destruction of the Office of the Presidency," to justify his refusal to hand over all the subpoenaed material.

In the April 16, 1973, tape, the president discussed how to deal with the crisis that was engulfing the Nixon presidency.[1] The conversation was a critical one. Ziegler came to the president as emissary for several advisers who wanted Nixon to take strong action to protect his besieged presidency. Ziegler's mission was to convince Nixon that events that would soon unfold would deepen the crisis. Obviously hoping to get Nixon to make crucial and unpalatable decisions, Ziegler delivered some unwelcome news, a transcript of the tape revealed:

Ziegler: Just from a general standpoint for perspective. At the White House Correspondents' Dinner, ah, Rosenfeld, who is the metropolitan editor for the *Post*, who has been the man in charge of . . .

Nixon: Yeah.

Ziegler: Ah, the story.

Nixon: Yeah.

Ziegler: Because Woodward and Bernstein fall under the metropolitan side, ah, which is unusual. Ah, mentioned to Ray Price, who used to work for Rosenfeld at the New York . . .

Nixon: *Tribune* . . .

Ziegler: *Tribune*. Ah, that he has been agonizing over this matter, that they have a lot more information than has been printed. That Rosenfeld feels, ah, that the story will be told in its entirety. That they are tying together some loose ends now, but he insists that anything printed is tied down, is what he said. And that his concern is that it will, when the story unfolds and breaks by the *Post*, that it will hurt the Presidency, the current President, and the Office

---

1. The full text of this tape appears in the Appendix.

of the Presidency. Ray, recognizing his view on this type of thing, although he did not do anything but report this, points out that Rosenfeld is one of the few people in a high position on the *Post*, who is a conscientious . . .

Nixon: . . . Decent guy . . .

Ziegler: . . . professional, and indeed volunteered to Price, and I believe him, that he supported you . . .

Nixon: Yeah.

Ziegler: . . . for public office consistently, including the recent election. And makes that point to Price by saying that this is a story that will be told and must be told.[2]

Nixon: Yeah.

Ziegler: Now combine that with the discussion that ah, ah speechwriter, ah, [David] Gergen had with Bob Woodward and Carl Bernstein also at the White House Correspondents' Dinner, on the basis that Gergen and Woodward were former college chums. Woodward made the point separately that the *Post* has far more information than they have reported and that they are tying up ends now. And that anything less than full disclosure at this time . . .

Nixon: Yeah . . .

Ziegler: . . . would pose, ah a problem. Now, that is consistent with what I sense from Woodward's inquiry, Woodward's inquiries too.

Nixon: In other words they've got a few more things—they don't know what we know now.

Ziegler: I don't believe so, but I think they're running down that line. They're running down the line, I think

---

2. Ziegler was building up my credibility through overstatement. At the *Herald Tribune* I did not outrank Ray Price. He was in charge of the editorial page and I oversaw foreign news, a more modest position. Ray would not have said he reported to me. Furthermore, I did not support Nixon in any campaign and certainly never said so to Price.

we can assume, specifically on the post-trial information, because they've already had a story on that.

Nixon: Yeah . . .

Ziegler: Now . . .

Nixon: That's a big story right there.

Ziegler: Yes sir. That's correct. Now, ah, Woodward also, Gergen said, had some, you know, hang-ups, to the degree that Gergen feels Woodward is into something that is bigger than he could handle. But in any event, both men made the point that they have additional information, ah, broader in scope, than anything that has appeared. And Woodward went so far as to say to Gergen that he would like to sit down with him and go over this with him, just to, which Gergen did not do.

Nixon: Maybe he should.

Ziegler: Well, I don't know . . .

Nixon: Maybe.

Ziegler: My view is that the activity of the *Post* over the last five or six days suggests that they are hovering on the outer fringes here, waiting to assess what move the White House will take, and then drawing the conclusion as to whether or not to discredit that move . . . so we have to keep that in mind.

Nixon: Good point.

It is obvious from the context of the tape that Ziegler used the correspondents' dinner encounters with Price to leverage the president to take bolder action as opposed to the "modified limited hang out" the White House sometimes favored to assuage public opinion by restricting the amount of information they would make public.

Instead of minimal measures, Ziegler maneuvered the conversation to an alternative that would lead to the dismissal or resignation of at least John Dean, the president's counsel, Bob Haldeman, the president's chief of staff, and with a bit less emphasis, John Ehrlichman, the president's chief domestic adviser.

Ziegler: My point on John Dean is that based on the information that you have obtained, you are now aware that the information that he could have provided to you both post- and pre-trial which has just now come to your attention. Now the only action that people can relate to on the part of, anyone, when you become aware of that information is decisive action. In other words, the man did not do right.

Nixon: Yeah, the problem you've got there is this: Making Dean, Dean the scapegoat or something I'm thinking works. And would he make up with regard to Haldeman or to be quite candid, see what I mean? I know what you're suggesting.

Ziegler: Of course, of course Dean would not necessarily be the scapegoat on this.

Nixon: See I'd have the right way to do it in a situation where I don't say Dean withheld information from me.

Ziegler: And that Dean did have information that suggested, ah, the corruption of ah justice or something of that sort. And, the reaction to that would be, if he did not tell you . . .

Nixon: Yeah.

Ziegler: . . . then you should have been aware of that, so, particularly from your counsel, if he had that, probably assumed that you could move against him. If he did tell you . . .

Nixon: I didn't fire him.

Ziegler: See, in other words, there's no, there's no positive way out of it.

Nixon: Yup.

The conversation between press secretary and president continued over the pros and cons of different remedies, including Ziegler's proposal to take action that would checkmate the Ervin committee "and put it out of business." Later on in their taped discussion, they talked about Haldeman's vulnerability because of his control of slush funds used for political purposes. Ziegler argued for the chief of staff to resign.

> Ziegler: In other words, Bob establishes himself in public opinion, in the country, as a man who was not responsible, who was not guilty of illegality, but a man who recognizes that the things he did got out of hand and steps up to the problem.
>
> Nixon: Um hum.

So, Ziegler argued that in the "bold play versus the minimum play . . . the broad play, if taken, must be taken in its entirety." In making this point, Ziegler was working to convince Nixon that the plan for the top people temporarily to step aside, suspended from their White House duties, would not suffice. This was the action that Haldeman and Ehrlichman thought would be taken.

> Ziegler: After nine months of all this press speculation . . .
>
> Nixon: Yeah, yeah . . .
>
> Ziegler: And leaks and so forth, much of which in this particular case [the infamous slush fund] . . .
>
> Nixon: . . . is accurate.

After Ziegler and Nixon went back on forth on taking minimal versus bold action, their conversation ended on a stark note.

> Ziegler: In cold terms, I'm thinking of the presidency.
>
> Nixon: Well, let me tell you this, also going have to, I don't know which, but I want to talk to Rogers, and ah consider all these things, but you can be goddamn sure that a man will protect himself.[3]

---

3. William P. Rogers, the secretary of state, was acting as Nixon's adviser as the Watergate cover-up unraveled. He expressed doubts about White House denials on Watergate and urged a top-level housecleaning. Probably the straightest arrow still in the upper levels of the Nixon administration, Rogers was forced to resign in August 1974.

The day after the Ziegler meeting, Nixon showed he had gotten the message. John Dean was told that he would not be given immunity. Three days after that, obviously aware what was coming down, Dean announced he would not accept the role of scapegoat the White House had in mind for him.

Two weeks after the Nixon-Ziegler taped meeting, the president revealed to the nation all he claimed to know about Watergate and its fallout, which kept the cover-up going.

Nixon called it "one of the most difficult decisions of my presidency," and he said, "I accepted the resignations of two of my closest associates in the White House—Bob Haldeman and John Ehrlichman—two of the finest public servants it has been my privilege to know." He also announced the resignation of another old comrade, U.S. Attorney General Richard Kleindienst, whom he praised as "a distinguished public servant."

On the other hand, John Dean was dismissed without any ceremony. Nixon said, "John Dean has also resigned." That's all a designated fall guy warranted. President Nixon told the American people that he took full responsibility for what his hired hands had done, implying that it had been without his knowledge.

The next day, May 1, was sunny and warm. In the afternoon, Ziegler, who had led the denunciations of Woodstein and the *Post,* apologized to the reporters and the paper. Early in our Watergate reporting, Ziegler had deflected questions from the press corps about what the *Post* had published, by stating, "I will not dignify with comment stories based on hearsay, character assassination, innuendo, or guilt by association." When Ziegler ate crow, the Associated Press called the *Post* for comment and reached me. I suggested they contact Bradlee, Simons, or Mrs. Graham. None of them was available. So for the first news cycle my comment was used. It was not as pithy as the occasion called for. I said, "I will dignify with comment Mr. Ziegler's apology. I think this late-in-the-day tribute to a free press ought to encourage all of the press to continue to play the watchdog role that our Founding Fathers probably had in mind for us." Later that day Mrs. Graham spoke for the *Post,* saying she welcomed the apology.

Harry and West Coast Correspondent, Leroy Aarons, on the sound stage of the film "All the President's Men" in Los Angeles in January 1975. It was a near-perfect copy of the *Post's* newsroom.

The man who was Harry. Jack Warden, who portrayed him in the film "All the President's Men," with Harry at an event in Washington, D.C. in 1975. Photo credit: *The Washington Post*.

At the Kennedy Center reception before the premiere of "All the President's Men," Dustin Hoffman tells a very funny, dirty joke to Ben Bradlee and Harry, who appreciate the actor's sense of humor. Photo credit: *The Washington Post*.

Katharine Graham, the publisher of *The Washington Post*, at one of the going-away parties for Harry in 1978. This party was held at the home of George Solomon, the Sports Editor of the *Post*. Photo credit: *The Washington Post*.

Woodstein's gift, a satirical representation of Nixon's San Clemente estate, presented to Harry on leaving the *Post*. San Clemente was Richard Nixon's oceanfront property in California, remodeled at substantial taxpayer expense. The inscription on the back reads: "To our friend & boss." Photo credit: *The Washington Post*.

Harry at age 50 when he left *The Washington Post* to take over the newspapers in Albany, New York. His hair was full and only a trifle gray at the temples. Both attributes were doomed. Photo credit: *The Washington Post*.

Annie and Harry attend the December 17, 1987, film premiere of Albany novelist William Kennedy's *Ironweed* at the Palace Theatre in downtown Albany. Photo credit: The *Albany Times Union.*

Governor Mario M. Cuomo on one of his regular visits to the *Times Union* for a meeting with the editorial board. Photo credit: The *Albany Times Union.*

Harry addresses Albany's Congregation Beth Emeth's 60th Anniversary observance of Kristallnacht in November 1998. Photo credit: The *Albany Times Union.*

Annie and Harry at a Mary Lou Whitney event in Saratoga Springs.

The Rosenfeld family gathers in Lake Placid to celebrate Harry's 65th birthday in summer, 1994. Counterclockwise from top left: Susan, Stefanie, Harry, Amy, and Annie.

To Anne Rosenfeld
Best Wishes,   Bill Clinton.

At a White House Correspondents' Dinner Reception, Anne Rosenfeld chats with President Clinton about his recent knee operation., 1997. Photo credit: The White House.

Harry during an editorial board meeting at the *Times Union*. Photo credit: The *Albany Times Union*.

18

After the Pulitzer

Bradlee succeeded in maneuvering the Watergate entry for the Pulitzer Prize into the Public Service category. The jurors for the National category had made it their third choice, likely because they were suspicious of the confidential sources that studded our reporting. Between the time that they voted and when the Pulitzer Board considered their selections, McCord's letter about pressure on the burglars to plead guilty and facilitate the cover-up became public. As a result, the Pulitzer Board felt differently about the bona fides of our work than the jury had, regardless of the confidential sources. The board had the authority to reject the jury recommendations and did so, selecting Watergate for the Public Service award. They also had to move the entry that earlier had been placed at the head of the Public Service list to another category. In turn, that entry shift displaced another excellent *Post* candidate, a series written by Metro staffer Bill Claiborne about a riot in the D.C. jail in which he had been held hostage.

The Pulitzer Prizes were announced May 7. *Washington Post* chief political writer David Broder also won for commentary. The Gold Medal, regarded as the greatest of the journalistic Pulitzers, was a first for the *Post*. In an interview for the paper's in-house newsletter Bradlee said: "Harry Rosenfeld's Metropolitan Desk handled this story impeccably." In a memo to his National staff, Harwood wrote: "We salute them [Metro] and envy the job they've done. The continuing story of the Watergate investigation remains their story." He then outlined a battle plan for National staffers to pursue, and concluded: "The point is that the national staff has a role to play in this case and I hope we do it as well as our colleagues across the room."

That was a generous acknowledgment from National, which in the ordained order of the newspaper universe was at the top of the food chain. Watergate for a while played topsy-turvy with the convention. We also heard from people around the country, and they offered primarily praise. National reporters already were heavily engaged in Watergate follow-ups, as their April front-page articles demonstrated. The altered landscape that was outlined in Harwood's memo to his staff was anticipated by me a couple of weeks earlier, when I suggested to Simons and Harwood how future coverage might be divided between Metro and National. I proposed Metro would do the daily story out of the Senate Select Committee hearings, with Larry Meyer encoring his successful trial coverage, while Woodstein would provide analysis and look for spinoff stories.

As for the interpretation and analyses of the political consequences—how the hearings impacted the presidency and national politics, including both political parties—I noted that "[t]his is clearly a National story and the Metro staff could not bring to it the political background that several National reporters easily could." It was my recognition that in the future the Watergate story was no longer solely Metro's but was becoming a manifold undertaking in which National had to play a lead part. As additional events shook up the federal government—with accompanying resignations and appointments, hearings and court cases—National's contribution increased to fifty-four front-page stories compared to Metro's thirty-three. During this stretch, Woodstein provided a dozen stories, among them many exclusives. They included the revelation that the Nixon administration launched its clandestine illegal and quasi-legal operations in 1969. Among other disclosures were these: The administration had tapped the phones of two reporters; the Justice Department was investigating how the Watergate trial prosecutors handled their case, with intimations that they had pulled punches; and FBI officials had warned their interim director Pat Gray that there appeared to be a cover-up underway. Gray did not go to Nixon with this information, as FBI officials wanted him to do.

Of the evidence massing against the White House, perhaps none was more to the point than that of the Deputy Director of the CIA, Lieutenant General Vernon A. Walters. In May 1973, he testified in person and in memoranda to Senate committees that Haldeman had ordered him, in the name of the president, to invoke the need to protect intelligence activities to ward off investigation of aspects of Watergate. The date that the instruction was given was June 23, 1972, less than a week after the break-in. Five days later, CIA Director Richard Helms followed up and ordered Walters to request the FBI to restrict its investigation to those "already arrested or under suspicion."

Walters's disclosure came early in the congressional probes, and its substance would eventually bring down the Nixon presidency. But an underling's word was not nearly enough. It took the so-called "smoking gun" tape recording of the president ordering the cover-up that finally forced Nixon to resign.

That month, too, Howard Simons heard that Seymour Hersh, the investigative reporter who had broken the My Lai massacre story and now worked in the Washington bureau of *The New York Times*, was going around town boasting that his paper, which had been left behind at the beginning of Watergate, was "supermobilizing" and "would bury the *Post*." Howard's note to Harwood and me continued: "This may be Hersh at his most manic but I think it's more than an idle threat. Therefore, I want a task force put together to counter the *Times* effort OR even if the *Times* unmaking said effort to ensure that we maintain our hitherto excellent coverage." In one swoop, under the pressure of outside competition, Howard stowed Bradlee's concept of creative tension on an out-of-reach shelf for the duration. In Bradlee's view, tension had a creative dimension derived from the competition it engendered between news departments, all to the benefit of what appeared in the newspaper. The downside of that method, in my opinion, was an ambience of hypercompetitiveness in the newsroom. The reporters and editors that flourished at Bradlee's *Post* were comfortable with the stresses and demands of creative tension. Many good people were not and departed when they had enough. At least some of those who chose to leave found fulfilling careers in journalism elsewhere.

Howard's task force idea evolved into Watergate Central, with Harwood and me sharing an office along with Sussman and monitoring the Senate hearings on TV. The FBI'S role in Watergate remained on my mind, as Senate testimony shed light on the various conflicts that played out after J. Edgar Hoover's death. One of my earlier suggestions in Central mode was that the task force do a story on how in the later Hoover days, when people supposedly in power and in charge remained reluctant to take action against a man who was possibly in the early stages of senility or who might be considered borderline mentally ill. In this context there was a memorable phone call in Bradlee's office, which was put on speaker phone. A crowd of us listened as Bradlee pumped Henry Kissinger about what I recall was Kissinger's role in the wiretapping of some of his staffers. What remains rooted in my mind from that conversation was the secretary of state denying all allegations in his German-accented English. He described the dearly departed Hoover as that "maniacal fag."

Despite what Woodward had told me, I could not let the thought rest that FBI discordance was crucially involved. I followed my earlier story proposal quickly with another, saying Central should look into the scenario that an FBI veteran rather than an outsider would be placed in the directorship permanently. I made note of the retirements of high-ranking FBI officials, including Mark Felt—although at the time I did not know he was Deep Throat. I repeated the suggestion of working on this story angle almost weekly. Two months later, I was still asking that it be looked into. The National partner in Watergate Central was best equipped to pursue this inquiry, but did not. Perhaps the spirit of Hoover, who had died in May 1972, survived to continue to intimidate the press. He was fearsome and beyond the reach of criticism when he was alive. Reporters, editors, and publishers all shared a rational concern that an attack on him would result in his use of FBI files reveal their own best-kept secrets. It wasn't that Watergate Central was especially productive as much as that it was necessary in a situation where two desks were involved in the ongoing coverage. In that regard, Watergate Central had reasonable success.

Among the scoops Woodstein scored in June was their report that Dean would testify that Nixon knew of the cover-up plan because the president had discussed it with Dean or in his presence no fewer than thirty-five times. Testimony before the Senate Select Committee brought out that the original Watergate prosecutors wanted to suppress testimony about cash payments made to the break-in defendants. Woodstein scored again with a story on how Hunt had tried to blackmail the White House. It was a month of steady revelations for which Metro provided the heaviest firepower with forty-seven front-page stories, including eighteen by Woodstein. National had an off month with twenty-five Page 1 Watergate stories.

June brought still more awards and acknowledgments. The American Veterans Committee, an organization founded after World War II by veterans who were not of the American Legion stripe presented us with the Eleanor Roosevelt Citizenship Award. I was designated to go to Atlantic City where the AVC was holding its convention to accept the honor. In my remarks, I noted that Bradlee had been active in the AVC in its formative days as it was scrounging for members. Next came an invitation to speak at the CLIO Awards in New York City where outstanding advertising leaders were honored. I was introduced by Clay Felker, then the editor and publisher of *New York*, a magazine that had begun life under Felker's direction as *The New York Herald Tribune*'s Sunday supplement. We were friends from those Trib days and he arranged for my appearance. I could not resist pointing out to the ad executives how many top White House officials implicated in Watergate, including Haldeman, came out of the advertising industry. I asked them to reflect on the role their highly successful job skills had played in Watergate. "The whole notion of selling the president needs to come under your review," I said, indulging in wishful thinking.

During this time of accolades, Metro received kudos from a delegation of French journalists from *Paris Match*, the popular weekly magazine. They wanted to be briefed on how our metropolitan operation worked. Upon their return home, they wrote that they were going to implement the concept of regional coverage.

While the major concentration was on Watergate, our staff covered other important breaking news as well as coming up with notable enterprise stories. Bill Claiborne's courageous behavior and account during a riot in the D.C. jail was the most dramatic in breaking news. The prisoners in cellblock No. 1 on October 11 "had seized nine hostages and wanted to talk to me," Bill recounted. The prisoners obviously were impressed by Claiborne's coverage of prison issues. The felons had sent a written message: "We want to negotiate with Hardy and Claiborne." Kenneth Hardy was the director of D.C. Corrections, and after some deliberation he decided to go along with the inmates' demands to enter the cell block they were holding. Both were taken hostage. Hardy and other prison officers were brutalized. Claiborne was used to carry a message of the prisoners' "revolution" and demands to the outside world. The uprising ended after twenty-two hours. Claiborne was done out of the Pulitzer Prize he almost had in his hand.

In the enterprise category was Karlyn Barker's exploration of the quality of care in Washington's most important public mental institution, St. Elizabeths. She had been covering St. Elizabeths and wanted to look into reports of unacceptable conditions there. Karlyn volunteered to pose as a woman in need of treatment and arranged to have herself committed to the hospital. During her hospitalization, Maureen Joyce—my secretary and a close friend of Karlyn's—and I visited her posing as family members. We found her attired in a long off-white gown of rough cotton. Her hair was stringy. She acted her part by staring wide-eyed and rapidly working her fingers in agitation. For the five days she was there, she inhabited the role she was playing—no small achievement. When she emerged from that stressful situation, she wrote a series of articles combining her experiences and observations. It was impressive work, and I took it to Bradlee with great pride. Bradlee liked it too, it quickly became apparent. In fact, he liked the series so much so that he wanted to give it to Style or *Potomac* magazine, where he said the articles would get stronger display than on Page 1. I was outraged and did not hide my anger. I argued fiercely and Karlyn's first article distinguished the front page of *The Washington Post*. I resented Bradlee's efforts to hand off Metro's best work to editors who played no role in making it happen. Of course, he got a little bit even by playing the remaining Barker articles inside the paper.

Among other major stories in Metro at this time were those produced by Ronald Kessler. He left *The Wall Street Journal* to join the Metro staff in 1970 as an investigative reporter. Metro got such an experienced reporter by default. His recruiter, National editor Ben Bagdikian, did not have a slot for him. So Kessler was parked at Metro with intimations that he would join National eventually. On Metro, Kessler took his opportunities where he found them. He did a thorough investigation of the financial shenanigans at the District's most prominent hospital, the Washington Hospital Center. The series of articles published in the fall of 1972 revealed how costs were padded, uncovered conflicts of interest among its managers, and detailed how medical care operated as a business. This story had to jump many hurdles, including the lobbying of Bradlee's physician and friend, who tried to use his personal connection to undermine our reporting. He charged the *Post* with bias against the hospital over the years. We took his complaint seriously, searched our archives, and found that we had printed only slightly more unfavorable articles than favorable ones. The negatives were almost all reports on labor negotiations and hardly supported the allegation by Bradlee's friend.

Meanwhile, the *Post*'s public relations department decided that it would be good for the paper to involve itself more actively with the general community. Finding the right cause to champion was difficult, because if any of its doings turned out to be questionable or worse, the paper would have to report on them. To forestall such an unwelcome and counterproductive development, the P.R. people decided that the least controversial and most feel-good project for the *Post* was to support a hospital caring for kids. Kay Graham agreed to head a fund drive for Children's Hospital.

In December 1972, Kessler was working on another story about problems at a hospital. This one, of course, involved Children's Hospital. I approved his pursuit of a lead he had picked up that the hospital's proposed $500 million building plans were being challenged because of high construction cost overruns and for not meeting fire safety standards. I said nothing to anyone as Kessler continued his reporting, not being sure that there was a there there. When the reporting matured to the point that a publishable story was in the offing, I knew I had to tell Mrs. Graham.

As she would from time to time, one day Kay walked through the newsroom and stopped in my office to say hello. The moment had come. I informed her that her community project likely would wind up as the subject of a critical article in her newspaper. She looked at me, unsmiling. She said few words in response. They were: "Be sure you're right." She turned on her heel and left.

The publication of the Children's Hospital story created a firestorm. The staff at the hospital was outraged, and we heard from them. When Kay hosted a fundraiser for the hospital at a cocktail party at her home, its executives were present in force. She insisted that I attend, in place to be berated by them in person. I had to figure out how to defuse their anger as much as possible without backing down from our work. To make matters worse, one of the senior hospital executives was on crutches, making it appear as if the paper had picked on a disabled man—however temporary his handicap.

19

Diversions High and Low

Before, during, and after Watergate there were commonplace hurdles to jump over. In my long years in newspapering, in times of turmoil and of serenity, there was one type of story that was a favorite of the advocates of the good news school of journalism to mollify readers. It catered to the public's enchantment with animal stories—a matter in which I struggled against a relentless tide. I regarded them as a misuse of always scarce reporter and newsprint resources, an indulgence in anthropomorphic sentimentality. A minor scourge of my Metro assignment was coping with the fascination of executives and editors when it came to the Chinese pandas in the National Zoo. The creatures were a major attraction, drawing large crowds, and therefore coverage of them was an easy way to cater to readers inclined to whine about the bad news they had to confront each day in the *Post*.

The public was particularly fascinated with the pandas' mating, or rather their abstention therefrom. There was hope that the two pandas would produce at least one heir and increase their population by 50 percent. The animals continued to disappoint. Considered from the panda point of view, the constant public leering could not have helped. Panda performance anxiety.

In contrast, to my mind the coverage of crime legitimately consumed considerable resources as a valid staple of local news, in terms of public safety and interest. We were so avid in pursuit of crime news that we upset D.C. Police Chief Wilson. He wrote me a letter saying that he understood our need for news and getting the facts right, but was unsettled by the number of times our reporters called him in the dead of night to get information they could have acquired earlier or from someone else in the department. "As a rule of thumb, Harry," he wrote, "I think your reporters should not wake me and my family for a story unless they think it's important enough to wake you and your family." This was a modest and appropriate solution.

Beginning in the summer of 1973, another major story occupied the Metro staff that had implications for what was happening in Watergate, as a new scandal increasingly involved the White House. In August, Richard Cohen, our top Maryland reporter at the time, and Bernstein reported that Vice President Spiro Agnew was being investigated for taking kickbacks while he was governor of Maryland. We deployed eight reporters to cover this story under the capable direction of Maryland editor Irna Moore. Carl continued to contribute memos as did others on the staff not working on Watergate almost full time.

As the investigation advanced and federal investigators dug deep into corruption in Maryland politics, Agnew, who had insisted for months that he was innocent, resigned on October 10, 1973. A court later revealed that Agnew had received an envelope containing bribe money in the vice president's office in the White House. Added to Watergate, which was still being investigated when Agnew stepped down, the vice president's disgrace could be read as a portent of even worse things to come.

On the other hand, when a friend asked me whether I thought Nixon would be impeached, I replied, no way. I did not think the political system would tolerate the removal of both vice president and president, an assessment soon enough contradicted.

June 1973 wrapped up with John Dean concluding five days of testimony before the televised hearings of the Senate Select Committee at which he fingered Nixon. About two weeks later, John Mitchell, the former attorney general and Nixon campaign manager, came before the senators and a national TV audience for three days to defend himself and the president. The man who more than anyone personified the Nixon administration's vaunted law and order mantra was asked by Sam Dash, the committee's chief counsel, why his sworn words should be given credence when they contradicted testimony he had given under oath in a deposition the year before.

The back and forth testimony that pitted Dean against his former White House colleagues reached a decisive point in the middle of the month. It was then than Woodward learned from contacts on the Senate Watergate Committee of the voice-activated taping system that Nixon had secretly installed in the Oval Office—as well as in other places including the cabinet room and Camp David. This was done a couple of years earlier. The device in the cabinet room could be shut off with a switch. The others were not set up that way. The system's existence was, according to Woodward, so secret that many of the president's top aides did not know of it. For me, it did not seem odd for a president to require a verbatim record of talks he was having with, say, a foreign leader or other important person, where the taking of notes might not serve the occasion or the flow of the conversation. The only striking aspect of the Nixon taping system to me was its voice activation. Five other presidents before Nixon had secret recording systems—Franklin Roosevelt, Harry Truman, Dwight Eisenhower, John Kennedy, and Lyndon Johnson—but they were used much less and had to be manually triggered to record. Nixon logged 3,700 hours of conversations compared to Johnson's 850 hours and Kennedy's 264 hours.

Shortly after Woodward alerted us, testimony about Nixon's elaborate recording system was delivered to the committee. The secret tapes, if they had functioned as intended and had not been tampered with, could provide conclusive evidence of "what the president knew and when he knew it," in the evocative locution of Senator Howard Baker of Tennessee, the ranking Republican on the committee. Because Nixon was anything but stupid, reliance on a voice-activated system was an act of supreme hubris—unless he had nothing to hide.

The effect of the revelation by former White House aide Alexander Butterfield was that the Senate committee, as well as special prosecutor Archibald Cox, subpoenaed the tapes. Nixon's steadfast refusal to turn them over resulted in a historic showdown in the Supreme Court. Afterward, I concluded that Nixon set up the system to assist him in writing his memoirs in retirement. Haldeman, in a tell-all book written after he and Nixon had severed their relationship, wrote that Nixon had the taping system installed for that reason, but also so the president could have a record of what his own advisers had told him when. This especially applied to Henry Kissinger, although ostensibly the two were close.

John Ehrlichman ended the month of June 1973 undergoing five days of strenuous questioning. The president's men sought to maintain the wall of deniability around the complicit Nixon. Former chief of staff Haldeman followed, doing his utmost to pile the blame on Dean. The hearings confounded the president, who felt himself beleaguered by hearsay and innuendo as the evidence against him mounted. His popularity plunged in the polls and the first impeachment resolution was introduced in the House of Representatives. It was premature but prognostic.

In August, Woodstein delivered a big story expanding Nixonian wrongdoing as they unearthed sixteen additional White House investigations ordered against perceived enemies, including the Smothers Brothers, popular liberal entertainers, and the producer of an anti-Nixon film. It also encompassed a probe to undermine Senator Ted Kennedy through his Chappaquiddick incident. They followed up a couple of weeks later revealing that the White House used not only the FBI, the Secret Service, and the Internal Revenue Service to spy on political rivals, but it also tapped the resources of the justice, commerce, defense, and interior departments.

Watergate was a story with international appeal, as Annie and I learned in August 1973 during a tour of England and Wales. We did this on the money Annie earned as a nursery school teacher, and it was her treat for our twentieth wedding anniversary. The trip was made possible by Annie's mother, who came from New York to stay with the girls and the obstreperous mutt we had adopted from a pound and hoped against all odds to civilize. In London we rented a shift car (the only kind then readily available) that had extremely squeaky brakes. When we drove into a small town we made disturbing noises. Driving on the left side of the road proved difficult to master, especially when navigating roundabouts. Many an exasperated British driver shook a fist at us for failing to observe the (unnatural) rules of the road.

We spent most of our time outside of London. We stayed at bed and breakfasts and thatch-roofed guest houses. One was across the road from the ruins of a castle once occupied by Henry VIII. We became acquainted with the ritual of an English tea, the likes of which is not rivaled anywhere, and enjoyed the varieties of cakes. We traipsed through the Lake District and thought of Wordsworth. We met up with our friends Victor Zorza and his wife Rosemary. They took us to mansions where she made the point that all the opulence was constructed within a society that hanged a man for poaching a rabbit. In Llandudno, Wales, we ran across a theater and decided to get tickets at the last moment. Hoping to impress the man in the ticket booth, I handed him my business card in the expectation that would buy us good seats. We wound up sitting in the last row in the balcony and thoroughly enjoyed the play, not least for the fact that the ticket seller had a prominent role in the performance. We met a lot of English folks and had the best of times with them and appreciated their outstanding hospitality wherever we turned. At one stop, I received a phone call from the London office, which I took in the hall of the residence. The other guests could hear me talking and learned that I was with *The Washington Post*. They were quite aware of the *Post*'s role in exposing the Watergate scandal. They were not only glad to meet me but practically cheered our Watergate work. Some asked for my autograph. One man said, "Our chaps here do the same kind of corrupt things, but no one calls them to account." That differed from what I encountered at the beginning of our tour in London when I appeared on a radio panel with British journalists. To a man they regarded Watergate as an unnecessary and destructive distraction for a great nation. They thought the American press was making too much out of stuff that all governments routinely did. The contrast from what we heard from ordinary people and the commentariat was striking and instructive.

Back in the office, I studied a memo from Len Downie outlining the problems that predated my departure and had worsened in my three weeks abroad. Most important was that the editing structure set up at the District operation was led by people promoted out of their experience level because Sussman was tied up with Watergate and Downie was doing two jobs, his and mine. The people we threw into the breach needed more time in grade to learn how to deal with reporters and especially how to mentor the inexperienced ones who we believed had potential but needed tending.

As avidly as the presidential tapes were pursued through the courts and by investigators, Nixon adamantly maintained he would not turn them over under the doctrines of executive privilege and separation of powers. He did dangle offers of summarizing or making available certain tapes under restricted conditions. All these efforts failed to deflect the path to a constitutional confrontation. The constitutional showdown loomed on October 20, when President Nixon discharged special prosecutor Archibald Cox, who had refused his orders to stop pursuing the tapes in the courts. Nixon accepted the resignations of his Attorney General Elliot Richardson and his Deputy A.G. William Ruckelshaus, each of whom in turn refused to fire Cox. Republicans in the House, where impeachment proceedings would have to be initiated, told the president they would not support him unless he gave the tapes to the court. These events decisively moved the coverage of Watergate into the bailiwick of the National desk.

Metro's major contribution during that momentous month had begun the preceding June. Back then, I assigned Ron Kessler to look into Nixon's finances in the wake of Government Accountability Office reports on lavish spending of public funds on the president's personal homes in San Clemente, California, and Key Biscayne, Florida. Kessler worked for months on the project. He had to rewrite articles in the series more than once because his reporting was connecting Nixon's finances to an alleged history of shady dealings. By the fall of 1973, I thought he had finally gotten the stories into good shape. I took the latest version to Simons and Bradlee. Bradlee continued to question the validity of the conclusions, which alleged that Nixon had intricate ties to the Teamsters and even the mob. Kessler kept working on revisions, not wanting his long months of reporting to go to waste. Howard Simons recommended that we no longer wait on the still-unfinished series (that was eventually scrapped) and publish one installment. It was about Nixon's friend Bebe Rebozo, a banker, who was alleged to have cashed $91,500 worth of stock in 1968 that an insurance investigator had told him was stolen. The story was published in October. Kessler relied on a deposition under oath given by the investigator. Rebozo denied he had been informed the stock was stolen. He sued the *Post* for libel. Rebozo was arguably a public personage and entitled to redress only if the article had been published in reckless disregard of the truth. The paper's defense was buttressed by questions I had written in the margin of the copy, which indicating careful editing. The case dragged on in the courts and was still underway five years later after I had left Washington for Albany. I was preparing to travel to Miami to testify when an out-of-court settlement was reached. Both sides agreed to donate a sum of money to a charity and that was it. Contrary to Republican charges throughout Watergate, the decision not to publish the Nixon finance investigation showed that the *Post* was not hunting for the presidential scalp. If the facts weren't sufficiently confirmed, the story was spiked.

Both President Nixon and his personal secretary made news in November 1973, when White House lawyers said two key tapes, of presidential conversations with John Mitchell and John Dean, did not exist. The disclosure was a bombshell. Woodstein followed with one of their four Page 1 contributions that month. It was a heads-up article that revealed that there were problems of "inaudibility" with some of the seven tapes the President had under great pressure agreed to release to the Federal District Court. Their White House sources were troubled that this would be another long-burning log feeding the flame of public suspicion. The next day Rose Mary Woods, Nixon's personal secretary, publicly confirmed Woodstein's scoop. Nixon added fuel to the fire by claiming he could not find one of the subpoenaed tapes. All this was prelude to the revelation of the renowned 18½ minutes of blank tape that could not be explained by the White House, but was surely perceived by the public as part of a cover-up. The month played out with an official explanation and Ms. Woods took the fall. She said she had erased the 18½ minutes accidentally.

The appointment by Nixon of a successor to the special prosecutor he fired made clear that the conflict over the tapes would not be resolved on the president's terms. Leon Jaworski was hired with a Nixon commitment not to again exercise his claimed right to fire this presidential appointee without the agreement of the leadership of the Senate and House as well as the top Democrat and Republican on the House and Senate Judiciary Committees.

During this time of Sturm und Drang, I had been invited to speak at the convention of the Associated Press Managing Editors in Orlando, Florida. I belonged to the organization but had not planned to attend the meeting in November because of the demands of work. Still, I could hardly turn down the opportunity to tell the "how-we-covered-Watergate" story to our newspaper colleagues. More than any other audience, these editors would comprehend the range of challenges we had to overcome. I gave the convention as detailed an accounting as time and good reason allowed. It was a well-received presentation, as my mail afterward showed. The best tribute came after I ended my talk, when Seymour Topping, a top editor at *The New York Times*, rose to say that he had not heard a better description of a newspaper at work. (Many years later, when he was the administrator for the Pulitzer Prizes and I was editor in

Albany, I was twice chosen as a juror. In all, I served on four juries over the years. Pulitzer Jury service is deemed a high honor in the newspaper trade).

President Nixon was a featured guest at that convention, where he agreed to participate in an hour-long question-and-answer session. I took Woodward to lunch before leaving for Orlando to pump him for what to ask the president, if I was given the chance. We went over a number of possibilities, but what Bob wanted me to ask was what he was working on. This involved Donald Nixon, the president's brother, and Donald's possible connection to some sleazy schemes. The subject had been broached in September in the *Post* and unconvincingly explained by the White House as relating to the protection of the First Family. Although I preferred to ask whether any president has the constitutional authority to order others to break the law in the name of national security, I considered that my obligation was to help Woodward and to ask the question he suggested. Deep into the televised press conference, I finally had a chance to leap out of my seat to seize the microphone.

"Mister President, Harry Rosenfeld of *The Washington Post*. Sir, there have been reports that the Secret Service was asked at your direction or authorization to tap the telephone of your brother, Donald Nixon. Is this true, sir, and if so, why?"

The president answered, "That, of course, is a question that has been commented on before; it will not take long to respond to it. The Secret Service maintain a surveillance. They did so for security reasons, and my brother was aware of it.

"And, may I say to my friend from *The Washington Post*, I like your sports page."

Rosenfeld: "Thank you, Mr. President."

Nixon: "Be sure Povich isn't paid too much for what I just said then."

When I attempted to follow up, I found my microphone had been turned off. The White House staff had not managed to screen who got to ask questions, but they had the ability to cut me off. Although I was silenced, Nixon came under strenuous questioning, memorably responding to the tenor of the inquiries by declaring, "I am not a crook," guaranteeing that would be the front page headline across the country. Of course, he lied about that as well, if a crook is defined as someone who breaks the law.

As bad as things looked for Nixon toward the end of 1973, with Gallup polls warning of a strong anti-Republican tide in the elections the following year, the Southern Republican Conference strongly defended the president. They also laughed at a joke that was making the rounds in the House cloakroom. "What we got to do," it went, "is get crime out of the White House and back into the streets where it belongs."

In early 1974 a former colleague at the *Herald Tribune* phoned me. He was an Australian correspondent who used the facilities of the *Herald Tribune* News Service as his base office as long as the paper survived. Over the years many different reporters had the job and I became friendly with all of them. The call was a request to go to dinner with his boss who was visiting from London. It was Rupert Murdoch. Annie was invited, as was Mrs. Murdoch. We had a fine dinner that Murdoch hosted and afterward we took our hosts to the cabaret where Mark Russell performed his deft satire of Washington's sacred cows and cherished rites. If Murdoch had a purpose in mind, as was likely, it was left for me to speculate what it might have been. He asked a few questions about Watergate and I certainly was not going to share any insider information even with such an eminence in our business. If, on the other hand, he was sizing me up for some job I obviously failed the screening, for nothing ever came of it. At least I can say that the media mogul bought me lunch and dinner— albeit many years apart.

For Howard Hunt, 1974 brought release from prison while his sentence was under appeal, and three Watergate burglars were granted parole. The prosecutor who helped to jail them, Earl Silbert, was promoted to interim United States Attorney for D.C. The 18½ minute erasure of a discussion between the president and his chief of staff in the June 20, 1972, tape was the focus of unease among congressional Republicans. The president insisted that he would serve out his term—and reiterated it in his State of the Union address at January's end, saying "one year of Watergate is enough." The members of the House and Senate applauded him thirty-three times and twice rose to their feet to do so.

Nevertheless, actions spoke louder than applause.

In February 1974, the House Judiciary Committee voted unanimously, followed by a House vote of 410 to 4, to proceed with its impeachment inquiry. Special Prosecutor Jaworski publicly contradicted President Nixon's claim that he had received all the information that was required and Nixon refused to provide more tapes and documents. Herbert Kalmbach, Nixon's personal lawyer and frequent bag man, pleaded guilty to raising millions and bartering ambassadorships as Woodstein reported that about $6 million had been collected for a secret political fund. At this juncture the Senate Watergate Committee, after having postponed reopening public hearings several times, decided not to hold any more sessions. This action cleared the field for the House Judiciary Committee and the special prosecutor. The Justice Department stated that "a constitutional confrontation of the highest magnitude would ensue" if the president persisted in withholding evidence. On the last day of the month, Nixon's lawyers were trying to dig a moat around the president. They argued that impeachment could only occur for indictable crimes.

The slow wheels of justice took another turn in March 1974, when a federal grand jury indicted seven top Nixon aides, including Haldeman, Ehrlichman, Mitchell, and Charles Colson, the former special counsel, for covering up Watergate. The grand jury also provided Judge Sirica with a secret report on Nixon's role that Woodstein reported was obstruction of justice. These revelations accelerated the impeachment momentum.

Meanwhile, indictments from another federal grand jury descended on Ehrlichman, Colson, and Liddy and three of the Cuban burglars for the break-in at Daniel Ellsberg's psychiatrist's office. In response, Nixon toured the nation seeking friendly audiences at which he cast himself as the victim. He told the loyalists that "I will not be party to the destruction of the presidency. . . . Resignation is the easy way out."

The trees in the forest kept falling in April as Dwight Chapin, Nixon's former appointments secretary, was convicted of lying about his ties to Donald Segretti, the political saboteur. The House Judiciary Committee on April 11, 1974, subpoenaed Nixon to hand over forty-two presidential tapes, a historic assertion of constitutional powers. The committee gave him two weeks to comply. Good news for Nixon in the month came when a federal jury in New York acquitted John Mitchell and Maurice Stans of all counts of conspiracy, obstruction of justice, and perjury in the matter of a secret $200,000 contribution made by Robert L. Vesco, a notorious financier then on the lam. After initially reaching a majority calling for conviction, the jurors changed their minds when they doubted the credibility of the former Nixon associates who had a personal stake in testifying against the president.

Having missed the stated deadline, Nixon told a national TV audience that he would release edited transcripts to the judiciary committee in place of the tapes. These numbered 1,308 pages. It was, Woodstein reported, an attempt to blur the focus of the Watergate probes, and Nixon drew a line in the sand. The tactic was intended to bolster Republican and public support while painting the Democrats as implacable partisans. The offer was immediately rejected by the Democrats and formally seconded in a largely party line vote by the House Judiciary Committee.

In April, the Newspaper Guild struck the *Post* and began a labor action that it asserted withheld the "excellence" of its reporter and editor contributions to the paper. The union did not establish a picket line. This meant that the craft unions that produced the newspaper, such as the printers and press operators, could come to work. The result was a newspaper in name, even in fact, but it was clearly not *The Washington Post*. The National, Business, and Style desks could rely on wire copy to fill their pages, but for Metro that was not possible.

For sixteen days, union-exempt managers and staffers worked extremely long hours, with perhaps one day off a week. My secretary Maureen Joyce sat by my side and worked the telephones as I filled the role of editor for the District, Virginia, and Maryland desks, whose editors were among those on strike. To write stories we had the help of Simons, Bradlee, and Geyelin as well as assistance from the business side of the *Post*. These good helpers had journalistic exposure in college or high school and some lacked even that rudimentary knowledge. They performed admirably and saved us from disaster.

We fleshed out small developments with information obtained from our library files. We listened to the radio for breaking news and used every piece of the skimpy Associated Press copy that emanated from our metropolitan area. One copy editor handled columns of text and headlines that exceeded by far what one person normally did. One day, Maureen took a phone call from a reader who complained that one of his favorite local features was missing. When told the reason was that the paper was on strike, he confessed he had not noticed.

The irony of the strike was that when it occurred, the *Post* was paying the highest wages in the nation. I urged Katharine Graham to send each striker the factual details of the dispute, including accurate wage and benefit figures. I cautioned that such a communication should not have the faintest whiff of propaganda about it, for that would undermine its credibility. Management issued such a statement and its factuality countered the distortions that the union leadership presented its members. In the end, the strike petered out and the reporters and editors, their "excellence" in tow, came back to work where they should have been all along, had they weighed the facts rationally. Not only were the strikers well compensated, they worked in a modern office with new furniture and fine art hanging on the walls.

The rewards of Watergate did not let up. In April 1974 I was contacted by my old boss, the former editor of the *Herald Tribune* News Service. Keith Spalding, now the president of Franklin and Marshall College in Lancaster, Pennsylvania, asked me to help persuade Bradlee to accept his invitation to deliver the commencement address and receive an honorary degree.

It wasn't hard for me to convince Bradlee, and Keith asked that I provide intimate biographical information for the citation. My assessment noted the characteristics that made Ben a great editor. I wrote: "At The *Post*, Bradlee is clearly the person who leads the charge. He blows the bugle and he is first over the top." He was a difficult man to sum up in a few words. I added:

> First he has guts. That doesn't mean he is foolish, it means that he can figure out the dangers ahead and if the cause is right—as in the Pentagon Papers or Watergate—he moves forward defying the risks.
>
> Second, he is smart. He has wide understanding of many things and is comfortable with the disparate political, social and intellectual issues of our times.
>
> Third, he has stamina. He keeps going under pressure, works around the clock if it's called for. . . . He is capable of the transcendent gesture that cuts through the fatty tissue of corporate tradition to get to the bony truth. . . . If I were a college, I'd give him an honorary degree, too.

Ben wanted Annie and me to accompany him and Sally Quinn to Lancaster for the ceremony. The college sent a limousine so the four of us were close company for the two-hour drive each way. It could have been awkward and tiresome for us all. Instead, it turned out to be rather pleasant.

On commencement day, rain forced the ceremony indoors. Ben was the only one in the academic procession whose head was uncovered when he was summoned to receive his honor and give his talk. As he rose to speak, his eyes found me sitting in the audience and he nodded in evident acknowledgment of the sentiments I had provided for the citation. His short response to his doctorate was an evocation of what he was, a courageous and committed editor. He received a sustained standing ovation from the faculty, graduates, their parents, and friends.

Woodstein contributed eight important articles during May. Their coverage focused on comparison of the edited transcripts the president first offered to the actual tapes, which fixed "expletive deleted" into the national lexicon. Carl and Bob reported many glaring inconsistencies with what Nixon had stated previously as well as in repeated misrepresentation by the White House about what the tapes upon close examination in fact contained. Informed sources told them that there were a series of mysterious gaps in the tapes themselves. The National staff demonstrated its dominance of the story by producing seventy Watergate and related front-page stories that month, and Metro, apart from Woodstein, added twelve.

The president's best-laid plans misfired as Republican disgust with the Nixon presidency built through the month as close scrutiny of the actual tapes revealed discussions of payoffs. Nixon's explicit threats to harm the *Post*'s TV ownership in retaliation for its Watergate coverage had been cut out of the edited transcript. There were reports of ethnic slurs uttered by the president on the tapes. In growing numbers, Republican officeholders called on Nixon to step down. Senator Barry Goldwater, Republican of Arizona, by stating his belief that Nixon would resign if he was impeached kept Republican calls for resignation somewhat in check. The House Judiciary Committee formally opened impeachment hearings as it subpoenaed forty-five more tapes. Dwight Chapin, the president's appointment secretary, was sentenced to ten to thirty months in prison for perjury and his former deputy campaign director, Jeb Magruder, got ten to forty-eight months.

National continued to expand its coverage role as other matters came to the fore in the lead-up to impeachment, including putative offenses that were related but not closely tied to the Watergate break-in and cover-up. These included various trials connected to the Pentagon Papers, illegal campaign contributions by Robert Vesco, the fugitive financier, and Howard Hughes, the business mogul. Metro's story count was substantial in some months, less so in others, but always outnumbered by National, even as the Senate and House hearings, as well as other legal maneuvers aimed at getting Nixon to give up the tapes, kept Watergate and its byproducts on the nation's front pages. Nonetheless, a survey of the Senate found that a majority was not for conviction of the president for "high crimes and misdemeanors" at that time, although by a reduced margin. Senator Goldwater's bold voice spoke out on behalf of the president's cause. He wanted *The Washington Post* to face criminal prosecution for publishing leaks of confidential FBI memos.

Charles Colson's unexpected guilty plea to one felony in a bargain with prosecutors that dropped other charges discomfited the White House, Woodstein reported. Nixon's people were worried about what information Colson was prepared to give up in exchange for leniency. Colson received one to three years, the stiffest sentence up to that time. Technical experts who examined the 18½ minute gap in the Nixon tapes contradicted White House claims that it was the result of a faulty recording machine. The erasure was deliberate, the experts concluded.

Woodstein's best scoop of June (among several) came in their report that the Watergate grand jury had earlier voted to name the president as an unindicted co-conspirator in the Watergate cover-up. With troubles mounting, President Nixon did what presidents usually do when under heavy political pressure at home. He went abroad. Nixon visited Arab countries and Israel, stopped over in Vienna, and after a brief stay in Washington returned to Europe at the end of June to meet with Soviet President Leonid Brezhnev. Back home, Nixon's lawyer, Herbert Kalmbach, got six to eighteen months for his part in raising illegal money for congressional candidates.

The struggle over the release of the tapes between the White House on one side and the courts, the special prosecutor, and the Congressional committees on the other was not a successful standoff for the president. Bit by little bit, in addition to edited transcripts and some tapes, Nixon tactically gave up more. This made public additional admissions of wrongdoings. Meanwhile, in July it was revealed that Ehrlichman had told the Senate select committee staff that he had pressed the IRS to investigate the tax returns of Democratic Party Chairman Lawrence O'Brien while that agency was being pressured not to pursue Nixon's buddy Rebozo. A federal court jury found Ehrlichman guilty on charges relating to the Ellsberg break-in, as were Liddy and the three Cubans. The House Judiciary Committee probe found that two of Nixon's secretaries of the treasury threatened resignation over attempts to use the IRS against political enemies.

The Senate Watergate Committee issued its final report, documenting improper and illegal activities and proposing major reforms to prevent a repetition of the Watergate scandal. The committee's chairman asserted: "The presidential aides who perpetrated Watergate . . . were instigated by a lust for political power itself." The House Judiciary Committee cleared the path toward impeachment, laying out exhaustive documentation gathered over eleven weeks of hearings. Seven articles of impeachment were proposed. Their essence was that Nixon "brought disgrace and disrespect to the office of the presidency, failed to honor the Constitution of the United States and the laws enacted thereunder, imperiled the civil liberties of the American people, and attempted to undermine the legislative and judicial branches of government, thereby jeopardizing the constitutional system of government in which the people of the United States have placed their trust." In the historic debate that followed, the committee in bipartisan votes approved three articles, discarding issues that were important but tangential.

John Dean, the man who declined the role of scapegoat and became Nixon's accuser-in-chief, was sentenced to one to four years for his crimes.

At a time when only fourteen out of 187 Republican House members opposed removing the president from office, the plan was for the full House to begin the impeachment debate on August 19. In diehard Republican hearts, hope still flickered that Nixon could be let off with no more than a censure.

20

Nixon's Final Hours

The no longer avoidable denouement unfolded when the Supreme Court, in a unanimous decision, instructed the president to surrender sixty-four tapes to U.S. District Court Judge Sirica for use by the special prosecutor in the trials of Nixon's chief aides. Days later, when those tapes were handed over, the president confessed to withholding incriminating information from the judiciary committee. The smoking gun tape was recorded on June 23, 1972, six days after the Watergate burglary. On it, Nixon explicitly ordered Haldeman to deploy the FBI and the CIA to frustrate the investigations that were beginning to bear early fruit. This recording answered in full Senator Baker's succinct question about what the president knew and when he knew it. Enough and right away, the tape showed.

At this point late in the constitutional standoff between Congress and the president, Senator Goldwater's steadfast defense of Nixon finally gave way. In light of the damaging revelations, the senator told his bloc of supporters that he favored resignation. On August 8, Richard Milhous Nixon announced his resignation as of noon on the following day, thus avoiding the humiliation of certain impeachment.

It was a solemn moment in the life of the nation. The change in leadership took place with no soldiers with fixed bayonets in the streets to keep civil order. The nation accepted the departure of its disgraced president and welcomed his successor peacefully. There was no rioting as for the first time in history the nation's president resigned his office. By this demonstration of national cohesion alone, America deserves to be hailed as a shining example to other nations.

It was not a time for gloating. For me, as for everyone at the *Post*, I'm sure, it was the end of a very long road, the most momentous event that Watergate had shaped. I remembered the bitter assaults on our investigative reporting and its confidential sources, and the generally hostile reaction from the public, as well as caviling from in-house colleagues. I came to recognize our perseverance in the face of opposition as the objective lesson for newspaper women and men.

Over the years, I have been questioned about whether National could have handled Watergate had the story been its responsibility. My polite answer has been, "Of course." In my heart, I was never so certain. National had the advantages—and the deficits—that come with experience covering the three branches of the federal government. The National editors and reporters knew their way around political Washington. They had very good sources among officialdom. On the other hand, they had perhaps grown too comfortable and close to those sources. They liked their lifestyle, going home in the evening or to a cocktail reception where they would consort with the influential people they covered. I suspected they would not have been inclined to devote the endless hours or maintain the single-minded pursuit of the story with Woodstein's energy. Most likely, National would have produced an extensive, very handsome, and well-written package for the Sunday paper—and then moved on, distracted by another issue. This may be ungenerous, but I believe it is more on the mark than the notion that they would have persevered through the long period of stonewalling that Woodstein managed with sustained persistence to overcome.

To my mind, two great failings afflict journalists. One is to know too little and thereby produce inaccurate and distorted reportage. The other is to know too much, and thereby overlook truth and alternatives to conventional wisdom. In many ways, the latter is arguably more dangerous than the former. A reporter too long steeped in one assignment gains the advantage of comprehension at the risk of being co-opted by the perspectives of those he or she is charged with critically observing. In other words, the danger lies in reporters coming to see the world through the eyes of those they are covering, and thus tending to slight any viewpoints that differ.

Watergate deserves a summing up. In the end, what does it mean? In speeches over the years I have described it essentially as the "arrogance of power." From the first moments of his presidency, Richard Nixon unleashed or tried to unleash the powers of the federal government against persons and groups he deemed his enemies. In his paranoia he regarded opponents as enemies. The press as a group (with some exceptions) was so classified. While his aides sometimes deflected his inner rages, on too many occasions they were willing executors of his disordered obsessions. Congressional investigations disclosed that Nixon felt himself thwarted, and that the whole world conspired against him. That led to clandestine operations in which numerous laws and constitutional rights were routinely violated at the behest of a lawyer fully knowledgeable about those laws and rights. This made his criminal intent all the more grave. It would not surprise me if most or maybe all presidents at one time or another are tempted to resort to some of these same abuses of power. No other president has as yet been shown to have committed anything approximating the range of Nixon's offenses. The very temptation provided by such power cries out for a vigilant press—and a public that is skeptical and paying attention—to hold people in high office to the professed and accepted standards. In this framework, *The Washington Post* earned its Gold Medal for Public Service and Woodstein merited the accolades that have come to them, along with the others on Metro and later on National, who worked with dedication to expose this "cancer on the presidency." Under resolute publisher Katharine Graham, her *Post* staff created a model standard for journalism and validated the aims of the First Amendment.

Woodstein's book *All the President's Men* became a best-seller and the inspiration for a film that reached a wide audience. During this time, Carl and Bob were busy traveling around the nation to promote their book with newspaper interviews and TV appearances. Woodstein attained a level of celebrity that enshrined them in journalistic lore. If their colleagues were jealous of their fame, I never heard anyone say so. There was wonder but no complaint about the money that blasted them way out of the universe of the working press. Who am I to judge whether the report that Carl became friends with Elizabeth Taylor is true in all its implications? In the longer term, Bob handled the vagaries of fame better than Carl. From my point of view, Carl overcame rough patches in his personal and professional life and hung in there to dig himself out of often self-inflicted difficulties. After all, he was always a smart kid.

21

New Assignment

After Nixon resigned, I was vacationing that August with my family on Cape Cod when Ben Bradlee phoned to ask me to fly to Washington to meet with him and Howard Simons. The confidential meeting would be held over lunch in Bradlee's apartment in the Watergate complex. Typical of Bradlee's need for instant gratification, he could not wait for me to finish our family holiday. The purpose of the summons was to discuss their plans for shifting editors. At the meeting, it was decided that I would take over from Dick Harwood as AME/National. Dick would head off to New Jersey to edit the *Trenton Times*, recently purchased by The Washington Post Co. Bradlee had offered me that assignment and I had turned him down, much to his disappointment. "I've been to Trenton and have no desire to return," I told him. My previous exposure to that tired city had come when I was in basic training at nearby Fort Dix.

Although I had been pondering what might be next for me, I had not asked for the National job. I was in my fifth year as head of Metro and would not be content to go on forever in that role. National had not been one of the possibilities I considered, because Harwood was probably Bradlee's favorite for any job in the place. My reservations, which increased when I had more time to reflect, gave way to Bradlee wanting me for the assignment. Having turned him down for the Trenton job, I did not relish courting his certain displeasure so soon again by saying no to National.

The assignment was a logical move for me. There was one major sticking point. In order to facilitate the changes, Peter Silberman, who was Harwood's No. 2 and popular with the National staffers, needed to be provided a soft landing. While he was deemed not suitable to become the AME/National (Harwood later said to me, "There's a difference between Silberman on tap and Silberman on top") Peter was penciled in by Bradlee and Simons to take over my job and title at Metro. Although Peter was a friend whose work I admired, along with his dry wit, I objected. When they tried to talk me out of my resistance I insisted that I could not take the job unless Len Downie succeeded me at Metro. To my mind, he had earned the promotion through his hard and smart work as my longest-tenured deputy.

At the luncheon I made a further stipulation, the kind that job applicants often pose for effect but which I meant because of the rocky history of previous National editors and other problems I might have to face. I asked Bradlee and Simons to evaluate my work periodically so that I would know whether I was fulfilling their expectations. If problems arose, I could correct course. They assured me they would provide such reviews. They never did, not once. Thinking that silence was tacit approval of my performance, I foolishly did not press them on the matter.

After lunch, Howie and I walked along the banks of the Potomac discussing salary and other practical matters. Later in the afternoon I flew back to my family, having departed as AME/Metro and returning as AME/National-designate. Bradlee, in his devotion to three-cushion billiard shots, quickly found a spot for Silberman. The story goes that one day he opened the door to the office of Hobart Rowen, AME/Financial, stuck his head in and simply said, "Bart, I'm going to need your title." Rowen was a financial columnist as well as a top editor and he would join National as chief economic editor and columnist.

As I reflected on what the future at National would hold for me, the first matter to consider was that National editors under Bradlee did not last long, not even his friends. Second was the reality that National was Bradlee's bailiwick, his best love. His scrutiny would be intense and his interference certain and frequent. In this area he had especially good connections and sources (a real benefit) and the most definite ideas (not categorically a benefit). I was leaving myself open to steady second guessing.

A third reason for caution was the fact that I was coming to take command of National after leading a Metro staff that had beaten it on the biggest national story, if not of all time, certainly in the history of the *Post*. Residual resentment would be natural from a staff that collectively constituted the more senior reporters and writers, many with reputations as the best of breed in their specialties. Backing up my assessment was National's initial denigration of our Watergate work. Also, I suspected that some National staffers were inclined to coast because they had already arrived. Skimpy in their reporting (been there; done that) there was a disposition to rely on personal perspective in place of the type of shoe-leather reporting I championed at Metro. It appeared that some of these writers were more content commentating for a weekly polemical journal than reporting for a daily newspaper that was then still focused on being the major bearer of breaking news to its readership.

At least I was going into the new assignment with my eyes wide open.

To fill the National Editor job, the No. 2 position, I thought long and hard before settling on Lee Lescaze, who was then Foreign Editor. He welcomed my invitation. I had known and admired Lee from my first days at the *Post*. We had worked well together on the foreign desk. He had sound news judgment and had demonstrated his reportorial and writing skills. His temperament differed from mine. Lee was calm and his modulated voice was never raised in criticism or praise. He embodied the low-keyed WASPy virtues and its manners. I thought that those National staffers uncomfortable with me would be more at ease with Lee.

Furthermore, I thought Lee had a good shot at one of the two top newsroom editorships. My own hopes for moving up had faded, especially after Howard Simons on more than one occasion assured me I would never make it. Howard's assessment did not upset me. For one thing, Howard was not inclined to encourage possible competitors for his job. In any event, it would not be his call. More importantly, Simons was a first-rate Managing Editor and we were both in our mid-forties at the time. There was no chance that I would displace him nor did I aspire to do so as long as he was upright and taking nourishment. Bradlee's Executive Editor position was completely off the charts of attainability. He and Mrs. Graham were bonded. I understood that opportunity for promotion depended on other prospects presenting themselves, such as either Bradlee or Simons leaving of their own accord, which was highly unlikely. Most probably, I would age out with them.

On the other hand, a tour as the National No. 2 would be another stepping stone for Lee. He was ten years my junior and therefore of a generation that would be ready to take over when the incumbent leadership retired.

With Lee on board, that was as promising a start as I could make given my catalogue of concerns. Bob Kaiser, then doing a fellowship at Duke University, wrote that "there are a couple of old members of your fan club down here in Norf' Carolina who are mightily pleased this morning [about the published announcement on 9/11/74]. You earned it, needless to say, but that didn't mean you'd get it. The fact that you did is a tribute to all concerned, but particularly to you." Sig Harrison, who had left the *Post* to take a position with the Carnegie Endowment for International Peace, wrote: "You know how I feel about you and you know how I felt about Dick, so it goes without saying that the latest musical chairs news was very musical indeed."

From the beginning there were challenges that blindsided me. For instance, I was surprised to learn that Sanford Ungar had resigned in Harwood's last days to work for the *Atlantic Monthly* magazine. I had hired him on Metro and he had moved to National to cover the Justice Department. He was a diligent and savvy reporter with whom I had a great working relationship. And he was only one of the many National staffers that would turn up missing during my tour. Bradlee and Simons had not told me about Sandy's departure (although Simons forced it), nor did they share with me commitments for leaves of absence that they had made with many reporters. It was mismanagement for the top editors to permit so many key people to go off at overlapping times, for various durations but some for as much as a year or more.

Among those off the playing field were Morton Mintz, who scrutinized the drug industry from the consumer's point of view and also covered issues of corporate misbehavior and industrial safety. He was well known for his watchdog journalism. Lou Cannon was off writing a book about Ronald Reagan's years as California governor. Larry Stern, a former National editor, embarked on a personal writing project. Reporter Bill Chapman was also on leave that first year. Woodward and Bernstein, once they were assigned to National, were largely preoccupied with getting the manuscript of their second book, *The Final Days*, into shape. Even when present, they functioned largely in conformity with their whims, a status their Watergate success had bestowed on them.

Somewhat later, William Greider, among the best writers on the *Post* and one of the most penetrating intellects in journalism, went off to the French countryside to write a book. His completed manuscript was lost shortly before his return to the United States. Another brilliant writer and thinker, Haynes Johnson, also had leave. Our West Coast correspondent, Leroy Aarons, worked full time on a film script.

The bottom line was that during my editorship too many of the National staff were working on personal projects. It meant that we had to integrate Metro reporters. Talented and ambitious as they were, they lacked the experience and background that would distinguish their work from the start and permit the National staff to make its mark. The irony was that in the 1974 Pugwash, which took place in January, there was unanimous agreement that personal leaves should be sharply limited, say one per department per year. So much for the endurance of Pugwash decisions.

If all these leaves of absence were intended to refresh the staff, they should have been offered to Metro, less so to National. And if they were symptomatic of a post-Watergate letdown, it is hard to understand why National staffers should have been particularly afflicted. Someone else did the heavy lifting, and National got to go on R&R.

To quote a favorite poet, A. E. Housman:

> The world, it was the old world yet,
> I was I, my things were wet,
> And nothing now remained to do
> But begin the game anew.

The new game was soon underway. Bradlee, it was understood, approached national coverage in terms of personalities, of winners and losers, the ones who were in and the ones who were out, and the perpetual shifts and fluctuations among those wielding power. It fascinated him and he soaked up tidbits, hints, rumors, and facts—anything that fed his passionate interests. My own view, which I found was shared by others on the National staff, was inclined to systemic coverage, to try to find out how ably government and its agencies performed by measuring them against their mandates and established regulations. The advent of the computer and data-driven reporting made this approach ever more plausible. These efforts at detailed data analysis were derided by Bradlee, who wanted to learn the "skinny." Such dichotomy pretty much assured trouble.

The idea to launch a project to examine how the congressional committee system functioned, how staffers were deployed, and how large sums of taxpayer money were being spent, was suggested by

Walter Pincus, a former and future *Post* reporter. He proposed collaboration between the *New Republic* magazine, of which he then was the Managing Editor, and the *Post*, with the paper providing the essential technology. Pincus was well acquainted with the issue, having explored the subject a dozen years earlier for the *Saturday Evening Post* magazine. Now he needed help to do a comprehensive payroll analysis.

Steve Isaacs was assigned to look into the proposal. Soon he came back with an intriguing memo outlining the likely abuses and a battle plan that would expose in detail what was transpiring in the congressional committees. This involved enlisting the paper's technical expertise with the newly arrived computers to do research much faster and more penetratingly than reporters could before computers. The Isaacs memo was enthusiastic and demonstrated his familiarity with the potential of the new technology. With the help of a researcher and a person from the paper's data processing department, Steve produced a series of articles, entitled "The Capitol Game," that laid bare how the Senate committee system exploited a steadily growing budget to misuse federal funds for personal or political benefits. Whereas in the Eighty-Third Congress of 1953–54, $8.7 million had been authorized for the committees, by the Ninety-Third Congress in 1963–64 it was up to $54.3 million. The potential for abuse would only increase as well.

Isaac's well-researched stories, published in February 1975, were limited to the Senate because it, unlike the House of Representatives, recorded the basic data required for computer analysis. The articles reported on how power in Congress often derived from the ability to control assigning staff and office space. It was an important series in the company town. For all that, it was hardly the kind of story to spin Bradlee's propeller. In many aspects it was innovative but deficiently sexy. Actual sexy Congressional abuses of power would come to light later in another *Post* exposé.

In December 1974, the Democratic Party held a midterm mini-convention in Kansas City. We dispatched six staffers, led by our premier political correspondent David Broder. An issue before the convention was a drive by women, blacks, and Latinos for the adoption of an affirmative action formula that would grant their constituencies representation more commensurate with their numbers in the party. Before the team of reporters left for the convention, we discussed coverage at a staff meeting. I asked that we keep in mind the general reader not beguiled by inside-the-Beltway machinations. I wanted our stories to explain the arguments over affirmative action that threatened to divide the Democratic Party. Broder afterward told me that was old news, but he said the opposite at our planning meeting. When our coverage did not explain in a straightforward way why the conservative wing of labor stood in opposition to the affirmative action recommendations, I asked for an article spelling out the conflict.

Shortly after the *Post* delegation's return to the newsroom from Kansas City, Broder sent me a memo that scathingly denounced my editing style and compared me unfavorably with National editors that had preceded me. He said these editors had also been demanding and also enlarged the political coverage. But they did not commit the crime that he charged was mine alone. He accused me of attempting to impose my judgment on the reporters, moreover reflecting my personal ideologies.

His four-page memo said that he was reminded of his bad old days at *The New York Times* that he had left behind. It was a thunderbolt. Broder was more than a top-line reporter. He was an eminence, the eight hundred–pound gorilla whose dominance was never to be regarded lightly. Barely into my third month as AME/National I had made an enemy of the most celebrated member of the staff. After a couple of days to review the articles published, I rejected his charges, most firmly the one that I told reporters what to write. I happily acknowledged that my editing style was to raise questions. All I wanted was consideration of those questions by reporters. I reminded him that he had made the point in our planning discussion that affirmative action was the crucial issue. His reportage made clear why the blacks, women, and Latinos wanted quotas but gave a mere twenty-five words to explaining the argument of those opposed. I did not deem that sufficient explication of the issue.

Obviously, the planning discussion I considered a dialogue he deemed a diktat. I wrote: "For you to come to make such a devastating accusation [of imposing my ideology on a story] without talking to me face to face suggests that something else must have aroused your hostility to me." My most serious complaint, and deepest disappointment, was that this wide gulf of his unhappiness had been permitted to grow to such proportions. In my response I did raise the possibility that he did not appreciate being edited, in fact corrected, by the new kid on the block. I asked him why he did not speak to me rather than send me a memo. In the future I suggested he do that and invited him to join me in working to overcome the communications gap between us.

From that time forward our relationship was correct but never warm, but then it hadn't been notably warm to begin with. When I wrote in my response that "something else" must have upset him, I had no idea what it might have been, for we had virtually no contact with each other before I joined National. In going over boxes of documents in preparation of this memoir, I came across an item involving his wife. Years earlier, Metro was doing a story on a Virginia political campaign and had a photographer take pictures. At the office, it was noticed that a principal figure in the photo was Mrs. Broder. Standard practice at the *Post* was not to publish a news item that might appear self-promoting. So a new photo session was set up with the campaign. We then heard from the campaign that our action in not publishing the photo of Broder's wife was a demonstration of sexism.

Broder's memo to me was private, as was my response. I never discussed it with Bradlee or Simons, but someone did. A few weeks later, Simons made a smiling reference to it, in a tone that suggested to me that he appreciated the difficulty of life with an eight hundred–pound gorilla.

There were postscripts to the Broder incident. While at Duke University, my daughter Amy took a course taught by Broder and they hit it off. After I had left the *Post* and Amy had graduated, she wanted to work a year before beginning law school. Broder hired her as a researcher for the book he was working on and later wrote her a letter of recommendation to the University of Chicago, where she wanted to pursue her law studies.

Many years after that, I had the opportunity to hire one of David's sons, Matthew, as a beginning reporter at the *Times Union*. He was doing very well when he decided to take a job at the New Haven, Connecticut, paper. In the end, Matthew left the business and our trade lost a good man. And I more than once picked David's brain about how to pursue political coverage in Albany. Without fail, he was helpful. In his own words, written much later on, he referred to our relationship as "an old friendship." I was delighted to read that description.

An illustration of what I faced in my National editorship came in May 1975, when Bradlee called me into his office at 7 p.m., right after our second front-page conference of the day. He closed the door, which was unusual for him. He asked me, "What is the story every-one in town is talking about?" I said I didn't know. Ben said, "It's who killed Kennedy." "Which Kennedy," I asked. "Both of them," he answered. He said it was a mystery that would not go away and that we should commit large resources to it. We started to brainstorm and Bradlee came up with the idea of going outside the *Post* to partner with the *Boston Globe* and the *Chicago Tribune*. Each paper would chip in a reporter for the project that he expected might take two years. I asked why he wanted to invite them in and he said because of the high costs.

Ben said the project would need its own editor, which I didn't like. I pointed out that this plan was a variant of an earlier agree-ment we made that Bill Greider would do a story on why the Jack Kennedy assassination story wouldn't die. That's when I found out that Greider was going off on leave and that Woodstein would be back in late September. I asked whether they would join National. He said, "If I were you I'd take Woodward," and taking Bernstein might be unavoidable.

We spent time going over different possibilities of who would be a good *Post* editor and reporter for the Kennedy assignment. Who would have the psychic stamina to endure not being pub-lished for two years? Bradlee said, "We are talking in this room among ourselves. . . . You can't even tell Annie." This came from the most notorious leaker in the building, who was known to share confidential information with copy boys. Then I said we needed to figure out what we could expect from this undertaking. First, I ques-tioned whether the whole town was talking about it (or just Bradlee's Georgetown coterie). He said I was wrong, that he had two calls about it only that day. Second, I said the reason the story won't die should be relatively easy to explain. It was the inability of people to assimilate such a grievously shocking event. I reminded him that he occasionally referred to a book that he read when he was fourteen, titled *Who Killed Lincoln*. On the other hand, we could report on the inadequacy of the supposedly definitive Warren Commission Report by reading through all twenty-six volumes, tracing its investigations and interviewing conspiracy theorists. It would be tough since many principals had died.

Just before we ended the meeting he said, "Don't be against this project." I replied, "I am not against it, but I want to know what we could expect from our investment." If there was something there to uncover, I was eager to find it; but it had to be more than table talk. I saw my responsibility to him to mean that I needed to translate his enthusiasms into practical terms. It was no small feat.

That summer, a friend who was a vice president at the World Bank told me that to curry favor with the oil-rich Arabs, the bank was demoting or sidelining executives who were Jewish. I turned to Bart Rowen, the economics expert on staff, to look into it. He did not have time as he was departing for Europe to cover an economic conference. So we gave the assignment to Isaacs, who had contacts with the Jewish lobby, and he found no support for the allegation. Then one of the Metro reporters filling in was assigned to check with the World Bank officers. Although not equipped with Rowen's array of contacts and sources, he did a credible job asking obvious questions of people, including Jews, who vigorously denied any such thing was happening. We did not write a story.

In Europe, Rowen ran across a lead distantly related to the tip. It involved a deal for an official Arab news operation to edit a forth-coming World Bank publication intended for Arab consumption. On Bart's return, he began intensive interviews on all aspects, including the bank's relationship with OPEC, the oil cartel, which was a source of dissension within the bank. The upshot was a harsh confrontation involving Rowen and the head of the World Bank, Robert McNa-mara. McNamara fiercely denied allegations of anti-Semitism (which Rowen had neither made nor alluded to) but would not respond to Rowen's questions about the pervasive fear of McNamara among bank staffers and their disagreement with his policies. Instead, he harped on the falsity of the anti-Semitism charge. No one had pub-lished anything about anti-Semitism; in fact, our reporting had found no validation for it. But the bank people were offended by our hav-ing raised the issue through our reporting efforts, saying that was a problem by itself. And it served McNamara's purposes to focus on what had not been published to try to undermine what would be.

McNamara was a very close personal friend of Katharine Gra-ham's and I counseled Rowen to put his encounter with McNamara into a memo and keep a record of all contacts he made in the course of exploring the story. He did so. Three articles appeared in July, which aroused much criticism of the *Post,* including from Henry Kiss-inger. McNamara turned to his friend Kay Graham to discredit the reporting before and after publication. Kay was thereby involved, but I heard nothing from her about the matter.

On another occasion, a tip came to me from a person in position to know that contradicted the public announcement about the cancer afflicting Senator Hubert Humphrey, who was undergoing treatment at Bethesda Naval Hospital. The source was a Navy officer who stated that contrary to the upbeat information released after the senator's hospitalization, Humphrey suffered from a serious case of cancer of the bladder. The officer, a physician, said he had seen the biopsy slides. Humphrey was then thinking about once more seeking the Democratic nomination for president. As the source could not supply the slides for checking with experts, I turned the story over to the senior science reporter, Vic Cohn, sharing with him the information I had obtained without revealing my source. He pursued the story at the hospital and in particularly with Humphrey's personal physician, Dr. Edgar Berman, who was also his political adviser. Berman denied the gravity of Humphrey's illness and no one else at Bethesda Naval would tell us anything. Because we had no other way to confirm the allegation, the article that was published quoted Berman as saying that Humphrey "should be perfectly cured of cancer" following treatment. As it turned out, Humphrey did not do well in the opening rounds of the campaign and withdrew. But the source who tipped us had been right. In October, Humphrey checked in at Memorial Sloan-Kettering Cancer Center in New York, a month before the election. He died less than two years later, which would have coincided with his term as president had he been elected. This underscored the danger of denials made by supposedly responsible people who do not hesitate tamper with truth on behalf of their interests, which often are narrowly construed. Dr. Berman's stonewalling could have drastically impacted the nation. In his capacity as a politically savvy friend and physician, he could and should have urged Humphrey to make the severity of his ten-year illness known publicly or else give up seeking the nomination. Why didn't our source stand up in support of what he knew to be true? He was a low-ranking officer who felt that he would face retribution for going against what was being officially said.

In August 1975, I sent a memo to Bradlee and Simons that reflected on my year-long tenure as AME/National. I detailed the strengths and deployments of the staff. The memo emphasized the need to write about how policies are made and how Washington worked as well as to scrutinize the White House, the cabinet departments, the Congress and the federal agencies, along with the courts.

After reciting the accomplishments in these areas, I cited some problems. We needed to develop more flexibility from reporters who had been on their beats for a long time. There was a problem in "the lack of energy, a consequence of age and status. The combination resulted in reporters taking longer to do stories than required by the difficulty of the assignment and a reluctance to do the necessary nitty-gritty of newspapering, shoe leather reporting, as every one of them surely had to do at more than one point in their career. There is a strong sense of having arrived when one is part of the National Staff of *The Washington Post*. This seems to lead some to behave as if, having arrived, not so much should be asked of them."

I remarked on the special relationships some staffers all too obviously enjoyed with Bradlee and Simons, undermining the morale of others less favored. I asked Ben and Howard to help improve the atmosphere. At that point, I still hoped to convince Peter Kann to forsake *The Wall Street Journal* and join us.

At this time, in 1975, Robert Redford was making the film of *All the President's Men.* He visited the newsroom and chatted everyone up. When Redford dropped by my office, presumably sophisticated journalists paraded past the office window to steal a look. In time, Dustin Hoffman joined him. He had learned that when I was Metro editor I insisted that male reporters possess a necktie. They didn't have to wear it in the office, but it should be handy in a desk drawer to don when an assignment required it—based on my sensibilities. Ties were mandatory when meeting with prominent people and interviewing recently bereaved persons, for example.

Hoffman, who played Bernstein in the movie, had no tie with him, if he actually owned one. When he found out about my rule, he went out and purchased a tie and wore it to the office to show it off to me. Later on, the actor who was to play me came along. Jack Warden had been a late pick because the role had been difficult to cast. Had they asked me, I would have been delighted to make suggestions, something along the line of Brian Aherne. You know the type if you know Aherne. Some of the people working for me had another candidate: Ernest Borgnine. I thought that Raquel Welch would have made a perfect Katharine Graham, no fool I. Warden was chosen after his performance in *Shampoo*. When Bernstein and Richard Cohen saw that film, they looked at each other and said, "That's Harry." The producers evidently concurred.

Warden showed up in the spring of 1975 weeks after Redford and Hoffman. He sat in my office quietly observing me at work. We hit it off and played a round of tennis. Only one round, because Jack pulverized me on the court and at the time I was considered a pretty good player. There was utterly no need for an encore. It was plain to anyone watching that neither Redford nor Hoffman did anything noticeable to make Jack part of the group. Annie and I entertained him at dinner with close friends and took him to a large dinner event at which he met a number of important people, danced with their wives and talked to celebrity stalkers among the Washington Establishment. Soon enough, Jack Warden made a circle of acquaintances in Georgetown that made life more pleasant for him socially in Washington.

While we were sitting in my office talking, he offered me a cigar. It was of a caliber way beyond my pay grade and it smoked that way. He told me that he would be playing a role and was not impersonating me. He said this, I am sure, to allay any unease I might have about being portrayed in a film. However, he did adopt some of my mannerisms. I wore my tie loosened and pulled down to half-staff. So did he in the film. The cuffs of my shirtsleeves were turned up twice. So were his in the film. When my children and grandnephews asked whether I used the salty language Warden uttered on screen, I assured them it was only a film.

While the Hollywood celebrities were in town, being entertained by Kay at her home, among other diversions, Bradlee and I one day stood outside his office wondering what the future held for Woodstein, now on the cusp of undreamed-of fame. I thought Woodward would probably expire from too much lovemaking, as this account has to phrase it. I had a different fate in mind for Bernstein. "I'm going to kill him," I said. Bernstein doing his best work still managed to remain irritating.

Redford was concerned about getting permission to use the names of the people portrayed in the film. Katharine Graham did not want hers used. While in Florida on vacation I got a call from Redford wanting to know how I felt about it. I told him I had no objection but would abide by whatever decision was made at the *Post*. In July 1975, I received a letter from Redford explaining that his production could not use fictionalized names because it would impinge on the "authenticity and impact of the film." He wrote:

"Within the constraints of the motion picture medium, each of you is portrayed factually as a responsible individual involved in the unwinding of this important and newsworthy series of events." All names were used except Katharine's, who, because of her reservations, was not depicted in the film.

Later that month, we were on our usual vacation in South Wellfleet on Cape Cod, where we had been going for many years. While there I received a special communication from Mrs. Graham. (It was always Mrs., not Ms., and she insisted on her title of Chairman and not Chairwoman, never mind Chairperson). Her note was mailed to our rental agent's office, where we checked in every couple of days. She wrote on her personal notepaper about some money she had been awarded. She went on:

> I have asked the American Public Service Awards Committee to split the award between you and Howard. *The Post* and I together already give a lot to causes. And anyway I prefer people.
>
> Of the big six involved most closely in the Watergate (including me I guess)—we have all received psychic or actual income in varying amounts from those years. It seems to me you two received the least of the latter.
>
> So this comes from the Committee via me to you with love & thanks. It will hardly make you millionaires like some we know—but I hope it will make you the possessor of a souvenir you will keep—be it only a few shares of Post stock!
>
> Love
> Kay

Her thoughtfulness resonates through the decades that have passed since those gracious words were written.

Toward the end of summer in 1975, an incident occurred that was the buzz of Washington. A secret report prepared by the House Intelligence Committee on the CIA had been acquired by broadcaster Dan Schorr. His employer, CBS News, deemed it too hot to handle and declined to air it. At the paper, we wanted to lay hands on a copy to see if, as seemed probable, it contained a valid story. Larry Stern and Walter Pincus, close friends themselves and close socially to Bradlee, were charged with getting a copy. They were not successful despite their vaunted Washington insider connections. So I took matters into my own hands. At a reception for visiting Israeli Prime Minister Menachem Begin I ran across Schorr, whom I had known since I visited Bonn in the mid-1960s when I was with the *Herald Tribune*. Over canapés I told Schorr that I wanted the *Post* to have that document. He did not reject my overture out of hand and we talked about CBS sitting on the story and about the possibility of Dan writing an article for one or another magazine. He began to bargain with me, saying I needed to commit the *Post* to publishing the entire report. I told him there was no way we could agree to publish something we had not laid eyes on.

He said that in any event he would not give up the copy he had, presumably because he might need it for that magazine article or CBS might change its mind and do something with it in the future. To accommodate him, I said we would photocopy it at our office or, if Schorr did not want to surrender custody of the document, we would cover the cost of his having it photocopied. That concluded the conversation and nothing came of it.

Except that something did. A while later, either Pincus or Stern came to my office to tell me that Schorr had told Pincus that I had offered him money for the document. The conversation took place in a cab the two men shared with their children who were being escorted to their private school. Schorr told Pincus that he was disturbed by the implications of what I had done and was only reluctantly informing Pincus. That account was also carried to Bradlee.

I told Bradlee, Stern, and Pincus precisely what had happened. I thought that was the end of it. At the time I could not see what else I should have done to set the record straight. I was still angry with Schorr when a while later we met at a reception for the publication of Len Downie's book. Schorr came up to me and said, "Harry, we've been friends too long to let this incident interfere with it." He apologized for the misunderstanding, as he termed it. He also told me that Bradlee, who had been in California promoting the sale of his own book as well as lecturing at colleges, was exploiting the anecdote in his talks. He was depicting it to students to illustrate what he did for a living, how he had to rein me in and made me back out of a deal that was unethical. Paying for news is often, though not always, a violation of newspaper ethics, such as they are. In fact, Bradlee had not chastised me.

The next day I went into Bradlee's office. He was seated behind his oval desk, which had been Phil Graham's. He leaned back in his leather chair and looked up at me as I repeated what Schorr had said about him. Again, I recounted all that happened and I was emphatic about not appreciating a bogus story being spread that implied anything else. Bradlee continued to smile, said nothing and merely nodded his head. There it finally did rest.

As I reflected on it, there was no reason for Schorr to be unkind to me. We simply did not have any relationship beyond a superficial acquaintance. Regarding his relationship to Pincus or the *Post* or Bradlee I had no clue. There had been no way for him to misconstrue my words. He distorted what I said to him for purposes unknown to me. He may have done it for no more than the pleasure of causing trouble. Trouble came to him after he sold the report to the *Village Voice,* which published it. The proceeds of the sale were to go to the Reporters' Committee for a Free Press. Nevertheless, contrary to his professed sensibilities, the report was not given, it was sold. He was suspended by CBS after his collaboration with the *Village Voice* and his already fragile status was never to improve, leading to his departure from the network.

22

A Strike and Other Troubles

On October 1, 1975, the *Post* was struck by the pressmen's union, in a hallmark action that defined labor relations in newspapers from then on. At issue, basically, was who had the right to control the newspaper's production operation: the unions or the management. Costly featherbedding and make-work was prevalent under union rules. The *Post* decided to meet the issue head on and to position itself to integrate new production technologies that would inevitably lead to staff reductions and union hostility. The result was an unconventional walkout not limited to leaving the building and establishing picket lines. The pressmen did both but added something extra, which struck at the heart of the First Amendment and aroused widespread resentment. On their way out of the *Post* building, they sabotaged the printing presses. Public opinion was instantly aroused against their cause. While other blue collar unions respected the picket lines, members of the Newspaper Guild, the union that represented the news, circulation, and advertising employees, for the most part did not. The strike, which spurred the modernization of American newspaper production, lasted nearly five months.

The presses were quickly repaired and I was in the pressroom when Katharine pressed the button to make them roll again. It was a stirring moment. For the duration of the strike, all of the newsroom managers did double duty. At the conclusion of a customarily long work day, I changed into chinos, sport shirt, and sneakers and went to the production departments to help make it possible for the paper to publish.

My first strike job was in the pressroom, squatting on a low wooden stool at the junction of two tracks on which press plates rolled toward their destination. I had to make sure that there was no pileup and that the plates, numbered with chalk, were heading toward the right presses. At other times, I worked in the engraving room going over the negatives of pages from which plates would be made, filling in with black ink pinpoints of white that remained on the negatives. Later in the night, I worked in the mailroom taking the bundles of printed papers off the rolling feeder system and placing them in delivery trucks.

The most important of my strike duties was working through the night until the last edition, overseeing the placement of articles into the pages, making sure that headlines fit, and trimming stories appropriately. I took pains not merely to chop from the bottom, which was the customary way to edit in the backshop. (This explains the newspaper tradition to put the most important information in the lead, with other facts and information added in descending order of importance for the rest of the article. It was also why in the era of hot type many newspaper paragraphs consisted of one sentence.)

The strike coincided with the last days of Francisco Franco, the long-lived dictator of Spain, who was tenaciously drawing out his mortal illness. The last chore late each night was to prepare an alternate front page, leading the paper with a banner headline on Franco's death that would be ready to go with a brief insert. That page could be quickly substituted ("replated") to catch the remaining press run, needing only the insertion of time of death. For that, and for my insistence throughout the night that the strike paper look as professional as possible, I became known as "Replate Rosenfeld."

However important my production work was (many times I spent the night and slept on a rollaway cot in my office), it was no more so than my responsibility to help keep the reporters and editors crossing the picket line to come to work. Only two National staffers stayed out.

During this time, Bradlee's personal world was measurably expanded as his relationship with *Post* feature writer Sally Quinn flourished. Under her guidance, his wardrobe sharpened up and he started to wear bespoke suits and shirts, putting behind his sometimes rumpled look. When the relationship was still at the stage where they took some care to disguise it (not with perfect success), I had occasion to tease Bradlee. I told him I had insider information that he and Sally lunched at Tavern on the Green in New York's Central Park. He demanded to know how I knew. I told him I would never, ever reveal my sources. Now it can be told: Annie and her mother were lunching there at the time and went unnoticed by the couple, who were oblivious to anyone else near them.

With Sally, Bradlee's circle was enlarged somewhat to the right. She came from a military family. Her father was a lieutenant general, with ties to the right wing of the Republican Party. Senator Goldwater, a friend of General Quinn, became a friend of Ben's. A certain irony resided in this new association. At the height of the Watergate clashes in Congress, the Arizona senator called on the press to reveal its sources, and called specifically for the criminal indictment of the *Post*. Had his extremist recommendation carried the day, the Nixon cover-up would have been vastly empowered, thus impeding our Watergate investigation and possibly halting it.

A predictable byproduct that affected the *Post* from the Sally and Ben relationship was the immediate doubling of sacred cows in the newsroom. Bradlee excised a sentence about him and Sally from a Style story while leaving untouched unflattering references to other colleagues. On one occasion, Sally intervened on behalf of her father, then retired and a consultant, who was implicated by congressional investigators in a probe of defense contractors.

During the 1976 presidential election campaign, Howard Simons talked to me about temporarily putting a Style writer on our staff. He felt that Myra MacPherson was most experienced in political coverage and would provide the kind of human touch that was not abundant on National. I was glad to get the help. Bradlee regarded this move as contrary to his preference. He thought, as did Sally, that Sally should have been chosen. I faulted myself for having been so unthinking about the in-house political impact of my decision. Working with Sally would have brought with it the difficulties of editing the boss' special friend, who also was headstrong. On the other hand, she was talented, equipped with insight and enterprising energy that produced attention-getting articles.

It occurred to me that I had been used in maneuvering between Simons and Bradlee. I believe Simon's concern was staff morale. Sally's selection likely would have appeared as nepotism that would alienate newsroom trust. Simons wanted to save Ben from himself, as it was his obligation to Ben and the newspaper to do.

Another National campaign coverage decision irritated Ben. It was Broder's proposal to write in-depth profiles of the candidates seeking the presidential nomination. David's vision likely was influenced by the scholarly work of James David Barber of Duke

University. The premise of Barber's seminal book *The Presidential Character* was that you can get an understanding of what kind of president a candidate would make by examining his character. In the light of the Nixon presidency that notion was particularly apropos for the election of his successor. That meant devoting a huge amount of reporters' time (about two weeks for each profile) and a large amount of space in the newspaper as there were many presidential aspirants. I stood with Broder on this.

In March 1976, the *National Enquirer,* a tabloid devoted to celebrity gossip and scandal, was about to publish a story with the ingredients of a quintessential Washington exposé, the kind that Bradlee savored. Its cast of characters included John F. Kennedy, the charismatic young president assassinated about a dozen years earlier, and a beautiful divorced woman alleged to have been his mistress. The article told of their trysts in the White House while Jackie was out of town. Also featured were CIA connections and an unsolved murder. The article was based on an interview with a former *Post* editor and corporate executive, who was perceived as mentally disturbed.

Bradlee, then vacationing with Sally in the Virgin Islands, thought the *Enquirer* story was "'bullshit." He emphatically didn't think it was worth a story in the *Post.* Of the occasions over the years at the *Post* that I was in conflict with my boss, this was the one with the most severe consequences. I strongly disagreed with Bradlee's assessment and determined to act according to what I saw as my duty to the *Post,* to Bradlee himself, and in keeping with the spirit of the Watergate investigative reporting that had earned the paper international distinction. I could not walk away from what I had to do, particularly because the *Enquirer*'s account was in some ways questionable and needed to be put in context.

The questions and concerns were ample. Until recently, Bradlee had been the brother-in-law of the woman in the alleged JFK affair, Mary Pinchot Meyer. Ben and his former wife, Antoinette Pinchot Bradlee, who was known as Tony, divorced not long before, had been intimate friends of the Kennedys during the White House years and before. Bradlee had not written of the Meyer-JFK relationship in his 1975 book *Conversations with Kennedy* beyond two anecdotes that demonstrated Mary Meyer's membership in the president's circle of personal friends. There was no allusion to any aspect of the *Enquirer* allegations.

There was more in the mess stewing in this kettle that demand-ed action on the paper's part. During the Watergate investigation the *Post* was accused of embarking on a witch hunt against the Nixon administration on behalf of the Democratic Party. Although our Watergate reporting turned out to be good as gold, the notion was still abroad in the land that we did it with added verve because the target was Richard Nixon. Bradlee's close ties to the Kennedys were noted frequently by *Post* critics. All we could do in response was to repeat tirelessly that we would have devoted ourselves equally to the task were the president and his men Democrats.

It was clear to me that the *Post* was compelled to deal with the *Enquirer* article and get ahead of it at the start rather than being forced to do so by media coverage that was sure to follow. Remaining silent would confirm those who accused us of practicing vigorous journalism when it coincided with our self-interest and not when we were implicated. From aspects principled and self-interested, dealing with the allegations up front was the better choice, even though for Bradlee it was a truly painful one.

As soon as I was sure that we had to do a story, I phoned Bra-dlee at Caneel Bay. The conversation was brusque and to the point. Subsequent efforts to make contact were unsuccessful because he refused to take my calls. He did talk with the reporter I assigned to the story, which underscored his extreme anger with me. Only once did he call me back, when he thought a press emergency call placed by me concerned the welfare of his kids in Washington. In that very brief talk he did not countenance my attempts to convince him that doing the story was by far the better course of action for the sake of his professional reputation and for the paper's journalistic stand-ing as well. In my mind, his legacy as a courageous editor was at stake.

To make certain that our story would be skillfully handled, I chose Don Oberdorfer, who had returned months earlier from a tour as Tokyo bureau chief. He was one of the senior reporters on staff. I also picked him because he had a reputation as a straight arrow with uncommon intelligence. With Don on the story, we were assured that he would report and write without straining to either embar-rass Bradlee or give him special consideration. He would produce a thorough, fair account and tie up loose ends left hanging by the *Enquirer,* and in the process provide balance and context.

The prospective article troubled not only Bradlee but also publisher Katharine Graham. The reason for her discomfort was that the chief source for the *Enquirer* story was James Truitt. Truitt's most recent association with the *Post* had been as an editor-consultant when the paper created its Style section. Previously, Truitt had been connected with *Newsweek*, also owned by the Grahams, and he had functioned as an aide to Phil Graham when he was president of The Washington Post Co., which owned both the newspaper and the magazine. As such, Truitt served at times almost as a caretaker of Phil Graham during periods of erratic behavior that eventually led to Graham's suicide at age forty-eight. Mrs. Graham knew about Truitt's mental instability even as she appreciated his past service to the family. At this time widowed for nearly thirteen years, she was concerned that because of Truitt's connection to Phil Graham our story might stir public talk about her husband's last, unhappy days. She shared these views with Howard Simons and me as the three of us sat at a table in the company cafeteria on the second floor of the L Street building. It was the day before we planned to publish on the front page our version of the *Enquirer* account. She worried whether we were doing the right thing. Howard and I discussed with her the interests of the paper in urging publication. Both of us assured her that there was little likelihood that Phil Graham's troubles would come to the fore again. The three of us were fully conscious of Bradlee's vehement opposition to publishing the story. She looked deadly calm, weary, and serious and did not order us not to publish, however much she might have preferred that course. Neither, for that matter, had Bradlee, to his credit.

Throughout, Howard and I had discussed how to handle the story. After our meeting with Kay Graham, we talked in Howard's office. Looking me straight in the eyes, he said, "You know Harry, Ben is not going to settle for getting mad. He's going to get even." I answered, "Howard, I know. In conscience, do we have a choice?" We had none, and what we were about to do was guaranteed to enrage Bradlee and incite his craving for revenge. In Howard's words, Bradlee was like the Kennedys in that he had a compulsion to look at the world in personal terms and to not leave unsettled outstanding scores. Leading up to this decision, Annie tried to keep me from proceeding, warning of Bradlee's vengeance. She knew her Bradlee. As husband, father, and wage slave, I did pause for a moment in the face of the clear necessity for staying the course.

The *Enquirer* piece, of which we got an advance copy, contended that Jack Kennedy while president had a love affair with Mary Meyer that lasted for two years. It said that once he had hidden a slip belonging to Mary in the White House safe. During that time they made love in the White House and smoked marijuana in the bedroom. After they had smoked a second joint, the story said, Kennedy "leaned back and closed his eyes. . . . He lay there a long time, and Mary said she thought to herself, 'We've killed the President.'" After the third joint, Kennedy said, "No more. Suppose the Russians did something," according to the *Enquirer*. This passage underscored the national security issues that trumped the salacious aspects.

Mary kept a diary and asked her sister Tony along with the then-wife of Truitt to destroy it if anything were to happen to her. This wish led to the involvement of the Central Intelligence Agency's counterintelligence chief, James Jesus Angleton, a Meyer family friend. Furthermore, Mary's ex-husband was Cord Meyer Jr. who had operated in the agency's dirty tricks and propaganda departments. When Mary was killed walking on the towpath in Georgetown on October 12, 1964, eleven months after Kennedy's death in Dallas, Tony Bradlee found her sister's diary, which allegedly contained an account of her relationship with the president. Tony turned it over to Angleton for destruction. Tony Bradlee's reactions were quoted in the *Enquirer*. A statement she gave to the Associated Press and a brief comment she made to our reporter were ambiguous, which underscored the need for the *Post* to address the matter. Some of Tony Bradlee's comments could be read as implying the Meyer-Kennedy relationship might have been amorous. She did not explain why she had turned the diary over to Angleton instead of disposing of it herself, when Ben was at her side.

The Meyer story was published on Page 1 and made its appearance after another affair conducted by Kennedy within the White House had been widely publicized. That tryst involved Judith Campbell Exner, who was introduced into the president's entourage by Frank Sinatra, allegedly a former lover of Exner's. A complication was that Sinatra also set her up with Sam Giancana, a Chicago crime boss. So at one point the President of the United States was sharing a girlfriend with a top mafioso. This story, which broke in 1975, was published by Bradlee in *The Washington Post*.

Undoubtedly figuring in Bradlee's firm opposition to printing anything about the Meyer affair was that its main source was a man with a history of mental problems. Conservators had been appointed by a U.S. District Court to oversee Truitt's financial matters. Over the years, since his last stint at the *Post* in 1969, Truitt supposedly had threatened Bradlee, among others, with exposure of alleged scandals.

Bradlee said nothing to me about our story on his return from the Virgin Islands. Neither did he mention it in subsequent weeks. After another of his lucrative lecture tours months later, he did make a passing allusion. He spoke in such a way that it seemed that he recognized we had done the right thing in publishing the story and that the *Post* was the better for it. I told him then that I had done him a favor all along. Many years later, when a major article appeared in the *New Yorker* on the occasion of the publication of his memoir, it stated that Bradlee "helped the *Post* on the story of the love affair in 1976, and then only after the *National Enquirer* had published its own account." In the pages of his own newspaper he had no comment for the story, though he did speak to the reporter on background. Bill Safire, the conservative columnist for *The New York Times,* told me how much he admired the way we handled the Meyer story. He said that he felt it was not believable that such a decision would have been made at Bradlee's direction. Keen observer, he.

Efforts to implement the plan I outlined for Bradlee and Simons at the end of my first year at the helm of National involved trying to encourage certain staffers to become less complacent and more curious and productive. Some reporters complained to Bradlee, although Ben never said anything to me, not after Broder, not even after the Schorr incident. It was a matter of fact that on the National staff there were reporters not partial to me. I had displaced Isaacs at Metro and my insistence that Downie take over from me in that assignment when I was promoted dislodged Bart Rowen from his AME title. Stern, I have no doubt, ran to Bradlee with Schorr's allegation of my offer to pay for a document. That was how creative tension also played out in the newsroom. Many of the players had been competitors before they ostensibly became teammates in the same news department. I almost never heard about these complaints directly. But third parties tipped me off.

In April 1976 Woodward told me that *Potomac*, the *Post* magazine, was working on a story about a woman employed by Democratic Representative Wayne Hays, who claimed she was being sexually exploited by the congressman from Ohio. Bob was working on several angles involving other sorts of dubious actions by Hays, who enjoyed power as the chairman of the Administration Committee. That committee played a role in how the various perks available to House members were bestowed. Bob's leads had petered out as he went off to promote the movie and his book. At this juncture Bradlee asked where Woodward stood with his Hays story. I told him he was stymied. The next time the subject came up was in May at our regular afternoon news meeting, when Bradlee alerted the news editor who had the weekend duty that a Hays story was coming up. Ben wanted it spread across the top of the front page with pictures. At first I thought it was a *Potomac* story and what Bradlee had in mind was a Page 1 key to the paper's magazine. After the meeting I asked Bradlee for clarification and he replied that it was a story for the news section and he would show it to me. He handed me a picture of a woman displaying ample cleavage.

The next day, Friday, he shared the story, which was co-written by two Style reporters, Rudy Maxa and Marion Clark. He asked me to identify holes in it. He said that he thought the story needed more details on the motivation of the whistleblower, Elizabeth Ray. He added that Ray was writing a book. My contribution was to suggest that instead of the paper flatly asserting the charges, have Ray allege them instead. I noted that there was no comment from two other members of the House who appeared to be in some ways involved in this sordid business. My contribution was pretty basic stuff.

In a follow-up note to Bradlee, I expressed concern that the story relied totally on Ray. We needed to do more reporting and talk to her co-workers. It was decided that since Bradlee was not coming to the office that Saturday, the story would be held for the following week. I briefed Lescaze, who was running the National operation that Saturday, and asked him to call me if anything changed. Lee phoned me on Saturday and said that the Style reporters had gone to see Bradlee at home and that Ben sent in a story that seemed to answer the questions I had raised, except for the motivation angle and the co-workers angle I had suggested should be added. In response to my suggestion, Lee said he would include something in the story about her book as an indication of motivation.

On Monday, Bradlee was euphoric. This was his kind of story. Howard described him as "manic." When Woodward came in later in the afternoon, he filled me in and then shared with Ben the accumulation of notes he had on Hays. As a result, Bradlee told me he wanted to set up a task force, with Larry Stern as editor. To my question why he was doing this, he said it was the best thing as I was busy with the political primaries and other matters. I pointed out that this was a major national story. At the time, rumors of my demise at National were more prevalent than ever. Although I had been aware of them for some time I decided not to run to Bradlee to defend myself. I would not debase myself with explanations. Either my work was good or it wasn't. But in light of the rumors, I told Bradlee that he was cutting me off above the knees. He responded, "You want me to do something to take care of you and I want that story and the task force is the only way to get it."

I answered, "If that is so then you have to go ahead as you planned."

Ben said, "Yes, but I surely would have liked your support." I was extremely upset by the exchange and so I called Annie and discussed with her what had transpired. As a result, I came to recognize that Ben was right. I went over to him at the water cooler and told him I would break my back to make the task force work. He thanked me.

After the first story appeared, Ray's unsavory reputation on the Hill emerged more clearly. There were second thoughts about having gone with only her version and not broadening our reporting. And that had been Bradlee's decision: he wanted the story in that Sunday's paper.

The task force comprised the two Style reporters, as well as Woodward and Scott Armstrong, by then hired by the *Post*, under Stern's direction. The copy would move through the National desk. There was disagreement between Stern and me on how to proceed but I had to defer to him. I thought he should pursue the Woodward angles of corruption and Larry wanted to focus on the culture of Congress that countenanced such exploitation. Subsequently, given the less flattering aspects of the accuser, I urged that we needed a lifestyle piece on Elizabeth Ray. When I suggested to Bradlee that we examine the sociological phenomenon of fishing off the company pier, he said, "I'm just the right guy to order a story about fishing off the company pier." He said it with a smile and agreed it was worth doing. That was Bradlee at his best.

From that point forward, the coverage was largely routine as Congress began to deal with the scandal. This involved National reporters assigned to cover Congress. Beyond the first article and perhaps one other, most of them were free of sensationalism. I was not pleased that there was no follow-up on Woodward's leads or exploration of other abuses being committed on Capitol Hill as a matter of business as usual. But Bradlee loved the running story and kept it on Page 1 for eleven days. Media critics deplored the *Post*'s making a major event out of a commonplace sin. One critic pointed out that while the *Post* was devoting unlimited space to the tawdry tale, it was not reporting, or skimpily reporting, on more consequential happenings on Capitol Hill. The critics were off the mark. The Hays scandal, involving a highly placed representative, was another in a series, the gift that keeps on giving, as congressional members find ever more creative ways to abuse the trust and responsibilities invested in their office. In the end, I conceded that Bradlee was right and I was wrong to worry about my status. A task force was the sensible way to go, though it failed to bust the story out of its initial parameters and make something more consequential out of it.

Very soon, this whole business was another straw in the wind for me in terms of my leading the National staff—the final straw. My fate as AME/National was sealed. Although the guillotine would not descend for a while—there was serious national political coverage to attend to—fall it would. By the beginning of July the date had been set. If Bradlee saw in the Meyer incident a plot to dethrone him, led by Simon and abetted by me, he was manifestly absurd. The bonds between Bradlee and Mrs. Graham that grew out of their mutual devotion to make the *Post* into a newspaper of the first rank far surpassed the usual relationship between publisher/owner and editor. No palace coup would have had the slightest chance of success, because Mrs. Graham would not have countenanced it in any guise.

I learned that my days running National were over not from the mouth of Bradlee or Simons, not from colleagues, but through an item in the "Ear" gossip column in the competing Washington *Star*, a paper edited for many months by my friend and former boss at the *Herald Tribune*, James Bellows. At a staff meeting of National editors that afternoon in my office, the news did not take long to show effect. One editor was particularly offensive, speaking to me in a dismissive manner that indicated he smelled blood in the water. He had never been so unpleasant. Harwood had picked him for the job. Although I found his work unimpressive and he was more of a bobblehead than an editor, I did not get around to changing his assignment. Sometimes I have tolerated problems that needed to be addressed more quickly.

Later that day, Bradlee came to my office and said, "I guess we have things to talk about," confirming what everyone had been able to read in that afternoon's editions of the *Star*. His idea was that I would return to the foreign operation as AME in charge. I had left that department at the end of 1969 as Foreign Editor, the No. 2 position. The new assignment suited me because of the many years I spent in foreign news. Bradlee's plan was quickly super-seded because Simons convinced Ben not to shift my first boss at the *Post*, Phil Foisie, who was still the AME/Foreign. Howard feared that Phil would not be able to handle being moved out (to become AME/Administration) after many years of devoted service. How-ard thought Phil might take his own life. Ben shortly returned to my office for another chat. Without looking me in the eye, he told me I would not get the AME/Foreign post. Instead, I would keep my AME title and head up the Sunday commentary section, called Outlook, as well as being in charge of daily book reviews and the Sunday Book World section.

I vividly remember that I felt as if I were being lashed. I turned my head from one side to the other involuntarily as I said to Bra-dlee, "You really do want me to leave." And he said, "Aw, no" and words that expressed a contrary sentiment—but not convincingly. Subsequently, Ben said that I had not done a good enough job at National. Howard agreed, saying that I failed to spark the National staff as I had the Metro staff. I said in that event, "I deserve a kick in the ass; not a kick in the head." After the Meyer tempest, however, all discussion was over. Had I been more assertive, I might not have lasted any longer running National but I might have produced more obvious successes. I should have copied what I did on taking over Metro and met with every National staffer privately, preferably over lunch or drinks. Looking back, I had to concede that in trying to manage a veteran staff I reined myself in more than I should have. Many efforts on my part to stir the National reporters out of their comfort zones failed more often than they succeeded, while these tactics increased their unhappiness with me as editor. After the ax fell, Woodward apologized to me and said that in my time of need he and Carl were away too often on their book project.

When I was already embedded in my new assignment, a for-eign correspondent, formerly one of my key Metro editors, wrote to complain about my dismissal and said, "I don't like what it says about the future of the paper." He added that he thought me "the best editor on the floor. . . . We had our differences, but at least we had them face to face and worked them out honorably."

I responded to his main point, saying that I had never had any ambition to be a long-term National editor. "What I wanted was another 18 months or so to finish what I started and what I felt was beginning to get underway."

23

Uncharted Waters

At the same time as my removal, Dick Harwood returned to Washington from Trenton, where he had edited the *Post* property, the *Trenton Times*. In his time on the job, he'd tried to impose a version of *The Washington Post* on Trenton, but his overhaul was out of tune with readership preferences in the capital of New Jersey. Harwood went so far as to have Sally Quinn write a column for Trenton; it did nothing for circulation, which declined, but surely pleased Ben and Sally.

In a move intended to undercut Simons, the other alleged conspirator, Harwood did not return under his old title. Rather, he came back as Deputy Managing Editor, a clear signal to Howard and the staff that Bradlee was hemming in Simons. Harwood had a deserved reputation for understanding the ins and outs of Washington politics and public affairs. He was an assertive editor with a lucid writing style. His other outstanding characteristic was his loyalty and dedication to Bradlee, without reservation or question. I would have described myself in the same words, except the last four. At times I challenged Bradlee, and I believed that to be an essential part of my responsibility.

Howard Simons expressed the difference between his and my relationship with Bradlee, compared to Harwood's. "If Bradlee asked the three of us to jump out the window head first, Harwood would open the window and jump." Howard continued, "You or I would first say 'Wait a minute, Ben, maybe there's another way to do this; maybe we can take the stairs or slide down a rope.'" An editor worth the name retains his independence of mind or risks the title. A former editor at the *Post*, J. Russell Wiggins, had a stylish aphorism to cover the situation: "An editor edits with his hat on."

Among the immediate reactions by the National staff, there must have been satisfaction among those who had paraded into Bradlee's office, some from nearly day one, to undermine me. The AME who lost her perch to accommodate my new role urged me to teach Bradlee a lesson by walking across town to join Bellows at the *Star*. My secretary had a more sober view. She said my curt dismissal warranted resignation except for the fact that I had two daughters in college and no independent income. That was the truth of it.

Don Graham, then in a management position, asked me out for coffee one afternoon at the Madison Hotel coffee shop across the street from the paper. We talked about other matters for a time before he broached the subject of my dismissal. Toward the end of the conversation Don looked at me and quietly said, "Harry, please don't leave." I responded by saying that there surely must be a way to make what are deemed necessary changes for the greater good of the paper without the need to spill so much blood. I promised Don, "I won't leave without talking to you."

Don respected my work but he also must have been concerned about the impact on the staff my leaving might have. We had worked together when he joined the Metro staff. To my relief and delight, Don Graham turned out to be a fine reporter and pulled his weight before moving onward and upward in the organization.

Later on, I came to understand that at times I must have been a trying subordinate. It is a reflection of his many facets that Bradlee put up with me. He was a complex man who harbored a mixture of motivations and feelings that were sometimes opaque. Despite our disagreements, Bradlee and I maintained a friendly relationship that lasted long past my time at the *Post*. My view of him always has been framed in affection and admiration for his transformative leadership that made the *Post* a great newspaper. Bradlee was an extraordinary editor. He also had warts, in the words of a news executive who stayed only briefly. Then again, who among us does not?

Before these contentious events played themselves out entirely and I took over the direction of Outlook and Book World, National had a presidential nomination campaign to cover. We followed up on Broder's character profiles, with mixed results because mining a politician for his character is an elusive undertaking. Politicians at all levels, no matter how long or short their time in the trade, regard the press as the enemy unless proven otherwise. They want the media to serve as an uncritical conveyor of their unchallenged ideas to the public. Any critical examination of their records and views that does not coincide with the image they wish to project is resented.

Governor Jimmy Carter, Democrat of Georgia, running in the 1976 campaign, was invited to a luncheon at Mrs. Graham's stately residence. A splendid table was laid out with linen and fine china. A select group of editors was invited along with wives. Rosalynn Carter accompanied her husband, as did a number of Carter's aides. I had a minor role at the lunch as AME/National. It was the first time Mrs. Graham and Don had met Governor Carter. What struck me in the discussion before, during, and after the meal was the hardness and colorlessness of the man, augmented by a lack of humor as he recited his policies. One of the *Post* executives asked Carter to comment on the *Post*'s coverage of him. He did not hesitate to denounce it as prejudiced against him because he was an outsider trying to break into Washington politics, which was a major theme of his campaign. When asked, he could recall only a single article to praise from among the work of all the media. While he had a slight difficulty in getting the reporter's name right, it was the long profile done on him by Don Oberdorfer. But Carter did not place him as being with the *Post*. It was my pleasure to make the point that Don was one of our staffers. What I did not say was that I had used the Oberdorfer article only reluctantly, because I judged it too worshipful and not sufficiently acute. The only reason that it was published in that form was that we had run out of time to do it over.

During both his campaign and his presidency, Carter played his religiosity card with fervor. In August 1976, when he taught Sunday school at his church in Georgia, our reporter, Helen Dewar, was excluded from the pool coverage because she was a woman. I wrote Carter that the *Post* urged that he "reconsider your agreement to the exclusion of women reporters" and that the press not be "subjected to such discrimination." It was an illustration of the self-righteousness that candidate Carter had displayed at the luncheon at Mrs. Graham's home.

Planning for the coverage of the two political conventions was extensive. The Democrats went first, in July in New York City, followed by the Republicans in Kansas City in August. With the input of reporters and editors, we drafted battle plans for each day, with specific assignments because conventions are highly scripted. We left room both in the plans and in our minds to abandon any part of the outline in response to breaking developments. At the conclusion of the Democratic convention, Katharine Graham hosted an elegant party in the rooftop rooms of the World Trade Center. Food and booze and fine cigarettes were plentiful. During the fete, I stood up to thank Mrs. Graham for the posh party and tacitly for the kind of boss she was. My well-intentioned thank you erupted into endless sycophantic outpourings by one staffer after the other. Mrs. Graham, who had contempt for suck-ups, surely was annoyed. Beyond that misfire, I remember clearly looking out a window in an adjacent room at the Statue of Liberty, illuminated from below against the darkness of the night, a powerful and emotional sight for me who had first glimpsed her upon arrival in New York Harbor as a refugee in 1939; but now I was fully conversant with her mythic symbolism.

The Republican convention followed. The highlight there was the battle between President Gerald Ford and Governor Ronald Reagan of California. Ford had the backing of most of the delegates and was all but assured of the nomination. That didn't keep the Reagan camp from putting up a ferocious fight, including the incessant blowing of infernal horns to drown out the speeches of their opponents. When the horns had sounded their last note, my tenure as AME/National effectively came to an end.

24

New Job, New Demands

As I took up my new responsibilities, I quickly came to appreciate that this assignment was a more welcome test for me than returning to the foreign desk would have been. I was able to use my reflective mind rather than the sheer nervous energy required to respond to the constant stimuli of breaking news. I committed to using Outlook as the vehicle to publish writing that was on the cutting edge of intellectual discourse and discovery, which in the normal course were not found in the pages of a newspaper absorbed with daily events.

In Book World, I began an effort to make it more attractive to readers and thereby to advertisers, whose scarcity in the section was all too apparent. The editor in charge was Bill McPherson, a prickly man but a gifted critic who was protective of his turf and who regarded me as an interloper. He never got over the fact that I was his boss.

McPherson's antagonism and resistance to my presence in his domain clashed with my insistence on being more than a wallflower. Seeing the lack of ads and beginning to understand the dynamics of the book review business, I decided to accompany the advertising salesman for Book World to New York City, the hub of book publishing. Because of the connections I had made in the book trade during Watergate, I had access to top people at publishing houses who otherwise would not have deigned to meet with our ad salesman—decent chap though he was. I got our foot in the door to make my spiel about the importance of supporting a book review publication to compete against *The New York Times Book Review,* a tabloid and by far the dominant book review newspaper supplement in the nation. McPherson's contribution to this effort was the overall quality of the section he edited, the impressive critics that he and his small staff enlisted, as well as the well-crafted reviews he and his associates contributed. In 1977, McPherson won the Pulitzer Prize for Criticism, reflecting the high esteem his work had achieved. We began to augment reviews with more profiles of authors and articles on the publishing industry.

After I had the chance to acquaint myself with the different aspects that impacted Book World, I produced for Bradlee an eight-page memo that outlined the tough challenges and recommended possible strategic responses. This memo noted that Book World had diminished since its earlier demise as a tabloid section, with the obvious suggestion that returning to tabloid format would help it, perhaps decisively. (It would not be a tabloid again until I was gone.)

I instituted a weekly conference, which I attended, at which the books were selected for both daily and Sunday presentation. I increased the pressure on keeping reviews focused and tight, which resulted in more being published, while their display on Sundays improved over time on the front of the section and on the inside. We started a local best-seller list, which proved popular. Because the slim four-page section was inserted deep inside the thick Sunday paper, anchored for much of the time as Section H, making it the seventh in the paper, it lent itself to being too easily overlooked even by interested readers. To attract them I pushed for the use of color on the front page of the section. At first, this was difficult to arrange because technical problems had to be overcome. Toward the end of summer in 1977, a front page with color on it became routine despite objections that it differentiated Book World from the rest of the black and white paper. Exactly my intention. I recommended that Book World increase its free distribution to more libraries and booksellers nationally, as well as to advertising agencies.

Our efforts paid off with McPherson's editorial triumphs and my contacts in publishing, with whom I mingled at annual book fairs in Bermuda and Atlanta as well as during my regular visits to New York. I did not neglect the Washington-area booksellers, and I went out to meet them frequently. The section sometimes doubled in size to as many as eight pages. In my first year, ad linage increased more than eighteen thousand lines. In June 1978, Mrs. Graham wrote me, "I am really amazed at how much you have increased retail advertising in this section and how good it is editorially. As I have said before, congratulations and many thanks." I was pressing so hard on ad sales, lobbying that the ad salesman should expand the number of his visits to the New York book trade, that the advertising director, Robert McCormick, struck a deal with me. If I backed off and left the ad business to them, he guaranteed that Book World (and Outlook) would have sufficient advertising. McCormick, his associates, and I became good friends and when I left for Albany they gave me a private dinner party.

Throughout my couple of years in that job, soliciting ads for Book World was an uphill battle. Publishers directed their advertising not primarily at readers, but at the agents for subsidiary rights such as films and television, leading the publishers to concentrate on Los Angeles and New York while throwing a crumb or two at other big cities such as Chicago. Washington did not then rank very high on their priority list; it had comparatively low book readership and lacked the retail base of other cities. That is why personal contact was especially important. When I took over, Book World had 9,300 lines of retail and 47,100 lines of national advertising. Just before I left BW, retail was at 65,280 while national had declined to 45,700, which was not as bad as it might have been. A prime reason behind the retail increase stemmed from publishers subsidizing retailer ads.

In December 1976, I was selected by default to receive the First Amendment Award of the Anti-Defamation League of B'nai B'rith in Los Angeles, honoring the film *All the President's Men*. The ADL had wanted Katharine, but she pleaded a full calendar. They then asked for someone else and Kay forwarded their letter to Bradlee, and wrote on it: "BCB—Maybe you can reply since you are in the movie." So it devolved to me. Annie and I flew out and attended a gala dinner at the Century Plaza Hotel. Senator Charles McC. Mathias Jr., Republican of Maryland, a person well known to me, was also honored. Robert Redford received an award, too, but he did not make it to the dinner and sent Jason Robards in his place. I was asked to speak briefly, with the briefly underscored. In terse remarks I said that "in every season, there are attempts—by legislatures, by executives, by the courts, and sometimes by public opinion—to alter the simple clarity of the forty-five words" of the First Amendment. I said that the amendment is both more and less than those words. It is less, because "absolutely applied" it can conflict with Sixth Amendment rights to trial by an impartial jury. It is more because it is "a perpetual goad to the press . . . into being courageous when it would be more comfortable to be something less."

I continued: "Watergate was a popular win. I hope that people and officials retain some of that good feeling about the rights and responsibilities of the press, against the day when the issue will be unpopular and the words of the messenger will not be pleasing to the ear."

On top of one of my bookshelves in my home office rests the award, which is a shofar, a ram's horn. It is cradled atop a rectangular block of polished wood, on which a citation states that the award was tendered because of my Watergate work in overseeing Woodstein. It has become a treasured keepsake because it combined two symbols important to my public and private lives: the First Amendment, which gave substance to my work, and the shofar, which speaks to my Jewish heritage. I wished I had possessed the quickness of mind to share with the black tie audience how honored I was especially because of the symmetry of the award's symbolism. Blow the shofar as hard as I might, I have never produced a sound. But two of my grandchildren, first Jonathan Wachter and later Melanie Aiken, have managed the difficult feat.

In late 1976 or early 1977 Bradlee offered me the job as No. 2 on the *International Herald Tribune*, which was published in Paris and in which the *Post* had part ownership, along with Whitney Communications and *The New York Times*. Annie did not like the idea for three reasons: we had two kids in American colleges, our widowed parents (her mother and my father) were living in New York City and given their advanced ages and health considerations, needed us not to be so far away from them. Finally, she felt I would spend, say, ten years in Europe and then return to Washington when I would be nearing my sixties. She rightly pointed out that my newspaper connections in America would weaken during the time in Paris. I would have to start over again, older and facing greater odds. Although what Annie said weighed heavily, I had a different reason for declining. The top job in Paris was held by Buddy Weiss, my old friend from *The New York Herald Tribune*. He had suffered a stroke and lost some speed. It was plain that Bradlee wanted me in position to replace Weiss, whose days as editor would then be numbered. There was nothing that could persuade me to take a job that would harm Buddy or help to push him out before he was ready to retire.

Along with my supervision of Book World, I was occupied doing the same sort of revamping of Outlook. There, too, I concentrated on story selection and on keeping articles as tight as possible. That emphasis was maintained throughout my association with Outlook. When it came time for me to depart for Albany, the small but effective Outlook staff gave me a present I have continued to use. It is a long pair of steel scissors, engraved with the command "Keep it Short!"

Outlook found grist for articles in academic, scientific, and political journals in which we found provocative ideas that we presented to the readers of the Sunday *Post*. We frequently adapted articles, sometimes solicited special contributions, or relied on contributions from staff writers. I also visited universities, institutes, and think tanks. A 1977 trip to West Coast institutions resulted in a sixteen-page memorandum, shared with my fellow AMEs as well as the Outlook staff. It outlined the studies that were then being pursued, methodologies of instruction that were being tested, and findings that had been made but not yet publicized. The memo was a cornucopia and resulted in articles for the *Post* that kept Outlook at the forefront of contemporary thought and stimulating for our readers.

Some articles for Outlook were done by a staffer who had been proposed by me as a rotating assignment, a form of internal leave of absence. My idea had good results, especially with Joanne Omang, a former foreign correspondent, who felt energized by her Outlook tour. It provided the reporter an opportunity to tackle the kinds of stories that she or he would not normally encounter in their work and served as a morale booster. Among the cutting-edge ideas we presented were a study of the impact of computers on society, including insight into the early days of nanotechnology. The Rand Corporation provided detailed briefings analyzing U.S. foreign and national security policies and the rise of mini-nationalisms around the world. A Nobelist at the Salk Institute briefed me on cutting-edge studies of cancer and viruses. At the Scripps Oceanographic Institute, I was told about the shrinking supply of fish as a food staple. And on and on it provided a long list of future stories for Outlook. One afternoon while in San Diego, Annie and I drove into Mexico and saw for ourselves the poor, chaotic, and decaying conditions that plagued its people. I wrote in my report: "The whole Mexican population problem will continue to grow far beyond" illegal border crossers.

In March 1977, a fringe group of Black Muslims, known as the Hanafis, seized three buildings in Washington and held 149 people hostage for almost forty hours. During their siege, they killed a radio journalist and a police officer. Bradlee and Simons assigned me to Downie as a consultant to this big breaking story, regarding me as a useful resource at this critical time. One of the hostages was a journalist friend of mine and he wrote a vivid account of his captivity for Outlook. I was happy to offer whatever help I could but Len Downie surely did not appreciate my being designated to assist him. Early on in his new job heading up Metro, he strode into my National office and out of the blue demanded that I cease interfering in his affairs. I was speechless because I had done nothing of the sort—not in thought, not in deed. At the time, I wrote it off to jitters or to someone maliciously messing with Len's head. When Len and I worked together on Metro, I was cautioned by people I knew well that he was no friend of mine. I had not given them credence. In his acknowledgments for his book *The New Muckrakers*, Downie wrote: ". . . Harry Rosenfeld, who taught by example what I know as an editor and especially impressed on me the great value of vigilant professional skepticism." As his star rose at the *Post*, some articles written by outsiders represented Downie as having a certain disdain for me. If so, he successfully camouflaged it during the years we were Metro's No. 1 and No. 2.

Decades before fundamentalist Muslims wreaked vengeance for a cartoonist's use of the figure of Mohammed, I had a foreshadowing encounter with what can happen when religion becomes a tool of political satire. Political cartoonist Vint Lawrence was a prime Outlook contributor. His work appeared regularly on Outlook's back page. Taking a half-page horizontally and nearly a half-page vertically, his caricatures appeared under the title "Heads & Tales." They were well drawn, witty, sometimes daring, and always on point. For the edition of June 19, 1977, the subject was the leader of the Soviet Union, Leonid Brezhnev. He was portrayed as a religious figure in the form of the Icon of Our Lady of Vladimir that depicted Mary the Mother of God, venerated by Russian Orthodox, Greek Orthodox, and Roman Catholics. In place of Mary gazing lovingly at the Christ child cradled in her arms, Vint drew Brezhnev, holding a child-scaled version of himself. He was attired in a black cloak. A head covering of the type worn by Orthodox nuns was decorated with the hammer and sickle on the brow of the cloak in place of a religious symbol.

On his chest were three Soviet medals and the child was holding a fourth to be added to the array. The title under the drawing was "Mother Russia."

It was a trenchant cartoon, admirable for its astute depiction of how Communist leaders used the captive church in Russia for their impious purposes. Because I thought it might offend believers, I consulted my Christian colleagues in Outlook. They assured me that I was being hypersensitive and that the cartoon's message was self-evident. With that reassurance, the cartoon was published. It did not take long for outrage to register. I received boxloads of mail from across the United States and from other settlements of the Russian Orthodox diaspora around the world. Other offended religious also protested. Apology was demanded because they believed the *Post* demeaned an icon holy to them. There was no practical way to respond to each complaint, so I chose a protest written by the head of a religious order to make our reply. I assured him that we had no intent to hold their faith up to ridicule and regretted any such impression the cartoon left. I outlined Lawrence's reasoning behind the cartoon and pointed out that it was a devastating comment about the atheistic Communist regime exploiting their religion. In turn, I received a letter accepting the explanation but seeking a more formal apology. I suggested that he should share my letter, which had satisfied him. The incident impressed on me the necessity for special awareness when it came to cartoons alluding to religious sensibilities.

One day in July 1977, Howard Simons asked in midmorning whether I was free to lunch with "Howard and Ben." We went to the Madison Lounge. I said I'd take the seat with my back against the wall. When seated, I picked up a knife, pointed it at them sitting across the table and asked, "Okay, what have you got in mind?" Ben laughed. Without delay, they said they wanted me to head a task force that would look into the activities of Tongsun Park, a Korean man about town, a friend and funder of politicians, shadily connected to people in high places in Washington. Congress was investigating South Korean efforts to influence U.S. policy through illegal means, including campaign contributions. A number of members of Congress were implicated and allegations were being pursued of connections between Park and Tip O'Neill, the Speaker of the House.

Among the outstanding questions was whether Park was an agent of the Korean Central Intelligence Agency, which was suspected of conducting clandestine operations in Washington. It was a story with many unexplored leads that the *Post* had been dealing with for some time. Bradlee said the story, which would acquire the epithet Koreagate, had started out belonging to *The Washington Post*, "but since then we've fallen down." *The New York Times* was now beating us. Part of the problem, Ben and Howard thought, was that the coverage was divided among newsroom departments. Ben complained that sometimes we wrote off a development in a sentence or two and missed its larger significance. When the *Times* played it up later, our reporters' alibis too often were "we've already had it." That cover-your-ass response exasperated Bradlee. Actually, it pissed him off something fierce.

"Howard and Ben" wanted me to pull the coverage together in addition to my existing duties. They said they selected me because of my experience and that I had "the clout." Harwood was on vacation and I was concerned about his being on board; after all, the task force would enlist two of his reporters. Ben said Dick would be told by phone and I noticed the famous Bradlee impatience emanating from his notoriously short attention span coming to the fore again. I asked what if Harwood objected. Ben responded, "He won't but if he does, tough." I had been there before so I knew how chancy this undertaking would be. But Howard said, "This brings you back into the daily operation more."

The task force included Maxine Cheshire from Style. No one was enthusiastic about working with her because she had a reputation for being difficult. She had been poking around the innards of the wheeler and dealer allegations as had Charles Babcock of the National staff, who was also on the team. We discussed a third prospect and T. R. Reid from National looked the most promising. A researcher was assigned to be part of the team. Babcock, who covered the Justice Department, quickly put together a complete summary of paths to pursue alongside the various congressional investigations underway and also those in the Justice Department.

A lot of copy was written over the next months, produced by the task force along with other National and Foreign staffers. As our investigative teamed chugged along, without coming up with a breakthrough story, the interest of the National reporters began to flag. By October, Harwood told me Babcock complained that I was pecking at him every time he did something out of the Justice Department not tied to Korean angles. Harwood reined in Reid's time commitment to the project. I said that was okay with me, but

Bradlee had to sign off on the proposed changes because the task force was his idea. When Harwood and I met with Bradlee, Ben was swayed by Harwood's complaints about the conflicting pressures on his staff and his need in National for their full-time services. The task force shrunk to Maxine, with Babcock and Reid making limited contributions. I said I would try to live with it. But I knew this was no pathway to success.

Back in my office, Simons came to ask what the three of us had discussed. When I told him, he complained that he had not been involved. Howard said he disagreed with Ben's decision. I showed Bradlee a list of stories we might pursue under the new arrangement and suggested that he relieve me of this assignment. I told him I was placing Babcock and Reid in the middle between the needs of the task force and those of the National desk, where their careers lay. But when Bradlee turned to them, Harwood and Stern told him that they had neither the time nor interest to handle the ongoing story or Maxine, who was a hardworking reporter but needed almost a full-time editor to supervise her. On further reflection, and with Howard's input, Ben felt it would look bad if his team approach were dropped.

Basically, I was left to work with Maxine, who had the ability to dig up all sorts of dirt but was not able to confirm it enough for publication. That didn't mean she wasn't on or near the mark. At the beginning of my assignment, she came to me for advice about an approach she was pondering to find confirmation for her discoveries. I vetoed her proposal to show a House committee investigator every note and document she had on a certain lead in hopes that he in turn would help us get the necessary backup. She could ask leading questions, I told her, but she should not turn over our work to a government investigator. A long time later, when we were nearly ready to publish a major story, I accompanied Maxine to the Central Intelligence Agency's headquarters to interview Admiral Stansfield Turner, the newly appointed director of the CIA. He insisted that as far as he knew, the American CIA did not assist either the Korean CIA or Tongsun Park. Maxine's byline was on the lengthy article summing up what we had spent so much time reporting. The lead paragraph read: "The American CIA had reason to know as far back as the early 1960s that Tongsun Park, a central figure in investigations of South Korean influence-buying on Capitol Hill, had ties with the Korean CIA."

In her assiduous hunt, Maxine was coming across insinuations and allegations linking Park and Speaker O'Neill, who in his public utterances denounced Korean efforts to suborn Congress. Her reporting attempted to tie together the associations of several different actors involved to prove the point, including, by implication, ties to organized crime.

Maxine's reporting was all over the lot and her submitted article reflected lack of focus and organization, although the tidbits were extremely enticing. The difficulty was finding the authentication required for publication. It was that sort of lingering uncertainty that hung over her diligent work that probably moved National and Metro to welcome my taking Maxine off their hands. In December 1977, I wrote her a two-page memo outlining the ways that our investigation could proceed and what further information was required to validate its putative findings. "I know you have worked very, very hard and long," I wrote, "and under tiring and straining conditions, bouncing up and down the eastern seaboard. I think you should rest and then pull together the evidence and proof; quotes, documents, attributions that we already possess so that we can see what kind of story we are prepared to write now; what needs further investigation; what holes, if any, need to be plugged. This is the moment of truth. Write and let's see what it looks like." In the end, unfortunately the lengthy story she produced was deemed not strong enough to be published. We will never know what might have been if Babcock and Reid were positioned to work alongside her.

Many breaking and some exclusive stories were produced by the task force, and they painted a persuasive picture of the corruption of members of Congress. Tongsun Park testified before Congress about his political contributions in April 1978. Thirty years later, he was still in business as a fixer and middleman for another client, Saddam Hussein, in a deal involving oil-for-food transactions before the Iraqi dictator's downfall.

A far different effect resulted from a single article published in Outlook on January 22, 1978. It surpassed in impact anything we had ever presented our readers in the Sunday opinion section, which included many extremely audacious and penetrating works. The article was headlined "The Death of a Daughter." It was written by Victor and Rosemary Zorza, close friends of mine over the years, whose home was in England but who lived for long stretches in America. Victor normally focused on international affairs. This essay was his most difficult to write for it recounted the death of Jane, his twenty-five-year-old daughter. He was uncertain about writing an article, but I encouraged him to at least try, for the catharsis that it might provide. As Jane realized what her cancer portended, the article stated, she said, "Now that I know, I want to enjoy every day I have left."

The article went on to tell her story with an emotional force that I have seldom if ever seen matched in a newspaper article. It brought tears to my eyes, as it would have even if I was not close to the Zorzas, and as it did to Bradlee when I showed him the article before publication. We displayed "The Death of a Daughter" across the top of Outlook and it occupied more than half of the front page before continuing inside. The outpouring of mail demonstrated the power and reach of Jane Zorza's story. I am certain it played a major role in the development of the hospice program in the United States.

In February 1978, the *Post* editors were off again to Pugwash, this one at Sanibel Island in Florida. For several days, when the other top editors were in Florida, I was left in charge of the paper. At long last I was in the position I always wanted to attain—albeit on a short leash and lease. A major story long in the works came together on my watch. H. R. Haldeman, President Nixon's former chief of staff wrote a book, *The Ends of Power,* that *The New York Times* bought for syndication. One of its customers was *Newsweek* magazine, owned by The Washington Post Co. The magazine paid some $125,000 for a thirty thousand–word excerpt. Under the cover of extraordinary security to keep its content secret from prying eyes, the Haldeman book, which was being touted as a tell-all account of the Nixon years, was eagerly bought by newspapers around the nation, including the *Washington Star,* the *Post*'s local competitor. *The Washington Post* did not buy into the expensive offering—but it was the first to bring its juiciest assertions to public view. We were able to do so through the savvy efforts of one of our Style reporters, Nancy Collins. She tracked the book to a Pennsylvania binding plant where it was being prepared. There she was able to acquire an extensive though not complete photocopy of the Haldeman book. The *Times*'s customers were restrained by a rigid contractual agreement imposed to assure that no one would jump the gun and publish early. The *Post* labored under no such restriction.

Before we would publish our account, I consulted our lawyer and was told we would be on safe ground in terms of any copyright issues that might arise. We deemed it fair game in the face of the bombast regarding the tight security arrangements surrounding the publication of the book, which was part of the promotional hype. Only a handful of people at the *Post* knew about our stealth operation to be the first to reveal what Haldeman had to tell the world about the secrets of the Nixon administration. Besides the three senior editors and me, the others in on it were Haynes Johnson, who was slated to write the story, Nancy, and Woodward and his buddy Scott Armstrong. They assisted Haynes as he put the story together. I closely read a photocopy of the Haldeman book material, making marginal notes before drafting a memo I shared with Haynes. When we were ready to go to press, we clued in a handful of others required to bring the project into the paper—under our own strictures to keep the secret to themselves. We published a smashing summary of the book. The article ran across the top of Page 1 under the headline: "Haldeman Accuses Nixon."

When the *Times* found out that we were poised to eat its lunch and preempt its costly exclusive acquisition, it was sure to attempt to restrain us with a legal order. Being fully aware of that possibility throughout, I refused to take phone calls from the *Times* or anyone I did not personally know. I also readied myself to dodge any subpoena servers who might show up in our newsroom. The frustrated *Times* editor involved, not being able to contact me, called Katharine Graham. She had not been informed about what we were doing and was not pleased that her paper was undermining the large financial investment her magazine, *Newsweek,* had made to acquire the rights for its national audience. The *Post's* scoop became not only a matter of worldwide attention, it also aroused outrage over the ethics of what we had done. It compelled the *Times* to lift its embargo of the five newspaper installments and publish them all in the next day's paper. It took an edge away from the *Washington Star*. So two competitors of the *Post*, one local and the other national, had been discomfited. Afterward, I apologized to Mrs. Graham and said that I had thought she had been filled in by Ben. She heard me out for a time and when she felt I was overdoing it, she told me to can it. Publicly she said, "*Newsweek* and the *Post* are very competitive, but sometimes it can be a pain in the neck."

Some days later, I was relieved by another editor who returned from the conference in Florida so that I could join the Pugwash discussions on Sanibel Island. My command of the paper had been brief, but eventful.

Other events stand out for me during the time I spent overseeing Outlook. In June 1978, Alexander Solzhenitsyn gave his famous Harvard commencement address in which he reproached Western democracy and its moral profligacy in ignoring the Supreme Deity. Outlook published an extended excerpt of the Harvard speech because of its singular distinction as the thoughts of a brilliant writer and hero of the resistance to communist tyranny. Right away, I solicited an article to respond to Solzhenitsyn from a distinguished figure. Henry Kissinger declined. I next thought of Arthur Schlesinger Jr., the eminent historian, who accepted. Schlesinger's rebuttal paid the Russian great honor, but noted the reverence for Christian despotism that characterized his jeremiad, which faulted Western history as far back as the Renaissance. I wrote Schlesinger to thank him for the excellence of his article and for how quickly he had put it together. He answered, "And I am grateful to you for stimulating me to put my random thoughts about Solzhenitsyn in some kind of sequence."

Between Outlook, Book World, the Korea task force, my travels, Pugwashes, participation in academic panels, and lunches with stimulating people such as historian Barbara Tuchman, CIA director William Colby, feminist Gloria Steinem, public intellectual and arch neoconservative Irving Kristol, my time was productively occupied. I recall a particular conversation with Tuchman. In a meeting with a group of editors, and in response to our prodding, she observed that newspapers seemed always to concentrate on the bad news. I took the opportunity to point out that her work—concerning wars and crises—also focused on what qualified as bad news. Obviously, there was ample justification for her to do so, because these events were the hinges of history. Bad news in newspapers, which studies have shown to be less than often charged, is judged to be pervasive often because the complainer's ox is being gored. It's their school, their bank, or their political organization that is held to account for some problematic activity that in their eyes makes it bad news. From the newspaper's perspective, the coverage is intended to bring focus attention on problems. However, the majority of those who complain respond to reports of societal malfunctions. They would much rather not have been alerted to the need for often difficult or costly rectifications. Complacency, or ignoring troubling issues, does not make the problems go away or foster solutions.

On another occasion, Warren Buffett, the financial wizard who had taken a large stake in *The Washington Post* when it went public and became a friend and adviser to Kay Graham, shared his views with us. What I remember clearly from that encounter was his observation that in investing the most important object is to keep one's capital safe and whole, forgoing interest if necessary.

25

Primed for a Fresh Start

Despite dealing with consistently challenging or absorbing concerns as AME, I was restless. I had been Foreign Editor, AME/Metro, AME/National, and AME overseeing Outlook and Book World. My work had been praised by Katharine and Don Graham ("Nother excellent week with Outlook," he wrote). Special assignments from Bradlee showed me I was out of the doghouse.

But all of these intellectual stimuli and overcoming workplace problems were not enough. I joined the downtown YMCA and ran the track when I found time. When a headhunter approached me in September 1977 I didn't mind listening to the pitch, because I was ready for a change. It was clearer to me than ever, despite my successes with Outlook and Book World, my record with Foreign and Metro, that my career at the *Post* was in a holding pattern. I would never rise higher than AME. More than anything, I wanted command of a newspaper. I allowed my name to be put up for consideration to edit the *Minneapolis Star,* an afternoon newspaper. It never got past the headhunter stage. Steve Isaacs got the job and within four years the *Minneapolis Star* was merged into its sister paper. Most afternoon metro dailies were shutting down as readers shifted to morning papers.

At the white tie and tails Gridiron Dinner in 1978, I was sitting across a narrow table from Harwood. I told him then I had thought it over and would now be ready to take the Trenton job that I had earlier rejected. Harwood shared my thinking with Bradlee. Ben thought it a good idea (it had been his in the first place) and asked Katharine. She would hear nothing of it. She was more than tired of editors from Washington failing to connect with the far different Trenton market.

Another consequence of my talk with Harwood was productive. Coincidentally, he was contacted by his former boss in Trenton, Roger Grier, who had moved on to become the publisher of the Capital Newspapers in Albany, comprising the morning *Times Union* and the afternoon *Knickerbocker News*. At the time, each paper had its own editor. Now the corporate owner, Hearst, and Grier wanted to install one editor in charge of both dailies. They were looking for someone who had the experience to upgrade the underperforming papers in New York State's capital city. Grier phoned Dick Harwood to pick his brain for prospects. Harwood told him about me. When Grier contacted me, I had no intention of leaving the *Post* for papers in Albany, but I thought there was no harm in taking a look. In the spring of 1978, I flew up to Albany, and was convinced that an intriguing challenge awaited me there. The papers cried out for improvement and I was confident I could help. Over two days, Grier and I had extensive and frank discussions in which we each offered our own analysis of the problems facing the papers and what needed to be done to improve them. Not only were Grier and I of like mind, I concluded that I liked Roger and could see myself working for him. Drawn-out negotiations began. At one time I would have considered a Hearst offer laughable because of its right-wing and yellow journalism reputation in the newspaper industry. Just about this time, I read an article that described the Hearst Corporation's new leadership and how it was transforming its chain of newspapers for the better, adopting standards of quality journalism to which previous management had paid insufficient attention. Validating these described changes was the fact that Jim Bellows, my ultimate boss at the *Herald Tribune*, had left the *Washington Star* to edit Hearst's *Los Angeles Herald Examiner*.

I asked Bellows what is was like working for Hearst. He said that within the constraints of the budget he was free to practice his kind of journalism. He did not minimize the firm grip corporate kept on the budget, but he said he was able to function well enough.

The negotiations continued while Hearst looked over two other candidates. Roger brought in Robert J. Danzig, the head of the Newspaper Division of Hearst. We met in New York, and afterward the Hearst executives indicated there would be more meetings. At that point, I said that although I was interested in making the move to Albany, there had been enough interviews and meetings and now it was up to them to make a decision. The indecision was not to my liking and there was nothing more I could tell them.

Roger flew to Washington and we had lunch at our house. He met my family, including the girls, who were home from college and school. He made an offer that he said was not negotiable. It was up to me to take it or leave it. After Roger left I still was not certain. My family was agreeable to a move to Albany and Amy argued that the proposed salary, which was about 50 percent more than I was making after twelve years at the *Post*, plus the additional benefits that came with the job, were good enough and might not come along in another offer soon again. And so I accepted. It was the kind of position I had been seeking and for which my time in grade in New York and Washington had prepared me. I did not want to wait on another possible offer from another possible headhunter. My future awaited me in Albany.

My first move was to seek out Don Graham to tell him, as I had promised I would. He heard me out and I could tell he was not happy. He teared up momentarily. Some years later I learned from Mark Meagher, who was president of the *Post* when I left, that Mrs. Graham had talked with him about "buying my contract" and topping the Albany offer. Mark told me he had advised Katharine to let me take the path I had chosen.

The announcement was made by Roger Grier with me at his side in Albany and the story was published simultaneously in Washington. The announcement led to a large number of congratulatory letters, many from colleagues, including several on the National staff and correspondents abroad, some of whom I had mentored on Metro. I also heard from Senator Daniel Patrick Moynihan, who wrote for me in Outlook and shared with me his take on Albany, which was all fine until Rockefeller's building mania ruined it from the senator's point of view, a perspective shaped while he was a long-time aide there. There were communications from an editor who fifteen years earlier was a member of the Press Institute seminar and remembered the clash over coverage I had with the *Times* representative, and from a man who had done the stint with me at Columbia University's PR department. Even Bill McPherson wrote that my leaving "actually made me sad."

The next-to-best letter came from Barnee Breeskin, composer of the hymn "Hail to the Redskins," who enclosed an autographed score "to remind you that we love you and admire what you did." I was a Redskins convert from the New York Giants, and a season ticketholder, and therefore was holier than the Pope in my devotion to the team. Breeskin pleaded that I not "get involved with the Buffalo football team."

The best letter came from Dick Wald, then a top news executive at the *Los Angeles Times*. He wrote that I did not have any idea how much I would enjoy the new job. He also dropped Frank Bennack, the chief executive officer of the Hearst Corporation, five lines, congratulating him on hiring me. "a first-rate editor and a first-rate man."

I interviewed people in Washington with Albany connections, including W. Averell Harriman, the former New York governor, whom I visited in his Georgetown mansion. He urged me to campaign for leaders in state government to reside in Albany. He felt that living in the suburbs detracted from the focus they should have. Ernest Boyer, a former New York State commissioner of education, had similar advice, not involving people but the location of the state office buildings in which they worked. State offices should be located in Albany, he strongly believed. U.S. Representative Sam Stratton, a long-tenured Schenectady Democrat and a powerhouse of a legislator, took me to lunch in the House restaurant.

We were not only leaving the *Post* but also our close circle of friends, and both partings were hard to bear. George Solomon, the Sports Editor and a close tennis-playing friend, attended a number of parties and hosted one to which Mrs. Graham came. I have a fine photo of Katharine and me sitting on a sofa in George's living room in Potomac, engaged in conversation. He jokingly compared the serial farewell events to the numbered Super Bowl games. The biggest one was thrown by the *Post*. Kay wanted to give it but Bradlee insisted that he had to. It was in a private room at Duke Zeibert's, a popular restaurant. In addition to people from the paper, some of our personal friends were invited. Roger Grier came down from Albany. Governor Hugh Carey was invited but could not attend. He sent a letter saying he looked forward to our meeting in Albany and telegraphed his "welcome to the winter capital."

There were a lot of speeches. I saved a copy of Bradlee's notes from which he spoke and that he gave me as a memento. Bradlee said: "And it took no time at all for us to feel Harry's impact, impact, impact. It turned out he had this unbelievable sense of history. Every time we decided to put one of Harry's stories inside, he would warn us that we were doing a dirty thing. 'You're going right into the history books if you put that inside. My friend Abe Rosenthal will probably lead the paper with it.' And he'd bet one of us and he'd almost always lose. That's one thing you've got to say about Harry. He's a good loser. . . . When you've got class as a loser, you've got real class."

He added, "Before we give you your present, I just want to get very serious, very briefly: One of the great things about this newspaper is that it asks great things of many people. And many people respond. Harry Rosenfeld is one of those who responded so well and so often for us in these last years. You are a complete newspaperman. You've done it all for this paper, with commitment and grace. We thank you, and we love you and we salute you."

I had been going over in my mind what I would say, searching for the words to express genuine feelings while keeping to the right side of sentimentality. It preoccupied me in the days leading up to the Bradlee dinner, even while I was jogging. It was wrenching for me to leave the *Post* given all my experiences, the good but also the not so good. I had worked in the company of champions.

Reflecting my hyper-emotionalism, I said something to the effect that in my heart, I would carry all of them with me to Albany. As the event broke up, Nora Ephron, then Bernstein's companion, asked me whether on my journey northward I minded dropping her off in New York. Carl said I was getting out gracefully.

In my letter of resignation addressed to Ben, dated September 27, 1978, I wrote that my last day would be September 29 and added: "I wish there were a way for me to catalogue the range of experiences that I've had at The Post these past 12 years and the lessons they have taught me. I thank you for hiring me, and for giving me assignments, each of which permitted me to do something different and learn something new. I am grateful for your counsel and guidance over the years, and for the many personal kindnesses you have shown my family and me.

"I leave to take up new challenges, but I will always hold dear *The Washington Post* and the people who have brought it to such high estate."

Simons did not leave the *Post* until 1984. I was well-established as editor in Albany when I was nominated to run for a seat on the board of the American Society of Newspaper Editors. During ASNE's annual convention in Washington I was at the opening cocktail party at the National Press Club, shaking hands and making pleasantries when Bradlee appeared. We greeted each other warmly and talked for a while. As he moved on, he turned to call out to me, "Tell your friend for God's sake to take the Nieman job." Howard had been offered the position to direct the prestigious Nieman Fellowship Program at Harvard University for mid-career journalists and was considering it. I said nothing about it to Howard, who did go off unprompted by me and quickly made a splash in Cambridge until his untimely death of cancer at age sixty. Downie succeeded him as Managing Editor of the *Post.*

As the first editor of both the *Times Union* and the *Knickerbocker News* in Albany, I reached the editing post I had long wanted. More than ready for the change, I was committed to the idea that quality journalism, sparked by enterprise and investigative reporting that scrutinizes those who wield power, was not a mission reserved for large metropolitan newspapers. It was, or should be, the domain of regional and small-city publications, even for community ones, in order to uphold the purposes of the First Amendment. Not only people in great cities were entitled to the benefits that vigorous journalism can provide. I was leaving my work on newspapers of national stature in New York and in Washington, where for twenty-five years I had served in subordinate though increasingly demanding positions. I left *The Washington Post* to confront the expanded duties as the Editor-in-Charge in Albany for nearly two decades to come. Now I could run the show without *Assistant* or any adjectival modifier before my title, totally in charge and totally responsible. It would be the third chapter in my professional life, the longest and the last.

Today, from the vantage of a newspaperman in his eighties whose career has spanned fifty years, looking back at my life I am able to see what only had been dimly apprehended throughout my earlier years—the connection between what I had experienced as a child growing up in the grip of a totalitarian regime and what I was to do as a grown man in a democratic America. The hindsight put into sharper focus how my Berlin childhood influenced the careers I did not choose and how I performed the one that I did. In coming to America, I ingested its inspirational myths and ethos and made them my own, which prepared me well to be a newspaperman. After I argued successfully with my parents to let me take that path, I never sought another way. That was my minor triumph, but a triumph nevertheless.

My major triumph was rooted as well in my childhood. Because the Hahn and Rosenfeld families had to flee Germany, Annie and I met. Had we been able to live out our lives in a tolerant Germany, we likely never would have crossed paths. She grew up in a small village in the provinces and I in the great city of Berlin. She was born into a Jewish family residing in Germany for more than two centuries. I was the child of Polish parents who at the time of our departure had lived in Germany only a couple of decades. The cultural separation between the German Jews and East European Jews was a barrier seldom breached.

So it was that because of a historic calamity, Annie and I found ourselves as young people in the same city. Even so, our meeting at a dance at a Bronx high school neither of us attended was not an opportunity likely to recur. Another instance of life-shaping good luck, but that doesn't mean our courtship was easy. Only unrelenting pursuit, refusing to take no or maybe for an answer, saw me through. In love and in my career, I never gave up. I was geared always to try harder. Nobody ever called me a quitter. And that is my life's major triumph, the one achievement that will be chiseled into my tombstone, that I was the husband of Anne.

After my retirement from the *Times Union*, two events came to pass that scaffold my story. When the sixtieth anniversary of Kristallnacht occurred in 1998, Scott Shpeen, the rabbi of the synagogue to which we belonged, invited me to speak at our congregation's commemorative Shabbat services on that occasion. Preparing my remarks rekindled in me fury at the vast cruelties of the Holocaust.

In front of a packed sanctuary, I recounted the sparse details I remembered of those days and nights. I summed up that evening this way: "Of this I am certain: That the values that I came to develop as an American and then as a journalist are buttressed by what I saw and felt as a child when the power of a hostile and hateful state overwhelmed us and nearly took our lives. That state ravaged our extended family, taking many uncles, aunts and cousins in Poland and in Germany, who did not have the chance to flee."

When the rabbi renewed the invitation on the sixty-fifth anniversary in 2003, I wanted to avoid going through the trauma again. But it was not possible for me to turn down Rabbi Shpeen. At first, I thought there was nothing left for me to say; the history of Kristallnacht had not changed for the better in the interim. Going over my earlier text, I concluded that I had not acknowledged enough my parents' role in those dangerous days. So I used my second presentation to largely the same audience to set matters right. I said: "My parents are my heroes because they remained steadfast and determined at a time when they had no way to know what the best decision would be. That was excruciating pressure to have to be under while striving to protect your family." I better understood this stress as a father than ever I had as only a son.

My parents' anguish was vividly brought to mind when I learned in 2005 what had befallen my boyhood playmate Gustav and his father. Four years afterward, a relative of Gustav and Roger Lowen, his American cousin, contacted me. The caller's son, Simon Lowen, was to become bar mitzvah. Simon wanted to have Gustav become bar mitzvah along with him. He did so under a twinning program established to remember murdered Jewish children deprived by the Holocaust the chance to observe this religious rite. In preparing, Simon asked me to tell him everything I could about Gustav, who was the first cousin of Simon's paternal grandfather. While the teenager was still undergoing instruction for the ceremony, another relative questioned whether Gustav was actually a Jew, since his mother was a Gentile. According to tradition dating back to the early years of the Christian era, Jewishness is determined either matrilineally or through conversion. In more recent times, that definition has been expanded by Reform Judaism to include descent through the father. Simon's family phoned me to ask my view.

Unfamiliar with the why and wherefores of the religious tradition, which differ among Judaism's different branches, I resorted to other reasoning. I said, "Gustav was killed as a Jew by the Germans. His identity card was stamped with a huge 'J' for all the world to see. Gustav was a Jew."

On July 11, 2009, some sixty-seven years after his death in a work camp in Estonia, Gustav, in the person of his cousin Simon, became bar mitzvah, son of the commandment, at Congregation B'nai Emunah in Tulsa, Oklahoma. To a man of my age and history, Simon's gesture continues to comfort me.

The other section of my story's scaffold occurred in 2005 when Mark Felt, the former No. 2 official at the FBI, revealed himself as Deep Throat. The former head of the regional FBI office based in Albany, Paul V. Daly, then retired, phoned me. We had become acquainted during his six-year Albany tour. He told me that he had some relevant information about Felt's actions as Deep Throat. Years before he was stationed in Albany, Daly was assigned to help prepare the prosecutors' case against Felt and others for illegal FBI break-ins directed at violent antiwar activists. Felt was convicted and later pardoned. In the course of his investigation, Daly learned in 1978 from a highly placed FBI official how he and two others of similar rank collaborated with Felt to leak information about Watergate to Bob Woodward at the *Post*. The four FBI officials regularly met in the afternoon to thwart White House efforts to halt the FBI probe then fitfully underway. I turned the tip over to *Times Union* Editor Rex Smith and he assigned his top investigative reporter Brendan Lyons. The ensuing story was spread across the top of Page 1. The article opened a window into understanding Watergate that had been shut all those many years since the break-in occurred in 1972. This was a revelation that *The Washington Post* in our exhaustive pursuit of the Watergate scandal had not reported.

Daly's disclosure was a postscript to an event that has shaped and reshaped American politics and society. It provides insight into how a free press functions to serve the public interest. A story of the consequential impact of Watergate lingers in the nation's communal consciousness. From time to time, bits and pieces emerge to enlarge or complicate our understanding of Watergate, as it did with Daly's belated speaking out. Predictably, the work of Woodstein and the *Post* was questioned over the years by revisionists. Despite whatever actual or alleged shortcomings, *The Washington Post*'s Watergate coverage was solid. Latter-day backbiting, nitpicks, and quibbles do not contravene the historical fact that the *Post* played a key role in assisting the ship of state to stay the course while navigating through the stormy waters of a constitutional crisis. The United States of America did not succumb to a leader who set himself above its Constitution. The newspaper stuck to its job, unearthing the truth about a law-breaker president, armed with the full arsenal of executive powers. It was a standard-setting demonstration of the indispensability of a free press in a democracy. Newspapering of such import, it must be said, can only be sustained with the owner or publisher standing behind the newsroom and committing the necessary resources, and having the guts, to sustain quality journalism.

To my mind, investigative and exploratory journalism are the soul of newspapering and the most taxing and rewarding part of the business. On the other hand, for a newspaper to blaze with a "hard, gem-like flame" all the time likely would result in burnout. For me, newspapering was mostly fun. It was never drudgery. I was modestly paid but amply compensated as I observed and recorded the absurd as well as the profound, the entertaining as well as the informative. When newspapers are on their game and are mindful of their limitations, they are handy and useful adjuncts to learning and understanding—as long as readers keep their skepticism at the ready.

Newspapering was my world and I was happy in it. I regard my five decades as a newspaperman as a down payment on a bill that can never be stamped "Paid in full." I owe America—for the lives of my families and for the opportunity to live my life as I wanted.

Epilogue

As I headed the unreliable family Dodge sedan north from Washington, it was quiet in the car. Annie and our youngest daughter Stefanie clearly were unhappy. There were tears of regret. Their unhappiness upset me because I had thrust this difficult and emotional relocation on them, even though they were all supportive of the decision when it was made.

Leaving Washington and our home in Kensington was a sea change for us all. For Annie, it was daunting, separating from close friends and starting from scratch to build a new life for us in a community much smaller than we were accustomed to and where she knew nobody. It was hardest for Steffie, then fourteen and about to begin high school. She was torn out of her circle of friends and comfort zone for reasons she probably could not fully understand. Her sisters were away at college, Susan at Boston University and Amy at Duke. The move did not impact the two of them in the same way. The transition from Washington to Albany was easiest for me, for I was fully engaged from the outset in my new job.

In Albany, at first we lived in a rented house while looking to buy. Since we did not know in which school district we would end up purchasing a home, Stefanie was enrolled in Girls Academy, an old and well-regarded private school. Her interest in art was spurred there and it became a primary focus of her college years at Ithaca College and New York University. Annie and I were introduced to a circle of acquaintances from which a core of close friends emerged. These new Albany friends became our local extended family as our grown children left town to pursue careers and establish their own lives.

I eagerly threw myself into my new responsibilities, clearly understanding how to carry out the mandate I was hired to execute: to raise the quality of the two newspapers. I spent the next nineteen years working at the task, the first sixteen as editor in charge of all newsroom activities, the final three in charge of the editorial pages, eventually under a new title, Editor-at-Large.

My self-confidence was not a sign of arrogance but reflected my long experience at two influential newspapers. At the *Herald Tribune* I was part of an effort to preserve the life of a once-substantial and still highly regarded newspaper as it struggled to ward off eventual closure. At *The Washington Post* I was part of a team that took a mediocre newspaper and elevated it to greatness. In Albany, I was again assigned to build up newspapers that in recent years had been neglected.

I began by imposing rigorous journalistic standards on the staff and the supervisory editors. Practices reeked of conflict of interest, and it was imperative to put everyone on the same page. To that end, I insisted that an ethics code be drafted and promulgated. At the same time, I recruited the best newspaper people I could find to help me reshape the papers. The first reporter I hired, Alan Miller, became the lead reporter on several major investigative projects. He went on to win a Pulitzer Prize for investigative reporting at the *Los Angeles Times* Washington bureau. The first news executive hire, Dan Lynch, was recruited from *Newsday*. He served energetically with notable skill as one of the *Times Union* managing editors as long as I was in charge of the news operation. He was a constant and major contributor to bringing the *Times Union* up to speed.

I was supported and backed by my publisher, Roger Grier, as our TU and Knick staffs began to execute the investigative and explanatory journalism that is at the core of a quality newspaper. The first order of business was to take on the entrenched Democratic political machine. Erastus Corning 2nd was the patrician face of the down and dirty machine, the longest-tenured mayor of any city in America. He died in his forty-second year in office. In several major projects over the years, our reporters detailed the political machine's corrupt practices and patronage abuses. Our reporting led the federal government to investigate the corruption of a local spawn of that Democratic machine, Jim Coyne, during construction of a county-owned sports arena in downtown Albany. Coyne resigned as Albany County Executive in time to be tried, convicted of nine felonies, and imprisoned for forty-six months.

We also took on state government with renewed vigor. When Governor Hugh Carey, who welcomed me to Albany by inviting me to a private breakfast in the Executive Mansion, complained he was underpaid, we revealed just how much he cost the state and we dubbed him "The Million Dollar Governor." We also investigated the operations of a home for wayward girls in Albany, run by a dedicated order of Catholic nuns. Our reporting uncovered that some of the nuns' practices were counterproductive and even abusive. Our work led to the home's leadership being changed and brought an end to its egregious practices.

Albany has a rich political history as a state capital with national aspirations as well as a city and county notorious for being able to deliver the votes for any Democrat its leadership supported. Politicians from near and far came to call, and the newspapers invariably were a stopover. Governors and mayors, U.S. senators and House members, candidates for president and vice president, and ambitious politicians at all levels regularly visited our newspapers' editorial boards, which developed a reputation for hard-edged questioning.

High culture occasionally dropped into our upstate province. Annie and I dined with and enjoyed the company of the Nobelist writer Isaac Bashevis Singer and the distinguished sculptor Louise Nevelson, among many renowned visitors.

Step by step, the newsroom's leadership team, formed from new hires and editors and reporters already in place, managed to effect widespread and profound changes for the better. I consciously rejected Bradlee's creative tension, which occasionally resulted in my living with problem employees longer than I should have.

Albany was not to be my only stop as an editor for Hearst. In 1985, I was assigned by corporate to take the helm at the *Los Angeles Herald Examiner*, whose editor had resigned. Hearst charged me with holding the wheel steady while corporate decided what to do with the economically troubled paper. This meant that I was simultaneously editor of three daily newspapers—two on the East Coast and one on the West Coast. That may have been some kind of geographical record for an editor's duties. During my temporary posting in L.A., circulation noticeably increased. The staff and I got along well. I was asked to take over the *Herald Examiner* permanently and was tempted. My battle plan for a better future for the paper was admired at Hearst headquarters but not funded. Although I enjoyed running the L.A. paper and learned a lot, I returned full time to Albany.

My standing with Hearst was demonstrated by my selection in these years to appear in three nationwide advertisements for the corporation. One celebrated the one hundredth anniversary of William Randolph Hearst launching his eponymous enterprise. The ad was a full-page painted illustration of people who had worked for Hearst over that century. I was the only serving newspaper editor or reporter among the fifty-four persons depicted, a collection that included Mark Twain and Jack London from The Chief's earliest years and the superstar Helen Gurley Brown from its modern era.

When Joseph Lyons succeeded Roger Grier as publisher about two years after I arrived in Albany, he quickly put on the agenda merging the *Knickerbocker News* into the *Times Union*. For years I resisted that proposition, even as periodically we were charged with making plans for integrating the afternoon daily into the morning paper. As time passed, my opposition weakened, because circulation figures showed that the Knick declined no matter what steps we took to hold it steady. The losses of the afternoon paper offset the gains made by the morning paper. On April 15, 1988, the *Knickerbocker News*, after 145 years, ceased publication.

My agreement to the merger was facilitated by corporate's commitment that we would keep virtually all of our reporters and editors. The result was that the *Times Union* became an even stronger newspaper that produced circulation numbers never before attained. We established an investigation team and a business news department and created coverage specialties in education, transportation, and health and science. We opened bureaus in adjacent counties. "The *Times Union* has legs," Frank A. Bennack Jr., chief executive officer of Hearst, once famously observed.

Throughout both the good times and then the worsening economic climate for newspapers, I held to the mission for which I had been recruited—to build up, not to scale back or tear down. During the cyclical economic downturns, acceptable cost controls included a hiring freeze and other nuanced belt-tightening reductions to keep within a reduced budget. That was par for the course. In 1989, when the Schenectady *Daily Gazette* announced that it planned to publish a Sunday paper, the immediate reaction by publisher Lyons and his management team was to make major cuts in the editorial budget.

In his view of the landscape, the *Times Union* had been delivering the Sunday paper for the *Gazette* these many years. Now that would end. His general manager told the newsroom managers working up the budget, "You guys just don't get it. Our revenues are going to take a major hit and you will have to downscale." The reaction of the newsroom was just the opposite: this was the time to increase the newsroom's firepower to keep our foothold in the *Gazette*'s circulation area. The newsroom won that argument, but not because we were persuasive. We won because the great-grandson of William Randolph Hearst was by that time the operations manager of the *Times Union*. George R. Hearst III, saw that the publisher's battle plan was buying into defeat. George went down to New York and told Frank Bennack that the *Times Union* was strong and could win the competition against the Sunday *Gazette*. Instead of cutting the editorial budget, as Lyons proposed, it should be increased. The result was that the *Times Union* halted the threat of the Sunday *Gazette* and even increased its circulation numbers in Schenectady.

The next publisher, Tim White, confronted tougher economic setbacks. Business downturns now appeared to be less cyclical. The publisher, who lived and died in the corporate world by his bottom line, wanted me to be an enthusiastic collaborator in what he was pleased not to call by its correct name, downsizing, preferring instead the spin merchant's rightsizing. By his calculation, this meant mostly cutting back on the size of the paper and editorial staff, whose accomplishments had earned the admiration of the highest echelons in Hearst headquarters.

Struggle and unrelenting tension accompanied my final years as editor as I chose to fight a rearguard action to preserve editorial quality and standards. It only ended with my retirement. Despite our fundamental differences, Tim White, who had spoken internally about replacing me nearly from the time he joined the paper, proposed and I accepted his offer to continue as a consultant, retaining my final title, Editor-at-Large, which I still hold. I had begun writing a Sunday column while I was editor and continued to do so after I retired. It was distributed through the Hearst Washington bureau to the other Hearst newspapers and by the *New York Times* news service to its clients nationwide. With the support of George Hearst, who was by then publisher and my boss, I suspended writing the column to begin to work full time on my memoir. I was eighty, and had to confront the deadline no human can circumvent.

In addition, over the span of these years I was appointed to serve on three separate committees to study the feasibility of cameras in the courts in New York State. I also was elected as vice-chair of the state's Fair Trial/Free Press Conference and worked alongside the Chief Judge of New York, who served as chair. As a happy consequence, I formed friendships that enriched my life with succeeding chief judges of the state, Sol Wachtler and Judith Kaye.

My newspaper work was honored over the years by my profession, my college, and religious and community groups in Washington and Albany and elsewhere. In the course of my career, I shook hands with five presidents, something beyond my imagination when I set foot in America. We came to America not for honors, not for religious freedom, not to find wealth. Simply said, we fled Germany to save our lives and we found a treasure—the American way of life and the remarkable opportunities that it spread before us.

The children and grandchildren of Martha and Sol Hahn, of Esther and Sam Rosenfeld over time settled across this nation. They now live between Boston and Miami, New York and California. The eight who found refuge on these shores have multiplied and thrived.

My sister Rachel is in her nineties and resides in Palm Springs. She is a mother of four, grandmother of eleven, and great-grandmother of eleven. After being known as Rosa, Resi, Ray, and Rachel, she acquired yet another name, GeeGee.

In my immediate family, Susan, our oldest, resides in the Boston area; Amy lives outside Chicago; and Stefanie makes her home in New York City. I never tried to steer my daughters into journalism, unlike my father, who wanted me to be a furrier. College for them was a foregone conclusion, and they all took it a step farther by earning graduate degrees. Each daughter chose her own path: Susan as a college admissions officer, Amy as an attorney, and Steffie as a graphic artist. Not a scribbler in the group.

Our grandchildren are on their way to charting their futures. In order of their age, they are: Sarah Wachter (Simmons College '09), Dana Kaufman (Amherst College '12), Jonathan Wachter (Syracuse University '13) and Jake Kaufman (Kenyon College '14). Melanie, Wil, and A. J. Aiken attend New York's public schools.

The promise personified by our children and grandchildren is the mother lode of the treasure we found in America.

I do not wear my acquired citizenship lightly. I tried to affirm my obligation as an American in my newspaper work. I donned with pride the uniform of my country. I am not a jingoist and I am keenly aware of the imperfections within our perfect union. Anti-Semitism is not impossible to find, although it has muted from my early days in the United States. Racism and other failings are all too evident still. For a country as rich as ours, there are too many poor and working poor. The founding ideal of *E Pluribus Unum* continues to need commitment and sweat labor. Each generation is duty bound to struggle to fulfill its promise. The point is that in this nation the people have the constitutional protections and traditions with which to constrain oppressive government, permitting them to scale the highest barriers to right wrongs.

Annie and I have buried our mothers and fathers in American soil; no longer Poles or Germans, they were Americans. "Land where my fathers died" now applies to us as much as to the native-born. America is my homeland, the place where I always breathed easiest and where, with luck, my last breath will be drawn.

Appendix

The Nixon-Ziegler tape was difficult to transcribe. Ziegler's voice was always audible, but Nixon's was hard to hear and occasionally indistinct. Equipment adjustments during several replays produced increasing clarity, although portions remained unintelligible. The tape was recorded on April 16, 1973, in the Oval Office, between 12:58 p.m. and 1:37 p.m.

Names Mentioned on Tape (In Order of Appearance)

Bob—H. R. Haldeman, president's chief of staff

John—John Ehrlichman, president's chief domestic adviser

Billy Griggs—unknown

Dick Moore—Richard Moore, special Watergate counsel

Len—Leonard Garment, special consultant to president

Chappie Rose—H. Chapman Rose, personal Watergate adviser to president

Rogers—William P. Rogers, secretary of state

Ray Price—Raymond K. Price Jr., chief speechwriter

Gergen—David Gergen, speechwriter

Dean—John W. Dean III, White House counsel

Petersen—Henry E. Petersen, chief of Justice Department's criminal division

Ervin—Senator Sam Ervin, Democrat of North Carolina

Magruder—Jeb Stuart Magruder, deputy campaign manager

Mathias—Senator Charles McC. Mathias Jr., Republican of Maryland

Dominick—Senator Peter Dominick, Republican of Colorado

Rikers—unknown

Segretti—Donald H. Segretti, political saboteur

Mitchell—John N. Mitchell, director of Nixon re-election campaign

Langston Hughes—poet and social activist

Eagleton—Governor Thomas F. Eagleton, Missouri Democrat, resigned as George McGovern's vice presidential running mate in 1972

Start of Transcribed Tape

Nixon: Hi Ron, come in.

Ziegler: Do you have a moment, ah, Mr. President?

Nixon: Sure. Just in case I brought a little something in, propagated cheap talk. Here.

Ziegler: Ah, Jesus. Couple of quick things. I had the meeting with Bob and John this morning, and . . .

Nixon: Did you go over to Billy Griggs?

Ziegler: No, I was meeting with them.

Nixon: Oh, right.

Ziegler: So I.

Nixon: We had a nice, nice reception.

Ziegler: Good.

Nixon: We talked about national defenses. Yup.

Ziegler: Well, couple very quick things. Ah, as you have been told, I think by John, um, I've been involved . . .

Nixon: Think they've got you working that scenario, right?

Ziegler: . . . with some meetings and so forth with Dick Moore, ah Len Garment and, ah, Chappie Rose.

Nixon: Yeah, yeah.

Ziegler: Len Garment, as Bob mentioned to you . . .

Nixon: Yeah, wants to see . . .

Ziegler: . . . Wants to see . . .

Nixon: But I'm gonna wait and let him see Rogers, if that's all right with you.

Ziegler: Well, I'd like to offer a point to you.

Nixon: Yeah.

Ziegler: Basically, I can get into some of Len's thinking with you if you like. I won't if you prefer not to.

Nixon: Yeah, yeah, yeah.

Ziegler: But I think it would, my judgment, which I would like to suggest, is that it might be good to see Len before Rogers, because Len may raise some points that I think would be good to check with [indistinct].

Nixon: Well, I've asked Len to write a little memorandum on it if he could, again he did this.

Ziegler: Well, what I told Len is that . . .

Nixon: You know, I told Bob to give him instructions on it, to write a memorandum on this before the meeting.

Ziegler: Well, I told Len, I said what you should do, Len, is . . .

Nixon: I gotta see it on a piece of paper so I can think about it.

Ziegler: Well, what I told him is, take the time now before he sees ya, just lock himself in his office, just sit down and block out on yellow paper or you know, his views, so that he can present . . .

Nixon: What'd he say?

Ziegler: . . . a solution. That's what he's doing right now.

Nixon: Good.

Ziegler: I said the President does not need any more facts.

Nixon: I've got, I've got more heat in this.

Ziegler: I said, that's what I told him. I said the President does not need any agonizing about the fact that we have a problem. All that you, all that he needs . . .

Nixon: Can I say please, that's the problem.

Ziegler: . . . all that he needs is your thinking, because you've been asked to steep yourself into this, as you say, and you have done that. And you have a recommendation to put to the President.

Nixon: That's right.

Ziegler: Do it, but do the recommendation and don't spend the time agonizing. So he's in that frame of mind.

Nixon: Right.

Ziegler: Therefore, I think, ah you know, he's asked for five minutes and, say, give him eight minutes or something. It would be good to get his view before Rogers, because I think Rogers would be a good person to . . .

Nixon: Try him out on.

Ziegler: . . . to try him out on.

Nixon: Good.

Ziegler: Ah, so that's the Garment, ah, file. Ah, now I can take your time with some additional thoughts now, or, or wait, ah, ah, whatever you'd prefer.

Nixon: What?

Ziegler: Well, ah, ah the following discussion with, with ah, John . . .

Nixon: Hello, hold on . . . I think that you should talk to him only about this. Hello, ah, Dennis [indistinct]

Nixon: The following discussion, go ahead.

Ziegler: Now he, John, fully, was very frank in our meeting this morning.

Nixon: Tell me something, he's gonna be, he could be, you hear me?

Ziegler: Well, he, he said he'd prefer for me to talk to you alone.

Nixon: Alright, fine. Go ahead. So . . .

Ziegler: So, ah, several things that should be provided to you so that you have in your mind, ah . . .

Nixon: Yeah, yeah.

Ziegler: . . . just from a general standpoint for perspective. At the White House Correspondents' Dinner, ah, Rosenfeld, who is the metropolitan editor for the *Post*, who has been the man in charge of . . .

Nixon: Yeah.

Ziegler: . . . the, ah, ah story . . .

Nixon: Yeah.

Ziegler: . . . because Woodward and Bernstein fall under the metropolitan side, ah, which, which is unusual. Ah, mentioned to Ray Price, who used to work for Rosenfeld at the New York . . .

Nixon: *Tribune.*

Ziegler: . . . *Tribune.* Ah, that he has been agonizing over this matter, that they have a lot more information than has been printed. That Rosenfeld feels, ah, that the story will be told in its entirety. That they are tying together some loose ends now, but he insists that anything printed is tied down, is what he said. And that his concern is that it will, when the story unfolds and breaks by the *Post*, that it will hurt the presidency, the current President, and the Office of the President. Ray, recognizing his view on this type of thing, although he did not do anything but report this, points out that Rosenfeld is one of the few people in a high position on the *Post*, who is a conscientious . . .

Nixon: Decent guy.

Ziegler: . . . professional, and indeed volunteered to Price, and I believe him, that he supported you . . .

Nixon: Yeah.

Ziegler: . . . for public office consistently, including the recent election. And makes that point to Price by saying that this is a story that will be told and must be told.

Nixon: Yeah.

Ziegler: Now combine that with the discussion that ah, ah speechwriter, ah, Gergen had with Bob Woodward and Carl Bernstein also at the White House Correspondents' Dinner, on the basis that Gergen and Woodward were former college chums. Woodward made the point separately that the *Post* has far more information than they have reported and that they are tying up ends now. And that anything less than full disclosure at this time . . .

Nixon: Yeah.

Ziegler: . . . would pose ah, a problem. Now, that is consistent with what I sense from Woodward's inquiry, Woodward's inquiries to . . .

Nixon: In other words, they've got a few more things to— they don't know what we know now.

Ziegler: I don't believe so, but I think they're running down that line. They're running down the line, I think we can assume, specifically on the post-trial information, because they've already had a story on that.

Nixon: Yeah.

Ziegler: Now.

Nixon: That's a big story right there.

Ziegler: Yes sir. That's correct. Now, ah, Woodward also, Gergen said, had some you know, hang-ups, to the degree that Gergen feels Woodward is into something that is bigger than he can handle. But in any event, both men made the point that they have additional information, ah, broader in scope, than anything that has appeared. And Woodward went so far as to say to Gergen that he would like to sit down with him and go over this with him, just to, which Gergen did not do.

Nixon: Maybe he should.

Ziegler: Well, I don't know.

Nixon: Maybe.

Ziegler: My view is that the activity of the *Post* over the last five or six days suggests that they are hovering on the outer fringes here, waiting to assess what move the White House will take, and then drawing the conclusion as to whether or not to discredit that move.

Nixon: Yeah.

Ziegler: So I think we have to keep that in mind.

Nixon: Good point.

Ziegler: Now, second, that is to put in perspective, at least the press side of it.

Nixon: Yeah, right.

Ziegler: The grand jury which . . .

Nixon: That's very good, that's very good to know.

Ziegler: . . . you know of. Now, in terms of the posture of the President and this was something talked about by Chappie Rose, who is a very sharp guy.

Nixon: Good man.

Ziegler: Um, Moore and ah Garment and myself. Ah, it seems that the minimum that should be done from the standpoint of the posture of the President . . . You have been informed of certain information by the Attorney General.

Nixon: Right.

Ziegler: You have become aware on you own initiative over the past period.

Nixon: Of certain information.

Ziegler: However, we, we, ah, however, that is, ah, mistaken. You face a situation where John Dean, your counsel, ah, who was placed in charge of this, provided you an accurate Watergate report, but not a complete one. Therefore . . .

Nixon: He says he didn't have a complete report.

Ziegler: But . . .

Nixon: Go ahead.

Ziegler: The facts that the President has been told, at least as I understand it, in terms of Dean, is that you were forced to make judgments based upon only thirty-two percent of the information that he had available to him. In all fairness to John, talking now about, ah, what will come out later.

Nixon: Well, Dean's report is basically, I said is anybody involved in the White House and he said no, and he still says that.

Ziegler: That's correct. So, I'm saying . . .

Nixon: The *Post* is what he's talking about.

Ziegler: Well also, ah . . .

Nixon: So I admit some general knowledge and all that, but I didn't ah, ah, I think the only point that I ever excluded, well go ahead.

Ziegler: No, the rationale is, yesterday or at some point, the Attorney General says to you that the grand jury is uncovering information that's . . .

Nixon: But I don't, I'm not going to hear the Attorney General, because we found that out ourselves.

Ziegler: No, alright, alright.

Nixon: That's what I'll say. Through our, through our investigation we were, we're turning it over and getting that out there, you know what I mean, by found ah, from Dean and others, so forth and so on. We turn this information over to the Attorney General. The Attorney General of course is in favor, not the Attorney General, but the U.S. Attorney. We turn over, turned it over to the Attorney General. But go ahead.

Ziegler: Well, however that . . .

Nixon: I want to be sure we get the precaution right. We've done something, too.

Ziegler: That's, absolutely.

Nixon: We weren't just dragged kicking and screaming in here by the U.S. Attorney.

Ziegler: That's a must. I agree with that. My point on, on John Dean, is that based on the information that you have obtained, you are now aware that he had information that he could have provided to you both post- and pre-trial which has just now come to your attention. Now the only action that people can relate to on the part of, anyone, when you become aware of that information is decisive action. In other words, the, the man did not do right.

Nixon: Yeah, the problem you've got there is this: making Dean, Dean the scapegoat or something I'm thinking works. And would he make up with regard to Haldeman or to be quite candid, see what I mean? I know what you're suggesting.

Ziegler: Of course, of course Dean would not necessarily be the scapegoat in this case.

Nixon: See, I'd have the right way to do it in a situation where I don't say Dean withheld information from me.

Ziegler: But the only choice you have, Mr. President is, in, in terms of . . .

Nixon: Yeah.

Ziegler: . . . of, of that, at some point . . .

Nixon: Dean claims he didn't have any information, didn't have all the information.

Ziegler: I understand that. But at some point the trial records, public trial records, will show that Dean did attend meetings, ah that Dean . . .

Nixon: Dean always attended meetings.

Ziegler: Right, ah that . . .

Nixon: But that was turned off long before and afterwards, afterwards I guess.

Ziegler: And that Dean did have information that suggested, ah, the corruption of ah justice or something of that sort. And, the reaction to that would be, if he did not tell you.

Nixon: Yeah.

Ziegler: Then you should have been aware of that, so, particularly from your counsel, if he had that, probably assumed that you could move against him. If he did tell you . . .

Nixon: I didn't fire him.

Ziegler: See, in other words, there's no, there's no positive way out of it. So . . .

Nixon: Yup.

Ziegler: The action now, in, in, in my view and in the view of this group, is at the minimum, ah, action.

Nixon: Well let me tell you, the U.S. Attorney is gonna tell me today and the ah, Petersen told me last night, that I said now look here, I said, get Dean's resignation. He said don't do it first of all, we're negotiating a plea with the department. You know, now if I, if I ah, if I, If I unloaded him today, they could say that with knowledge that it would jeopardize their efforts to get, you know, other issues. Now I, I can't lie.

Ziegler: I'm, well, I'm, see, that's where I . . .

Nixon: That's the problem.

Ziegler: . . . I'm not a lawyer, so I don't know.

Nixon: I, I already asked that question last night with Petersen. I said look, I, I've got this information and he said, oh, I gotta let it go very quick. And ah, told Dean right off of this information I have here this morning, said I'll give it to him, at the direction of Petersen. You know, which I can use at any time, which his point is that. I see your point. Let me see, with regard to action, though, do you got any other thoughts, though, other than just, you know, getting Dean? Do you see my point here?

Ziegler: Yes, absolutely.

Nixon: I've yet, I cannot jeopardize the prosecution.

Ziegler: That's correct.

Nixon: It's the prosecution . . .

Ziegler: Well . . .

Nixon: With what I know, crap, I didn't know in a good minute.

Ziegler: Minimum action, it seems . . .

Nixon: Yeah.

Ziegler: . . . is that the President announces awareness . . .

Nixon: Yeah.

Ziegler: . . . ah, developed over the last few weeks.

Nixon: That's right. Get the full report.

Ziegler: Ah, meeting with the Attorney General. Ah, you know, the action that you've undertaken here in the last, ah . . .

Nixon: That's right.

Ziegler: . . . forty-eight hours, which brings to your attention that you had before you less than all the facts.

Nixon: I'll say that? Yes, when I go out . . .

Ziegler: That, that . . .

Nixon: Seems to me that what I could potentially do is to go out to the pressroom and make that announcement.

Ziegler: Then, based upon the information that you have received, you have taken certain actions. Appointing the Special Prosecutor.

Nixon: No, we aren't going to focus, we can't.

Ziegler: Okay, okay.

Nixon: Regarding what I'm, what I'm taking the action of ah, accepting the Attorney General's, ah disqualification. So if I'm trying to get Petersen as being the man actively in charge of this thing, and he's reporting directly to me. Nobody else, nobody else, nobody else. Petersen is reporting directly to me. And don't worry, he's tough as a son of a bitch. That's, that's my . . .

Ziegler: Well, that's, that, that, I suppose that the Special Prosecutor really would not do any . . .

Nixon: It is the Special Prosecutor. We can't go to the outside. The difficulty going to the outside Ron is this, and this is the point Petersen made as well. The Special Prosecutor, he said it'd take him a month to learn the goddamn thing, and by that time he said *The Washington Post* and Ervin Committee would have it all out. It'd look like the Department of Justice hadn't done its job. He said now we have done the job, he, he says it's gonna look better if we do the job better than the Ervin Committee or the newspaper.

Ziegler: Petersen said that?

Nixon: Petersen said this to me. He's right, too.

Ziegler: Petersen is solid?

Nixon: Solid, you mean solid in what way?

Ziegler: Well I mean in terms of any prior contacts he may have had with Dean back in the previous . . .

Nixon: Oh, I think so. I think so.

Ziegler: Okay.

Nixon: He claims so, and I don't think that's going to be relevant.

Ziegler: Alright.

Nixon: Because now, the main thing is he's solid in going after this case. He's going after everybody Ron, believe me, everybody. He is competent. Told me last night that he thought I should get the resignations of Haldeman and Ehrlichman, as well as Dean.

Ziegler: Well, the Petersen thing is an action point.

Nixon: Yes, yes.

Ziegler: We're talking about minimums now. Ah . . .

Nixon: And, and they're reporting directly to me.

Ziegler: That's correct.

Nixon: And I'm, and I'm . . .

Ziegler: Ah . . .

Nixon: I wish there could be more. I'd like the Special Prosecutor . . .

Ziegler: Of course, then, then . . .

Nixon: . . . To, to, to just delay the case.

Ziegler: Then there's the Dean . . .

Nixon: It's moving too fast.

Ziegler: No, I think this is better than the Special Prosecutor.

Nixon: Alright, go ahead.

Ziegler: Then of course further action would be the Dean step. Which is the . . .

Nixon: Accept his resignation.

Ziegler: Accept his resignation. Or at least remove him publicly from any involvement in the case.

Nixon: Oh yeah, well I'll say that. I already did that two weeks ago.

Ziegler: Right, but no one knows that see.

Nixon: Okay, I see.

Ziegler: The public does not know that.

Nixon: I see.

Ziegler: Then, of course, there's the Magruder problem. However that is dealt with. From the, the . . .

Nixon: Well, Magruder could be removed. Ah, ah, he could be suspended. I don't know if anybody thought of that, but he should be, that again, I guess I'll ask Petersen whether he wants Magruder removed before Magruder testifies. See that's the point. I should say, since we know that he's involved I think we should just have him removed.

Ziegler: Well, that's something that . . .

Nixon: That'll tip off the case though. You see, they don't want to tip the case off to the press before they met Magruder.

Ziegler: Of course.

Nixon: Magruder's the one that pleaded guilty in open court.

Ziegler: Of course, one factor involved here is, ah, I understand they don't want to tip off the case, but if there's going to be bold . . .

Nixon: Yeah, I know.

Ziegler: . . . action from the part of the presidency . . .

Nixon: Right, right, right.

Ziegler: . . . ah, after the nine months when you did not have the complete facts . . .

Nixon: That's right, because we didn't have the facts.

Ziegler: Ah, we . . .

Nixon: Okay, I see.

Ziegler: . . . should be very cautious in not having the Justice Department cracking down.

Nixon: Alright, alright. Well I know, I'm, I'm, I'm very, I'm very aware of that and I'm going to hit Petersen hard on that, let's see, at one-thirty today.

Ziegler: Ah.

Nixon: Go ahead. That's a very, go on, go on.

Ziegler: Okay, well then.

Nixon: This is very helpful.

Ziegler: That is, that should be the, the ah, minimum and, and perhaps . . .

Nixon: Magruder option.

Ziegler: Well then, then also make the point the grand jury is the place to pursue this in fairness.

Nixon: That's right.

Ziegler: And maybe, ah, have a comment about the, the, ah committee itself, but those are things once you determine your course of action you can work out.

Nixon: They, that's, Mathias is going to the committee on this.

Ziegler: That's right. Keep in mind the public posture. For example, the news today on the Watergate is simply the fact that Mathias has associated himself with Ervin and White House aides who do not appear to be arrested to come onboard the committee.

Nixon: So what do you think we should do? Do you want us to say they're lawyered?

Ziegler: Well, I think whether or not you say that or have to say it depends on the course of action you've determined see, because . . .

Nixon: You're still against the third, aren't you?

Ziegler: Well, I think that as you said earlier becomes sort of irrelevant now, that ah, ah . . . I think action could be taken, or at least there's an option for action to be taken that could totally checkmate the committee and put it out of business.

Nixon: Ah, let me say this. Yeah, that's true. But we could say that the, um . . . I could say this, I could say under direct law, three of four of the committee stayed in session, including Dominick.

Ziegler: Under oath?

Nixon: Oh yes.

Ziegler: Alright, I saw the . . .

Nixon: [Indistinct]

Ziegler: Well, there's maybe.

Nixon: Of course then the committee will say that's not enough. It's gotta be resolved.

Ziegler: That's right.

Nixon: Should we say that all three or four of the committee on television? Just gave them the needle, in view of these developments?

Ziegler: Well, in view of these developments, ah . . .

Nixon: Is that what you'd say?

Ziegler: I think the decision regarding what we say and do about the committee rests on what your decision is and what to do about Dean, Magruder, ah, and how you intend to proceed. Ah.

Nixon: Yeah. In other words, ah, you know.

Ziegler: I think that is the last decision that you can make based upon what you've found.

Nixon: Yeah sure. This is the most important point. Ah, would you ask, be sure John Ehrlichman, ask him what he thinks we should do about the committee. Does he say that they, ah . . .

Ziegler: I think he would agree with my assessment.

Nixon: I see. Fine.

Ziegler: That, that is the last decision to make.

Nixon: Alright.

Ziegler: Okay. That's enough of, that's option one. There are others who in this group and in the discussion . . .

Nixon: Who want me to go at night, primetime session?

Ziegler: No, that.

Nixon: That I will promise you.

Ziegler: That would you take the steps which I've just mentioned.

Nixon: Yeah.

Ziegler: But also based upon the information which you have compiled, ah

Nixon: Yeah.

Ziegler: Over the last period, recommend that you suspend all members of the White House staff who have been mentioned to you as having some . . .

Nixon: Any contact.

Ziegler: Any contact. The problem with that, of course, is that you never recover.

Nixon: Well the problem with that is that you've condemned them on the basis of charges.

Ziegler: That's right. You never recover.

Nixon: You favor that?

Ziegler: No sir.

Nixon: That's, that's a final action.

Ziegler: That's basically it.

Nixon: You don't favor it?

Ziegler: Ah, I don't favor suspension, no sir. Because you, you're giving up, under that line, under suspension . . .

Nixon: You've condemned them all.

Ziegler: You've condemned them number one, but you've accomplished nothing.

Nixon: No.

Ziegler: Because you still have information coming out in the trial about the men. And secondly, you have information coming out in the press about the men.

Nixon: Yeah.

Ziegler: Which is the same result as to whether or not they're here or they're suspended. So . . .

Nixon: I accepted, I cleared the White House of the, of anybody who's open to question, maybe that's the point there now.

Ziegler: But you can't do that. You've cleared the White House of anyone having prior knowledge of the Watergate ah, ah burglary, but you have not cleared anyone in the White House of having even tangential knowledge of the post-trial, ah, ah post-arrest periods. And the facts as they seem to be stacking up are, that at some point, it may be May the fifteenth, it may be May the twenty-fifth, it may be this Friday, information is going to come out probably in the press regarding . . .

Nixon: . . . Haldeman.

Ziegler: . . . Haldeman and Ehrlichman. And I think if, and if it doesn't come out at that point, it will come out at the time of a trial, even though . . .

Nixon: Yeah but what, what can you do about that? I mean how do we, how do we anticipate that?

Ziegler: Well, I think any decision that is made has to anticipate that.

Nixon: Well Ron, I, I'm trying to get what you'd do, besides send blood pressure medication to Rikers. What do you think we should do about them, Haldeman and Ehrlichman? You would, ah, you wouldn't have their, you wouldn't suspend them now, is that right?

Ziegler: I would not suspend them, no sir.

Nixon: Why not?

Ziegler: Well, because you accomplish nothing through suspension.

Nixon: It shows the President is cleaning house.

Ziegler: It shows the President is cleaning house. But in order to make a decision on suspension, you've got to make a decision on losing the men. In other words . . .

Nixon: Oh . . .

Ziegler: . . . my point is . . .

Nixon: Oh, I, when you say suspended, I can say, ah, right, you can say they are suspended until they are cleared.

Ziegler: That's right, but having said that, you have to, you have to . . .

Nixon: Assuming they're getting back.

Ziegler: You'll never get it back. See . . .

Nixon: Continue . . .

Ziegler: So, the . . .

Nixon: So therefore, you want, the other point, I suppose the argument on the other side is, they say, well goddammit, they're going to be driven out.

Ziegler: Yes sir, that's a very strong argument. It, it comes down to, if I could . . .

Nixon: Go ahead.

Ziegler: . . . attempt the sunrise here.

Nixon: Go ahead, sure.

Ziegler: It comes down to limited action, which is the first option we talked about.

Nixon: Yeah.

Ziegler: Or total action.

Nixon: Yeah.

Ziegler: Now, there is nothing in between, in other words, suspension is not a good idea. Because . . .

Nixon: Yeah, yeah.

Ziegler: . . . suspension is really total action, but you do not as the President benefit the most from the suspended act, the suspension.

Nixon: Yeah, yeah.

Ziegler: Because everything that would result from the . . .

Nixon: It's my view that you can't act on Haldeman and Ehrlichman unless and until charges are made that are seriously impaired by the facts, and they've got to come in and say, we are, we ask to resign until we've had a chance to hear what they, I think that, that, is that what you would say? Or are you, maybe you'd wait? Because you have to, see by that, you see Ron, they're entitled to, whatever charge is made, they're entitled to their day in court.

Ziegler: Absolutely.

Nixon: And ah, they may not even be in, they may not even get there.

Ziegler: I don't think they will be.

Nixon: And, my mind is that, I, ah, I just feel that I can't, but on the other hand, their usefulness may be destroyed. You don't agree with that?

Ziegler: That's a very real, real possibility.

Nixon: That's a problem. So how do you handle that?

Ziegler: Well.

Nixon: And when? You wouldn't handle that now. That's the hold up. They're usefulness is not destroyed yet.

Ziegler: No.

Nixon: So.

Ziegler: So that's where the tough call comes in.

Nixon: Yeah.

Ziegler: Is between the minimum or maximum action. But under the minimum action, I think the point I'm making for your consideration, is that the minimum action at some point down the line . . .

Nixon: Yeah.

Ziegler: Information regarding Segretti and Haldeman, information regarding the $350,000 and Haldeman.

Nixon: Right.

Ziegler: Information regarding how it was transferred to the committee will come out.

Nixon: Yeah.

Ziegler: All of that is gonna come out as a result of testimony.

Nixon: Sure, sure, so?

Ziegler: That fact, in itself, in public opinion if not legally . . .

Nixon: . . . is enough to condemn . . .

Ziegler: . . . is enough to condemn Bob anyway.

Nixon: So.

Ziegler: So.

Nixon: What do you think?

Ziegler: Well, that's, that's, that's the tough call. Do, is the call that . . .

Nixon: He steps up now.

Ziegler: . . . is the call that you take minimum action and allow these events to unfold and then deal with the Haldeman situation as it um, develops? And is that fair to Bob? And is that fair to the presidency? Secondly, the suspension route is sparing no one.

Nixon: Your point is Haldeman should either resign or stay on?

Ziegler: Yeah, the Garment line is not to discuss this with Bob, very frankly.

Nixon: You said he should resign.

Ziegler: The Garment line is the broad approach to it. He rises above it, resigns and . . .

Nixon: Yeah.

Ziegler: . . . and carries the thing at the higher level. In other words, Bob establishes himself in public opinion, in the country, as a man who was not responsible, who was not guilty of illegality, but a man who recognizes that the things he did got out of hand and steps up to the problem . . .

Nixon: Um hum.

Ziegler: . . . and moves on that basis. Now, ah, I told Bob as I passed this view on to him, that I'm no one that can even draw a judgment on that, because I have . . .

Nixon: Yeah.

Ziegler: . . . ah, a longtime association with Haldeman.

Nixon: I know.

Ziegler: And it was tough for me, but I did feel a responsibility to . . .

Nixon: Yup.

Ziegler: . . . to tell him this.

Nixon: What did he think of that?

Ziegler: Well, if . . .

Nixon: You'd prefer the big play?

Ziegler: I don't.

Nixon: Be quite, be quite honest would you?

Ziegler: I'm not, I can't, I'm not prepared to give you a statement on that, Mr. President. But in making the judgment, it seems to me, that you should be candidly told by all of the people who have awareness of this that the story will come out in terms of not only the Magruder activities and the Mitchell activities, but also . . .

Nixon: Theirs, oh I know that.

Ziegler: . . . but also, but also the story regarding White House staff people at the highest level . . .

Nixon: That's right.

Ziegler: . . . will come out.

Nixon: Oh, yeah.

Ziegler: Now . . .

Nixon: No question about that.

Ziegler: At some point.

Nixon: It's just a matter of when.

Ziegler: Accepting that, what action does the President take to totally isolate the Oval Office from this, as it should be and is, so that the impression of public opinion after these nine months of cover-up . . .

Nixon: Yeah.

Ziegler: Cannot suggest further cover-up. Ah . . .

Nixon: Yeah.

Ziegler: So that bold play versus minimum play is um, ah, should take that into, should take that into account. Minimum ah, action on it ensures the fact that it is an ongoing story of revelation. Ongoing for how long and how dogged and distorted the scope is hard to predict, but it is ongoing. The committee, grand jury, leaks, trial testimony.

Nixon: I know.

Ziegler: The bold play, or the broad play, if taken must be taken in its entirety, and this is Chappie Rose's point.

Nixon: Yeah.

Ziegler: Because if a bold play, which is . . .

Nixon: Is Chappie for the bold play?

Ziegler: Um . . .

Nixon: Or is he just saying, ah, just putting out the options?

Ziegler: Chappie's for the bold play.

Nixon: You got Haldeman and Ehrlichman both as an anchor.

Ziegler: If not, ah Ehrlichman he would have Haldeman I think do it on a broader scale, you see. Now, the bold play or any play that does not tell the whole story is fraught with disaster.

Nixon: Yup.

Ziegler: You see, because as Bob for example would, would say . . .

Nixon: Yeah.

Ziegler: . . . give the honest picture. Ah, three hundred and fifty thousand dollars once a year and we didn't use it? Send it back to the committee. Disaster. Because in three weeks, maybe in a month, it's going to come out that the man took it in a suitcase and all that type of thing. Which in itself is not illegal, but the impression in the public opinion, wait—as I told Bob—my view is, that would destroy

Bob and would taint him as a person and in the country's faith.

Nixon: Yup.

Ziegler: So.

Nixon: You gotta lay it out for him, you know, the full scope. He's got to be sure what he, he—it takes a hell of a lot for him to do. So you gotta say that.

Ziegler: You asked me what do I think of the bold play or the minimum option. Ah, when I get to that point, my recommendation is not very good because I obviously get into the, ah . . .

Nixon: You see, there's another problem too you know which concerns me that ah, I didn't know about this thing, as you can be sure.

Ziegler: Absolutely.

Nixon: I didn't know about the three hundred fifty thousand dollars until weeks ago, you see. I didn't know. I mean, Dean didn't tell me, Haldeman didn't tell me, Ehrlichman didn't tell me. You know what I mean? I was, ah, business so forth and so on. Ah, I must, I must admit, I must have had some information. I read in the papers about [sounds like] Langston Hughes or whatever. I was a little busy during this period. That's been my problem.

Ziegler: See this goes to the argument that Chappie Rose makes in the, in the more, in I, I . . .

Nixon: About Dean?

Ziegler: The point you just made to me. Having become aware of this information

Nixon: Yeah.

Ziegler: After nine months of all of this press speculation . . .

Nixon: Yeah, yeah.

Ziegler: . . . and leaks and so forth, much of which in this particular case . . .

Nixon: Is accurate.

Ziegler: . . . is accurate.

Nixon: Right.

Ziegler: You will find out within a ten-day period or twenty-day period, that's your own admission.

Nixon: Yeah.

Ziegler: That a lot of that was right and you were not told about it. You were not told about it by Dean, you were not told about it from others.

Nixon: Even Haldeman.

Ziegler: Even Haldeman. What is the legitimate reaction not only of a president, but of a man who runs a company or a man who has any . . .

Nixon: Throw him out.

Ziegler: Other, other . . .

Nixon: Throw the, slight, slight situation of Governor Eagleton. Which is the question a couple people have is, ah, shock treatments, but he hadn't told the governor.

Ziegler: See, in other words, if yesterday afternoon, which is the, the case, information was provided to you that said to you that men, particularly in this case Dean, could have given you additional information for you to make judgments on . . .

Nixon: Dean and also somebody else.

Ziegler: . . . failed to do it, then the action that you take must be swift and must be bold. It's ah, it's something, something people can relate to.

Nixon: They'd like to.

Ziegler: Now, ah.

Nixon: It's all hard on the men.

Ziegler: It's very hard on the men. It's ah, it's, I've, you know, never been through something like this obviously.

Nixon: Oh, it's, it's, we'll survive.

Ziegler: The emot[tion], I, I, but you say it's hard on the men.

Nixon: They're not gonna . . .

Ziegler: Let me just say, I'm not thinking . . .

Nixon: You're thinking of this in the softest terms.

Ziegler: In cold terms. I'm thinking of the presidency, the presidentship. The . . .

Nixon: Well let me tell you this, we're gonna, also gonna have to, we're gonna have to I don't know which, but I want to talk to Rogers, and ah I'll consider all these things, but you can be goddamn sure that a man will protect himself . . .

Index